Emerging Giants

Emerging Giants

China and India in the World Economy

Edited by
Barry Eichengreen, Poonam Gupta,
and Rajiv Kumar

OXFORD
UNIVERSITY PRESS

Great Clarendon Street, Oxford, OX2 6DP,
United Kingdom

Oxford University Press is a department of the University of Oxford.
It furthers the University's objective of excellence in research, scholarship,
and education by publishing worldwide. Oxford is a registered trade mark of
Oxford University Press in the UK and in certain other countries

© Oxford University Press 2010

The moral rights of the authors have been asserted

First Edition published in 2010

All rights reserved. No part of this publication may be reproduced, stored in
a retrieval system, or transmitted, in any form or by any means, without the
prior permission in writing of Oxford University Press, or as expressly permitted
by law, by licence or under terms agreed with the appropriate reprographics
rights organization. Enquiries concerning reproduction outside the scope of the
above should be sent to the Rights Department, Oxford University Press, at the
address above

You must not circulate this work in any other form
and you must impose this same condition on any acquirer

Published in the United States of America by Oxford University Press
198 Madison Avenue, New York, NY 10016, United States of America

British Library Cataloguing in Publication Data

Data available

Library of Congress Cataloging in Publication Data

Data available

ISBN 978-0-19-957507-7

SUMMARY CONTENTS

List of Tables	xi
List of Figures	xv
List of Contributors	xix
Abbreviations	xxi
Introduction	xxv

Part I. China and India in the Global Economy

1. What Can Be Learned about the Economies of China and India from Purchasing Power Comparisons? 3
   Alan Heston

2. Trading with Asia's Giants 32
   Barry Bosworth, Susan M. Collins, and Aaron Flaaen

3. The Chinese Export Bundles: Patterns, Puzzles, and Possible Explanations 62
   Zhi Wang and Shang-Jin Wei

Part II. Contrasts in Development Experience

4. The Cost Competitiveness of Manufacturing in China and India: An Industry and Regional Perspective 87
   Bart van Ark, Abdul Azeez Erumban, Vivian Chen, and Utsav Kumar

5. Law, Institutions, and Finance in China and India 125
   Franklin Allen, Rajesh Chakrabarti, Sankar De, Jun 'QJ' Qian, and Meijun Qian

Summary Contents

6. China and India: A Tale of Two Trade Integration Approaches   184
   Przemyslaw Kowalski

Part III. Challenges to Sustaining Growth

7. China's Growth Model: Choices and Consequences   227
   Eswar S. Prasad

8. Deconstructing China's and India's Growth: The Role of Financial Policies   243
   Jahangir Aziz

9. Pollution across Chinese Provinces   281
   Catherine Yap Co, Fanying Kong, and Shuanglin Lin

10. What Constrains Indian Manufacturing?   307
    Poonam Gupta, Rana Hasan, and Utsav Kumar

References   343
Index   363

CONTENTS

List of Tables	xi
List of Figures	xv
List of Contributors	xix
Abbreviations	xxi
Introduction	xxv
China and India in the global economy	xxvi
Comparisons and contrasts	xxviii
Challenges for sustaining growth	xxix

Part I. China and India in the Global Economy

1. What Can Be Learned about the Economies of China and India from Purchasing Power Comparisons?   3
   Alan Heston

1.1 Introduction	3
1.2 The growth record in a comparative framework	4
1.3 Levels of GDP in China and India	8
1.4 PPPs and sources of past and future growth	22
1.5 PPPs and exchange rates	28
1.6 Conclusion	30

2. Trading with Asia's Giants   32
   Barry Bosworth, Susan M. Collins, and Aaron Flaaen

2.1 Introduction	32
2.2 Context	34
2.3 Services trade	39
2.4 Composition of goods exports	42
2.5 The role of multinational corporations	44
2.6 The role of distance	47
2.7 Effects of the US trade deficit	55
2.8 Conclusion	59

Contents

3. The Chinese Export Bundles: Patterns, Puzzles, and Possible
   Explanations   62
   Zhi Wang and Shang-Jin Wei

   3.1 Introduction   62
   3.2 Evolving sophistication in export structures: China
       vs. India   63
   3.3 What might explain China's precocious export
       sophistication?   69
   3.4 Conclusion   79
   Appendix 3A. Data   81

Part II. Contrasts in Development Experience

4. The Cost Competitiveness of Manufacturing in China and
   India: An Industry and Regional Perspective   87
   *Bart van Ark, Abdul Azeez Erumban, Vivian Chen, and
   Utsav Kumar*

   4.1 Introduction   87
   4.2 Unit labor cost as competitiveness measure   89
   4.3 International comparisons of productivity and unit
       labor costs   92
   4.4 Regional comparison of productivity and unit labor cost   96
   4.5 Convergence trends in compensation, productivity,
       and unit labor cost   107
   4.6 Conclusion   116
   Appendix 4A. Basic data for China and India regional
   comparisons   118

5. Law, Institutions, and Finance in China and India   125
   *Franklin Allen, Rajesh Chakrabarti, Sankar De, Jun 'QJ' Qian,
   and Meijun Qian*

   5.1 Introduction   125
   5.2 Evidence on China's legal and financial systems and
       growth in the three sectors   129
   5.3 Law, finance, and growth in India: Aggregate evidence   144
   5.4 Firms' financing sources in China: Aggregate evidence and
       cross-country comparisons   151
   5.5 Law, finance, and growth in the Indian corporate sectors:
       Firm level evidence   161

Contents

5.6 Survey evidence on the Chinese private sector	167
5.7 Conclusions	181

6. China and India: A Tale of Two Trade Integration Approaches — 184
   Przemyslaw Kowalski

6.1 Introduction	184
6.2 Main trade developments	189
6.3 Trade policy developments	206
6.4 Conclusion	223

Part III. Challenges to Sustaining Growth

7. China's Growth Model: Choices and Consequences — 227
   Eswar S. Prasad

7.1 Introduction	227
7.2 The composition of growth in China and India	229
7.3 Policy choices	232
7.4 The reform agenda	237
7.5 Monetary policy	239
7.6 Concluding remarks	241

8. Deconstructing China's and India's Growth: The Role of Financial Policies — 243
   Jahangir Aziz

8.1 Introduction	243
8.2 China and India's recent growth experience	248
8.3 China and India's economy as a neoclassical growth model	249
8.4 Calibrating the growth model	252
8.5 Simulating the Solow growth model	255
8.6 Investment wedge	257
8.7 Interpreting investment wedges as financial frictions	260
8.8 Financial sector reforms in India	272
8.9 Conclusion	276

9. Pollution across Chinese Provinces — 281
   Catherine Yap Co, Fanying Kong, and Shuanglin Lin

9.1 Introduction	281
9.2 Pollution and environmental policy in China	284

Contents

9.3 Data and empirical methodology	286
9.4 Analysis of results	291
9.5 Conclusion	304
Appendix 9A	306
10. **What Constrains Indian Manufacturing?**	307
Poonam Gupta, Rana Hasan, and Utsav Kumar	
10.1 Introduction	307
10.2 Stylized facts and preliminary evidence	312
10.3 Evidence from enterprise surveys	319
10.4 Econometric analysis	323
10.5 Conclusion	337
Appendix 10A. Data sources and construction of variables	339
References	343
Index	363

List of Tables

1.1.	Per capita GDP levels at 2000 prices from PWT 6.2	5
1.2.	Official, Maddison and Wu, and PWT indexes of per capita GDP	7
1.3.	The size of the world economy	10
1.4.	Preliminary World Bank estimates for 2005 of levels of China and India	11
1.5.	Rural–urban price differences by province (2004)	14
1.6.	Completed investment in China by quarters	26
2.1.	Trade with China and India, major industrial economies, 2005	37
2.2.	2005 services trade by type, India and China	40
2.3.	Correlations of bilateral commodity trade, 2005	42
2.4.	US affiliate activities in China and India, 1989–2004	45
2.5.	Japanese affiliate activity in China	46
2.6.	Gravity equations for global trade: United States, Japan, and EU-15	49
2.7.	Gravity equations for services trade: United States, Japan, and EU-15, 1999–2005	54
2.8.	United States top trading partners, 2005	57
2.9.	Combined gravity model for US, Japan, and EU-15	58
3.1.	Comparing export structures: China relative to the G-3 (1996–2005)	68
3.2.	Comparing export structures: India relative to the G-3 (1996–2005)	68
3.3.	Percentage breakdown of China's exports by firm ownership, 1995–2006 (%)	71
3.4.	Share of processing trade and policy zones' production in China's total exports, 1996–2005 (%)	73
3.5.	What explains cross-city export structure? Export structure dissimilarity between Chinese cities and the G-3 economies	76
3A.1.	Definition of key variables and data sources	82
3A.2.	Starting years of various economic zones with policy incentives	83

List of Tables

4.1.	Labor productivity, compensation, and unit labor cost, China and India, 2002, PPP converted	96
4.2.	Size distribution, China and India: A comparison	98
4.3a.	Change of ALC, ALP & ULC by industry groups and seven regions	103
4.3b.	Change in ALC, ALP & ULC by industry group and region—India	104
4.4a.	Relative level of ALC, ALP & ULC by industry groups and seven regions in 1995, all China = 100	105
4.4b.	Relative levels of ALC, ALP & ULC by industry group and region in 1993, all India = 100	106
4.5a.	Beta convergence, OLS regression results: China	109
4.5b.	Beta convergence, OLS regression results: India	110
4A.1.	Comparative levels of labor compensation, labor productivity and unit labor cost, 1990–2005	121
4A.2.	Industries and industry groups	122
4A.3a.	Provinces and regions—China	123
4A.3b.	States and regions	124
5.1.	Panel A: The largest 20 economies in the world: GDP and growth	131
	Panel B: Comparison of 2007 PPP GDP from different statistical sources	132
5.2.	Comparing legal systems and institutions	133
5.3.	Comparing financial systems: Banks and markets	136
5.4.	A comparison of the largest stock markets in the world (2006)	138
5.5a.	A comparison of nonperforming loans of banking systems	140
5.5b.	A cross-country comparison of banking system profitability	140
5.6a.	Growth rates of the state, listed, and private sectors	142
5.6b.	Employment in the state, listed, and private sectors	142
5.7a.	Types of common stock issued in China	155
5.7b.	Tradable vs. nontradable shares for China's listed companies	156
5.7c.	Ownership and control in listed firms of China	156
5.8a.	Summary statistics of Chinese listed firms	158
5.8b.	Ownership structures of Indian firms vis-à-vis other country groups	159
5.8c.	Comparing external financing, dividend, and valuation	160
5.9.	Comparing the state and nonstate sectors in India: 1990–2003	162
5.10a.	Evidence from the World Bank's investment climate survey data: Basic information	164

List of Tables

5.10b.	Financing sources and efficiency	165
5.10c.	Growth	165
5.10d.	Internal	167
5.10e.	Trade credit	168
5.10f.	Family/friend borrowing	169
5.10g.	Total informal financing	170
5.10h.	Growth of firms	171
6.1.	Selected indicators	187
6.2.	Trade in goods and services, world and China	190
6.3.	Changing structure of China's trade: Twenty-five top exports and their share in total exports	192
6.4.	China: Services trade composition	194
6.5.	Changing structure of India's trade: Twenty-five top exports and their share in total exports	197
6.6.	High technology exports	200
6.7.	India: Composition of services and trade	202
6.8.	China's average trade-weighted tariffs by trading partner and product at the time of accession to the WTO in 2001	207
6.9.	China's tariff structure	208
6.10.	FDI regulatory restrictiveness scores by country and sector	210
6.11.	India's tariff structure	211
6.12.	Top ten Indian imports	216
6.13.	Disposition of top ten Indian imports	217
6.14.	Doing business in China and India—Selected indicators, 2006	222
9.1.	Summary statistics, 30 Chinese provinces from 1987 to 2004	286
9.2.	Provincial unconditional rankings in various pollutants, 1987–1995	288
9.3.	Spearman rank correlation coefficients, thirty Chinese provinces from 1987–1995	289
9.4.	Fixed effects panel regression estimates	292
9.5.	Correlates of the estimated province-specific fixed effects in 1987–1995	303
10.1.	Pre- and post-reform performance of Indian manufacturing	318
10.2.	Single most important obstacle for operation and growth of the firm	322
10.3.	Growth of gross value added post-delicensing across industries	327

List of Tables

10.4.	Value added post-delicensing	330
10.5.	Number of factories	331
10.6.	Employment post-delicensing—results from equation 2	333
10.7.	Investment post-delicensing—results from equation 2	334
10.8.	Robustness tests	336
10A.1.	Summary statistics of the ASI data	339
10A.2.	Delicensing	340
10A.3.	Industry characteristics	341

List of Figures

2.1.	GDP per capita, China and India (constant 2000 international (PPP) dollars)	34
2.2.	Growth in output per worker: Sector and reallocation components 1978–2004	35
2.3a.	Mainland China's exports and imports to world, 1990–2006	35
2.3b.	India's exports and imports to world, 1990–2006	36
2.4a.	US exports to selected countries, 2005 with East Asia adjustment	53
2.4b.	US imports from selected countries, 2005 with East Asia adjustment	53
2.5a.	US service exports to selected countries, 2005 with East Asia adjustment	55
2.5b.	US service imports from selected countries, 2005 with East Asia adjustment	56
3.1.	Fraction of the HS-6 codes that the G-3 export but that China and India do not, 1996–2005	64
3.2.	Fraction of the HS-6 codes that G-3 economies export by at least a million US dollars but that China and India do not, 1996–2005	66
3.3.	Value-weighted fraction of HS-6 codes that G-3 economies export by at least a million US dollars but that China and India do not, 1996–2005	66
3.4.	China and India's export dissimilarity index (relative to G-3 economies), 1996–2005	69
4.1a.–c.	Relative levels of labor compensation per person employed (4.1a), value added per person employed (4.1b), and unit labor cost (4.1c), 1990–2005	95
4.2a.	Change in ALC, ALP & ULC by province for total manufacturing—all China	99
4.2b.	Change in ALC, ALP & ULC by state for total manufacturing—all India	100

xv

List of Figures

4.3a.	Change in ALC, ALP & ULC by industry for all China	100
4.3b.	Change in ALC, ALP & ULC by industry for all India	101
4.4a.	Coefficient of variation for ALC by industry, China	112
4.4b.	Coefficient of variation for ALC by industry, India	112
4.4c.	Coefficient of variation for ALP by industry, China	113
4.4d.	Coefficient of variation for ALP by industry, India	113
4.4e.	Coefficient of variation for ULC by industry, China	114
4.4f.	Coefficient of variation for ULC by industry, India	114
5.1.	A comparison of performance of stock indexes	149
5.2.	Investor protection and external financing: International comparison	150
5.3a.	Financing sources for the listed sector	152
5.3b.	Financing sources for the state sector	153
5.3c.	Financing sources for the private sector	153
5.4a.	Background information on survey firms	173
5.4b.	Financing channels of survey firms	174
5.4c.	Governance mechanisms of survey firms	174
5.5.	Comparing financing channels in emerging economies	176
6.1.	Annual GDP growth rate 1990–2006	185
6.2.	GDP per capita in China and India 1975–2006	186
6.3.	Shares in world exports	186
6.4.	China's current account structure	190
6.5.	China's top trading partners	195
6.6.	India's current account structure	196
6.7.	Evolution of India's export mix according to skill intensity (1996 and 2005)	201
6.8.	China: Exports to GDP and exports value added to GDP ratio	205
6.9.	India: Exports to GDP and exports value added to GDP ratio	205
6.10a.	Taxation of international trade: Duties as % of value of imports of goods and services	212
6.10b.	Taxation of international trade: Duties as % of GDP	212
6.11.	Percentage change in sectoral value added, 1991–2006, % of GDP	214
6.12.	Banking and insurance TRIs—India and selected emerging economies	218
6.13.	Telecom TRIs—India and selected emerging economies	218

List of Figures

6.14.	Distribution TRIs—India and selected emerging countries	219
6.15.	Doubling India's share of world trade: The size of the challenge exports in billions US$	220
7.1.	GDP growth	230
7.2a.	Base lending and deposit rates	231
7.2b.	Real lending and deposit rates	231
7.3a.	Rmb-US$ exchange rate	233
7.3b.	Real and nominal effective exchange rate for China	233
7.4a.	Rupee-US$ exchange rate	234
7.4b.	Real and nominal effective exchange rate for India	234
7.5.	Foreign exchange reserves: Flows and stocks	236
8.1.	China and India: GDP growth rate	249
8.2.	Changes in GDP components: 1990–2005	250
8.3.	China: Growth accounting	252
8.4.	China and India: Labor productivity	253
8.5.	India: Growth accounting	254
8.6.	China: Simulation with efficiency wedge	255
8.7.	China: Simulation with efficiency and Government wedges	256
8.8.	India: Simulation with efficiency and Government wedges	257
8.9.	China: Derived investment wedge	258
8.10.	India: Derived investment wedge	259
8.11.	China: Simulation with efficiency, Government, and investment wedges	260
8.12.	India: Simulation with efficiency, Government, and investment wedges	261
8.13.	China: Official estimates of NPLs created (end 2004)	263
8.14.	Derived cumulative capital income wedge	263
8.15.	China: Average effective tax rate	264
8.16.	China: Domestic savings by sectors	265
8.17.	Short-term bank loan to capital ratio	268
8.18.	China: Simulation with borrowing constraint	269
8.19.	Effective gross capital income tax rate	271
8.20.	India: CRR and SLR	272
8.21.	India: Domestic savings	275
8.22.	India: Simulation with SLR	276

List of Figures

8.23.	India: Simulation with SLR and CRR	277
8.24.	India: Simulating policy change	278
8.25.	China: Simulating policy change	279
9.1a.	Total industrial waste water per capita discharge (actual and estimated, 1987–1995)	294
9.1b.	Industrial COD per capita discharge (actual and estimated, 1987–1995)	294
9.1c.	Waste gas per capita discharge (actual and estimated, 1987–1995)	295
9.1d.	Industrial dust per capita discharge (actual and estimated, 1987–1995)	295
9.2a.	Total industrial waste water per capita discharge (actual and predicted, 1996–2004)	296
9.2b.	Total industrial dust per capita discharge (actual and predicted, 1996–2004)	297
9.2c.	Industrial COD per capita discharge (actual and predicted, 1996–2004)	297
10.1a.	Sectoral shares in GDP, India	308
10.1b.	Sectoral contribution to Indian GDP growth, 1951–2007	308
10.2a.	Cumulative share of industries delicensed	314
10.2b.	Average nominal rate of protection, 1988 to 1998	314
10.3.	Infrastructure investment, China and India	316
10.4.	Performance of Indian manufacturing	317
10.5.	Obstacles for operations and growth	320
10.6.	Areas for improvement	321

List of Contributors

Franklin Allen The Wharton School, University of Pennsylvania

Bart van Ark The Conference Board, University of Groningen

Jahangir Aziz Asia and Pacific Department, the International Monetary Fund

Barry Bosworth The Brookings Institution

Rajesh Chakrabarti Indian School of Business, Hyderabad

Vivian Chen The Conference Board

Catherine Yap Co Department of Economics, University of Nebraska at Omaha

Susan M. Collins The Brookings Institution and the University of Michigan

Sankar De Centre for Analytical Finance, Indian School of Business, Hyderabad

Abdul Azeez Erumban University of Groningen

Aaron Flaaen The Brookings Institution

Poonam Gupta Department of Economics, Delhi School of Economics

Rana Hasan Asian Development Bank

Alan Heston University of Pennsylvania

Fanying Kong Department of Sociology, Midland Lutheran College, Fremont, Nebraska

Przemyslaw Kowalski Organization of Economic Cooperation and Development

Utsav Kumar The Conference Board

List of Contributors

Shuanglin Lin Department of Economics, University of Nebraska at Omaha; School of Economics, Peking University, Beijing

Eswar Prasad Department of Applied Economics and Management, Cornell University, Brookings Institution and National Bureau of Economic Research

Jun 'QJ' Qian Carroll School of Management, Boston College

Meijun Qian NUS Business School, National University of Singapore

Zhi Wang Office of Economics, United States International Trade Commission

Shang-Jin Wei Graduate School of Business, Columbia University

Abbreviations

ALC	average labor compensation
ALP	average labor productivity
ASEAN	Association of Southeast Asian Nations
ASI	Annual Survey of Industries
BCA	business cycle accounting
BEA	Bureau of Economic Analysis
BLS	Bureau of Labor Statistics
BOP	balance of payments
BPT	Business, Professional, and Technical
BRIC	Brazil, Russia, India, and China
BSE	Bombay Stock Exchange
C, I, and G	Consumption, Investment, and Government spending
CEPII	French Institute for Research on the International Economy
CIS	Commonwealth of Independent States
CMIE	Center for Monitoring Indian Economy
COD	chemical oxygen demand
CPI	consumer price index
CRR	cash reserve ratio
CSRC	China Securities Regulation Committee
CV	coefficient of variation
EDI	Export Dissimilarity Index
EKC	environmental Kuznets curve
EKS	Elteto, Koves, and Szulz
EPCG	export promotion of capital goods
EPZ	export processing zone
ESCAP	Economic and Social Commission for Asia and the Pacific

Abbreviations

ETDA	Economic and Technological Development Areas
EU	European Union
FDI	foreign direct investment
FIE	foreign invested enterprise
FOB	Free on Board
GAO	General Accountability Office
GATS	General Agreement on Trade in Services
GCP	gross city product
GDP	gross domestic product
GK	Geary–Khamis
GNI	gross national income
GNP	gross national product
GVA	gross value added
HKSE	Hong Kong Stock Exchange
HS	Harmonized System
HTIDA	Hi-Technology Industry Development Areas
IAS	International Accounting Standards
ICOP	International Comparisons of Output and Productivity
ICP	International Comparison Program
ICRIER	Indian Council for Research on International Economic Relations
ICS	investment climate survey
ICT	information and communication technology
IDA	Industrial Disputes Act
IMF	International Monetary Fund
IPO	initial public offering
IT	information technology
LC	labor compensation
NASDAQ	National Association of Securities Dealers Automated Quotations
NBS	National Bureau of Statistics
NPL	nonperforming loan
NSE	National Stock Exchange
NSSO	National Sample Survey Organization
NYSE	New York Stock Exchange
OECD	Organization for Economic Cooperation and Development
PBC	People's Bank of China

Abbreviations

PCA	private credit agency
PPI	producer price index
PPP	purchasing power parity
PSU	Public Sector Undertaking
PWT	Penn World Table
RBI	Reserve Bank of India
RCA	revealed comparative advantage
SEBI	Securities and Exchange Board of India
SEC	Securities and Exchange Commission
SEPA	State Environmental Protection Administration
SEZ	special economic zone
SHSE	Shanghai Stock Exchange
SITC	Standard International Trade Classification
SLR	statutory liquidity ratio
SME	small and medium enterprises
SOE	state-owned enterprise
SZSE	ShenZhen Stock Exchange
TFP	total factor productivity
TRI	Trade Restrictiveness Index
TUA	Trade Union Act
TVE	Township Village Enterprises
ULC	unit labor cost
UVR	unit values ratio
VC	venture capitalist
WDI	World Development Indicators
WPI	wholesale price index
WTO	World Trade Organization

Introduction

China and India are the two most populous countries in the world and now also two of the fastest growing. In 2007, China and India together contributed nearly as much to global growth as the United States. Their share in global output has risen from barely 3 percent in 1980 to more than 7 percent in 2007 in current US dollars, making these two economies important players in the world economy. Their combined share of world trade has risen even more dramatically—from 1.5 percent in 1980 to 9 percent in 2007. By sheer virtue of the fact that China and India are home to 2.4 billion people—two-fifths of the world's population—the rapid growth of their economies has far-reaching implications not just for global living standards and poverty reduction but also for competitiveness and distribution of income in the rest of the world.

Reflecting these facts, there has been a surge of interest in the nature and implications of China and India's economic growth. Our goal in assembling this book has been to bring together the best such research and to place the issues in a comparative perspective. Academics and practitioners, more so perhaps in India than in China, routinely compare the two countries as a way of assessing their economic performance and characterizing their economic development strategies. They use comparative evidence to gauge whether India is poised to experience a sustained growth acceleration similar to that seen in China. More recently, and with more novelty, they have also begun to ask whether China can draw lessons—for example, for its political and financial reforms—from the experience of India.

The reality, of course, is that simple-minded comparisons conceal as much as they reveal. China and India are both home to ancient civilizations that have bequeathed distinctive attitudes, institutions, and traditions. Both have very large populations. Both have performed well economically for more than two decades. But as soon as one transcends these generalities, important differences become apparent. China started

Introduction

the current reform process in 1978—that is, almost fifteen years before India. The two countries have very different political systems. Their development models differ fundamentally as well. China has opened up much more than India to foreign trade and foreign direct investment, while India has a better developed banking system. Growth in the two countries has been driven by different sectors—Chinese growth by manufacturing and Indian growth by services.

While both China and India are increasingly regarded as success stories, both confront serious challenges to sustaining economic growth. China's challenges include the need for comprehensive financial sector reform, greater exchange rate flexibility, more environment-friendly growth, and a better balance between consumption and investment. India, for its part, needs to grow its manufacturing sector, reform its labor laws, invest in infrastructure, and further liberalize its foreign trade. While some of these challenges overlap, the two economies are likely to remain a study in contrasts.

Our analysis of these issues falls under three headings: The roles of China and India in the world economy; contrasts in their development experience; and challenges to sustaining growth.

China and India in the global economy

Any discussion of the role of China and India in the international system must start with reasonable estimates of the size of the two economies. It is also important to have a sense of the size of the two economies in order to form reasonable predictions about the future course of events. In Chapter 1 of this book, Alan Heston develops estimates of the relative size of the Chinese and Indian economies. Going back to the 1950s, Heston points out the difficulty of precisely calibrating their size owing to the poor quality of data on growth rates. As he observes, the estimates constructed by previous researchers differ a great deal. Heston concludes that, irrespective of the differences in exact numbers, it is reasonable to say that though China and India started at a similar level of income in the 1950s, since 1978 there has been a dramatic divergence, with the Chinese economy growing much faster and becoming much larger as a result of the first wave of reforms. Heston also considers estimates of the size of the Chinese and Indian economies at purchasing power parities, drawing on the most recent (2005) data provided by the United Nations' International Comparison Program (ICP). These

Introduction

estimates show both economies to be smaller than previously thought. In attempting to reconcile these estimates with earlier figures, Heston points to new estimates of price levels, the way the different regions are linked, and downward adjustments to the productivity of the public sector.

As already noted, China and India play an increasingly prominent role in global trade. In China's case attention has focused on the rapid growth of processing exports and the country's bilateral current account deficit with the United States, while in India's case concern has centered on the outsourcing of services and its implications for the employment of skilled workers in the United States. In Chapter 2, Barry Bosworth, Susan M. Collins, and Aaron Flaaen examine US trade with both countries. The authors first note that the US trade deficit is due more to unusually low US exports than to unusually high imports from China and India. In seeking to understand these low US exports, they find that the US competes head to head—often less than successfully—with Japan and the EU-15 in the Chinese market. Another explanation for the relatively low level of US exports to China and India is the limited presence of US multinationals in the two countries—multinationals typically constituting an important conduit for exports. The authors also use a gravity model to show that the distance of the United States from Asian markets does not have much to do with its disappointing export performance. Finally, they observe that the low level of US exports is a global phenomenon and not limited to the Asian economies. Their findings thus go some way toward dispelling the notion that the unfavorable trade balance of the US in China and India is due to unfair trade practices.

In the final chapter of this first part, Zhi Wang and Shang-Jin Wei document the rising sophistication of Chinese exports and analyze the country's evolving export structure. They measure the sophistication of Chinese exports in two ways: The overlap between its export structure and that of developed countries; and the unit value of exports within each product category. They find that both measures point to significant increases in the sophistication of China's exports. Insofar as China has moved from exporting mainly relatively low-tech, labor-intensive goods to exporting medium- and high-tech products, it is now competing more directly with the advanced economies. As for what explains the growing sophistication of China's exports, the authors point to human capital accumulation and to Government policy, such as the creation of tax-favored high-tech zones. To be sure, both processing trade (that is, the assembly of imported parts and components for re-export) and foreign

Introduction

investment enterprises have played roles in the growing sophistication of China's exports, but they are far from the entire story.

Comparisons and contrasts

The next set of chapters offers a series of comparisons and contrasts. Bart van Ark, Abdul Azeez Erumban, Vivian Chen, and Utsav Kumar compare productivity in India and China at the industry and provincial levels. They find that productivity in Chinese industry has been increasing over time and that this increase is quite uniform across provinces. In comparison, productivity growth is slower in India, and there is considerable heterogeneity across provinces. The authors attribute these differences to faster implementation of market reforms in China and to lower factor mobility in India.

Franklin Allen, Rajesh Chakrabarti, Sankar De, Jun 'QJ' Qian, and Meijun Qian compare the legal and financial systems of the two countries and explore their implications for economic growth. As they show, China's legal and financial systems are underdeveloped by almost any metric. India presents an anomaly of a different sort: Despite the origin of the legal system in English common law and the presence of an independent judiciary—on the basis of which many economists would expect favorable financial development—investor protection and the quality of financial institutions remain weak. And yet, despite these financial weaknesses, the two economies have registered high rates of growth in recent years. The authors point to informal finance and relational lending as mechanisms by which the two countries have surmounted financial obstacles to growth.

Przemyslaw Kowalski compares the trade integration processes of the two countries. While China has liberalized its manufacturing trade and FDI to a much greater extent than India, important constraints remain on the growth of the services sector in the form of a high level of public ownership and regulatory barriers. India, for its part, has reduced tariff and non-tariff barriers to trade, but continues to apply important limits on import competition with domestic manufacturing. The result has been two quite different sectoral patterns, with trade and growth led by manufacturing in China and by services in India. The author's simulations show that the implementation of China's General Agreement on Trade in Services (GATS) commitments would create important gains for China itself as well as for its trading partners. In India's case, further expanding foreign

Introduction

trade will require removing residual barriers at the border, implementing internal reforms, such as relaxing labor laws, promoting interstate labor mobility, and improving infrastructure.

Challenges for sustaining growth

The third part considers the challenges to sustaining growth in the two countries. Eswar Prasad first analyzes China's macroeconomic and structural policies. Jahangir Aziz then considers the challenges to financial sector development in the two countries. Finally, Catherine Yap Co, Fanying Kong, and Shuanglin Lin focus on environmental degradation in China, while Poonam Gupta, Rana Hasan, and Utsav Kumar look at the factors inhibiting the growth of India's industrial sector.

Prasad observes that Chinese officials will have to complete a demanding reform agenda in order to successfully sustain recent growth performance, not just because of the economy's internal weaknesses but because integration with the world economy will mean greater susceptibility to external shocks. Making growth more resilient will require a stable macroeconomic policy framework and a more efficient financial sector. This in turn would require an effective monetary policy, a more flexible exchange rate, and slow but steady movement in the direction of a more open capital account. Prasad points out that earlier efforts to limit the flexibility of the exchange rate were facilitated by the tight regulation of domestic as well as international financial transactions, something that has already begun to change and whose pace will now accelerate as the economy continues to open. He recommends greater exchange rate flexibility and the adoption of an explicit inflation target as a nominal anchor for monetary policy. He cautions that further movement in the direction of exchange rate flexibility should precede further opening of the capital account and that, insofar as there is now a tendency for the capital account to open spontaneously, there is no time to waste.

Aziz underscores the importance of financial reform for sustaining growth in both China and India. He observes that the cost of capital is significantly distorted in both countries. In China it is depressed by the authorities' permissive policies toward nonperforming loans and the retention of profits by state-owned enterprises. Among the consequences, he notes, is an inefficiently high level of investment. In India, in contrast, the cost of capital is elevated by limited financial sector competition and the absorption of resources by the state. The result, equally predictably,

Introduction

has been an inefficiently low level of investment. After long periods of little or no growth, both countries were able to prosper despite the presence of these financial distortions. But now that the low-hanging fruit has been picked, Aziz emphasizes the urgency of comprehensive financial reform.

Co, Kong, and Lin examine the environmental implications of China's growth. Their findings suggest that pollution is correlated with industrial activity, with the prominence of the public sector in production, and with the fiscal position of local Government. *Ceteris paribus*, provinces in the north of China and those with lower levels of industrial activity have less pollution. But all else is not equal: Provinces with more state-owned enterprises appear to suffer from greater environmental degradation. Moreover, the worse the fiscal condition of local Government, the less it appears to invest in environmental protection and the higher the priority attached to industrial growth (which is a source of revenue growth). The authors recommend more stringent enforcement of environmental protection legislation by the central Government and stronger incentives for local Government to encourage environment-friendly growth, for example, by tying central Government transfers not only to local output growth but also to environmental outcomes.

Finally, Poonam Gupta, Rana Hasan, and Utsav Kumar discuss the distinctive sectoral transformation of the Indian economy, comparing a service sector whose share of GDP has been growing rapidly with a manufacturing sector whose share of GDP has stagnated. This phenomenon is puzzling insofar as the reforms of the past fifteen years have focused mainly on manufacturing. Using data on formal manufacturing enterprises at the three-digit level of disaggregation, the authors find that labor-intensive industries, sectors dependent on infrastructure, and activities in which productivity requires support from the financial sector have shown a tendency to lag. They interpret their results as indicating the importance of infrastructure investment, financial development, and labor market reforms to enhance the growth and competitiveness of Indian manufacturing and, thus, create the industrial employment that will more widely spread the benefits of the country's growth.

Though both China and India have seen millions lifted out of poverty through successful economic growth, continued progress in this direction is not assured. While the two countries are increasingly mentioned in the same breath, a key message of this volume is that they face quite different challenges going forward. Challenges emanate from the fact that growth in the two countries has been concentrated in a few sectors, has relied on unsustainably high levels of capital accumulation in China, and has not generated adequate employment growth in India. China needs to rebalance its growth away from investment and exports, move toward a more rational pricing system for land, power, and fuel, enforce more stringent environmental standards, implement significant reforms of the financial sector, and adopt greater exchange rate flexibility. India needs to grow its manufacturing sector, reform its labor laws, invest in infrastructure, further liberalize its foreign trade, and strengthen its financial system by reducing the dominance and influence of the public sector. The main thing that these two agendas have in common is that both are ambitious and will be difficult to complete.

The conference at which the initial drafts of the chapters were presented in New Delhi in December 2007 was sponsored by the Indian Council for Research on International Economic Relations, the Konrad-Adenauer Foundation, and the International Monetary Fund. For help with organization, we thank Manmeet Ahuja, Neena Bhatia, Anil Kumar, and Laxman Rao. We also thank Anil Kumar and Laxman Rao for preparing the manuscript of the book.

Part I

China and India in the Global Economy

1
What Can Be Learned about the Economies of China and India from Purchasing Power Comparisons?

*Alan Heston**

1.1 Introduction

Comparisons of India and China have been a media and scholarly staple since 1950 with academic antecedents in the orientalist tradition and more popular precursors in accounts of famine, floods, and disease. Since 1950 there have been economic comparisons by Wilfred Malenbaum, T. N. Srinivasan, S. Swamy, and A. K. Sen among others. Scholars, whose principal interest was China, have been wiser, perhaps, in concentrating their attention on the Chinese experience, rather than in comparisons. My research interests for the past forty years have concentrated on purchasing power estimates across regions and countries so, not surprisingly, this paper adopts a comparative framework.

Section 1.2 of the chapter discusses the interrelationships of purchasing power conversions of GDP to economic growth. Section 1.3 looks at both China and India in the 2005 round of the UN International Comparison Programme (ICP) that was coordinated by the World Bank, the Regional Banks, and Economic Commissions.[1] The 2005 ICP round

---

* I am indebted to Surjit S. Bhalla and other participants at the conference on India and China's role in International Trade and Finance and Global Economic Governance, Indian Council for Research on International Economic Relations (ICRIER), New Delhi, December 6–7, 2007 for useful comments.

[1] The first round of the ICP was initiated in 1968, when the author joined the work, and involved 10 countries, including India, for 1970. The 2005 round involves 146 countries including all India and a less satisfactory estimate for all of China.

provides estimates of purchasing power parities (PPPs) of currencies and real product per capita for 146 countries, and the results for China and India are discussed in the context of the size of these economies. Section 1.4 discusses possible insights that the ICP provides into the sources of past and prospects of future economic growth in China and India. Section 1.5 concludes with a note on PPPs and the 'appropriate' exchange rate, the subject in the past several years of a number of writings involving analysis, policy recommendations for China, and likely scenarios in the future.

1.2 The growth record in a comparative framework

Most discussions of growth rates consider in their comparisons only the national statistical record without taking account of the levels of economic output at the beginning and end of the growth journey for the countries being compared. Consider, for example, the following illustration from the Penn World Table (PWT), which has attempted to monitor the performance of China and India along with most of the worlds' economies. The distinctive feature of PWT has been to use purchasing power parities to move from GDP and its major components at national currencies to a common international unit that we have termed international dollars; and to provide a time series of these estimates. In the latest version, PWT 6.2, the estimates run for some or all the years, 1950 to 2004, for some 168 countries.[2] This version, which is under revision, incorporates the 2006 official revisions of China's national accounts based upon new service sector surveys and Chinese official growth rates. Table 1.1 presents the per capita GDP of China and India in 1978 and 2000, in 2000 dollars converted at PPPs in columns 1 and 2. Columns 3 and 4 express these relative to the United States. If taken individually the economic performance of each country over this period might not raise eyebrows. But when China is compared to India, the estimates become implausible moving backward from 2000 (column 5): In 1952 using official growth rates of both countries, an admittedly questionable excursion, India is 2.43 times China's per capita GDP.

Scholars, such as Clark (1965), Eckstein (1977), Malenbaum (1982), Swamy (1973), and others who have looked at both countries over the

See: http://web.worldbank.org/WBSITE/EXTERNAL/DATASTATISTICS/ICPEXT/0,,pagePK: 62002243~theSitePK:270065,00.html and World Bank (2008).

[2] See pwt.econ.upenn.edu.

The Economies of China and India

Table 1.1. Per capita GDP levels at 2000 prices from PWT 6.2

Year	GDPpc China (1)	GDPpc India (2)	As % of US China (3)	As % of US India (4)	Ratio India/China (5)
2003	$4,970	$2,990	14.3%	8.6%	0.60
1978	$669	$1,318	3.2%	6.0%	1.97
1952	$326	$794	2.7%	6.3%	2.43

past fifty years, might have given India a slight edge in 1952; China was emerging from civil war to a frosty international reception, while India had gained its independence, written its constitution, and launched its first Five-Year Plan with international assistance. However, despite the ups and downs of China until 1978, observers would put China above India at the start of reforms in 1978; this conclusion would be based on a variety of real measures like caloric consumption, energy consumption, primary education, and health status. Further, there are purchasing power studies around the beginning of reforms in China that clearly put Chinese per capita GDP above India by 20 to 50 percent.[3] Clearly official growth rates for both countries do not describe their comparative experience within acceptable margins, and may not be a very good starting point for understanding their growth experience or the lessons they provide for other countries.

What is the explanation?

Most literature puts the blame on China's official growth rates. However, the discussion often gets complicated.[4] For example, it is frequently argued that if anything, China has underestimated its GDP, so how can

---

[3] Eckstein (1977) put Indian per capita GDP in 1952 at $50 and that of China at $60. Hollister (1958) undertook a bilateral PPP comparison of China and the US, for 1952 and 1955, placing China at $146 in 1955. In PWT, India was $145 in 1955, both in current prices. The closeness of these two numbers is totally by chance, but certainly places China in a similar position to India. Kravis (1981) carried out China–US PPP comparison that put per capita GDP at 12% of the US in 1975, and that of India, 6%, again very different than implied by official growth rates going back from 2000. Ahmad (1983) carried out a PPP study for 1981 that also included India. It implied that in 1981 China's per capita GDP was 50% above that of India. The study used by Maddison (1998) in his work on China is based on Ren Ruoen and Chen Kai (1995), that, less so than Kravis suggests, China's economic position was higher than implied by official growth rates.

[4] The discussion here focuses on growth rates, but there has also been a fairly heated discussion between Carsten Holz and Angus Maddison (Holz 2006) regarding the latter's adjustments to levels of Chinese GDP.

5

it have overstated its growth rates? The answer, in fact, is that the two phenomena are quite compatible.[5] Critics of Chinese growth rates have argued that the Chinese price statistics have underestimated the degree of inflation while defenders (Klein and Ozmucur 2003) have pointed out that China has not made corrections for quality improvements, so in fact price indexes have a tendency to overstate inflation.

The recent paper by Harry Wu (2007) has focused on the official incorporation by China of their 2006 revisions of national accounts and he proposes a more plausible explanation. In the official revisions the current price statistics were adjusted upwards to reflect previously unrecorded output, particularly in the service sector. This was followed by a constant price series that is the basis for the estimation of growth rates of GDP. What Wu shows is that the official growth rates were maintained throughout the 1990–2005 period, while the current price production statistics showed some decline in the 1997–1998 period in response to the Asian financial crisis. The only way to achieve the planned growth rates was to adjust the deflators of GDP downward in an inexplicable and undocumented way, so as to preserve the planned level of growth.

Put another way, OECD members and many other countries including India have followed the UN System of National Accounts over the past forty years, and compute real GDP growth series by dividing estimates of current production by independently estimated price deflators. The rate of growth is thus a residual. What Wu is arguing is that in China, current production and planned growth rates are taken as truth, and the GDP deflator is residually derived.[6] In contrast to China, Indian planning shortfalls have historically been freely reported with the opposition blaming policies of the current Government, and with the current Government blaming external factors, such as the monsoon. None of this necessarily puts into question the increasingly accepted view that China is now, or soon will be, the second largest economy in the world. However, this

[5] Many adjustments that raise the level of GDP or major components are done once only, but many require substantial adjustments in earlier years too. Suppose older series put GDP at 50 in 1990 and 100 in 2005, with the service sector being 15 and 30 respectively. A new survey raises the service sector to 50 and GDP to 120 in 2005, and to 30 and 65 in 1990. The old growth showed a doubling (100/50) of output in the 15 years, and the new growth rate, an 85% increase (120/65−1)*100. This amounts to a slower growth than before correcting for undercounting of the level of services in GDP.

[6] China derives its constant price series from the production side of the accounts which means that there are different deflators for the major sectors like agriculture, industry, services and the like. The implication of Wu's analysis is that the deflators of some of these sectors take up the slack. Section 1.4 discusses the likely case that deflation of the tertiary sector is a suspect and the implication this has for understanding future growth prospects in both China and India.

The Economies of China and India

Table 1.2. Official, Maddison and Wu, and PWT indexes of per capita GDP

Year	Official China (1)	Maddison & Wu China (2)	PWT62 China (3)	PWT62 India (4)	Ratio Maddison & Wu India/China (5)	Ratio PWT62 India/China (6)
1952	6.9	11.2	6.6	26.5	1.00	2.43
1978	13.6	20.4	13.5	44.1	0.91	1.97
1990	31.7	39.0	33.6	63.5	0.69	1.13
2003	100.0	100.0	100.0	100.0	0.42	0.60

discussion of growth rates is intended to question some of the projections of growth for China into the future for two reasons, one because of likely overstatement, and two because of structural factors to be discussed in Section 1.4.

Maddison and Wu (2007) have suggested lower growth rates than official rates, namely 7.85 percent per annum vs. 9.60 percent for total GDP. This growth restatement is based primarily on adjustments to the official rates for industrial production and services. Table 1.2 presents in column 1 the official levels of GDP per capita for China where the value in 2003 is set as an index of 100; columns 2–4 do the same for the Maddison and Wu estimates and the PWT 6.2 estimates for China and India. Column 1 suggests that compared to 2003 levels of 100, per capita GDP at constant prices was 6.9 in 1952 and only 13.6 at the start of reforms.[7]

The adjustments proposed by Maddison and Wu are incorporated in column 2. Column 3 is close to, but not identical to the official series in column 1; the difference arises because PWT applies slightly different weights than contained in the official statistics to the growth rates of the four expenditure components, consumption, investment, Government, and the net foreign balance.[8]

Column 5 asks the following question? If India and China had equal per capita GDPs in 1952, what would be the relationship of India to China in subsequent years assuming the PWT values for India and the adjustments of Maddison and Wu for China? So in column 5 for 1952 the

---

[7] Official Chinese statistics present a time series of national accounts beginning in 1978. However, the State Statistical Bureau and the Hitotsubashi University (1997) put the national accounts of China in the form of the UN system of national accounts (SNA) from 1952 to 1978. These estimates were based adjustments of the older national accounts of China that used the Material Product System of national accounts used in Soviet bloc countries.

[8] The relation of the indexes of India to China may appear larger in Table 1.2 (column 4 to 3) than in Table 1.1; this is because in Table 1.2, 2003 is set at 100 for both countries. Because the level of per capita GDP in China is much larger than India in 2003, it is not really appropriate to compare the two indexes.

Alan Heston

ratio of GDP per capita of India to China is taken as 1.00. Even though China experienced much larger swings during the Great Leap and Cultural Revolution the experience of China and India over the whole period 1952 to 1978 was fairly similar, namely slow growth. In the column 5 scenario, China pulled significantly ahead of India after the reforms began in 1978 reaching a per capita GDP in 2003 that was more than double that of India.

Column 6 is simply a restatement of the last column of Table 1.1, filling in the rows of Table 1.2 for years in addition to 1978 that are used by Maddison and Wu. As noted, column 6 relies on official series in China and India, using PPPs for GDP that are somewhat different than those of Maddison and Wu to obtain the starting levels of GDP per capita. The conclusion is that the growth rates of China implicit in column 5 provide us with a much more plausible comparison of the economic performance of China and India than provided by column 6.[9]

The discussion of growth rates so far has focused on consistency over the past thirty to fifty-five years. But our conclusion clearly has implications for projections that are based upon past growth rates. For example, *The Economist* (June 30, 2007, p. 31) presents a Goldman Sachs GDP forecast, beginning at a lower base than PWT, that puts the total size of the Chinese economy as passing the United States by 2025, when both would have $20 trillion in 2006 prices. Such forecasts are based on past official growth rates, which if overstated, bring into question the value of such projections. There are other reasons that past growth, at official or other rates, may not be a guide to future experience, which are taken up in Section 1.4.

1.3 Levels of GDP in China and India

China and India have been leaders in advocating that their votes in the IMF should be based upon their GDP converted at PPPs; while at the same time maintaining that the United Nations should continue the use of exchange rates for determining their contributions. This is hardly surprising since votes in the UN are primarily by membership and in the World Bank and IMF by size of the economy. Compared to exchange rates, the use of PPPs would in 2003 raise China's GDP by a factor of 4.2 and India's by 5.7 relative to the United States in PWT.

[9] In PWT 6.3 it is proposed to provide series for China using both sets of growth rates.

Another way to express this relationship is the national price level, the PPP/exchange rate expressed as a percentage. In 2003, these estimates in PWT were 17.5 in India and 23.9 in China, meaning it would take $0.175 in India and $0.239 in China to purchase what a dollar would buy in the United States over the bundle of goods that make up GDP. The fact that nontradable goods like construction, education, personal services, and general Government comprise over half of GDP helps make such differences easier to comprehend. The PWT estimates of PPPs for China and India are approximately the same as those used in the World Bank and in the IMF for its World Economic Outlook. One point that emerges is that China's price level is not different from that of countries at similar levels of income, a point not usually made clear in the discussions of whether the exchange rate of China is undervalued.

More recent PPP estimates

The price levels quoted above are at the lower end of the spectrum of estimates that have been put forward in recent years for China and India. That is, they place the GDP of these countries higher than others who on plausible grounds argue for numbers that are often two-thirds or half of that in PWT or the World Bank. The good news is that the final report of the 2005 ICP has been released and includes new estimates of real GDP levels for both China and India. The other news is that the results have generated a fair amount of controversy primarily because they substantially lower the position of a number of countries in Asia, China and India included, relative to the OECD countries.

SOME BACKGROUND TO THE 2005 ICP ESTIMATES

India participated in the first round of the ICP covering ten countries for 1970 (Kravis et al. 1975), and like a number of other countries, has had a love–hate relationship with the project over the years. In contrast, China has never fully participated in the ICP, which has given rise to what might be termed partial surveys (see footnote 4). Full participation requires that a country provide a detailed distribution of expenditures for about 130 basic headings like rice, public transport, and residential construction. For each heading countries must also provide national annual average prices of three to six product specifications per heading. This price collection is the truly international characteristic of the work that permits estimation of PPPs at both detailed and aggregate levels.

Alan Heston

Table 1.3. The size of the world economy

GDP 2005 ($ billions)	ICP 2005 GDP @PPP	Previous GDP @PPP WDI	GDP @ ExRates
World-146 countries	54,975	59,712	44,306
High income: OECD	31,422	31,726	33,342
Africa	964	1,264	486
Asia and Pacific	10,971	16,367	4,221
CIS	2,269	2,171	970
South America	2,698	2,911	1,411
West Asia	1,158	932	588

Source: Constructed using data from Table 1 of the ICP 2005 Report.

THE 2005 ESTIMATES

The Asian Development Bank coordinated the twenty-four Asia-Pacific countries, including China and India, who participated in the 2005 ICP comparisons for which the World Bank served as the Global Office. The Final Global results, released in May 2008 for the 146 countries, are summarized in Table 1.3. Column 1 provides the results of ICP 2005 and column 2 the totals in the World Development Indicators (WDI) of the World Bank, aggregates that are similar to PWT though there would be differences for individual countries. Both columns 1 and 2 are much closer to each other than to exchange rate totals as given in column 3, a result found in all rounds of the ICP since 1970. What has caught the attention of many commentators is the smaller share of a smaller World GDP of Africa and particularly Asia, the latter accounted for mainly by China and India. Turning specifically now to China and India, the new results are provided in Table 1.4 for China, India, and select countries including the earlier estimates from PWT. The World Bank Report discusses some important reasons for the 40 percent reduction in the positions of China and India compared to the previous WDI (and PWT) results. The discussion below examines several of these issues and suggests how users familiar with the earlier estimates might want to think about the new estimates in terms of the place of China and India in the world economy.

One reason offered for the large changes in Table 1.3 for Asia, Africa, and West Asia is that participation in the 2005 ICP was 146 countries, and all benchmark comparisons for countries in these three regions were non-existent or over ten years old.

Table 1.4 presents the final estimates of the Bank placing China as the second largest economy in the world, with Japan third, and

The Economies of China and India

Table 1.4. Preliminary World Bank estimates for 2005 of levels of China and India

Country	GDP pc (billions) $ at Exchange Rates	Price Level US = 100	GDP (billions) $ at PPPs	GDP pc $ at PPPs	Population (thousands)	Exchange Rate Local currency/$
China	1,721	42	5,333	4,091	1,303,720	8.19
India	707	33	2,341	2,126	1,101,318	44.10
United States	41,674	100	12,376	41,674	296,497	1.00
Japan	30,290	118	3,870	30,290	127,800	110.2
World	7,230	81	54,976	8,971	6,128,000	

Source: Constructed using data from Table 1 of the ICP 2005 Report.

Germany fourth, just above India. These results are a major departure from exchange rates, but also considerably lower than the numbers in PWT or previous bank publications. The resources devoted to this round of the ICP in terms of regional consultations and price validations were much more than in previous comparisons. The 2005 round should be much improved, so the question arises as to whether there are reasons that the new numbers are so much lower than previous estimates for China and India.

THE 2005 RESULTS AND EARLIER BENCHMARKS

This section provides four reasons why the 2005 round might lower Asia's position in the world economy in comparison with previous rounds. We begin with the urban nature of price collection in China; second is the treatment of Government administrative services and other non-priced output; third is the linking of regional comparisons into the world economy; and fourth is the treatment of the net foreign balance.

(1) National average prices

China agreed to participate in the ICP in the 1993 and 2005 comparisons but on a limited basis providing mainly urban prices. In 1993 the plan was to compare Shanghai with Tokyo and Guangdong with Hong Kong; the Shanghai comparison was never made public but the Guangdong comparison was completed and was described in the publication of ESCAP (1999). Of course, that leaves the question of how you go from Guangdong to all of China, and in the ESCAP publication, this was not attempted. Interestingly there is a long tradition of such

11

city to city comparisons going back to a Shanghai–Tokyo comparison for 1955.[10]

The price collection by China in 2005 took place in eleven cities and their surrounding areas. The expenditures refer to all of China and the prices were moved to an all China basis to replicate the inputs of fully participating countries. Like the 1993 comparison, the relationship of urban to rural prices is the critical step and the method used in 2005 did not involve any price information beyond that provided to the ICP. There have been no official studies of rural–urban price differences. There are urban and rural expenditure surveys that permit comparisons of unit values of many food items and several non-food item, such as tobacco, fuels and power, and transport. Some research has been carried out with these expenditure surveys but permission to make any results of these studies public has not been forthcoming. Further, even if these results were available, the consumption items for which price differences appear largest are items like housing, medical, and personal services.[11] These are precisely the items that have not been surveyed or measured very well in most studies.

One early argument was that price collection in China was organized in a way that provided prices that were too high because of some combination of choice of brand, outlet, or center for collection. The price collection by China in 2005 took place in eleven cities and their immediate surrounding areas that had some rural and some urban characteristics. In their review of the Chinese results for the purpose of producing new poverty lines Chen and Ravallion (2008, Figure 1) concluded that the provinces of eleven ICP cities represented the range of urban poverty lines in all provinces, an encouraging finding. Their conclusion is based on rural and urban poverty price levels that they independently estimated by province for 2002. In that study the eleven urban provinces used in the ICP had an average poverty line of 1,243 yuan, which may be compared to an all province urban average of 1,195 yuan, and an average rural line of 849 yuan. This line was based upon actual region-specific food bundles and so it can be interpreted as price differences between rural and urban

---

[10] See Mizoguchi (1968). This study found that the urban price level in Japan was about 30% higher than in China. The study was also consistent with Colin Clark's estimates in Clark (1965; 1976).

[11] For example, Aten (2006) shows that for the US, prices of commodities increase only slightly as you move from low-income small urban areas to higher-income centers, such as New York or San Francisco, whereas service prices rise fairly sharply. Overall prices differ by over 60% across the 38 BLS centers that are surveyed.

The Economies of China and India

areas for a poverty bundle. It is clear that the eleven ICP provinces were only slightly more affluent than all cities.

However, it is unlikely that the eleven cities represented the price levels of urban centers in their provinces. For example, Chen and Ravallion report that the National Bureau of Statistics (NBS) chose those cities because they were most likely to have outlets carrying the types of products and brands in the ICP specifications. Chen and Ravallion also note that the rural areas were closer to what would be suburbs than rural areas, and of the 1,700 outlets sampled (an impressive number in ICP practice) about 22 percent were in these 'rural' areas. They conclude that a downward adjustment of 35 percent is required in the 2005 results for China for purposes of approximating prices in rural areas in their poverty analysis.

Brandt and Holz (2004) have made the most comprehensive set of comparisons of rural-urban and regional price levels in China for 1990 updating the results to 2004.[12] As more and more of the urban housing is market priced, the rural-urban differentials for rented and owner-occupied housing have increased in China. However, in their work Brandt and Holz only approximate rental differences by the cost of construction taking no account of the scarcity value of land. If there is a direction of error in their estimates, it is to understate the difference between rural and urban prices in China. Table 1.5 presents a summary of the Brandt-Holz estimates.[13] For a common or joint basket of goods that holds quantities equal, the cost in rural and urban areas for 2004 is given in columns 1 and 2. Urban prices as a percent of rural prices are given in column 3. Several points are worth noting.

First there appears to be much more difference between prices across the provinces than between rural and urban areas within provinces. For example, the joint basket in rural Beijing is 84.7 percent higher than in rural Chongquing. The largest urban-rural difference across provinces is 43.5 percent in Chongquing. The costs of a common basket in urban Beijing is 50.9 percent higher than in urban Chongquing. Table 1.4 highlights why it is difficult to move from urban to national prices in a large country like China.

---

[12] The Brandt-Holz estimates have been used by Sicular et al. (2007) to compare the rural-urban income gap in China.

[13] In their paper they prefer an adjusted CPI index for rural areas to update their 1990 base estimates. These estimates only go to 2002. In column 1 their estimates have been extrapolated to 2004.

Alan Heston

Table 1.5. Rural–urban price differences by province (2004)

Area	Rural Prices Adjusted (1)	Urban Prices Official CPI (2)	Urban/Rural (%) Extrapolated (3)
Nationwide	1,486	1,924	129.5
Beijing	2,240	2,627	117.3
Tianjin	1,795	2,120	118.1
Hebei	1,320	1,807	136.9
Shanxi	1,451	2,028	139.8
Neimenggu	1,429	1,864	130.4
Liaoning	1,393	1,963	140.9
Jilin	1,414	1,814	128.3
Heilongjiang	1,425	1,867	131.0
Shanghai	2,197	2,586	117.7
Jiangsu	1,611	2,061	127.9
Zhejiang	1,541	2,076	134.7
Anhui	1,663	1,843	110.8
Fujian	1,561	2,127	136.3
Jiangxi	1,489	1,883	126.5
Shandong	1,473	1,968	133.6
Henan	1,427	1,805	126.5
Hubei	1,627	2,011	123.6
Hunan	1,835	1,956	106.6
Guangdong	1,819	2,569	141.2
Guangxi	1,655	1,819	109.9
Hainan	1,873	2,474	132.1
Sichuan	1,471	1,911	129.9
Guizhou	1,924	1,862	96.8
Yunnan	1,857	1,922	103.5
Xizang	1,654	1,846	111.6
Shaanxi	1,911	1,953	102.2
Gansu	1,792	1,828	102.0
Qinghai	1,547	1,951	126.1
Ningxia	1,683	1,871	111.2
Xinjiang	1,637	1,860	113.6
Chongqing	1,213	1,740	143.5

Consider the 1993 urban comparison that was made for Guangdong–Hong Kong. This comparison, which involved statisticians from both countries, estimated that the PPP of Rmb/HK$ over GDP was 0.466 when the exchange rate was 0.743, implying a price level 62 percent of that in Hong Kong. These estimates were done with considerable care but often the attempt to compare the same qualities may have led to selecting items in China that were not commonly consumed. This is particularly true in clothing and footwear where it was estimated that the price level in China was 64 percent above that of Hong Kong. Further, these bilateral price levels also tend to overstate the prices in China compared to what happens in a multilateral comparison. But even allowing for these factors the price level for Guangdong is likely to have been 55 percent that of Hong Kong in 1993, much higher than the all China price level of 25 percent that PWT and the bank are using. Are such differences between urban and national price levels plausible?

Looking at Table 1.5, urban Guangdong prices are 73 percent above the average for rural China and 34 percent above urban China. If these factors were used if would suggest the price level in all of China was 35 percent of Hong Kong circa 1993. Hong Kong was in turn, 82 percent of the price level of the United States in 1993, so a price level of China that was under 30 percent of the US is consistent with these numbers.

The Brandt–Holz work is based on unit values and has other limitations that leads one to ask whether the differences they report by region are high relative to other countries. Aten (2006) reports that for the 38 urban centers used by the US for the CPI the differences between small southern urban areas and San Francisco are large, 80 vs. 130 percent of the US average in 2003. From the million plus prices collected, Aten is able to obtain about 25,000 annual average price observations for 256 entry-level items collected by the BLS from which price-level differences over all of consumption can be estimated. This is a rich data set that has now been updated to include 2004 and 2005 with similar findings, so that we can be fairly certain that the range across US urban areas is around 60 percent, suggesting that the Brandt–Holz estimates for China are not unreasonable. Aten also finds that the gradient of prices from low to high is not large for goods, but it is much steeper for services, a common finding of previous rounds of the ICP across countries. Unfortunately, it is service items, such as housing, medical, and personal services, that have not been surveyed or measured very well in the ICP, or the expenditure surveys that underlie the Brandt–Holz study.

But is the situation of price collection for the ICP so different in China from other large developing countries? There are other large countries, such as India, Nigeria, Egypt, Brazil, Bangladesh, or Indonesia, where the extent of coverage of price collection, or adjustment to national averages, is not as clear. For the ICP, India uses prices in a number of cities broadly covering the most important regions of the country and modifies these based upon their rural labor price index. However, in rapidly growing countries like India or China, price collection is not being carried out in an economic environment where spatial differences are close to being in long-term balance. That is, disparities are probably larger than they will be in less interesting times, and less well measured than they will be when the framework for price collection catches up with the economies. And the big differences by region are not for commodities, which are easier to price, but for services, where differences can easily be 50 percent or more. The main reasons for service price differences are site rent, which means services provided in large urban areas including housing, must cost more than smaller cities, less accessible regions, and rural areas; and the lower wage rates of service workers in these areas.

This raises a more general question for the ICP as between large, diverse countries and smaller city states. National average prices for countries, such as Hong Kong, Singapore, and Luxembourg are quite fully covered in the outlets used for their CPIs. However, for large countries, such as Brazil, China, or India, this is less likely because prices within a country will move in unison over time so the CPI does not require full country coverage. This means the framework for collecting prices for nontradable services does not adequately reflect internal price differences within large developing countries compared to very small countries or more affluent highly urban economies. This factor tends to bias price levels in large developing countries upward.[14]

Until there has been more analysis of the detailed ICP results not much more can be said about how we should interpret price levels between small and large developing countries as reported in the 2005 ICP.[15] One approach to this is to compare unit values from expenditure surveys in ICP countries, that do cover the whole of countries, with corresponding ICP prices. We do have estimates noted above that prices in rural China may be 35 percent below those in urban areas for a poverty bundle. For all of China, however, this effect for rural–urban price difference is likely to be less because for those not in poverty, a higher proportion of the purchases are for goods for which price differences are less. However,

---

[14] This would tend to lower the volume of services if the national accounts adequately capture the expenditures on some of these services, for example, the site rent involved in rural housing. Since the national accounts may well miss some of these expenditures, the bias in price collection may well be partially offset, so that volume comparisons are less affected.

[15] Large high-income countries, such as the US, France, or Australia, essentially provide urban prices for commodities and services. While this is similar to what is done in many of the lower-income countries in the ICP, the consequences are not large because the higher-income countries are more urban and make more purchases in urban areas or online. The EU asks countries to supply an adjustment factor to move urban prices to a national level, but the factor used for most items is 1.0 meaning no adjustment. There is a directive in the EU for Eurostat to estimate regional price levels within countries but this has not been funded or implemented. An important exception is housing, where EU countries collect rents on several sizes of apartments and houses, with different amenity combinations on a more national level. The US estimates a hedonic regression using the appropriate specifications to supply rent price levels.

regional differences appear to be large in China, and it would appear that price collection took place in urban areas with higher than average prices so there would be an added downward regional effect that also should be considered. It should be noted that China has been very clear on where they would price for the 2005 comparisons, and the real problem is how to interpret the results. While these comments may sound critical of the 2005 benchmark, it is important to understand that we are only able to raise these questions because the 2005 comparison has been better documented by individual countries and by regions compared to the 1980 and subsequent benchmarks, when regional comparisons and fixity were introduced.

A final point relates to the quality of items compared across the wide range of economies in the ICP. On one hand, the average quality of goods entering into the CPI tends to be lower in poorer countries so it can be argued that they may match lower-quality items with higher-quality items in richer countries, making their price levels too low. This is more likely to have occurred in earlier ICP benchmarks. In contrast more effort was made at Regional meetings to insure an exact matching of items in ICP 2005. This effect was reinforced by the fact than many of the qualities available in the CPIs of poorer countries are not available in higher-income countries, while the qualities in the CPIs of richer countries can also be found in poorer countries. Also, the higher-quality items are frequently international brands while regional or brand less products are more important for lower-quality items. The consequence is that higher-quality items tend to dominate the actual list of items compared in the ICP. These items will often not be in the CPIs of poorer countries nor necessarily available in the outlets normally sampled in their CPIs, the consequence being to raise price levels of poorer countries.

The first of the two effects, the use of prices of lower-quality items in poorer countries, was more prevalent in the earlier ICP benchmarks, and the opposite was more frequent in the 2005 ICP because of the stress on and validation of exact matches of specifications within the countries of a region and between regions. The net impact on comparisons is that the price levels in the 2005 ICP for lower-income countries tend to be too high in some expenditure groupings, especially as compared to earlier benchmark comparisons. More research is needed to evaluate what the net effect of the quality factor on the overall comparisons is. The conclusion drawn from this long discussion of national average prices is that there is some upward bias in the price levels of China, and to a lesser extent, India, compared to more affluent countries.

(2) The equal productivity assumption

How does one compare the output of civil servants, health and education workers across countries? Because these outputs are not typically priced, in past ICP rounds volumes have been derived by dividing compensation by a PPP that was derived from a detailed comparison of salaries for specific occupations. It had been recognized that this procedure assumed equal productivity across countries in a given occupation, which was unlikely given very different amounts of capital per worker and opportunity costs of labor across countries. Very low wage economies have little inducement to organize work to improve productivity of their employees, including in administrative, health, and education services. In the 2005 benchmark, the range of countries was much greater than in previous rounds, and some consequences of the equal productivity assumption loomed much larger. In Asia, for example, salaries for the same occupation differ by a factor of 100 between Laos and Hong Kong. Similar differences exist between Yemen and Kuwait in the western Asia comparison. Without some adjustment for productivity, the resulting per capita volumes in Yemen or Vietnam would greatly exceed those of its richer neighbors. Such adjustments have been considered before by the OECD and the ICP, but the 2005 Asian comparison is the first actual case where the equal productivity assumption has been significantly modified.[16]

Asia, West Asia, and Africa have also carried out such adjustments based on estimates of capital per worker in the whole economy of each country. In Asia, for example, it means that the volume of GDP of China and India relative to Hong Kong or Singapore will be lower than in previous ICP rounds. This poses a problem of comparability across regions in 2005 because EU-OECD-CIS and South America have not made such adjustments. Further, because capital per worker data were not available for many countries, it was often necessary to apply the same adjustment factor to low-income countries that were at different stages of development.

What does this mean for comparing the 2005 results for previous benchmarks? In previous benchmarks, the volume of administrative, health, and education services for very low wage countries in Africa, Asia, and West Asia would have been substantially lowered if the 2005 procedure

---

[16] The report on the 1975 ICP round (Kravis et al. 1982, 140) compared PPPs of unpriced services with those of priced services, and the latter are systematically higher for low-income countries. However, it is difficult to substitute priced for unpriced services because most countries do not collect an adequate number of prices for purchased services, but it would be an improvement on the equal productivity assumption.

The Economies of China and India

had been adopted in those years. Everything else the same, the methods adopted for these sectors has the effect of producing a smaller spread in real GDP per capita between rich and poor in 2005 than in previous benchmarks.

What is the consequence for the 2005 comparison of the mixed application of an adjustment for productivity? A sense of this can be gained from the magnitude of the adjustment for China and India and the importance of compensation in GDP. Government administrative services and individual services for health and education were 5.2 and 6.7 percent of GDP in China and India in 2005. Average reported wages were 26 and 22 percent of the 'productivity adjusted wages' in China and India. This means that compared to higher-income countries where no adjustment was made, GDP could have been lowered by as much as 30 percent.[17] However, a conservative estimate is that China and India would be at least 10 percent higher with respect to OECD countries without the productivity adjustment. This is not an argument against a productivity adjustment, though the actual implementation was of a 'one size fits all' nature; rather it helps us better understand where the new view of the position of China and India in the Global economy of 2005 is coming from.

(3) Linking of the regions

In previous global comparisons linking of regions has often been through only one or two countries, in which case the results can be quite sensitive to which are the link countries.[18] In 2005 a method that was less sensitive to the choice of countries was adopted for linking regions at the basic heading in the ICP.[19] These basic heading parities in each region were used to convert the national currency expenditures in each country to a volume in the currency of the numeraire country of a region, like Oman in western Asia. The next step is to aggregate these expenditures and parities

---

[17] The adjustment factors for China and India are taken from Appendix Table D in the Preliminary Report but were not reproduced in the final report. It is not possible without computations with all of the input data, which will only be made available to researchers at a later date, to make a more precise calculation at the GDP level.

[18] Also the linking can be done at a detailed level or an aggregate level. When it is done at an aggregate level as in 1985, it is particularly sensitive to the link countries, e.g. Japan was used to link Asia to the OECD.

[19] In the parlance of the ICP there were eighteen Ring countries from the five regions that undertook special pricing. Based on prices from these countries parities at the basic heading level were estimated for the Ring countries that could be linked to each of the five regions. Russia served as the link country between the OECD and the CIS countries in a separate exercise carried out by the OECD.

for each region to a total, like consumption or GDP. In the 2005 this was done by the Elteto, Koves, and Szulz (EKS) method, which in effect gives equal weight to Africa, Asia, OECD, South America, and western Asia. PWT, in contrast, uses a method that weights each country by its GDP converted at exchange rates.[20] Without going into the merits of each approach, let it be said that the PWT approach would tend to increase the share of output of Asia in the global GDP by 13–14 percent or more compared to the 2005 ICP. And within regions this would have the effect of lowering incomes for countries like Japan and raising them for China and India within Asia. China would be about half the size of the US economy and India under one-fourth the US, but fourth largest just above Germany, but still well below Japan.

However, there was another important difference in the way EKS was applied in the 2005 round related to the practice of fixity. Initiated by the EU in the 1980 benchmark, fixity requires the relationship between countries within a region, say Germany and France, to be preserved for each level of expenditures in the results involving non-member countries, like OECD non-EU countries, including the US. In the 2005 ICP, each region adopted fixity, so a method for aggregating the world was required. The method adopted was to treat each region as a unit, with aggregate expenditures in the prices of the region as one input with a regional PPP at each basic heading as the other input. The advantage of this approach is that it preserves the relationships of each country within the region without any further adjustment. The disadvantage is it makes no use of information comparing countries from different regions, for example, Brazil and China. An alternative is to use EKS or Geary–Khamis (GK) where each country is a unit, and find the total output of each region. If fixity is required, then relationships within a region can be preserved by distributing the regional total according to the results within each region.

It in fact turns out these two applications of EKS produce fairly large differences in the totals for some regions. The ratios of the regional totals of GDP using unrestricted EKS to the published totals are: Africa 1.00; Asia and the Pacific 1.10; CIS 1.16; OECD-EU 1.02; South America 0.99;

[20] While the bank and PWT are closer to each other than to the 2005 ICP for China the comments in this section only apply to PWT. The World Bank uses a different method to obtain their WDI numbers. Also, with respect to the next point to be taken up, the net foreign balance, the comments only apply to PWT. The WDI for 2005 relied on extrapolation of 1993 results at the GDP level. This means that if exports are constant but their prices fall, as in the case of micro chips for Singapore, GDP growth will overstate the ability of Singapore to convert current production into current domestic expenditures in 2005 that underlies their benchmark estimate of GDP. Other changes in the terms of trade will similarly drive a wedge, positively or negatively, between extrapolations and current price PPP conversions.

The Economies of China and India

and western Asia 1.04. As can be seen, using unrestricted EKS would raise Asian countries relative to the OECD by about 8 percent, and 11 percent relative to South American countries. Thus the change in the exact application of the same aggregation method, EKS, explains away one-fifth of the observed declines in the positions of China and India in the world economy. While there is a political rationale for the practice of fixity, the academics are solidly behind unconstrained methods of aggregation and so would argue that the method used by the bank should be reconsidered in the next round of the ICP scheduled for 2011.[21]

(4) Exports and imports

In the 2005 round the net foreign balance is converted at exchange rates, a practice common in the OECD countries. In fact it has long been recognized that the proper way to deal with trade is to deflate exports by a PPP based on export prices and the same for imports. However, to do this requires collecting of another large set of producers' prices, making an already formidable task appear too daunting. PWT does not do it right either as discussed in a recent paper (Feenstra et al. 2009).

Are there alternative approaches to a full PPP conversion of exports and imports? What is being done in PWT is to convert the net foreign balance at the PPP for domestic absorption. This has one major advantage for the GK approach used in PWT, namely that it is symmetric with respect to whether a country has a trade surplus or deficit.[22] In Feenstra et al. (2007) it was found that there was a significant difference for a number of high-trade countries between GDP based on expenditures as in PWT and GDP based on production taking into account the difference in parities and volumes of exports and imports. However, among the 146 countries in the 2005 ICP there are a number in Asia, Africa, and western Asia, where this difference can be quite large.

What conclusions can be drawn about where China and India fit into the world economy based on the 2005 benchmark? The largest source of difference from past practice is the productivity adjustment for Government, which certainly is a change in the right direction. However, my judgment is that these adjustments produced too large a reduction for

---

[21] It should be pointed out that the way in which the EU links in associate members and other countries is highly constrained, so even in the OECD comparisons, the positions of members and non-members would be different without the restrictions that are imposed.

[22] In PWT the aggregation is over C, I, and G, and the net foreign balance is handled as a separate item. In EKS as usually carried out, the net foreign balance is included in the aggregation with the exchange rate as the parity for that entry. Other conversion factors could also be used within EKS, or for that matter in the GK approach.

China and India. In addition because the adjustments were not carried out in the OECD, the most important region for comparison, the overall results for Asia are understated in this round. The difference in aggregation methods also operated to reduce Asia substantially in the world, and there is legitimate disagreement on whether this was appropriate. But even the EKS method in the 2005 ICP was applied to five regional aggregates, not the individual countries as in most applications. If countries had been used as in the past, this would have raised the position of Asia by 8 percent compared to the OECD.[23] While there are reasons for aggregating by region, the cost seems high, namely reducing meaningful comparisons of countries across regions.

Moving down the list, the difference in treatment of foreign trade is in any event not a large effect. The special pricing in China may well have produced prices that were on average higher than for other large countries, such as Brazil or India. A rough guess as to what might be the net impact of defensible changes in the preliminary results including applying EKS to countries would be to reduce price levels of China and India relative to the US by 25 percent plus or minus at least 5 percent. Put another way at least half of the much publicized reduction of the incomes of China and India of 40 percent can be explained by improved data and changed methods and the productivity adjustment for those expenditure headings where PPPs have been based on relative wages.

1.4 PPPs and sources of past and future growth

Do the ICP results provide any insights into the sources and prospects for future growth in China and India? We have already noted that when one converts China or Indian GDP from local to a common currency using PPPs it makes future levels of output more obtainable compared to the use of exchange rates. Beyond this, the discussion will concern only two of the common explanations for growth and limitations on future growth, diminishing marginal productivity of capital and structural changes during economic development. The literature is large and we will only take up two recent studies of past growth, both of which compare China and India. Bosworth and Collins (2007) covers the period 1978 to 2004,

---

[23] An EKS was run on the individual countries and regional aggregates were summed up and compared with the regional aggregates that are part of the 2005 Final Report. Compared to the OECD, Asia-Pacific rose by 8% and South America declined by 1%. This means that a comparison of India to say Brazil would put India 9% higher if the EKS were applied to countries not regions.

and Herd and Dougherty (2007) that which goes from 1952 to 2005. Herd and Dougherty, both of whom have been involved in the country studies of China and India of the OECD (2005; 2007a), and Bosworth and Collins provide a review of the literature on sources of growth for the two countries; readers are referred to either paper for a fuller discussion.

Some conclusions drawn in the studies are given below.

1. Growth of physical capital has accounted for more than twice the share of total growth in China compared to India.
2. Total factor productivity has been a more important source of growth in China than in India in absolute terms in the period of reforms. However, in the 1950–1980 period, it was stagnant in China compared to India. Relative to total growth, Bosworth and Collins find it is also more important in China than India, and Herd and Dougherty the opposite.
3. Both papers estimate the contribution to total growth of the reallocation of the workforce from the lower productivity primary sector to the higher productivity secondary and tertiary sectors. Both studies find this shift in resources an important source of growth in both countries, more important in China than India during the reform period.
4. Bosworth and Collins put the output per worker in China in the secondary sector as seven times the primary, while in India secondary is less than five times higher than primary. Further, output per worker is higher in both sectors in China than in India, providing China with more potential gains from shifting resources.
5. However, in India the output per worker in the formal sector is almost twenty times as high as the informal sector (agricultural plus informal secondary and tertiary employees), suggesting major potential for output gains.

In looking to the future, aside from the common emphasis on maintaining high rates of investment, there are differences in the two studies. Bosworth and Collins see the potential for both China and India to maintain their recent rates of growth so long as they continue their reforms and participation in the international economy. Herd and Dougherty believe that there are more constraints on future growth in China than India, so long as the latter can achieve major labor market reforms. The discussion below considers the conclusions of these studies from the perspective of purchasing power research that focuses heavily on relative prices.

Alan Heston

Role of capital and relative price of investment goods

In explaining the sources of total factor productivity (TFP) growth in China and India, capital accumulation is seen to play a major role. India makes official estimates of capital stock in rupees but not China. Therefore both studies make independent estimates of the capital stock in China, and allow for both labor quantity and quality in their analysis, albeit with differences in the adjustments they make. These capital stock estimates are in national prices that tend to overstate the role of capital formation.

China and India follow a common pattern of relative prices that at first may seem paradoxical, namely their prices of investment goods are relatively high. Since both countries are major exporters of producers' durable equipment, how can their prices be high? The answer is we are referring to relative prices. We can illustrate this using the GDP price levels of China and India of 23.9 and 17.5 noted above for 2003 from PWT; and the same pattern was found in the 2005 ICP. In comparison the price levels of investment goods including construction are 32 and 35 respectively; so investment goods are still inexpensive with respect to world prices, but not compared to other expenditures in GDP, namely Government and household consumption. In contrast, investment goods are relatively inexpensive in countries like Japan and the United States compared to consumption.

This means that in national currencies the share of investment in countries like China and India is overstated and therefore their ratio of capital to output is overstated compared to higher per capita income countries. Rather than 43 percent of GDP, PWT would estimate China's investment share at 32 percent in 2004. That is, the real amount of physical capital that is being put up each year compared to the quantities of other goods is smaller. This is an aspect of relative prices that is frequently overlooked in international comparisons of productivity. The effect of using comparable measures of capital to output across countries does not have to decrease contribution of capital to growth but that is certainly a working hypothesis.

However, this finding is related to another unusual aspect of the Chinese economy, the reported 47 percent consumption out of GDP in 2005, and a correspondingly high rate of savings. Savings can be measured as the (1) net additions of owned assets by the enterprise, household, and Government sectors of the economy; or as (2) the difference between GDP and consumption expenditures of households and Government; or as (3) the sum of foreign and domestic investment expenditures. Most countries are able to independently check estimates from all of these sources, where often (2) is considered the most reliable. In China, GDP is estimated from the production side, and the expenditure side of the accounts is more problematic, with differences that must be allocated to various expenditure headings. It is a common conjecture that China's savings estimates are much too high and consumption levels too low.[24]

Financial repression and the efficiency of capital use

In his chapter, in this book, Jahangir Aziz asks the question of whether estimated growth from a model without financial frictions tracks actual experience and compares to a model that does introduce wedges in financial markets. He finds that a financial repression model does the better job of tracking Chinese experience. He considers the wedge as a borrowing constraint on smaller privately-owned firms as well as due to a repressed banking system replete with nonperforming loans. The very high savings rates in China represents a tax on consumers and on small businesses that must seek financing from their own savings. Consumers must save more because the returns they can earn on assets is low because of the low cost of capital made available to state-owned enterprises (SOEs). And small firms are constrained in access to credit so they must rely on a great deal of internal financing. In contrast, Aziz argues that when account is taken of subsidies for energy and other costs, SOEs effectively have negative borrowing rates so if they can make investments, the incentive is there to invest at any positive return.

Perkins and Rawski (2008) have made a related argument that the investment choices made by the SOEs and other Government-related entities have generated a very inefficient use of capital because of the absence of incentives to optimize choices when the cost of capital is so cheap. Is this claim that China's investments have been poorly allocated consistent with the TFP studies cited above? The answer is yes because high rates of investment have been associated with high growth of output, but probably not the source of this growth to the extent implied by these studies. The labor force reallocations have been underestimated because of residential permit system, this latter source of growth has probably been underestimated.

---

[24] Kraay (2000) provides an analysis of Chinese savings that, while several years old, makes points about overstatement that are still timely.

Alan Heston

Table 1.6. Completed investment in China by quarters

Year	1975	1990	2000	2002	2003	2004	2005
Q1 + Q2	33.8	28.3	31.1	33.7	35.3	37.3	37.2
Q4	42.6	48.3	44.4	39.9	37.8	35.1	35.1

Source: Constructed using data from Perkins and Rawski (2008) Table 20.9.

One piece of evidence cited by Perkins and Rawski (2008, Table 20.9) is the seasonal aspect of investment in China. Table 1.6 shows that in pre-reform China in 1975, over 40 percent of investment occurred in the fourth quarter while only one-third of annual investment took place in the first two quarters. Rawski argues that this illustrates the situation where SOEs had more funds than good ideas and so made a rush to invest in poorly planned projects in the last quarter of each year. The evidence in Table 1.6 suggests this seasonal pattern was maintained or even more exaggerated in the first fifteen years of reform and only in the more recent years when the share of private investment has increased has the allocation become more evenly distributed.

There are two possible qualifications to this argument. First, it might be argued that this investment pattern is somehow seasonally related to weather conditions, construction conditions being unfavorable in the first quarter of each year. To check on this provincial investment patterns were related to January and annual average temperatures, and indeed there is the expected relationship. However, correcting for this, there still remained a substantial excess of investment in the fourth quarter compared to the first quarter in all provinces.[25]

A second qualification is that if current price investment is growing due to either price changes or real changes, then one would expect fourth quarter investment to be higher than first quarter investment. It is easy enough to allow for this effect by calculating expected levels in each quarter using quarterly growth rates derived from the annual increase in a given year. For example, in 2006 the expected national ratio of first quarter to fourth quarter investment was 0.849 whereas the actual

[25] The coefficient on January temperatures was positively and significantly associated with the ratio of first to fourth quarter investment across the 31 provinces in 2003 and 2006, the only 2 years examined. The equation did a good job of prediction for the colder provinces like Jilin, Liaoning, Heilongjiang, and Inner Mongolia. However, the residuals were much larger for provinces with above freezing January temperatures, and may be related to the extent of private investment in the province. If we made an upward adjustment in first quarter investment for those provinces with negative January temperatures, the overall effect would be to raise the national ratio by under 0.01, say 0.37 to 0.38 in 2006.

ratio was 0.367, a clear indication of the crowding of investment into the fourth quarter. Of more relevance is whether continued high rates of investment can contribute to future growth as much as in the past. When economies are reallocating from low to high output per worker sectors, the impact of the new investment is likely to be higher than when additional investment is directed to increasing capital per worker within a sector. In the Soviet Union and Eastern Europe it was commonly felt that continued high rates of investment in the 35 percent range would run into diminishing returns as pools of low-productivity labor dried up. This is a potential constraint on growth faced by China and, to a somewhat lesser extent, India. Herd and Dougherty also believe that India has not freed up its labor markets as much as China since 1978; they conclude there remains more potential for growth from moving labor to higher-productivity sectors in India than China. In conclusion, we would argue that TFP studies show that China and India can gain from additional investment but that the notion that it is the desirable engine of growth seems problematic. Efficient use of capital coupled with facilitating continued movement of low-productivity labor to more productive sectors would move both countries much closer to their production possibility frontier.

The tertiary sector

One of the curious findings of Bosworth and Collins is that output growth in the tertiary sector of China is higher than in India. This appears paradoxical as China is viewed as producing commodities for the world and India is the call center for the OECD. Maddison and Wu (2007) suggest one factor that may help us understand what is happening here. Transportation and commerce services in China were 12.4 percent of GDP in 2003 and 'non-material' services 15.8 percent. Officially, output per worker rose by 4.8 percent in transport and commerce and 5.1 percent in 'non-material' services during the period 1978 to 2002. There is little explanation of how one would arrive at that type of labor productivity growth for 'non-material' services that include general Government and health and education. 'Non-material' services are very difficult areas of national statistics to pin down, but in general they are thought to be subject to Baumol's disease, where productivity increases are difficult to achieve.

It would be understandable in the case of India for the increase in the proportion of service workers in IT type activities to lead to increases in output per worker. However, in the case of 'non-material' services, which have declined as a share of the tertiary sector, the type of labor productivity growth assumed in China since 1978 seems much too high. One conclusion is that without further explanation of how China arrives at its high productivity growth for 'non-material' services it seems much more likely that this sector will serve as a constraint on growth rather than being a high-growth sector.

Returning to Baumol's disease, there is every reason to believe that both China and India will face the same problems of many OECD countries. As income per capita increases, demand shifts to sectors where productivity gains have been harder to achieve than in manufacturing. In this context, it is interesting that one of the productivity gains in marketing in the last twenty years has been reduction of the supply chain from producer to consumer, through direct purchases by final retailers, or one level of wholesalers. In India, resistance to the big box stores has been pushed by the small retailers and taken up by some political parties to pass laws restricting their entry. This was a familiar battle in the United States in the 1930s and beyond leading to legislation that provided some restrictions on large retailers. Many of the restrictions of the Robinson–Patman Act had the desirable effect of reducing the types of price discrimination that do not increase efficiency, but only redistribute gains of reducing the supply chain.

1.5 PPPs and exchange rates

In this section the PPP of China is discussed in the context of whether China's currency is being undervalued compared to what it would be if it freely floated. One of the least understood arguments in international economics relates to exchange rates and the purchasing power parity doctrine. After the First World War, Sweden was concerned as to how it should return the kroner to the gold standard, which led Cassel to propose that the Swedish authorities be guided by the purchasing power parity of the kroner relative to other currencies defined in terms of gold. This advice was summed up as follows:

I propose to call this parity *the purchasing power parity*. As long as anything like free movement of merchandise and a somewhat comprehensive trade between two countries take place, the actual rate of exchange cannot deviate very much from this purchasing power parity. (Cassel 1918, 413)

Samuelson has suggested that if the Nobel economics prize had been awarded in the 1920s, Cassel would have received it for this insight. And surely Cassel would also have modified his views as world financial markets changed and capital movements have come to dwarf trade in goods and services. There were no national accounts in Cassel's world, so the notion of a PPP for GDP as opposed to one only for traded goods was not in the vocabulary of his day.

Put another way, PPPs are a sensible way to make quantity comparisons across countries by converting expenditures by the relative prices of the items entering into the expenditures. However, the relation of PPPs over GDP to exchange rates is not direct and so is not a simple guide as to the level of a country's exchange rate. In the long run, *the purchasing power parity doctrine* in its relative form which states that inflation rates, PPPs, and exchange rates will move in parallel does tend to hold.

What can be said is that both China and India have ratios of PPPs to their respective exchange rates that are not out of line with countries at similar levels of per capita income. This was true in both the older and even more so for the 2005 ICP comparison. In fact a principal finding of the ICP is that the price level (PPP/exchange rate) and the price of nontradables relative to tradables rise with per capita incomes, with the usual explanation being the Balassa–Samuelson effect.[26] However, the variation about this relationship is especially large for high-income countries, with the price level of Hong Kong in the draft Global Report 73, Japan 118, and Switzerland 140 in 2005 with the US at 100.

One implication of this wide range of price levels of high-income countries has become clearer in recent months. Policymakers in the euro bloc have recently become even more vocal about the exchange rate of China than the United States. From the Chinese point of view this is mostly a reflection of the rise of the euro relative to the dollar rather than any policy of the Chinese. Certainly the asymmetric position of the dollar in international monies complicates this discussion. Again the results of purchasing power studies do not provide any special perspective on this issue nor on the larger issue of why China wants to maintain such large foreign exchange holdings. However, the chapter by van Ark et al. in this book does make a strong case that unit labor costs in China and, to a lesser extent, India have been highly competitive since 1990 compared to peer countries like Hungary, Korea, Mexico, and Poland. And the slow

---

[26] This is discussed a number of places, e.g. Summers et al. (1994).

but steady appreciation of the renminbi in the past two years is certainly consistent with their findings.

1.6 Conclusion

Purchasing power studies provide a comparative perspective on the volumes of GDP in a common measure across countries and therefore a reading on how well national growth rates tell the same story over time as do two cross-section readings. The chapter concluded that compared to India the growth rates of GDP place China at much too low a level at the beginnings of reform and earlier. Much more reasonable results across time and space emerge from use of the Maddison–Wu adjustments for China than from official series. One conclusion is that past official growth rates are not necessarily a good guide to the future for China, even if everything else remains the same. Results from the 2005 global PPP comparisons suggest a much lower GDP than the World Bank or PWT had been using, but it is not clear whether this has any implications for the discussion of Chinese growth rates.

One concern about the China comparison was discussed in some detail, namely the limitation of price collection to eleven urban centers and surrounding rural areas. In addition both China and India share similar problems in adequately representing their national price structure compared to small countries, such as Hong Kong or Singapore. Further the linking of the whole Asian region to the other regions is quite different in the 2005 Global Report than in PWT. In this the bank followed the methods used in Eurostat and the OECD. The overall impact of the new bank ICP for 2005 is to lower the share of Asia compared to the OECD, a different world economic view than previously held.

The adjustments of Maddison and Wu also call into question the results of TFP comparisons that suggest the service sector has grown more rapidly in China than India. The tertiary sector typically has very slow growth in productivity leading to what has been termed Baumol's disease, where as economies become more affluent they demand more services. But services productivity does not grow as rapidly as in manufacturing and even agriculture, so this becomes a constraint on growth. As Maddison and Wu point out the apparent exceptional behavior in China appears to be due to assumption about the growth of labor productivity not due to measured productivity increases. Both China and India will face this structural shift to services in their economies, which may constrain their future growth.

In both countries the price of consumption relative to investment is lower than in higher-income countries, which is likely to overstate the past contribution of capital, as well as its likely future contribution. Further, it has been argued that the measurement of capital stock is in national prices in both countries, which are higher compared to prices of consumption goods. This may account for the large role that capital accumulation appears to play in studies of TFP in India and even more so in China where the movement of labor to higher output sectors has been understated. Another major source of post-reform growth has been the allocation of a larger share of the workforce from lower to higher productivity sectors. This will clearly become a constraint on rapid rates of growth in the medium-term future and is already showing itself in China by outsourcing some items to cheaper Southeast Asian countries. It does seem likely that India does have more potential for growth from such allocation shifts than does China because of the very low productivity in informal enterprises in the secondary and tertiary sectors.

2
Trading with Asia's Giants

*Barry Bosworth, Susan M. Collins, and Aaron Flaaen**

2.1 Introduction

Strong economic gains in China and India have captured an extraordinary amount of global attention, and the potential spread of economic prosperity to the world's two largest countries is a truly momentous development. At the same time, however, the United States' large and sustained trade deficit with Asia raises concerns in the US about its competitiveness in the region. In recent years most of the focus has been on the bilateral trade balance with China; however, a different but equally contentious set of issues—centering on business services—is emerging with respect to US trade with India. The purpose of this chapter is to examine the patterns of the US trade relationships with China and India, and the factors that are influencing their evolution. In particular, the public policy discussion has focused on imports from the region, while largely ignoring the role of US exports. Much of our discussion compares these two economies as markets for US exporters.

We begin with a brief review of the trade flow patterns that motivbreak ate this study. The large bilateral imbalance in US–China trade is well known. While the overall magnitude of US goods trade with India is much smaller, that bilateral trade deficit is also substantial in percentage terms. Our review highlights two important aspects of these trade relationships. First, despite all the focus on fears of job loss associated with US imports from China, those imports do not stand out as particularly large when compared with European and Japanese imports from China.

---

* Research for this chapter was financed by a grant from the Tokyo Club Foundation for Global Studies.

Instead, what stands out is the comparatively low level of US exports to both China and India. Second, US trade data shows services trade to be even larger with China than it is with India. With both countries, the bilateral services trade balance seems to be in balance or in slight surplus. These findings are surprising in light of all of the expressed fears about outsourcing of services jobs to India. Throughout the analysis, we explore US trade with both India and China by contrasting it with their trade with the other two major industrialized economies of Japan and the EU-15.[1]

The main body of the chapter evaluates the trade relationship from three perspectives. First, we look at the composition of US exports to the two economies. Do the products the US exports to China and India differ from the products for which it appears to have a comparative advantage in world markets more generally? Such a finding could be interpreted as suggesting the existence of various import barriers. How does the composition of US exports compare with that of Japan and the EU-15?

Second, we look at the role of multinational corporations because of the often cited link between foreign direct investment and subsequent trade flows. Multinational firms are believed to focus on the creation of production and distribution networks that facilitate trade. Are American business firms as actively involved in India and China as implied by their operations in other economies? Do they serve as sales agents for their own imports into these countries?

Finally, we undertake a more structured analysis by estimating a set of simple 'gravity equations'. This enables us to examine trade with India and China in the context of bilateral trade patterns more generally and to control for a variety of country characteristics including the distance between trading partners. Perhaps the problem is simply that India and China are far away? If so, this would shift the puzzle from why US exports are so small, to why imports into the United States are so large. In this context, we examine patterns of services trade as well as the more traditional focus on goods trade.

---

[1] The EU-15 refers to the fifteen members of the European Union prior to its May 2004 expansion to 25 countries. For comparative purposes, the EU-15 group corresponds more closely in income levels to the United States and Japan. The expanded EU includes a number of Eastern European states with significantly lower income levels and limited links to the global economy. The 15 are: Austria, Belgium, Denmark, Finland, France, Germany, Greece, Ireland, Italy, Luxembourg, Netherlands, Portugal, Spain, Sweden, and the United Kingdom.

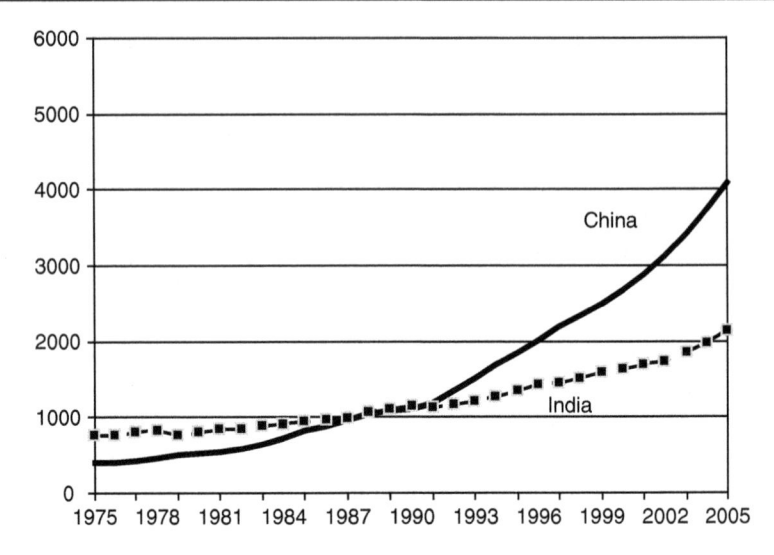

Figure 2.1. GDP per capita, China and India (constant 2000 international (PPP) dollars)

Source: Constructed using data in World Development Indicators World Bank, 2006. This purchasing power parity measure of GDP standardizes for differences in the prices of common products across countries and over time.

2.2 Context

While it is often reasonable to consider the roles of China and India together in evaluating the growth of trade with Asia, it is also important to recognize their differences. Economically, China is a much larger country and has far greater interactions with the global economy. The acceleration of economic growth began much earlier in China, and over the past quarter century, average incomes have risen well above those of India. This gap has continued to widen in recent years, as GDP and trade have advanced more rapidly in China than in India. Figure 2.1 shows the growth of income per capita in the two countries.[2] It makes clear the extent to which China has leaped ahead, with average income now twice that of India. A summary of the sector composition of growth is provided in Figure 2.2. China has achieved a faster growth of labor productivity in each of the three major sectors of agriculture, industry, and services,

[2] The comparison is based on the new 2005 estimates of PPP. The new estimates reduced the level of GDP per capita by about 40% relative to the earlier estimates that were used by the World Bank. While the relative income levels of the two countries were not significantly altered, the absolute levels of income in 1978 seem even more implausibly low.

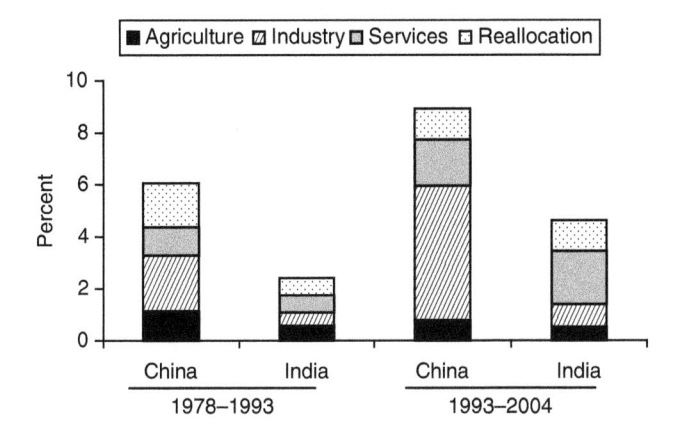

Figure 2.2. Growth in output per worker: Sector and reallocation components 1978–2004

Source: Constructed using the data in Bosworth and Collins (2008).

but industry stands out as the largest source of difference. India matches China's growth only in the services producing sector. At the same time, the two countries have experienced roughly equivalent gains from the reallocation of labor from low- (agriculture) to high-productivity sectors (industry and services). By international standards, both economies have been growing at extraordinary rates, but China's growth is broader and has been sustained for a much longer period.

Figures 2.3a and b provides a simple overview of the historical trade performance of China and India. China's role in the global trading system has been complicated in recent years by a sharp shift in its global trade

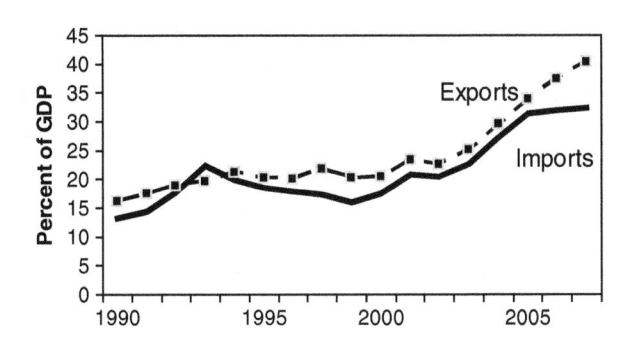

Figure 2.3a. Mainland China's exports and imports to world, 1990–2006 (goods and services trade, % of GDP)

Source: Constructed using data in the IMF's Balance of Payments Statistics.

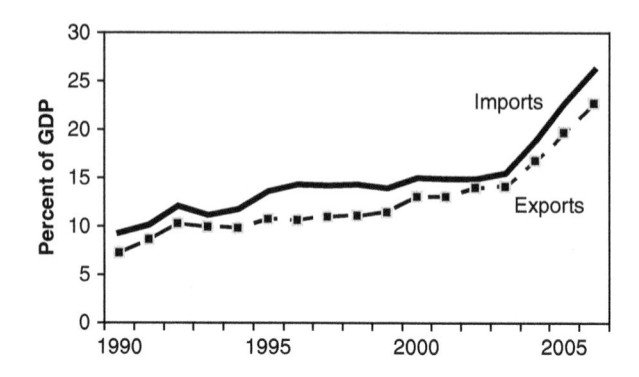

Figure 2.3b. India's exports and imports to world, 1990–2006 (goods and services trade, % of GDP)

Source: Constructed using data in the IMF's Balance of Payments Statistics.

balance. As shown in the top panel, China's external trade was a stable share of GDP throughout the 1990s, as exports and imports averaged about 19 and 18 percent of GDP respectively.[3] After admission to the WTO, both exports and imports grew rapidly, reaching 31 percent on the export side and 29 percent for imports in 2004. In addition, mainland China typically generated small trade surpluses averaging about 2 percent of GDP over the period of 1990–2004, and exceeding 3 percent only briefly in 1997–1998.

All of this changed after 2004 when the trade surplus began to grow at a rapid pace. The balance for mainland China increased from $32 billion in 2004 to $102 billion and $178 billion in 2005 and 2006 respectively. The surplus for 2007 is projected to approach $300 billion. The emergence of a large trade surplus has been a considerable surprise since many countries believed that they had extracted major concessions from China as part of the negotiations leading up to its admission to the WTO at the end of 2001. Some commentators have traced the change to the termination of the Multifiber Arrangement at the beginning of 2005.[4] However, as evident in the figure, the break in the prior pattern of trade, measured as a share of GDP, appears to be on the import side: While exports continued their rapid growth, the import share has flattened out.

---

[3] The stable trade share is itself a notable contrast to frequent assertions that China's rapid growth has been driven by export promotion policies.

[4] The opening of the market did lead to an extraordinary surge of apparel imports from China, but was followed by the reimposition of quantitative limits in mid-2005.

Table 2.1. Trade with China and India, major industrial economies, 2005 (billions of US dollars)

GDP		United States 12,417		Japan 4,534		EU-15 12,765	
		Goods	Services	Goods	Services	Goods	Services
Global trade							
	Exports	904.3	367.8	594.9	110.3	1,459.2	514.0
	Imports	1,732.5	281.6	515.2	134.3	1,581.7	454.8
	Balance	−828.3	86.2	79.7	−24.0	−122.5	59.2
Bilateral trade with:							
China	Exports	58.2	13.4	116.0	10.5	87.8	23.7
	Imports	269.1	12.1	110.0	14.2	205.0	17.7
	Balance	−211.0	1.4	6.0	−3.7	−117.3	6.0
India	Exports	8.0	5.2	3.5	0.8	25.6	6.5
	Imports	19.9	5.0	3.2	0.3	23.3	5.8
	Balance	−11.9	0.1	0.3	0.4	2.3	0.7
Percent of GDP							
China	Exports	0.47	0.11	2.56	0.23	0.69	0.19
	Imports	2.17	0.10	2.43	0.31	1.61	0.14
	Balance	−1.70	0.01	0.13	−0.08	−0.92	0.05
India	Exports	0.06	0.04	0.08	0.02	0.20	0.05
	Imports	0.16	0.04	0.07	0.01	0.18	0.05
	Balance	−0.10	0.00	0.01	0.01	0.02	0.01

		Goods	Services	Total	GDP
Global trade					
China	Exports	1,054.5	146.8	1,201.3	
	Imports	930.8	119.4	1,050.1	2,406.6
	Balance	123.8	27.4	151.2	
India	Exports	102.2	55.8	158.0	
	Imports	134.7	48.0	182.7	785.5
	Balance	−32.5	7.8	−24.7	

Source: Constructed using data from IMF's database Directions of Trade Statistics for goods trade, and OECD for services trade.

India, in contrast, has long had a much lower share of trade in GDP and the rapid growth in trade is of a more recent origin, beginning after 2003. In 2003–2006, however, India's trade grew at a more rapid rate than that of China—in excess of 30 percent per year. Furthermore, India has also had a consistent trade deficit, financed by private remittances and capital inflows.

Some basic statistics covering US trade with China and India in 2005 are shown in Table 2.1, and contrasted with Japan and the EU-15.[5] The

[5] Our definition of China combines the trade data for the Mainland, Hong Kong, and Macao.

unusual size of the US merchandise trade deficit with China is very evident. However, despite the emphasis often placed on imports from China, the middle panel indicates that goods imports from China are a smaller share of GDP for the United States than in Japan (2.2 vs. 2.4 percent). Instead, the bilateral relationship seems unusual in the small magnitude of US exports to China. US merchandise exports to China comprise only 0.5 percent of GDP compared to 2.6 for Japan. In fact, Japan has had a consistent trade surplus with China. Compared with the US, the EU-15 also exports a larger share of its GDP to China, and combined with its lower share for imports, has a significantly smaller trade imbalance.

The precise size of the bilateral trade imbalance between the United States and China—and to a lesser extent, China's global trade balance—has been a subject of some dispute. Issues involving differences in the measurement of bilateral trade flows have been extensively explored in a series of prior papers.[6] Most of the confusion is caused by the transhipment of goods through Hong Kong. Not only do exporters often not know the true destination of such products, there is also a significant change in value due to the additional margins added by the Hong Kong traders. Both the United States and China alter the source of imports that pass through Hong Kong if they judge that greater value was added prior to arrival in Hong Kong.

However, both report Hong Kong as the destination for much of their own exports. Fung and others (2006) obtain an estimate of the US bilateral merchandise trade deficit with China of $172 billion in 2005 compared with official estimates of $202 billion published by the United States and $114 billion published by China. We avoid some of the problems that they identify by focusing on trade with the combination of China, Hong Kong, and Macao.

India represents a sharp contrast to China in the small size of its goods trade.[7] Although India's GDP is a third that of China, its global trade is only about 12 percent as large while its trade with the United States is less than 10 percent as large. Even more striking, Japan's trade with India is less than 5 percent of its trade with China. Only in the case of the EU-15, does the relative size of the bilateral trade seem proportionate to the size

---

[6] The issues were clarified in a series of papers by Feenstra et al. (1999), Fung and Lau (1996; 2003), Fung et al. (2006), and Schindler and Beckett (2005). A recent paper by Wang and others (2007) uses a highly flexible algorithm to reconcile China's trade data with all of its major trading partners.

[7] A detailed comparison of the global trade performance of the two countries is available in Panagariya (2006b).

of the two economies. For example, EU-15 exports to India are three times those of the United States. Similar to China, the United States has a large bilateral trade deficit with India, while both Japan and the EU-15 have small bilateral trade surpluses.

2.3 Services trade

Surprisingly, China's global trade in services is substantially larger than India's, although the two countries' service trade ratios are roughly proportionate to their GDPs.[8] As evident from the data shown in Table 2.1, India's services exports are about 7 percent of its output, compared with 6 percent for China. Of course, given China's size, this translates into a much greater dollar value. Thus, despite extensive media to the offshoring of service jobs to India, the United States reports a larger volume of services trade with China than India, and a positive services trade balance with both countries. The EU-15 countries report services imports from both China and India that exceed those of the United States, but they too show a bilateral surplus. In contrast, Japan's reported services trade with India is quite trivial.

Table 2.2 shows the composition of services trade for both countries, which is indeed quite different. While computer- and information-related services account for nearly 40 percent of India's services exports, by far the largest category, these products are less than 2 percent of the total for China. Other business services are the largest category for China and the second largest for India. But this primarily reflects trade-related services for China (fully one-quarter of China's services exports) vs. non-trade-related services for India. It is important to note, however, that while this latter category accounts for 24 percent and 9 percent of exports from India and China respectively, it amounts to roughly the same dollar value of trade. In terms of services imports, the main differences are the much more important role for travel and travel-related services as well as royalties and license fees for China, and for transportation and other business services for India.

India's estimate of $56 billion in services exports includes $43 billion for other services, excluding transportation and tourism. We would expect most of this trade to be with the high-income economies of the

---

[8] See Nikomborirak (2007) for a discussion of the service industries in the two countries.

Table 2.2. 2005 services trade by type, India and China (billions US dollars)

	Credits		Debits	
	China	India	China	India
Total	146.8	55.8	−119.4	−48.0
Transportation services	36.1	5.7	−39.1	−20.1
Travel services	47.6	7.5	−35.4	−6.0
Other services	63.1	42.6	−44.8	−21.8
Communications	1.5	2.0	−1.8	−0.7
Construction	2.9	1.0	−1.9	−0.7
Insurance	1.0	0.9	−7.9	−2.2
Financial	6.5	1.5	−1.6	−1.1
Computer and information	2.1	22.0	−2.1	−1.6
Royalties and license fees	0.4	0.1	−6.6	−0.8
Other business services*	47.7	14.6	−21.9	−14.2
Trade-related services	34.6	1.2	−12.6	−1.4
Other business services	13.1	13.5	−9.3	−12.8
Other services	1.0	0.5	−1.0	−0.6

Source: Constructed using data from IMF's Balance of Payments Statistics database.
* The composition of trade in other business services is proportionally allocated based on data from the mainland only.

EU-15, Japan, and the United States. However, as shown in the middle of Table 2.1, these countries together report services imports from India totaling only $11 billion. It is difficult to discern the strong performance of India's services sector from these statistics. The US, EU-15, and Japan together report $44 billion in services imports from China—four times that from India. This is also well below the totals reported by China (Table 2.2), but we might expect China's services trade to be somewhat more dispersed.

There are, however, major concerns about the international comparability of statistics on services trade. The measurement of services trade is more difficult than that of goods because in many cases the services transactions cannot be tied to any physical movement across a national border. Instead, the transactions are defined in terms of the residence of the buyer and seller, but residence can be a vague and easily changed standard. An additional complication arises because the United States reports services trade in two categories—affiliated and unaffiliated. Affiliate transactions refer to intra-firm trade between parent firms and their affiliates. The United States does not report the country pattern of affiliate trade for the detailed categories of computer and other business services because it believes that the multinational companies cannot accurately account for their detailed intra-firm trade by country.

In recent years, India has consistently reported a level of exports to the United States in the category of Business, Professional, and Technical (BPT) services that is more than twenty times that recorded by the United States as an import—$8,700 million vs. $402 million, for example, in 2003. The General Accountability Office (GAO) sent a team to India and issued a report in 2005 that identified most of the discrepancies.[9] To begin with, the US estimates are too low: The Bureau of Economic Analysis (BEA) reports country-specific data only for unaffiliated trade. Given the importance of affiliated trade in total BPT services, it would be reasonable to increase the US estimate by a factor of three to four. Also, the importation of computer software that is embedded in imported computers is classified as part of goods trade, rather than services. However, because India is not a major exporter of embedded software, the different treatment is probably not a major contributor to the discrepancy.

Issues with the Indian data account for most of the remaining discrepancy. The Indian balance of payments deviates from US practice in two major respects. First, the earnings of Indian workers who reside in the United States are included in India's service exports, but excluded in the US data if they intend to stay more than one year. That activity is believed to represent about 40 percent of India's total BPT exports. Second, India reports the internal sale of services to local affiliates of US firms as part of its exports. That is estimated to be about 30 percent of the BPT total. Thus, the GAO concluded that, relative to US standards, the level of service exports to the United States was overstated, by a factor of two to three in the Indian data.[10]

Measuring trade in services accurately is thought to be more challenging for the importing country because consumers tend to be considerably more diffuse than producers. Since there is no counterpart to customs reports on goods, the United States relies heavily on surveys of service-importing firms. In contrast to exporters, these are spread over a large number of industries and can be difficult to identify. From the Indian side, exporters are a more readily identified producer group. At the present

---

[9] They have authored two reports on the issue. See United States General Accountability Office (2004) and (2005).
[10] Some of the issues for computer services are discussed from the Indian perspective in Reserve Bank of India (2005).

Barry Bosworth, Susan Collins, & Aaron Flaaen

time, however, India and the OECD countries appear to be reporting very different concepts of services trade.

2.4 Composition of goods exports

The weak performance of US exports to China and India is a long-standing phenomenon. The United States has had a consistent trade deficit with both countries dating back to the mid-1980s. In this section, we compare the commodity composition of US exports to both countries with the composition of US exports to the world more generally. Perhaps the low level of US exports to these countries reflects differences in the types of goods the US exports to each relative to the types of goods it exports to the world as a whole. We also compare the composition of US exports with those of the EU-15 and Japan as an indicator of the extent to which they are competitors in these markets.

Measures of the correlation of commodity composition of trade with China and India and the world as a whole are shown at the level of 237 3-digit SITC codes in the top of Table 2.3. The simple rank correlation is reported on the left, and the correlations based on shares of total trade are shown on the right. First, it is notable that the composition of US exports to China seems very similar to the composition of its global exports, a rank correlation coefficient of 0.84. We obtain a matching result for the EU-15 countries, and the correlation is even more evident for Japan (a rank correlation coefficient of 0.92). We interpret this result as implying

Table 2.3. Correlations of bilateral commodity trade, 2005

	Rank Correlation of Commodity Trade		Correlation of Trade Shares	
	China	India	China	India
World/Country				
United States	0.84	0.77	0.78	0.69
Japan	0.92	0.88	0.67	0.51
EU-15	0.84	0.78	0.72	0.26
Competitors				
US/Japan	0.74	0.71	0.61	0.27
US/EU-15	0.78	0.82	0.72	0.52
Japan/EU-15	0.78	0.81	0.72	0.15

Source: Constructed using data from United Nations Comtrade database. Correlations based on 3-digit SITC commodity classification, with a total of 237 codes. Commodity share is the value for each code divided by the relevant bilateral total.

that the Chinese market is about as open to industrial country exports as world markets are more generally. The rank correlations are lower for India, but large differences do not emerge until the correlations are computed on the basis of shares of total exports. The large drop in the correlation for trade between the EU-15 and India compared with the EU-15's trade with the world results because 30 percent of their exports to India are accounted for by shipments of precious stones for polishing and finishing. The deletion of this single commodity category would raise the correlation from 0.26 to 0.60. This commodity group accounts for 5 percent of US trade with India and zero for Japan.

Second, the table shows that the three high-income economies export very similar products to China, and therefore appear to be strong competitors in that market. The rank correlation between US and EU-15 exports to China is 0.78, declining only modestly to 0.72 for the correlation of actual commodity shares. However, the correlations fall dramatically for shares of exports to India. Again, this is largely due to the dominant role of precious stones in EU exports. In other respects, export patterns accord with areas of specialization: The US is strong in aircraft, computing, and telecommunications equipment; Japan has a prominent role in motor vehicles and various machinery categories; and EU-15 exports other than gem stones are concentrated in aircraft and telecommunications. However, outside of these dominant areas, there is very little overlap in what these economies export to India.

Overall, there is little that we find unusual about the commodity composition of US trade with India and China. It is similar to US trade with the world more generally. It is also evident that the industrial economies are strongly competitive with one another in both markets; but the competition is more extensive in China.

We conclude that the low level of US exports to both China and India cannot be attributed to restrictions that distort the commodity pattern of trade.

Finally, statistics on the commodity composition of trade can also be used to contrast the export performance of China and India. Panagariya (2006b) argues that the composition of China's exports has rapidly shifted toward an emphasis on labor-intensive manufactures, while the composition of India's exports has remained more haphazard. He also points out that, at the 2-digit level of commodity trade flows, there is very little overlap between the exports of China and India. We obtain much the same result using the more detailed 3-digit classification. The rank correlation between their global exports is only 0.59 in 2005, and there is no correlation between the commodity share distributions. The correlations of the two countries' global imports are also quite low: The rank correlation is 0.77, but the correlation of 3-digit commodity shares falls to 0.42. Currently China and India are not close competitors in either export or import markets, and given the large differences in the size of their trade sectors, they occupy quite different positions in the trading system.

2.5 The role of multinational corporations

The foreign direct investment (FDI) of multinational companies in emerging markets is believed to be important because it provides a beachhead from which to promote bilateral trade. From this perspective, it is notable that US investments in both China and India are very small. Although the US imports a large volume of goods from China, US firms invested over the period of 2000–2006 an average of only $5 billion per year, split equally between Hong Kong and Mainland China, or only about 3.5 percent of US global FDI over the period. Investments in India were even smaller, averaging $0.75 billion, or 0.5 percent of the global total. While US retailers, such as Wal-Mart and Mattel, have large imports from China, they do not deal with American multinationals in China. Instead, a large portion of their purchases are from foreign invested enterprises (FIEs) that originate from other countries in Asia, or from Chinese contract manufacturers. Similarly, the information and communication technology (ICT) trade with India appears to not pass through US affiliates.

A summary of the activities of US affiliates in China and India is shown in Table 2.4. The data are drawn from the benchmark surveys of US multinational corporations that are conducted at five-year intervals. The top panel reports the results for China, and, as with the trade data, it combines the information for the mainland and Hong Kong. First, although affiliate sales started from a very low level, they have grown at a rapid pace.[11]

Total affiliate sales expanded at a 14 percent annual rate between 1989 and 2004, and the growth has been concentrated among affiliates on the mainland. Second, affiliate sales are focused on the domestic market, which accounts for 60 percent of total sales in 2004. Approximately 30 percent of sales are directed to other countries—largely in Asia—and only 12 percent are sales back to the United States.

---

[11] Exports have also grown rapidly in recent years, 15% annually in the 2000–2006 period.

Table 2.4. US affiliate activities in China and India, 1989–2004 (in millions of US dollars)

	1989	1994	1999	2004
China:				
US multinational affiliate sales				
Total sales	16,664	32,954	67,635	123,531
Sales to the US	3,554	4,638	10,405	14,297
Local sales	7,438	19,289	42,565	73,602
Sales to other foreign countries	5,672	9,027	14,665	35,632
US exports of goods to affiliates	2,261	5,719	7,533	5,402
US imports of goods from affiliates	3,071	4,021	8,500	9,719
Total US trade with China				
Exports	12,111	20,732	25,670	50,530
Imports	23,139	51,504	97,499	220,308
India:				
US multinational affiliate sales				
Total sales	323	983	4,554	13,100
Sales to the US	(D)	28	138	1,582
Local sales	(D)	934	4,327	9,914
Sales to other foreign countries	13	21	89	1,604
US exports of goods to affiliates	23	33	331	508
US imports of goods from affiliates	(D)	28	77	373
Total US trade with India				
Exports	2,463	2,296	3,666	6,095
Imports	3,551	5,663	9,598	16,437

Sources: Constructed using data from BEA Surveys of US Direct Investment Abroad, and IMF Directions of Trade Database.
Notes: Data for China includes Hong Kong. Sales are those of majority-owned companies. '(D)' indicates that the data has been suppressed to avoid disclosure of data of individual companies.

Furthermore, as shown at the bottom of the table, only 10 percent of US exports to China pass through the affiliates, and only 5 percent of imports originate with affiliates. Clearly US multinationals operate in China with minimal trading links to their US operations. They are not directly utilizing China's low labor costs for exports back to the US market.

Comparable data for India is reported in the bottom panel of Table 2.4. The contrast in scale of the operations with that reported for China is similar to the prior analysis of trade flows. US affiliate sales in India in 2004 were only 10 percent of the total for China. The emphasis on the local market is even greater—75 percent of total sales—primarily because of the trivial amount of sales to third countries. Despite all of the discussion of the offshoring of IT services, little of it appears to involve affiliates of US multinationals.

Table 2.5. Japanese affiliate activity in China (in millions of US dollars)

	2002	2003
Japan multinational affiliate sales		
Total sales	27,515	43,524
Sales to Japan	9,506	13,062
Local sales	9,665	18,497
Sales to other foreign countries	8,349	11,772
Japan exports of goods to affiliates	6,270	8,305
Japan imports of goods from affiliates	3,685	5,077
Total Japan trade with China		
Exports	65,390	87,398
Imports	63,211	76,907

Source: Constructed using data from the Japanese Ministry of Economy, Trade, and Industry, and IMF Directions of Trade Database.
Note: Data include mainland China and Hong Kong.

For comparison purposes, we have also compiled some data on Japanese affiliate operations in China that are presented in Table 2.5. Japanese affiliate sales are considerably smaller than those of the United States, but they are expanding even more rapidly. They are less focused on the local market (about 45 percent of sales), and export a larger percentage of sales back to Japan. However, like US firms, the affiliates are not used as vehicles to promote exports from Japan—sales to affiliates are less than 10 percent of exports to China. In its published material, the Japanese Ministry of Economy, Trade and Industry does not identify India, presumably because the affiliate activities are very small, commensurate with the scale of its trade.

An alternative set of data from the OECD on the outstanding stock of FDI in 2005 provides additional information on the relative involvement of the three large industrial economies in China and India (OECD 2007b). The United States is the largest investor of the three with investments of $55 billion in China and $8.5 billion in India; but as noted above, they represent very small shares of its global investments. The EU-15 is of similar importance with $51 billion in China and $6.5 billion in India. Japan has a substantial investment base in China, $31 billion; but is very small in India, $2 billion.

Branstetter and Foley (2007) conclude that affiliate activity in China is very much in line with US operations in other countries and that it is motivated by both the size of the domestic market and favorable tax treatment. We find that same emphasis on the domestic market in India with only a weak linkage to trade.

It seems clear that US firms operating in China and India do not serve as vehicles for exports, although a loose linkage seems to be a common feature of US affiliates throughout the world. US global exports to affiliates of multinationals represented only 5.6 percent of affiliate sales in 2004. The 4.5 percent reported for affiliates in China and the 4 percent in India are not appreciably different. In comparison, Japanese exports to their affiliates in 2002–2003 were 6 percent of sales at the global level and 20 percent in China.

2.6 The role of distance

The simplest explanation for a low level of exports between the United States and the Asian economies is that they are far away. However, distance does not provide an obvious explanation for the asymmetry of the US trade relationship that is so evident for trade with China and India, small exports but large imports. In this section, we use econometrics to explore its role more formally.

The use of gravity equations to explain the pattern of bilateral trade flows dates back to the work of Jan Tinbergen in the early 1960s. In their simplest form, the volume of trade between any two countries is modeled as proportionate to their economic size and various measures of 'trade resistance'. Measures of trade resistance have included distance between the two trade partners, the presence of a common language or membership of preferential trade associations.[12] We use the gravity model framework to examine the extent to which such a model can account for the differential importance of China trade for the United States, Japan, and the EU-15.

The empirical analysis is based on a very simple formulation in which economic size is measured by the combination of a country's population and its income per capita. In addition, the trade (distinguishing between imports and exports) between a country and its trading partners is estimated separately for the United States, Japan, and the EU-15. The base

[12] A useful review is provided by Deardorff (1998). Helpful recent discussions of linkages between the theoretical formulations and the empirical analyses are those of Anderson and van Wincoop (2004), Feenstra (2002), and Helpman et al. (2007). For a recent application and discussion the estimation issues, see Coe and others (2007).

regression is:

$$\ln T_{ij} = \alpha + \beta_1 \ln POP_j + \beta_2 \ln Y_j + \beta_3 \ln D_j + \beta_4 \ln X_{i,j} \qquad (1)$$

Where T_{ij} = trade (imports or exports) from country i to country j,
POP_j = population of country j,
Y_j = GDP per capita of country j,
D_{ij} = distance between country i and country j, and
X_{ij} = other measures of 'trade resistance'.

Normally, the relationship would also include the population and income per capita of both country pairs, but in our analysis the relationship is estimated separately for each of the three base economies (the United States, Japan, and the EU-15).

Goods trade

The annual trade data are taken from the Direction of Trade Statistics of the International Monetary Fund and cover the period 1980–2005. GDP and population are from the World Development Indicators of the World Bank. The trade data are scaled by the nominal dollar GDP of each of the base economies and the GDP per capita of the trading partners is measured in 2000 US dollars. The measures of distance and the other bilateral pairing variables used to proxy 'trade resistance'—such as language, contiguity, and colonial link—were obtained from the French Institute for Research on the International Economy (CEPII).[13]

The basic results are reported in Table 2.6 and cover 162 countries over 26 years. All of the equations are estimated with a fixed effects formulation to allow for shifts in the constant term over each of the twenty-six years.[14] The number of observations varies slightly across the individual regressions because the few countries in each sample for which no trade is recorded have been dropped. Also, while the individual countries of

---

[13] The distance measure is the weighted distance measure of CEPII, which reflects the bilateral distance between the major cities of each country. The definition of a common language that we use states that a language is shared if it is spoken by at least 9% of the population in both countries. A country shares a language with the EU-15 if this is true for any of the 15 countries.

[14] The use of fixed effects estimation had no significant influence on the estimated coefficients, but it does reduce the evident autocorrelation of the error term. These year dummies adjust for a variety of factors that may be changing over time, such as overall openness and degree of exchange rate overvaluation.

Table 2.6. Gravity equations for global trade: United States, Japan, and EU-15

	United States				Japan				European Union (15)			
	Exports/ GDP (1)	Imports/ GDP (1)	Exports/ GDP (2)	Imports/ GDP (2)	Exports/ GDP (1)	Imports/ GDP (1)	Exports/ GDP (2)	Imports/ GDP (2)	Exports/ GDP (1)	Imports/ GDP (1)	Exports/ GDP (2)	Imports/ GDP (2)
Weighted distance	−1.02 (−29.2)	−0.60 (−11.3)	−1.16 (−31.9)	−0.71 (−13.0)	−1.11 (−26.0)	−1.55 (−24.0)	−0.61 (−10.7)	−0.65 (−7.7)	−1.06 (−48.7)	−0.74 (−26.3)	−1.15 (−43.9)	−0.79 (−23.3)
Population	0.90 (106.0)	1.05 (81.8)	0.90 (108.2)	1.05 (82.5)	0.82 (88.6)	0.93 (64.0)	0.86 (90.8)	1.00 (68.0)	0.79 (124.4)	0.90 (110.6)	0.79 (125.1)	0.90 (110.7)
GDP per capita	1.06 (98.2)	1.15 (70.6)	1.05 (98.7)	1.14 (70.2)	0.98 (83.0)	1.13 (63.2)	1.01 (85.9)	1.18 (67.2)	0.87 (97.6)	0.90 (78.3)	0.87 (97.2)	0.90 (77.8)
Common language	0.70 (20.1)	0.71 (13.6)	0.67 (19.6)	0.69 (13.2)					0.26 (8.0)	0.26 (6.4)	0.30 (9.2)	0.29 (6.9)
Colony									0.32 (7.0)	0.24 (4.2)	0.38 (8.2)	0.28 (4.7)
East Asia region			0.56 (11.8)	0.51 (7.0)			0.89 (13.1)	1.61 (15.8)			0.25 (6.1)	0.15 (2.8)
Constant	−37.17 (−100.1)	−44.12 (−78.9)	−35.97 (−95.1)	−43.06 (−74.7)	−33.90 (−72.8)	−33.46 (−47.1)	−39.39 (−63.7)	−43.36 (−46.6)	−32.98 (−139.6)	−37.83 (−124.5)	−32.28 (−123.4)	−37.41 (−110.8)
adj_R2	0.858	0.760	0.863	0.763	0.812	0.714	0.820	0.733	0.886	0.841	0.887	0.841
Observations	3,577	3,532	3,577	3,532	3,626	3,534	3,626	3,534	3,367	3,367	3,367	3,367

Source: Estimated by authors as described in text. All of the regressions are estimated within a fixed effects model allowing for shifts over years. All variables are measured as logarithms except for the categorical variables of common language, colony, and the East Asia region. T-statistics are in parentheses.

the EU-15 are included in the regressions for the United States and Japan, regressions for the EU-15 exclude intra-group trade. The regression results are very consistent with similar estimates in the literature: The elasticity of trade with respect to the two measures of economic size is very close to unity and there is a strong role for distance.

There are also significant econometric issues that we have not addressed (see Helpman et al. (2007) for a discussion). In our data set, which is limited to the trade of the large economies, we do not have a significant problem with zero bilateral trade entries, which have to be excluded in a logarithmic estimation. In addition, the distinction between intensive and extensive trade should be important for us only on the import side, and we do not yet have an effective estimation method.

Of greatest relevance in the current context, the distance coefficients are very large and significant in all of the regressions. Unexpectedly, there is evidence of an asymmetric effect on US trade: The distance coefficient for US exports is markedly greater than that for imports. A similar, though smaller, asymmetry also exists for the EU-15; but the asymmetry is reversed for Japan where the coefficient on distance is largest in the import equation. The coefficient on distance is interpreted by some researchers as a measure of global integration. From that perspective, importers to the United States appear to have been considerably more successful than US exporters in overcoming trade barriers associated with distance from the US market. Furthermore, the reversal of the relationship for Japan implies that Japan has been more successful in overcoming barriers to its exports than others have been in overcoming barriers to their exports to Japan. It is also notable that the effects of distance on exports from and especially imports to Japan are significantly larger in magnitude than for either the US or the EU-15.

Thus, the results from the gravity equations do have a major effect on our conclusions about the magnitude of US trade with Asia. This is particularly true for trade with China, which is far away from the United States (11,000 kilometers), but close to Japan (2,000 kilometers). An elasticity of distance near unity implies that the US export share in GDP would be very similar to that for Japan if the two countries' distance from China were equalized. Thus, distance can fully account for the differences in the importance of exports to China. However, if the distance were equalized, the hypothetical level of US imports from China would also increase by a proportionate amount.[15] India is even further away from the United States (13,500 kilometers).[16]

In testing the robustness of the results, we examined a wide range of alternative formulations. For example, we included categorical variables for each of the three major economies in the trade relationships of the others. Canada and Mexico were also included directly in the US equations. While those variables were all significant, they had no substantial effect on the size of the other coefficients in the regressions, such as distance. Furthermore, we found a more general pattern in which all of the East Asian economies had positive residuals, implying a larger volume of trade than indicated by the simple distance variable.

The results with the categorical variable for East Asia are shown in a second set of regressions in Table 2.6. The East Asia coefficient is large and positive in the US regressions, raising the predictions for both exports and imports; but surprisingly, there is no significant change in the coefficients for the other variables including distance. Also, the magnitude of the regional effect seems to be similar for both imports and exports. There is some decline, however, in the magnitude of the asymmetry of the coefficient on distance between the export and import equations. A similar result is evident for the EU-15, although the coefficient on the Asia variable is only half as large. The regression results for Japan are quite different, however, because the coefficient on the East Asia region is extremely large, twice the magnitude shown for the United States; and the coefficients on distance decline dramatically. It is evident that an important regional trading pattern has emerged within East Asia that is not well represented in a simple focus on distance. This formulation did not work, however, when we tried to expand the definition of the categorical variable to include South Asia.

Several commentators have raised questions about the consistency of the results over time and the possibility that the effect of distance in particular may have declined. As a partial test of the hypothesis, we refit the regression estimates to five-year subperiods. While we have not reported all of the results, the regression estimates were remarkably stable across the subperiods. For the United States, the coefficients on population and GDP per capita had standard deviations of 5 percent or less across the

---

[15] The distance elasticity for imports from China is less than for exports, but the level of imports is much larger.

[16] The distance from Japan to India is 6,000 kilometers, and for the EU-15 the average distances are 6,800 kilometers to India and 8,300 to China.

five subperiods. The coefficients on distance did vary over a wider range of 10 percent, but the coefficient in the export relationship became more negative over time, contrary to our expectations, and the magnitude of the asymmetry between exports and imports increased.[17] The magnitude of coefficient changes for the EU-15 and Japan were very similar to the results for the United States, except there was no uniform pattern of change over time.

The actual and predicted results for US exports and imports in 2005, based on the regressions with the East Asia variable, are shown in Figure 2.4. Because exports to Canada and Mexico are so dominant, they are excluded from the figure to focus on exports to the other countries. The figure highlights two important results of the analysis. First, within a gravity equation framework, both exports and imports from China are larger than expected. In 2005, the export relationship, shown in the top panel, produces a 50 percent underestimate of exports to China that is markedly less than the large overestimate of trade with countries like the United Kingdom and Japan. In contrast, imports from China, shown in the lower panel, exceed the predicted values by about 70 percent. US trade with India is so small that it is difficult to identify in the figure. However, the predicted and actual values are very similar: The error in 2005 for exports is zero and the predicted level of imports is above by 5 percent.

Second, the figure brings out the point that, while exports to China may be a small share of US GDP, they are relatively substantial compared to US exports to other countries. The basic problem is that, except for Canada and Mexico, the United States has a low level of exports to all countries. Within that framework, exports to China are comparable to those to Germany and the United Kingdom. In other words, while US exports to China are small in comparison to those of other countries, they are not small within the context of US exports to other countries.

Services trade

Traditionally, gravity equations have been applied to bilateral trade in goods. In recent years, however, the OECD has begun to publish data on the bilateral services trade flows of its members. We obtained data covering the seven years from 1999 to 2005 for exports and imports of

---

[17] To explore whether changes in the distance coefficient over time were statistically significant, we ran full sample regressions that interacted distance with dummies for each 5-year time period. The changes were highly significant (1% level) for exports, but not significant for imports.

Trading with Asia's Giants

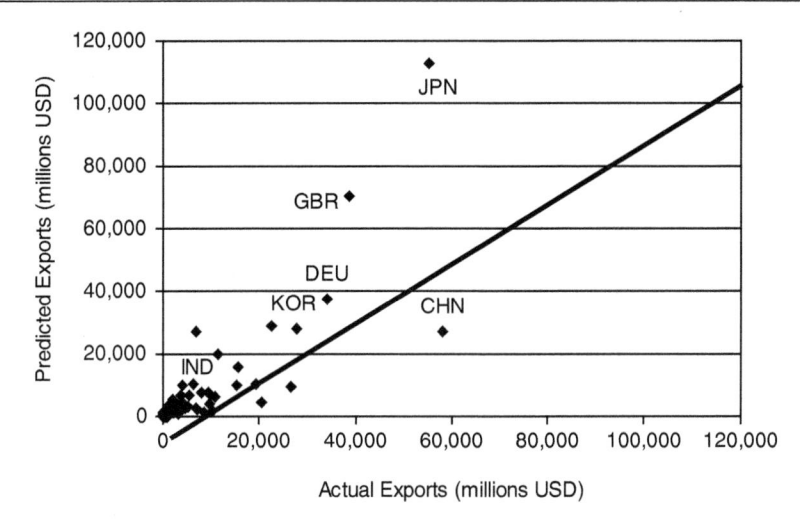

Figure 2.4a. US exports to selected countries, 2005 with East Asia adjustment (in million USD)

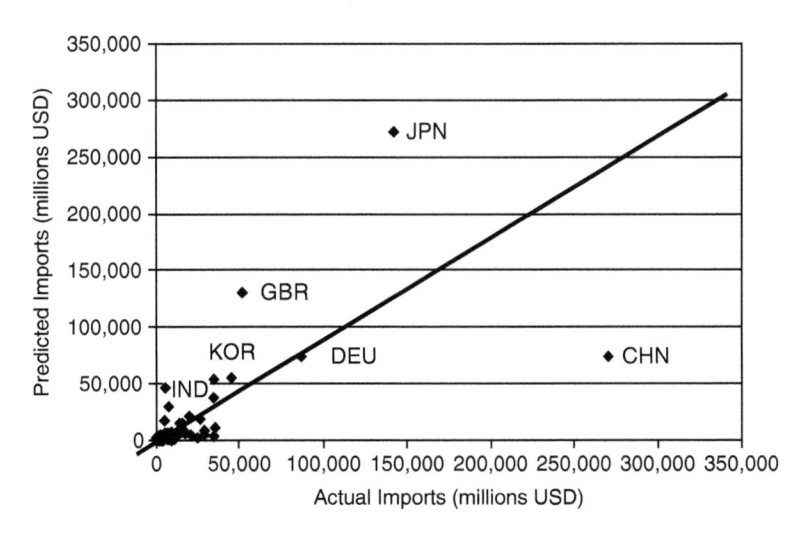

Figure 2.4b. US imports from selected countries, 2005 with East Asia adjustment (in million USD)

Source: Computed from equations of Table 2.5. Values for Canada and Mexico are excluded from the charts.

53

Table 2.7. Gravity equations for services trade: United States, Japan, and EU-15, 1999–2005

	United States		Japan		European Union (15)	
	Exports/ GDP (2)	Imports/ GDP (2)	Exports/ GDP (2)	Imports/ GDP (2)	Exports/ GDP (2)	Imports/ GDP (2)
Weighted distance	−0.56	−0.57	−0.25	−0.32	−1.08	−0.87
	(−14.7)	(−10.0)	(−1.9)	(−3.3)	(−20.9)	(−13.5)
Population	0.71	0.78	0.84	0.79	0.74	0.81
	(40.1)	(29.2)	(15.5)	(20.2)	(40.5)	(35.2)
GDP per capita	0.90	1.01	1.11	1.19	0.77	0.78
	(41.6)	(31.2)	(18.0)	(26.0)	(31.1)	(25.0)
Common language	0.30	0.40			0.13	−0.23
	(8.0)	(7.1)			(1.8)	(−2.6)
Colony					0.29	0.23
					(3.8)	(2.4)
East Asia region	0.49	0.57	1.68	1.71	0.73	0.92
	(11.2)	(8.7)	(9.5)	(13.2)	(8.4)	(8.4)
Constant	−37.37	−40.11	−45.36	−44.34	−31.19	−34.02
	(−55.6)	(−39.7)	(−22.5)	(−30.1)	(−62.4)	(−54.0)
adj_R^2	0.879	0.794	0.681	0.805	0.882	0.850
Observations	420	420	187	196	265	265

Source: Estimated by authors as described in text. All of the regressions are estimated within a fixed effects model allowing for shifts over years. All variables are measured in logarithms except for the categorical variables of common language, colony and the East Asia region. The data are from the OECD and cover 31 trading partners for the United States, 28 for Japan and 38 for the EU-15. T-statistics are in parentheses.

total services for the EU-15 and Japan.[18] The data for the United States were obtained from the Bureau of Economic Analysis and cover the years 1992–2006. We applied the same gravity model, outlined in equation (1), to the services trade of the United States, Japan, and the EU-15 (excluding intra-EU trade). Those regressions are reported in Table 2.7.

The results are very similar to those reported for goods trade in that distance, size, and income per capita again have large and highly significant elasticities, and the regressions fit the data very well. The coefficients on distance, however, are generally smaller and show more variability. In part, that is due to the smaller sample sizes; but we also estimated a set of parallel regressions for goods trade that was restricted to the same countries and years for which we had data on services trade. For the United States and Japan, the distance coefficients for services trade are smaller than for goods trade, but they were larger for the EU. It is notable

---

[18] The data on trade in services by partner country is available at http://stats.oecd.org/wbos/default.aspx. At present, disaggregated partner country data below the level of total services is not available.

Trading with Asia's Giants

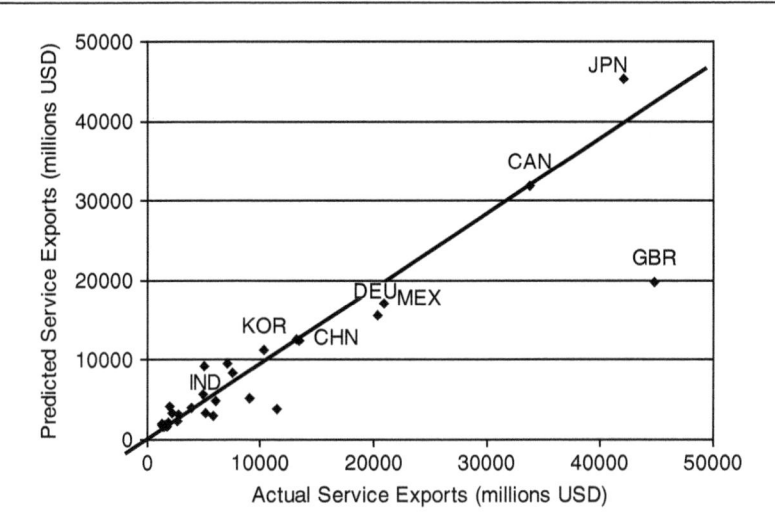

Figure 2.5a. US service exports to selected countries, 2005 with East Asia Adjustment (in million USD)

that there is again a special positive effect for the East Asian economies of equal magnitude in both the export and import regressions. The United States' services trade with East Asia is substantially greater than would be predicted by the standard gravity equation.

As with goods, we are surprised by the magnitude of the distance variable as it can have little to do with freight costs. In fact, we re-estimated the US regressions excluding travel and transportation, the components one would expect to be most sensitive to distance-related transport costs: This had no significant effect on the parameters. Figure 2.5 shows the distribution of US trade in services by partner country. The largest errors for both exports and imports are an under-prediction of services trade with the United Kingdom and an over-prediction for Japan. The high level of trade with the United Kingdom is related to financial services because both countries are important global finance centers. Trade with China and India is very close to predicted.

2.7 Effects of the US trade deficit

One interesting issue, shown in Figure 2.4, is that US exports to China and India are not small if the comparison is limited to US trade alone. They are small only in comparison with other countries' trade. This issue

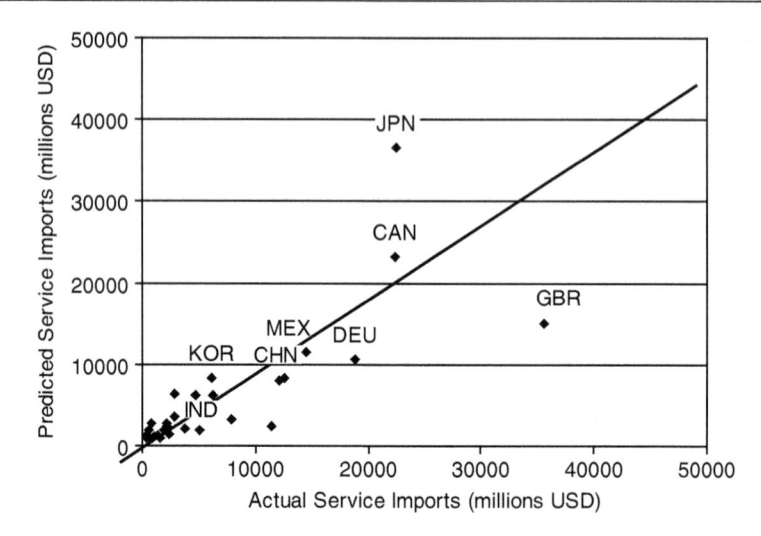

Figure 2.5b. US service imports from selected countries, 2005 with East Asia adjustment (in million USD)

Source: Authors' calculations as in text.

can be developed more clearly with the ranking of US trade with partner countries shown in Table 2.8. While China is the second largest source of US imports behind Canada, it is also the fourth largest export destination. In the comparison with Japan and the EU-15, the striking feature is the small share of total US exports as a share of GDP.

As shown in the lower part of the table, total exports are only 7.3 percent of GDP in 2005, compared to 13.1 and 11.4 for Japan and the EU-15 respectively. In contrast, the United States actually imports a slightly larger share of its GDP than either Japan or the EU-15. The table shows the extent to which the comparison of the relative importance of exports is distorted by the large overall trade deficit of the United States. Given that the overall trade deficit of the United States is equal to 90 percent of total exports, the comparison of US trade with most partner countries is bound to appear unfavorable.

It is sometimes alleged that US firms, provided with access to a large domestic market, are insufficiently interested in the development of export opportunities.[19] In addition, the US Government was criticized

---

[19] Admittedly, this is a more popular argument outside of the United States, but American multinational firms have also been willing to use foreign affiliates as an alternative to exports from the United States. The sales of foreign affiliates less their purchases from US parents, $3.9 trillion in 2005, far exceed the comparable measures of net sales of foreign firms in the United States, $2.3 trillion (Lowe 2008).

Trading with Asia's Giants

Table 2.8. United States top trading partners, 2005 (in billions US dollars)

Country	Exports	Percent	Rank	Country	Imports	Percent
EU-15	182	20.1		EU-15	308	17.7
Canada	211	23.4	1	Canada	292	16.9
Mexico	120	13.3	2	China	270	15.6
China	58	6.4	3	Mexico	172	10.0
Japan	55	6.1	4	Japan	142	8.2
United Kingdom	39	4.3	5	Germany	87	5.0
Germany	34	3.8	6	United Kingdom	52	3.0
Korea	28	3.1	7	Korea	46	2.6
Netherlands	26	2.9	8	Venezuela, Rep. Bol.	35	2.0
France	23	2.5	9	France	35	2.0
Singapore	21	2.3	10	Malaysia	35	2.0
India	8	0.9	20,17	India	20	1.1
Total	904			Total	1,733	
Trade deficit	−828					

Country	Exports	Percent of GDP	Country	Imports	Percent of GDP
US	904	7.3	US	1,733	14.0
Japan	595	13.1	Japan	515	11.4
EU-15	1,459	11.4	EU-15	1,582	12.4
incl. intra-EU	3,688	28.9	incl. intra-EU	3,810	29.9

Source: Constructed using data from IMF Direction of Trade Statistics and authors' calculations.

in past years for restricting the exports of those technology products for which the United States has a comparative advantage. As a simple exploration of this idea, we combined the data for the EU-15, Japan, and the United States, and fit a common gravity equation. The basic result is shown in columns 1 and 3 of Table 2.9. As would be expected from the regressions in Table 2.6, the imposition of common coefficient values for all three industrialized regions has little effect. In columns 2 and 6, we added a categorical variable for the United States. In essence, the US performance is evaluated against a peer group composed of an average of the EU-15 and Japan. The coefficient is negative and highly significant in the export equation but zero in the import equation. The results are at least suggestive of the view that the United States is a weak exporter relative to other high-income economies, but that its imports are quite normal.[20]

---

[20] A similar point about the weakness of exports accounting for the deterioration of the US trade balance is advanced by Baily and Lawrence (2006, 228–36). Using a different methodology, they demonstrate that the weakness cannot be attributed to lack of growth in US export markets or the commodity composition of trade.

Table 2.9. Combined gravity model for US, Japan, and EU-15

	Exports/GDP (1)	Exports/GDP (2)	Exports/GDP (3)	Imports/GDP (1)	Imports/GDP (2)	Imports/GDP (3)
Weighted distance	−1.102	−1.098	−1.123	−1.020	−1.020	−1.007
	(−61.2)	(−62.6)	(−63.4)	(−39.7)	(−39.7)	(−38.6)
Population	0.831	0.837	0.838	0.976	0.976	0.975
	(172.3)	(178.0)	(178.8)	(139.5)	(139.4)	(139.4)
GDP per capita	0.973	0.974	0.972	1.062	1.062	1.063
	(153.1)	(157.4)	(157.5)	(116.6)	(116.6)	(116.6)
Common language	0.258	0.529	0.544	0.562	0.562	0.554
	(10.9)	(20.7)	(21.3)	(16.7)	(15.0)	(14.7)
Colony	0.556	0.156	0.326	0.698	0.699	0.610
	(21.9)	(5.2)	(9.2)	(19.3)	(16.0)	(11.6)
East Asia region	0.400	0.407	0.414	0.755	0.755	0.751
	(15.1)	(15.8)	(16.1)	(19.9)	(19.9)	(19.8)
United States		−0.586	−0.609		0.000	0.012
		(−24.2)	(−25.1)		(0.0)	(0.3)
Log average exchange rate*			−1.119			0.586
			(−8.7)			(3.1)
Constant	−34.325	−34.249	−28.940	−38.490	−38.490	−41.276
	(−170.8)	(−175.1)	(−45.1)	(−133.9)	(−133.8)	(−43.6)
adj_R2	0.840	0.848	0.849	0.762	0.762	0.762
Observations	10,570	10,570	10,570	10,433	10,433	10,433

Source: Estimated by authors as described in text.
Notes: All of the regressions are estimated within a fixed effects model allowing for shifts over years. All variables are measured as logarithms except for the categorical variables of common language, colony, the US, and the East Asia region. * Computed as a simple average of the prior 5-year trade-weighted real exchange rates. Data taken from JPMorgan. T-statistics are in parentheses.

We also sought to determine if we could explain some of the variations in US performance as related to exchange rate effects. We do not have effective exchange rate measures covering all of the trading partners, and in particular, we do not have a means of accounting for competitor effects in third markets. However, as a partial measure of changes in competitive conditions over time, we included the multilateral real exchange rate for each of the respondent countries. Since there is no variation across the partner countries, the exchange rate has to substitute for the fixed effect estimation.

The results are presented in columns 3 and 6. The exchange rate elasticity is a negative—1.1 for exports and a positive 0.6 for imports. This smaller effect on the nominal value of imports is expected, since a rise (appreciation) in the real exchange rate promotes a rise in the quantity of imports, that is partially offset by a decline in price. No such offset exists on the export side.[21] Strikingly, the inclusion of the exchange rate does not alter the size of the coefficient on the US categorical variable however. Evidence of relatively poor US export performance persists even after adjustment for the exchange rate.

As shown in Table 2.8, the US trade deficit is roughly equal to total exports; and if we projected a future adjustment that restored a trade balance, the export share would roughly double as a share of GDP. If we also adopted the reasonable assumption that the adjustment would spread in proportionate terms across all trading partners, the Chinese and Indian markets would be much more important to the United States.

2.8 Conclusion

The large US trade imbalance with Asia is a frequent topic of concern in the US media and policy discussion. There is a perception that the imbalance is somehow the result of unfair trade practices. The trade issues take on added importance with respect to US economic relations with China and India, who are emerging as global centers for manufacturing and business services respectively. In this chapter, we have argued that it is the low level of US exports to the region, not the magnitude of imports, that appears puzzling. Thus, we have examined various possible explanations for the low exports, focusing on trade with the two economic giants, China and India, with whom we have particularly large trade deficits. US imports from China, for example, scaled by US GDP, are similar to those of Japan and EU-15 imports from China as a share of their own GDPs. In contrast, the US exports a much smaller share of its GDP to China than either the EU-15 or—especially—Japan. Indeed, US exports to China are still less than a quarter of its imports, while Japan exports more to China than it imports. Even though US exports to China have been growing rapidly since 2002, this growth is from such a small base that it would take a long time to have much effect on the bilateral balance. Our analysis also highlights the importance of trade in services with China, which appears to significantly exceed the more publicized services trade with India.

---

[21] In reality, the adjustment process would be more complex, in part because of the need to take account of possible limits of the pass-through of exchange rate changes into export and import prices. See Cline (2005) and Mann (1999) for more detailed discussions.

Our main findings are as follows. First, the poor performance of US exports of goods does not reflect an unusual export composition. Like Japan and the EU-15, the distribution of commodities that the US exports to China is quite similar to the basket it exports to the rest of the world. Furthermore, with the exception of agricultural goods and raw materials, the mix of commodities that the US exports to China is very similar to the exports from Japan and Europe. Thus, the US is clearly competing with these countries, especially in the Chinese markets for capital goods and electronics. We find no evidence that the composition of US trade with China is distorted. The situation is less clear-cut for India where the composition of US exports is less correlated with its global trade and with the exports of the EU-15 and Japan.

Second, small US exports to China and India may be due in part to the relatively small presence of US multinationals. Operations of these affiliates to date have largely focused on serving the domestic markets of both China and India, with relatively little trading links to their operations in the US. In any case, US FDI to both countries is now growing rapidly, though from a very small base.

Third, our more formal econometric analysis using gravity equations highlights both expected and unexpected dimensions of the importance of distance. Like the large prior literature that uses the gravity framework to explain trade flows, we find distance always to be a very important and significant determinant. Since China and India are far away from the US, one would expect that controlling for distance would help explain the relatively small US exports to China, with the large imports emerging as an outlier instead. Quite surprisingly however, we find that US exports to East Asia and imports from the region are both unexpectedly large. Even after adjustment for the East Asia region, US exports to and imports from China are both larger than expected. Trade with India is about what would be predicted, however.

Finally, our most important finding is that the low level of US exports is a global phenomenon and not one limited to trade with the Asian economies. At present, the United States has a trade deficit with nearly every country of the world, and the imbalance with the Asian economies stands out primarily because they account for a large proportion of total trade. At 7 percent of GDP, US exports are only about half the level of its imports and only half the share of GDP reported for Japan and the EU-15. Most of the concerns about trade with the Asian economies would be resolved by an adjustment of the US global trade balance. However, we note that the last two decades have also been notable for the strong expansion of US multinational firms. Ownership-based estimates of trade, which take into account the net earnings of foreign affiliates, imply a significantly smaller trade imbalance for the United States.[22] Thus, US firms have been very active and successful in the global economy, even though they have not done it through an emphasis on exports.

It is important to stress that the relatively weak US export performance we have identified is not a reflection of weak US industrial performance overall. In contrast, overall growth and gains in TFP were strong during the 1990s and early parts of this century, such that the US played a substantial role as an engine of growth for the global economy. This context makes relatively small US exports all the more surprising. While we do not have a fully satisfactory explanation for the pattern of weak export performance, we conclude by suggesting some possibilities. J. David Richardson (1993) highlighted a variety of impediments to US exporters. His work stresses a deficiency of supporting infrastructure and lack of access to trade finance relative to our major competitors in global markets. Baily and Lawrence (2006) focus on the decline in the US export share, placing much of the blame on an overvalued dollar. While we too find an important role for exchange rates, our analysis does not suggest that this explains much of the fact that US exports are relatively low. Finally, it is often argued that many US firms display a limited interest in exporting, preferring to focus on a very large and expanding domestic market. Exploring these possible explanations further needs to be a focus of future research.

[22] The US Bureau of Economic analysis reports an ownership-based estimate of the trade deficit in 2006 of $584 billion compared to $758 billion for the conventional concept—available at http://www.bea.gov/international/xls/1982–2006table.xls.

3
The Chinese Export Bundles: Patterns, Puzzles, and Possible Explanations

Zhi Wang and Shang-Jin Wei[*]

3.1 Introduction

Both China and India are major success stories in their integration with the world economy, and in their fast economic growth rates. At this stage, China's goods exports are somewhat ahead of India's. China's exports in 2007 were valued at $1,218 billion according to statistics released by China's Ministry of Commerce, more than seven times India's estimated $155 billion in exports in the same year (IMF, 'India: 2007 Article IV Consultation-Staff Report'). On the other hand, India has been more successful in exports of business services and of information and IT services.

China exports a huge variety of goods in a way that makes the composition of its export bundles looks increasingly similar to that of rich country bundles. This has been documented by Fontagne et al. (2007), Hallack and Schott (2005), Rodrik (2006), and Xu (2007), is perhaps surprising to many. Using data on Chinese exports at the level of product-producing region-customs type, Wang and Wei (2008) investigated possible reasons behind the apparent rise in the sophistication of Chinese exports.

The current chapter has two objectives. First, it collects new product-level data on Indian exports and compares the evolution of export

---

[*] The views in the chapter are those of the authors and not the official views of the US ITC, or any other organization that the authors are or have been affiliated with. The authors thank Kyle Caswell and Chang Hong for their efficient research assistance, and Xuepeng Liu, William Power, and especially Galina Hale, for helpful comments.

sophistication for both China and India. Second, it summarizes the key findings of Wang and Wei (2008). Because we do not have comparably detailed data for Indian exports as we do for China, we are not able to replicate all of the analyses performed in Wang and Wei (2008).

The rest of the chapter is organized as follows. Section 3.2 documents the evolving export structure sophistication for both China and India. Section 3.3 explains the basic methodology, the underlying data, and the statistical analyses of Chinese exports. Section 3.4 concludes.

3.2 Evolving sophistication in export structures: China vs. India

To keep track of export sophistication, we adopt the methodology developed in Hallack and Schott (2005) by comparing the export structure of each country in question with those of the high-income industrial economies. Specifically, we use as a benchmark the collective export structure of the United States, Japan, and the European Union, which we will hereafter call the G-3 for short. The G-3 economies, on an *ex ante* basis, have a comparative advantage in producing and exporting the most skill-intensive products. Therefore, similarity in export structure to these economies is taken as a measure of export sophistication. By implication, if India and China's export structures become more similar to those of the G-3 economies over time, this should be taken as evidence that their exports have become increasingly more sophisticated.

This methodology allows us to avoid having to make a judgment on products' skill content, product by product. Since G-3 economies adjust their export structures over time in response to their evolving comparative advantage (and to competition from the rest of the world) the benchmark of the G-3 export structure is a moving target. In other words, there is no presumption that any developing country's export structure should automatically converge to those of the G-3 economies over time.

This definition of export sophistication has its drawbacks. First, even when China and India export the same type of product as do the high-income countries, they may not be producing the same variety within a given product category. Using unit value within a product category as a yardstick for the sophistication level of a variety, Schott (2006) and Wang and Wei (2008) confirm that the Chinese varieties tend to have lower unit values than those exported by the G-3 economies. Moreover, Wang and Wei (2008) showed that unit values tend to vary systematically across production by Chinese exporters. Private Chinese firms tend to produce the lowest unit values. Foreign invested firms that engage in processing exports, and that are located in high-tech development zones, tend to produce the highest unit values. Second, half of Chinese exports are from processing trade, which could muddle the sophistication content of Chinese exports. Taking into account the role of processing exports, Koopman et al. (2008) calculate that, on average, domestic value added as a share of Chinese exports is about 50 percent. Moreover, those sectors that are likely to be labeled as technically sophisticated, such as computers and telecommunications, tend to have even lower domestic content, on the order of 20 percent or less. These caveats about using export structure to judge a country's export sophistication should be kept in mind while interpreting subsequent results.

A preliminary look at export structure sophistication

We now start with a check on the sophistication of Chinese and Indian exports. The most detailed way to classify a country's exports while maintaining international comparability is to use the Harmonized System at the 6-digit level. With this classification, a country can export slightly over 5,000 products. Figure 3.1 plots the fraction of HS 6-digit level products that the G-3 economies export but that China (or India) does not over the period from 1996 to 2005. By this metric, only 2–3 percent

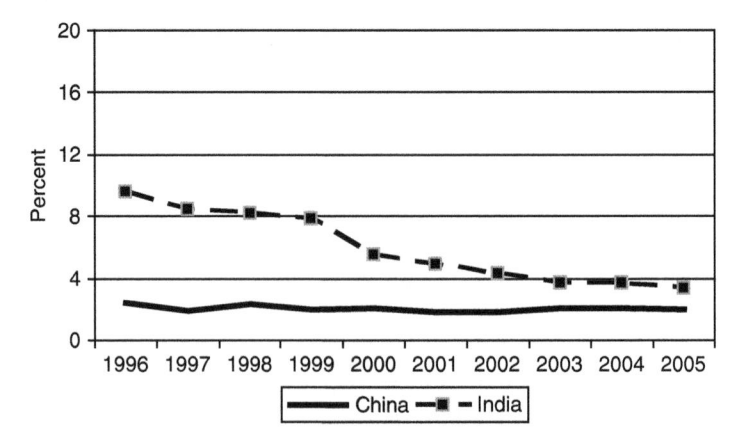

Figure 3.1. Fraction of the HS-6 codes that the G-3 export but that China and India do not, 1996–2005

Source: Authors' calculations based on official trade statistics from the China Customs Administration and UN COMTRADE data.

The Chinese Export Bundles

of all product lines fall into category for Chinese exports. In other words, there is very little difference in export bundles between China and the G-3 economies: China exports virtually all the things that the G-3 economies do. For India, the gap is somewhat more visible. In 1996, close to 10 percent of product lines that the G-3 exported were also not exported by India. The gap has shrunk over time, however, to about 3 percent by 2005.

We can also look at the flip side of the story, that is, the fraction of product lines that China or India exports but the G-3 economies do not. By this measure, overlap in the export bundles of China and the G-3 is astonishingly high. The overlap between India and the G-3 is only slightly less so but also very high. (These results are left out to save space.) From these admittedly naive measures, one might think that China and France are producing and exporting more or less the same bundle of goods, or at least moving fast in that direction. India is not doing so yet, but is following in China's path with a lag of roughly ten years.

This method suffers from one serious drawback, in that it only ticks off whether any particular good is exported or not. Since both China and India are large economies, they may export virtually all products, but for some product lines, only by a tiny bit. If China and India are more likely to export those relatively sophisticated products in only a trivial amount, this metric may exaggerate the degree of overlap in export bundles. As a refinement, we apply some cutoff level to the value of exports before it is deemed significant. We choose $1 million as our cutoff point. Specifically, we now look at the fraction of goods that G-3 export (in an amount of at least $1 million) but that China or India does not. The results are represented in Figure 3.2. As we can see, this number was 29 percent for China in 1996, and declined more or less steadily to 14 percent in 2005. The line for India also traces out a steady decline in the part of exports that does not overlap with that of the G-3 economies, from about 65 percent in 1995 to about 40 percent in 2005. Note the degree to which India's area of no overlap in 2005 was bigger than that for China in 1995. This suggests that India still has some catching up to do in the development of its exports' sophistication.

Rather than assigning equal weight to all products, one may assign a greater weight to products whose export values are greater. The results of this operation are presented in Figure 3.3. A pattern broadly similar to those shown above can be seen in this figure.

Rather than applying a blunt cutoff point, such as that employed in Figures 3.2 and 3.3, we could explicitly take into account the share of

65

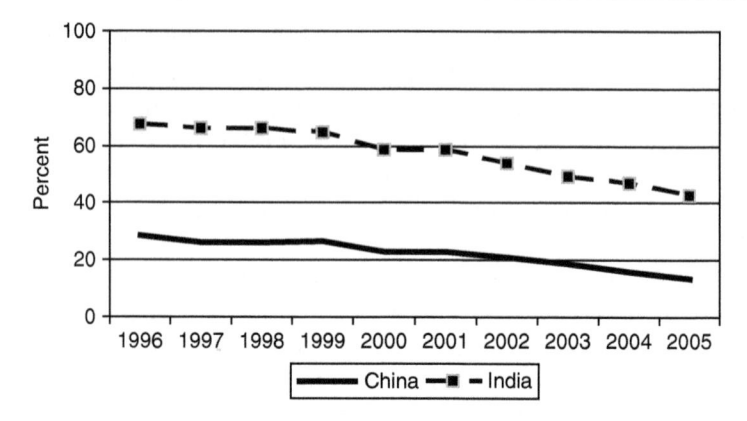

Figure 3.2. Fraction of the HS-6 codes that G-3 economies export by at least a million US dollars but that China and India do not, 1996–2005

Source: Authors' calculations based on official trade statistics from the China Customs Administration and UN COMTRADE data.

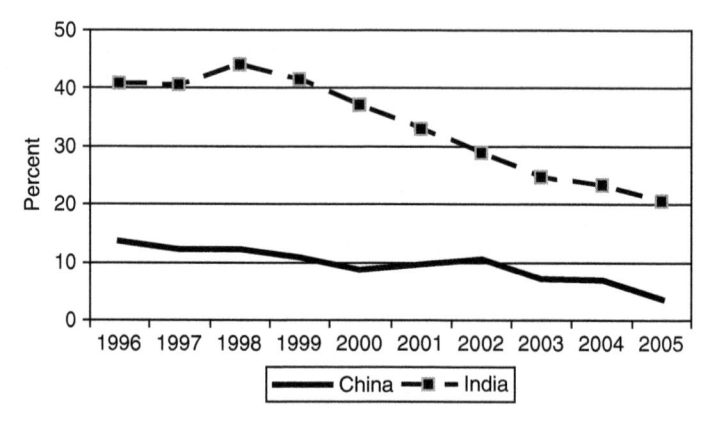

Figure 3.3. Value-weighted fraction of HS-6 codes that G-3 economies export by at least a million US dollars but that China and India do not, 1996–2005

Source: Authors' calculations based on official trade statistics from the China Customs Administration and UN COMTRADE data.

each product in the export bundle. We do this later in the chapter by constructing and analyzing an Export Dissimilarity Index (EDI). We note here, simply, that we arrive at broadly the same conclusions.[1]

---

[1] Xu (2007) noted that the unit values of China's exports tend to be lower than those of the same products from rich countries, indicating China's varieties are of lower quality and presumably of lesser sophistication. Fontagne et al. (2007, Tables 1 and 2) show that China's export structure, defined as in Schott (2006) but at the HS 6-digit level, is more similar to those of Japan, the United States, and the European Union than to those of Brazil and Russia.

A formal index of export structure dissimilarity

We define an index for a lack of sophistication in exports by the dissimilarity between the product structure of a region's exports and that of the G-3 economies' exports, or the export dissimilarity index (EDI) as:

$$EDI_{rft} = 100 \left(\sum_i abs \left(s_{irft} - s_{i,t}^{ref} \right) \right) \quad (2)$$

where

$$S_{irft} = \frac{E_{irft}}{\sum_i E_{irft}} \quad (3)$$

Where s_{irft} is the share of HS product i at the 6-digit level in Chinese city r's exports by firm type f in year t, and $s_{i,t}^{ref}$ is the share of HS product i in the 6-digit level exports of G-3 developed countries. The greater the value of the index, the more dissimilar the two export structures are. If the two export structures were to be identical, then the value of the index would be zero; if the two export structures were to have no overlap, then the index would take the value of 200. We regard an export structure as more sophisticated if the index takes a smaller value. Alternatively, one could use the similarity index proposed by Finger and Kreinin (1979) and used by Schott (2006) (except for the scale):

$$ESI_{rft} = 100 \sum_i \min(s_{irft}, s_{it,}^{ref}) \quad (4)$$

This index is bounded by zero and 100. If Chinese city r's export structure has no overlap with that of the G-3 developed countries, then the ESI is zero; if the two export structures have a perfect overlap, then the index takes the value of 100. It can be verified that there is a one-to-one, linear mapping between ESI and EDI:

$$ESI_{rft} = (200 - EDI_{rft})/2 \quad (5)$$

While ESI and EDI are linearly related, log ESI and log EDI are not linearly related. Wang and Wei (2008) show that in regressions, the sign of the coefficients associated with log EDI is more robust to small changes in specification than is log ESI. Therefore, we regard inferences drawn from log EDI as more reliable.

We compute the values of the EDI for China and India (relative to the G-3 economies) and report them in Tables 3.1 and 3.2, respectively. They

However, judged on unit values, Chinese exports are more likely to be on the low end of the market than are those of the high-income countries.

Table 3.1. Comparing export structures: China relative to the G-3 (1996–2005)

Year	Number HS6-digit level product lines that G-3 economies export	Of which China exports	Number of HS6 product lines that G-3 exports by at least US$ 1 million	Of which China exports by at least US$ 1 million	Share of no. HS-6 product that G-3 exports but China does not	Value Share of product that G-3 exports but China does not	Export Dissimilarity Index (EDI)
1996	4,143	4,042	4,126	2,942	28.7	13.7	133.7
1997	4,143	4,063	4,123	3,042	26.2	12.3	132.5
1998	4,143	4,046	4,121	3,041	26.2	12.3	130.8
1999	4,143	4,061	4,120	3,024	26.6	10.8	129.2
2000	4,143	4,059	4,116	3,172	22.9	8.8	125.5
2001	4,143	4,068	4,118	3,184	22.7	9.6	124.8
2002	4,213	4,135	4,184	3,306	21.0	10.5	125.4
2003	4,213	4,125	4,182	3,408	18.5	7.2	126.1
2004	4,213	4,126	4,186	3,515	16.0	6.8	123.1
2005	4,212	4,130	4,179	3,609	13.6	3.8	121.5

Source: Authors' calculations based on official trade statistics from the China Customs Administration and from UN COMTRADE data.

Note: In the last three columns, the smaller the value, the greater the overlap. Value share is the sum of the shares of G-3 product lines for which China's export shares are zero. A US$1 million cutoff is used in the second to the last column.

Table 3.2. Comparing export structures: India relative to the G-3 (1996–2005)

Year	Number HS6-digit level product lines that G-3 economies export	Of which India exports	Number of HS6 product lines that G-3 exports by at least US$ 1 million	Of which India exports by at least US$ 1 million	Share of no. HS-6 product that G-3 exports but India does not	Value Share of product that G-3 exports but India does not	Export Dissimilarity Index (EDI)
1996	4,143	3,746	4,126	1,324	67.2	40.8	154.0
1997	4,143	3,792	4,123	1,387	65.9	40.5	154.5
1998	4,143	3,803	4,121	1,371	66.1	44.0	156.4
1999	4,143	3,817	4,120	1,443	64.5	41.5	157.5
2000	4,143	3,916	4,116	1,685	58.5	37.2	152.3
2001	4,143	3,940	4,118	1,691	58.4	32.9	149.1
2003	4,213	4,057	4,182	2,107	48.9	24.7	144.2
2004	4,213	4,058	4,186	2,206	46.5	23.2	143.4
2005	4,212	4,072	4,179	2,381	42.3	20.4	139.9

Source: Authors' calculations based on official trade statistics from UN COMTRADE data.

Note: In the last three columns, the smaller the value, the greater the overlap. Value share is the sum of the shares of G-3 product lines for which India's export shares are zero. A US$ 1 million cutoff is used in the second to the last column.

The Chinese Export Bundles

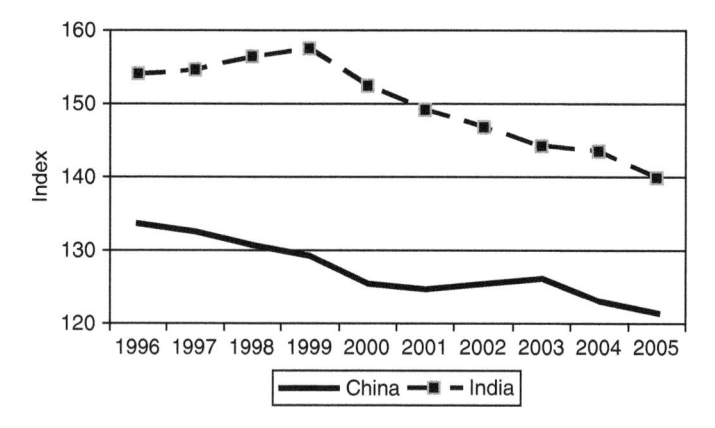

Figure 3.4. China and India's export dissimilarity index (relative to G-3 economies), 1996–2005

Source: Authors' calculations based on official trade statistics from the China Customs Administration and UN COMTRADE data.

are also plotted in Figure 3.4. A few features are worth noting. First, the dissimilarity index relative to the advanced economies has been declining for both China and India. For China, the dissimilarity index declined from 134 in 1996 to 122 in 2005. For India, it declined from 154 to 140 during the same period. Second, in contrast to the impression one gets from looking at the fraction of product lines that are common to China (or India) and the G-3 economies, this metric suggests that it is still premature to claim that China and France are exporting more or less the same bundle of goods. In fact, the value of the dissimilarity index (at 122 in 1995 for China) is a long way from consistency with an identical export bundle (i.e. a value of zero). Third, by this measure, India's export dissimilarity score in 2005 was still greater than China's in 1995. This suggests that it may take more than a decade for India to catch-up with China in terms of the export structure sophistication in manufactured goods.

3.3 What might explain China's precocious export sophistication?

While our calculation does not support the claim that China already has a similar export structure to France, Japan, and other high-income countries, it shows a clear trend in that direction. Moreover, as Fontagne et al. (2007) show, China's export structure is already more similar to those of the high-income countries than to those of Brazil, Russia, and middle-income countries. What could explain this precocious export structure sophistication?

Using detailed trade data at the level of product, producer location, producer ownership, and customs type (i.e. processing trade or not), Wang and Wei (2008) provide some useful clues to what the answer may be. As we do not have comparably detailed data for India, we are not able to conduct the same exercise for India. In this section, we summarize our methodology and some of the key findings of Wang and Wei (2008), and speculate over the implications for China.

Some qualitative priors

It is useful to think through some logical possibilities before we embark on a more rigorous analysis. First, the sophistication we have measured could be a statistical mirage due to processing trade. For example, both the United States and China may export notebook computers, but Chinese manufacturers may import the most sophisticated components of the computers, such as processors (CPUs) made by Intel or ADM in the United States. In such a case, Chinese producers may specialize in the unsophisticated stage of the production while the final product is classified as a sophisticated one. If one were able to classify a product further into its components, China and developed countries might be found to produce different components. That is, they might not compete directly with each other. In this scenario, there is very little for developed countries to worry about.

Second, as a variation of this scenario, China and the high-income economies may export the same set of product lines, but the two may export very different varieties within each product line, with China exporting varieties of much lower quality. The competition between the high-income economies and China, in this case, would be moderate.

Third, on the other hand, the Chinese authorities, including Governments at the regional and local levels, have actively promoted quality upgrading of China's product structure, through tax and other policy incentives. A particular manifestation of these incentives is the proliferation of economic and technological development zones, high-tech industrial zones, and export processing zones around the country. Their collective share in China's exports has risen from less than 6 percent in 1995 to about 25 percent by 2005. These policy incentives could

The Chinese Export Bundles

Table 3.3. Percentage breakdown of China's exports by firm ownership, 1995–2006 (%)

Year	SOE	Joint Venture	Wholly Foreign owned	Collective	Private
1995	66.7	19.8	11.7	1.5	0.0
1996	57.0	24.9	15.7	2.0	0.0
1997	56.2	23.9	17.1	2.5	0.0
1998	52.6	24.1	20.0	2.9	0.1
1999	50.5	23.2	22.2	3.5	0.3
2000	46.7	24.2	23.8	4.2	1.0
2001	42.6	24.1	25.9	5.3	2.0
2002	37.7	22.7	29.5	5.8	4.2
2003	31.5	21.5	33.3	5.7	7.9
2004	25.9	21.0	36.1	5.4	11.7
2005	22.2	19.9	38.4	4.8	14.7
2006	19.7	18.7	39.5	4.2	17.8
Average 1996–2004	39.8	22.7	27.8	4.7	4.9

Source: Authors' computation based on official trade statistics from the China Customs Administration.

increase the similarity of Chinese exports to those of developed countries, although it is unlikely the most efficient thing for China to do (unless there is significant positive externality from learning by doing). If this is the primary driver for China's rising sophistication, rather than the mismeasurement induced by processing trade, then China may increasingly be competing directly with developed countries.

Fourth, bearing on the two explanations, is the role of foreign invested firms in China. The share in China's total exports produced by wholly foreign-owned firms and by Sino-foreign joint ventures has risen steadily over time, from about 31 percent in 1995 to more than 58 percent by 2006 (Table 3.3). These foreign invested firms may choose to produce and export products much more sophisticated than those indigenous Chinese firms would. In this scenario, while China-made products may compete with those from developed countries, at least the profits from such production also contribute directly to the GNPs of developed countries. Besides this direct effect of foreign invested firms in China's export upgrades, it is possible that the presence of foreign firms helps indirectly to raise the sophistication level of Chinese exports through various spillovers to domestic firms (Hale and Long 2006). The above three possible explanations can reinforce each other, rather than being mutually exclusive. For example, a foreign invested firm may engage in processing trade while located in a high-tech zone.

To the best of our knowledge, direct evidence of the importance of these channels is provided only in Wang and Wei (2008). A key finding is that neither processing trade nor foreign invested firms play an important role in generating increased overlap in the export structures of China and the high-income countries. Instead, improvement in human capital and Government policies in the form of tax-favored high-tech zones appear to have contributed significantly to the rising sophistication of China's exports.

Specification and basic facts

To link China's export structure dissimilarity to potential underlying factors, our strategy is to make use of variations across Chinese cities in both export sophistication and its potential determinants. We consider several categories of the determinants, including the level of human capital, the use of processing trade, and the promotion of sophistication by Governments through high-tech and economic development zones.

To start with, Table 3.3 reports a breakdown of export value by exporter firm ownership. A number of features are worth noting. First, there has been a steady decline in the share of state-owned firms in China's exports, from 66.7 percent in 1995 to 19.7 percent in 2006. This reduction in the role of state-owned firms in exports mirrors the reduction of the state's role in the economy in general. Second, foreign invested firms (both wholly foreign-owned and Sino-foreign joint ventures) play a significant role in China's exports. Their share in China's exports has also increased steadily, from 31.5 percent in 1995 to 58.3 percent in 2005. The role played by foreign firms in China's exports is larger than that of such firms in most other countries with a population greater than 10 million. Third, exports by truly private domestic firms are relatively small, though their share in China's exports has also increased over time, from basically nothing until 1997, to 17.8 percent by 2005. Some of the growth in exports produced by domestic private firms has been achieved by a change in firm ownership. For example, when the laptop manufacturer Lenovo was first established, it was a partly state-owned firm. By 2003, it became a privately owned firm. By now, it has added foreign investment, acquired the original IBM PC division, and exported some of its products under the IBM brand.

Table 3.4 reports a breakdown of China's exports into processing trade, normal trade, and others according to exporters' customs declarations.

Table 3.4. Share of processing trade and policy zones' production in China's total exports, 1996–2005 (%)

Year	Special economic zones	Exports processing zones	Processing exports in high-tech zones	Normal exports in high-tech zones	Processing exports outside policy zones	Normal exports outside policy zones	All other exports[a]
(1)	(2)	(3)	(4)	(5)	(6)	(7)	(8)
1995	10.6	0	3.2	2.1	39.8	42.1	2.2
1996	8.7	0	3.9	1.8	45.2	38.3	2.0
1997	8.8	0	4.6	1.7	43.9	39.0	1.9
1998	8.2	0	5.5	1.9	45.5	36.9	1.9
1999	7.0	0	6.4	2.2	45.5	37.0	1.9
2000	7.1	0	7.0	2.6	43.3	38.2	1.8
2001	6.8	0.1	7.4	2.8	43.0	38.0	1.9
2002	6.2	0.7	8.0	3.0	42.2	37.6	2.3
2003	5.3	2.4	9.5	3.4	39.6	37.1	2.7
2004	4.4	3.6	11.0	3.6	37.7	36.4	3.2
2005	4.3	4.6	11.8	3.6	35.6	36.8	3.5
Average 1996–2004	6.3	1.3	8.0	2.8	41.7	37.4	2.4

Source: Authors' computations based on official trade statistics from the China Customs Administration.

Note: [a] This category includes international aid, compensation trade, goods on consignment, border trade, goods for foreign contracted projects, goods on lease, outward processing, barter trade, warehouse trade, and entrepôt trade by bonded area.

Processing exports come in three varieties: (a) those from export processing zones; (b) those from various high-tech zones; and (c) those from outside any policy zones. Collectively, their share in the country's total exports has increased from 43 percent (= 0 + 3.2% + 39.8%) in 1995 to 52 percent (= 4.6% + 11.8% + 35.6%) in 2005. As we lack information on the share of processing exports for other countries, we cannot conduct a formal international comparison. Our conjecture is that very few developing countries would have a share of processing exports as high as China's. On the other hand, we conjecture that a portion of China's reported processing trade may be exaggerated due to some firms' desire to evade tariffs on imported inputs that are actually used for domestic sale.[2]

Additional tables in Wang and Wei (2008) indicate that foreign invested firms are dominant in processing exports, accounting for 100 percent of exports out of export processing zones, 95 percent of processing exports out of high-tech zones, and 67 percent of processing exports from the rest of China. State-owned firms account for the bulk of the remaining processing trade. Therefore, processing exports are mostly the

---

[2] Fisman and Wei (2004) provided evidence of massive tariff evasion in China's imports.

domain of wholly and partly foreign-owned firms. The reverse is not true, in that foreign firms also engage in normal (i.e. 'non-processing') exports, accounting for 40 percent of non-processing exports out of high-tech zones and 24 percent of normal trade outside of policy zones in 2004.

For both wholly foreign-owned firms and Sino-foreign joint ventures, processing trade accounts for nearly 50 percent of exports produced. For state-owned firms and collectively owned firms, the share of processing exports in total exports produced is 18 percent and 13 percent, respectively. Domestic private firms engage in comparatively little processing trade, producing less than 7 percent of their total exports in this category.

China has established a number of special economic zones and areas where more incentive policies have been applied since 1979, as a part of its development strategy. Five special economic zones (SEZs) have been set up and are distinguished from other special economic areas. They include all of Hainan province, three cities (Shenzhen, Zhuhai, and Shantou) in Guangdong province, and a city (Xiamen) in Fujian Province. Other special economic areas are much smaller geographically, and classified as Economic and Technological Development Areas (ETDAs), Hi-Technology Industry Development Areas (HTIDA), and Export Processing Zones (EPZs). Some of these special incentive zones and areas fall within the five SEZs. We will also refer to these incentive zones or areas as 'policy zones'.

Among these policy zones, ETDAs and HTIDAs are tax-favored enclaves established by central or local Governments (with the approval of the central Government) to promote development of sectors that could be considered 'high and new tech' by some imperfectly defined criteria. There are differences in theory between the two types of zones. In practice, however, the line between the two is often blurred. Which firms should go into which type of zone is somewhat arbitrary. As a result, we group them together in our discussion. With progressively more ETDAs and HTIDAs being established in the sample, their share in China's exports has grown steadily, from only 4.3 percent in 1995 to 15.4 percent in 2005 (sum of columns 4 and 5 in Table 3.4). Since most cities still do not have such zones, an unweighted average of their share in a city's exports across all cities and years yields only 2 percent.

Dedicated export processing zones (whose exports are exclusively in processing trade) were established starting in 2001 and are present in only twenty-six cities today. In national aggregate, only 4.6 percent of

The Chinese Export Bundles

exports come from all the export processing zones taken together, by 2006 (Table 3.4, column 3). On simple average (across cities and years), only 0.04 percent of exports come from EPZs. This means that most of China's processing exports are produced outside an export processing zone.

Foreign invested firms dominate exports from EPZs and processing exports from high-tech zones in our sample period (99% and 95% respectively), and also took the lion's share in processing trade outside those policy zones (67%). State-owned firms are the major players in normal exports, accounting for 58 percent of normal exports from high-tech zones and 63 percent of normal exports outside policy zones during our sample period. Relative to processing trade, collectively owned and private firms also played an important role in China's normal exports, accounting for 8.5 percent of normal exports from high-tech zones and 18 percent of exports originating outside policy zones.

We relate the sophistication level of a local export structure to its plausible determinants including the role of processing trade, foreign investment, and local human capital. Formally, the econometric specification is given by the following equation (or some variation of it):

$$\begin{aligned}\text{Ln}(EDI_{rft}) = {} & city\_fixed + year\_fixed + \beta_1\, EPZ\_share_{rft} \\ & + \beta_2\, High\_tech\_zone\_processing\_Share_{rft} \\ & + \beta_3\, Processing\_outside\_anyzone\_share_{rft} \\ & + \beta_4\, High\_tech\_zone\_nonprocessing\_share_{rft} \\ & + \beta_5\, Ln(GDP_{rt}) + \beta_6\, SKILL_{rt} + other\_controls + \mu_{rft} \end{aligned} \quad (6)$$

Where Ln(*EDI*) is the log of a **dissimilarity index** between a Chinese city's export structure and the general export structure of the United States, Japan, and the European Union combined. β_1–β_6 are the coefficients to be estimated. μ_{rft} is the error term. Other regressors and the sources of the data are explained in Appendix Table 3A.1. Robust standard errors, clustered around cities, are reported.

Statistical results

The regression results are reported in Table 3.5. In the first four columns, the sophistication of a city's export structure is measured by its similarity to that of the G-3 high-income countries on a *year by year basis*. As a robustness check, in the last four columns, the city's export sophistication is measured against the export structure of the high-income countries in a fixed year (2004, the last year in our sample period). The change in

Table 3.5. What explains cross-city export structure? Export structure dissimilarity between Chinese cities and the G-3 economies

Explanatory Variables	Year by year benchmark				2004 benchmark			
	(1)	(2)	(3)	(4)	(5)	(6)	(7)	(8)
Export processing zone exports as a share of total city exports	−0.351*** (0.074)	−0.382*** (0.055)	−0.350*** (0.071)	−0.384*** (0.053)	−0.552*** (0.116)	−0.594*** (0.087)	−0.544*** (0.111)	−0.591*** (0.084)
Processing exports in high-tech zones as a share of total city exports	−0.065*** (0.018)	−0.070*** (0.020)	−0.067*** (0.018)	−0.073*** (0.020)	−0.083*** (0.020)	−0.089*** (0.023)	−0.082*** (0.020)	−0.090*** (0.023)
Non-processing exports in high-tech zones as a share of total city exports	−0.087* (0.045)	−0.108** (0.053)	−0.093** (0.044)	−0.115** (0.053)	−0.087* (0.049)	−0.116* (0.061)	−0.092* (0.049)	−0.122** (0.061)
Processing exports outside economic zones as a share of total city exports	0.005* (0.003)	0.004 (0.003)	0.004 (0.003)	0.002 (0.003)	0.006* (0.003)	0.004 (0.003)	0.005* (0.003)	0.003 (0.003)
Student enrollment in institutions of higher education as a share of the city non-agricultural population	−0.225*** (0.066)		−0.229*** (0.066)		−0.309*** (0.073)		−0.315*** (0.072)	
per capita GCP		−0.006** (0.002)		−0.007*** (0.003)		−0.010*** (0.003)		−0.010*** (0.003)
Gross city product (GCP)	−0.003** (0.001)	−0.003*** (0.001)	−0.003*** (0.001)	−0.003** (0.001)	−0.003* (0.001)	−0.003** (0.002)	−0.003** (0.001)	−0.003** (0.002)
Foreign invested firms' share in city exports			0.001 (0.006)	0.004 (0.006)			−0.004 (0.006)	−0.000 (0.007)
Joint venture firms' share in city exports			0.010*** (0.004)	0.010*** (0.004)			0.009** (0.004)	0.009** (0.004)
City fixed effects	Y	Y	Y	Y	Y	Y	Y	Y
Year fixed effects	Y	Y	Y	Y	Y	Y	Y	Y
Robust, cluster(city)	Y	Y	Y	Y	Y	Y	Y	Y
Observations	1981	1981	1981	1981	1981	1981	1981	1981
R-squared	0.98	0.98	0.98	0.98	0.98	0.97	0.98	0.97

Note: Standard errors in parentheses * significant at 10%; ** significant at 5%; *** significant at 1%.

The Chinese Export Bundles

the reference year for export sophistication does not turn out to matter qualitatively.

The coefficient on 'export processing zone exports as a share of total city exports' is negative and significant, implying that exports from EPZs tend to be more similar to those of high-income countries than do typical Chinese exports. However, as a majority of Chinese cities do not have EPZs, this does not contribute much to explaining cross-city differences in export sophistication.

The coefficients on the two variables describing exports from high-tech zones ('processing exports from high-tech zones' and 'non-processing exports from high-tech zones') are negative and significant, implying that the high-tech zones do contribute to raising the export structure sophistication of China. Comparing the two point estimates, however, one sees that non-processing exports from the two types of high-tech zone, in fact, contribute more to raising export sophistication than do processing exports.

The share of processing exports outside any policy zone is positive and significant: The more processing trade takes place outside any policy zone, the less sophisticated a city's exports become. Taking the discussion of the last three coefficients together, we might argue that the processing trade (outside policy zones) is unlikely to have promoted similarities between the Chinese export structure and that of the high-income countries. It is consistent with the intuition that processing trade in many areas of China, except in these policy zones, is relatively labor intensive in nature.

The coefficient on student enrollment in colleges or graduate schools as a share of a city's non-agricultural population—a proxy for a city's level of human capital—is negative and significant, consistent with the notion that a city with more skilled labor tends to have a more sophisticated export structure. In column 2 of Table 3.5, we use per capita gross city product (per capita GCP) as an alternative measure of a city's level of human capital. This variable also produces a negative coefficient, indicating an association between more human capital and a more sophisticated export structure.

In columns 3–4 of Table 3.5, we include measures of the presence of foreign firms in a city. The estimated coefficient for the share of exports by wholly foreign-owned firms in a city's total exports is not significantly different from zero. Interestingly, the share of exports by joint-venture firms has a positive coefficient: The more a city's exports come from joint-venture firms, the less the export structure resembles those of high-income countries. These results suggest that foreign invested firms in

China are not likely to be directly responsible for the rising sophistication of China's export structure, or at least not in a simple linear fashion (e.g. the more FDI, the more sophisticated China's export structure will be).

As we explained earlier, columns 5–8 of Table 3.5 replicate the first four columns except that the left-hand side variables are recalibrated against the 2004 export structure of the G-3 economies. The qualitative results stay essentially the same. To summarize the key findings that emerge from the series of regressions in Table 3.5, we find that:

(a) Cross-city differences in human capital are linked to cross-city differences in the sophistication level of the export structure. A higher level of human capital, measured either by per capita GDP or by college and graduate school enrollment, is associated with a more sophisticated export structure.

(b) The high-tech zones are associated with more sophisticated export structure. The higher the share of a city's exports coming out of high-tech zones, the more likely the city's export structure resembles that of the G-3 high-income economies.

(c) The export processing zones (EPZs) contribute to the rising sophistication of the export structure. However, since only a small fraction of the cities have any EPZs, they play a very small quantitative role in explaining the cross-city differences in export structure sophistication.

(d) Processing trade generally is not a major factor in explaining cross-city differences in export structure sophistication. This can be seen in two ways. First, for exports originating outside any policy zone (which represent the lion's share of all exports) more processing trade is in fact associated with less similarity to the export structure of the high-income countries. Second, for exports from high-tech zones, those products that are classified in processing trade do not appear to overlap more with high-income countries' exports than do products classified in non-processing trade.

(e) After controlling for exports from major policy zones, foreign investment does not appear to play a major role in explaining cross-city differences in the sophistication level of their export structures. If anything, joint-venture firms may create some divergence between a city's export structure and that of the high-income economies.

These findings reject the views that the rising sophistication of China's export structure is mostly generated by processing trade and/or foreign

The Chinese Export Bundles

invested firms. At the same time, it confirms the importance of human capital and Governmental policies in the establishment of the high-tech zones to promote the rising sophistication of China's export structure.

The specification used in Table 3.5 includes city fixed effects. This is the appropriate thing to do in a panel regression such as this. However, in order to make sure that the proposed explanatory variables—processing trade, foreign ownership, high-tech zones, human capital, etc.—collectively have enough explanatory power on their own to account for the observed cross-city differences in the export structure dissimilarity index, we have also run similar regressions without city fixed effects (the results are not reported here, to save space, but can be found as Appendix Table 8 in Wang and Wei 2008). The patterns on the signs of the coefficient estimates and the statistical significance are mostly the same as in Table 3.5. As important, the total R-squares in this set of regressions without city fixed effects are in the range of 66–68 percent. This suggests that much of the cross-city differences in export patterns are explained by the included regressors rather than merely by city fixed effects.

3.4 Conclusion

Are China and India's exports increasingly competing head to head with those of high-income countries? To address this question, this chapter undertakes two tasks. The first part of the chapter compares the product structures of China and India's exports with those of the G-3 economies (the United States, Japan, and the European Union). It finds that both emerging market giants have an export bundle that is becoming increasingly more similar to those of the high-income countries. However, by this metric, China is perhaps a bit more than ten years ahead of India.

The second part of the chapter sifts through various potential determinants of the rising sophistication of Chinese exports, drawing on our recent research (Wang and Wei 2008). The list of potential determinants includes Government incentives, the use of imported inputs, foreign invested firms, and improved human capital. The underlying methodology makes use of variations in the key variables across different cities in China. As we do not have access to comparable data for India, this exercise is not replicated for Indian exports.

The estimation shows that, for the country as a whole, China's export structure does increasingly resemble that of the advanced economies, and the unit values of its exports are also rising over time. If these patterns are generated entirely by the rising use of processing trade, then there may not be much genuine increase in the sophistication level of China exports. If there is a real increase in sophistication, where the increment comes entirely from foreign-invested firms in China, then the economic profit associated with the improved sophistication accrues to foreign economies rather than to China. Of course, the increased sophistication can also come from an improved level of local human capital, or Government policies such as high-tech policy zones set up specifically to promote the upgrading of the industrial structure. Regional variations in the use of processing trade, high-tech zones, and availability of skilled labor are used in this chapter to assess the relative roles of these factors.

The econometric analysis conducted in Wang and Wei (2008) provides evidence on the relative importance of the three channels:

(1) Cross-city differences in human capital are linked to cross-city differences in the sophistication of export structures. A higher level of human capital is associated with a more sophisticated export structure in Chinese cities.

(2) High-tech zones are associated both with more sophisticated export structures and with higher unit values. This means that the policy zones (especially ETDZs and HTIDZs) set up by the central and local Governments in China may have worked to induce firms to upgrade their product ladder to a higher level than it otherwise would have achieved. In other words, these policy zones may not only have promoted processing trade, but they may have promoted greater sophistication of China's exports, too.

(3) The export processing zones contribute both to the rising sophistication of export structures and to rising unit values. However, since only a tiny fraction of cities have EPZs and since most of their exports come from foreign invested firms, they do not contribute very much to explaining cross-city differences in export sophistication.

(4) Processing trade generally is not a major factor in explaining cross-city differences in export structure sophistication. This can be seen in two ways. First, for exports outside any policy zone (which comprise the lion's share of China's total exports, about 42 percent during our sample period) more processing trade is in fact associated with less similarity to the export structure of advanced countries.

The Chinese Export Bundles

Second, for exports out of the high-tech zones, those products that are classified as processing trade do not appear to overlap more with advanced countries' exports than do products associated with non-processing trade.

However, further analysis by Wang and Wei (2008) suggest that processing trade is significantly associated with higher unit values. How would one reconcile the findings on export structure and unit values? If most processing exports outside the policy zones are labor intensive, a higher share will increase the dissimilarity of the export structure between the Chinese cities and G-3 advanced economies. However, processing exports could still be of higher quality (of more sophisticated varieties) than normal exports in the same product line, because of the use of high-quality imported materials in the former. In other words, processing trade moves China into producing and exporting more sophisticated varieties within a given product category, but not necessarily in those product categories that overlap heavily with the exports of the G-3 advanced economies.[3]

(5) The export share of foreign invested firms in a Chinese city does not appear to play a major role in explaining cross-city differences in the sophistication level of export structure. If anything, joint-venture firms may create some divergence between a city's export structure and that of the advanced economies. However, after controlling for processing trade, both types of foreign invested firms are found to be strongly associated with higher export unit values. Therefore, foreign investment is conducive to raising China's within product sophistication.

Appendix 3A. Data

Data on China's exports at the HS 8-digit level (the most disaggregated level of classification made available by Chinese customs) are obtained from the China Customs General Administration. The database reports the geographic origin of exports (from more than 400 cities in China), policy zone designation (i.e. whether an exporter is located in any type of policy zone), firm ownership, and transaction

---

[3] It is possible that the higher unit values associated with processing exports simply reflect higher costs of imported inputs as compared to domestically made inputs. This leaves open the question of whether processing exports generate more value-added when compared with normal exports that use more local and domestic inputs.

Appendix Table 3A.1. Definition of key variables and data sources

Dependent variables	Description	Data Sources
$EDI_{rft} = \left(\sum_i {}^{abs}\left(s_{rft} - s_{i,t}^{ref}\right)\right)$	Absolute export structure dissimilarity index	Calculated by the authors from 6-digit HS level. Chinese City exports based on official China Custom Statistics. Data on US, EU-15 and Japan exports download from WITS
Explanatory variables		
GCP_{rt}	Gross City Product (10,000 yuans); note that this is a value added concept, making GCP conceptually similar to GDP.	China City data, China data online
$PCGCP_{rt} = 100\ GCP_t / POP_t$	per capita GCP (yuan)	China City data, China data online
$SKILL_{rt} = 100 *$ (no. of college students)$_{rt}$ /(non-agricultural population)$_{rt}$	Student Enrollment in institutions of higher education as a share of a city's non-agricultural population	China City data, China data online
EPZ_share$_{rft}$	Export processing zone exports as a share of total city exports	China Custom Statistics.
High_tech_zone_processing_share$_{rft}$	Processing exports in the two high-tech zones as a share of total city exports	China Custom Statistics
High_tech_zone_nonprocessing_share$_{rft}$	Non-processing exports in the two types of high-tech zones as a share of total city exports	China Custom Statistics
Processing_outside_anyzone_share$_{rft}$	Processing exports outside policy zones as a share of total city exports	China Custom Statistics
Expfiesh$_{rft}$	FIE firm exports as share of total city exports	China Custom Statistics.
Expjonsh$_{rft}$	Joint venture firm exports as share of total city exports	China Custom Statistics
expothsh$_{rft}$	Collective and private firm exports as share of total city exports	China Custom Statistics
expsoesh$_{rft}$	SOE firm exports as share of total city exports	China Custom Statistics

The Chinese Export Bundles

type (whether an export is processing trade by customs declaration) for the period from 1995 to 2005.

We link this database with a separate database on Chinese cities, including per capita gross city product, population, college student enrollment and FDI data, from China data online, managed by the China-Data-Center at the University of Michigan. Unfortunately, the coverage of the second database is more limited (240 cities from 1996 to 2004).

Note that a 'city', in our sample, refers to a geographic unit that includes a metropolis and adjacent rural counties under the jurisdiction of the metropolitan Government.

Data on exports by the G-3 economies at the HS 6-digit level come from the United Nations' COMTRADE database, downloaded from the World Integrated Trade Solution (WITS) site. We wish to focus on manufactured goods, not on natural resources, and therefore exclude the goods in HS Chapters 1–27 (agricultural and mineral products) and raw materials and their simple transformations (mostly at the HS 4-digit level) in other HS chapters.

Appendix Table 3A.2. Starting years of various economic zones with policy incentives

City code	City name	Special economic zone	Economic & technological development area	Hi-technology industry development area	Export processing zone
1100	Beijing CY		1996	1996	2001
1200	Tianjin CY		1996	1996	2001
1301	Shijiazhuang			1996	
1303	Qinhuangdao		1996		2005
1306	Baoding			1996	
1401	Taiyuan		2003	1996	
1502	Baotou			1997	
2101	Shenyang		1996	1996	
2102	Dalian		1996	1996	2001
2103	Anshan			1996	
2201	Changchun		1996	1996	
2202	Jilin			1996	
2301	Harbin		1996	1996	
2306	Daqing			1996	
3100	Shanghai CY		1996	1996	2001
3201	Nanjing			1996	2004
3202	Wuxi			1997	2003
3204	Changzhou			1997	
3205	Suzhou		1996	1997	2001
3206	Nantong		1996		2003
3207	Lianyungang		1996		2004
3211	Zhenjiang				2004
3301	Hangzhou		1996	1996	2001
3302	Ningbo		1996		2004
3303	Wenzhou		1996		

(cont.)

Appendix Table 3A.2. (*continued*)

City code	City name	Special economic zone	Economic & technological development area	Hi-technology industry development area	Export processing zone
3401	Hefei		2005	1996	
3402	Wuhu		1996		2003
3501	Fuzhou		1996	1996	
3502	Xiamen	1995		1996	2002
3601	Nanchang			1996	
3701	Jinan			1996	
3702	Qingdao		1996	1997	2004
3703	Zibo			1999	
3706	Yantai		1996		2001
3707	Weifang			1996	
3710	Weihai			1996	2001
4101	Zhengzhou			1996	2005
4103	Luoyang			1997	
4201	Wuhan		1996	1996	2001
4206	Xiangfan			1997	
4301	Changsha			1996	
4302	Zhuzhou			2000	
4401	Guangzhou		1996	1996	2001
4403	Shenzhen	1995		1996	2002
4404	Zhuhai	1995		1996	
4405	Shantou	1995			
4406	Foshan			1998	
4408	Zhanjiang		1996		
4413	Huizhou			1996	
4420	Zhongshan			1996	
4501	Nanning			1996	
4503	Guilin			1996	
4505	Beihai				2005
4601	Haikou	1995		1996	
4602	Sanya	1995			
5000	Chongqing		2002	2002	2002
5101	Chengdu		2001	1996	2001
5107	Mianyan			1996	
5201	Guiyang			1996	
5301	Kunming			1996	
6101	Xi'an			1996	2004
6103	Baoji			1997	
6104	Xianyang			2002	
6201	Lanzhou			1996	
6301	Xining		2005		
6501	Urumqi		1996	1997	

Note: Cities that do not have any of the policy zones during 1996–2005 are not on the list.

Part II

Contrasts in Development Experience

4
The Cost Competitiveness of Manufacturing in China and India
An Industry and Regional Perspective

Bart van Ark, Abdul Azeez Erumban, Vivian Chen, and Utsav Kumar *

4.1 Introduction

The large changes in the growth dynamics of the economies of China and India during the past two decades have led to a flood of literature on the competitiveness of the two economies in international and comparative perspective. Strikingly, however, there are very few studies that have gone into a direct comparison of the basic statistical material on output, employment, and cost levels between the two economies, in particular not at a detailed industry level. One reason for the limited number of studies in this area may be related to the difficulty, in particular in China, in accessing and using the detailed production statistics for this purpose. Another reason is that there are some major issues of comparability of the statistics between the two countries.

---

* Paper presented at conference on 'India and China's Role in International Trade and Finance and Global Economic Governance' organized by the Indian Council for Research on International Economic Relations (ICRIER), the Konrad-Adenauer Foundation (KAF) and the International Monetary Fund (IMF), December 6–7, 2007, New Delhi. The authors are grateful to Qin Xiao (formerly at The Conference Board China Center for Economics and Business) and Harry X. Wu (Polytechnic University of Hong Kong and The Conference Board China Center for Economics and Business) for their contribution to a companion paper (Chen et al. 2007) on which we have extensively relied for this study. We also acknowledge the OECD for their financial support to the University of Groningen for executing the India/Germany comparison of manufacturing productivity (Erumban 2007). The results presented in this chapter remain solely the individual responsibility of the authors.

Nevertheless a direct comparison between India and China is of great relevance, not only for policymakers and academia who are interested in understanding the main differences in the sources of growth in both economies. Such comparisons are also of great importance to the business sector, which needs to make crucial decisions on market access and investment opportunities. Such considerations go beyond macro comparisons between the two countries. Such analysis requires detailed insight at industry level and a regional perspective within each of the two countries.

The Conference Board has therefore launched a multi-year research project in the area of comparisons of productivity and (unit) cost measures in the manufacturing sectors of India and China. In Section 4.2 we briefly motivate our focus on this topic and describe our approach on the following main factors: Productivity, labor compensation, and unit labor cost levels.

The work done so far, as reported in the remainder of this chapter, involves two aspects. The first is an *international comparison* of productivity and unit labor cost levels of the two countries in a broader international perspective, which has been carried out in cooperation with the University of Groningen. Section 4.3 reports on the methodology for international comparisons of productivity making use of industry-specific output purchasing power parities (PPPs) which are used to convert output into a common currency. We motivate our preference for the use of an indirect comparison of productivity for China and India through the United States and Germany respectively. We then integrate this work into a comparison of unit labor cost levels making use of international measures of labor compensation. We find that even though China had somewhat superior productivity levels in manufacturing compared to India in 2002, it was at a slight disadvantage in terms of unit labor cost relative to India due to its slightly higher compensation level. It is important to recognize that China's productivity advantage relative to India is only very recent.

The second aspect of the work on which this chapter reports focuses the attention on an analysis of *regional and industry differences* in productivity, labor compensation, and unit labor costs across provinces and states in China and India respectively. For this purpose we developed a unique database for twenty-eight industries and up to thirty states and provinces and two benchmark years, one in the early/mid-1990s and one in the early 2000s. In Section 4.4 we briefly explain our sources and data

The Cost Competitiveness of Manufacturing

manipulations for the two countries and discuss our most important findings. We find that India's unit labor cost in national currency has increased over the decade, whereas China's ULC has rapidly declined. This is due to a faster increase in compensation relative to productivity in most Indian industries and states over the decade. In general labor cost and productivity have become much better aligned in China, so that today unit labor cost varies much less than in India. In Section 4.5 we show that, compared to India, Chinese provinces clearly show both a catch-up (beta-convergence) and regular (sigma) convergence pattern. We speculate that improved market performance in China has contributed to the catch-up and the convergence pattern. Finally, in Section 4.6 we summarize our main findings and indicate directions for future research activities in this program.

4.2 Unit labor cost as competitiveness measure

In this chapter we use a simple competitiveness measure, which is unit labor cost (ULC) defined as the cost of labor required to produce one unit of output. We prefer this measure which takes account of output and inputs, over comparing only the cost of the inputs. For instance, high wages do not mean the same thing in high- and in low-productivity sectors. In low-productivity sectors, high wages mean that production may become too costly and jeopardize the long-run profitability of businesses. In high-productivity sectors, however, high wages are often compensated by higher output levels per person and can be fully compatible with long-run profitability.

Unit labor cost can be expressed as labor compensation over output, but it is more instructive to observe how ULC is made up of labor compensation per person employed relative to output per employed person. Hence our analysis in this chapter focuses primarily on three indicators, average labor compensation (ALC), average labor productivity (ALP), and unit labor cost. ALC is defined as the ratio of nominal labor compensation (LC)[1] to total number of employees (E), while ALP is obtained as a ratio

[1] Note we are focusing on total labor compensation and not just total wages or earnings. The latter only represent take-home pay measures which provide an incomplete picture of labor costs. Total labor compensation is a more comprehensive measure of labor cost for the employer. In addition to wages and salaries, labor compensation includes payroll taxes paid by the company, including employer contributions to social security schemes, social benefits paid by employers in the form of children's, spouse's, family, education or other allowances

of gross value added (GVA) to number of employees. Finally, ULC is the ratio of ALC to ALP or simply the ratio of nominal labor compensation to gross value added.

Each of these indicators can be compared across countries, regions, provinces, or states. They can also be compared at different levels of economic activity, that is, for the whole economy, for industry groups (sectors) or for specific, more narrowly defined industries. Hence the level of ALC, ALP, and ULC for each individual industry i and country, province or state j can be expressed as follows:

$$ALC_{ij} = LC_{ij}/E_{ij} \qquad (1a)$$
$$ALP_{ij} = GVA_{ij}/E_{ij} \qquad (1b)$$
$$ULC_{ij} = ALC_{ij}/ALP_{ij} \qquad (1c)$$

Aggregation for each country, province, or state j across industries i is as follows:[2]

$$ALC_j = \sum_i^m LC_{ij} / \sum_i^m E_{ij} \qquad (2a)$$
$$ALP_j = \sum_i^m GVA_{ij} / \sum_i^m E_{ij} \qquad (2b)$$
$$ULC_j = ALC_j/ALP_j \qquad (2c)$$

The third dimension in our study is time, as comparisons can be made at between two points in time or on an annual basis. In this context, it is important to note that while labor compensation is expressed in current prices, the time series for output (gross value added) is deflated with output deflators. Thus, in the calculation of ULC, only the denominator (ALP) is expressed in real terms, while the numerator (ALC) is in nominal terms. This is standard practice in studies on competitiveness as ULC is supposed to measure the nominal cost per unit of real output. Hence the unit labor measure represents the current cost of labor per 'quantity unit' of output produced. The deflators for China and India are described in more detail in the data description in Appendix 4A.

When making comparisons of unit labor cost levels across countries, the level of wages or labor compensation is converted at the official exchange rate: It represents the cost element of the arbitrage across countries.

---

in respect of dependants, payments made to workers because of illness, accidental injury, maternity leave, etc., and severance payments (International Labor Office).

[2] To get the national level measures for each of the industries, we use the respective national level data to get the corresponding indicators rather than adding up the industry data across individual states.

The Cost Competitiveness of Manufacturing

In contrast, output or productivity relates to a volume measure as it resembles a quantity unit of output. Hence for level comparisons output needs to be converted to a common currency using purchasing power parity instead of the exchange rate, so that comparative output levels are adjusted for differences in relative prices across countries. For an analysis in terms of comparative levels between countries A and B (and leaving out the sign for industries) this implies:

$$ULC^{AB} = [(ALC^A/ER^{AB})/ALC^B]/(ALP^A/PPP^{AB})/ALP^B] \qquad (3)$$

where ER^{AB} is the official nominal exchange rate between countries A and B and PPP^{AB} is the purchasing power parity for output in country A relative to country B. Equation (3) can be rewritten to decompose the difference in unit labor cost between country A and country B into three components, i.e. the difference in nominal labor cost per person, the difference in nominal labor productivity (that is unadjusted for differences in price levels), and the differences in relative price levels (ER/PPP):

$$\log(ULC^A - ULC^B) = \log(ALC^A/ER^{AB} - ALC^B) - \log(ALP^A/ER^{AB} - ALP^B)$$
$$-\log(ER^{AB} - PPP^{AB}) \qquad (4)$$

All these components contribute in their own way to differences in cost competitiveness between two countries (or without the third term) for comparisons within countries. However, even for tradables, the ULC index should not be interpreted as a comprehensive measure of competitiveness for several reasons. First, ULC measures deal exclusively with the cost of *labor*. Even though labor costs account for the major share of inputs, the cost of capital and intermediate inputs can also be crucial factors for comparisons of cost competitiveness between countries.[3] Second, the measure reflects only *cost* competitiveness. In the case of durable consumer and investment goods, for example, competitiveness is also determined by other factors than costs, notably by technological and social capabilities, and by demand factors. Improvements in product quality, customization, or improved after-sales services are not necessarily reflected in lower ULC. Third, measures of cost competitiveness may be distorted by the effects from, for example, bilateral

---

[3] One might argue that with greater international tradability of capital and intermediate inputs, labor input is the key determinant of cost competitiveness as it is much less mobile across countries.

market access agreements, direct and indirect export subsidies, and tariff protection. However, we maintain that the relative importance of labor as a cost factor in competitiveness analysis, and the availability of statistical measures make the ULC still a good candidate for competitiveness studies.

4.3 International comparisons of productivity and unit labor costs

Before being able to compare productivity, labor compensation, and unit labor cost between China and India, it is useful to discuss the key limitation for this comparison. As indicated above, a fundamental issue concerns the adjustment for differences in relative price levels across countries (the third term on the right-hand side in equation 4). Using the official exchange rate for converting output into a common currency, say, US dollars, assumes no price differences across countries. Exchange rates are clearly inappropriate for this purpose given the impact of capital mobility and currency speculation on these conversion rates. Current analytical work has been highly dependent on the Penn World Tables (PWT) which relies on PPPs derived from the UN International Comparison Program (ICP). Some scholars applied economy-wide GDP PPPs at the industry level. This, however, introduces serious distortions especially for countries at lower levels of development for which GDP PPPs are heavily downwardly biased because of relatively cheap services due to the Balassa–Samuelson effect.

An alternative route followed in a range of studies under the International Comparisons of Output and Productivity (ICOP) project at the University of Groningen is to develop industry-specific purchasing power parities based on producer output data instead of final expenditure information (Maddison and van Ark 2002). For the manufacturing sector, the basic data sources for the calculation of these industry-specific PPPs are the industrial surveys or manufacturing censuses of the various countries. These contain product level data on quantities and output values, allowing for calculation of unit values for each item or group of items. For each matched product, the ratio of the unit values (UVR) in both countries is obtained. Subsequently these product UVRs are aggregated to an average UVR for manufacturing industries and for total manufacturing, using either gross output or value added as weights. Once these UVRs are obtained they can be applied to the output value for individual industries

The Cost Competitiveness of Manufacturing

to obtain output and (in combination with labor input data) productivity comparisons for two or more countries.[4]

Although there have been various studies using the ICOP approach for China and India relative to the United States,[5] there are few direct comparisons of productivity and unit labor cost levels between the two countries. The reason for this is the lack of sufficient product PPPs for such a direct comparison. The most recently published ICOP study on China/India by Lee et al. (2007) compares the two countries on the basis of 95 UVRs for 1985, whereas indirect comparisons between China/USA in 1995 by Szirmai et al. (2005) and India/Germany in 2002 by Erumban (2007) obtain 188 and 258 UVRs respectively.[6] We have therefore chosen to use the latter two studies, comparing China and India indirectly through a China/USA, India/Germany, and Germany/USA comparison of manufacturing productivity levels.

For China, the basic source used by Szirmai et al. (2005) is the *Third Industrial Census* for 1995, which provides data on value added, employment, and labor compensation for 'national independent accounting industrial enterprises at and above township level'. This source also provides measures on sales value and quantities on the basis of which UVRs could be computed.[7] For 2002, the estimates for China/USA were obtained by combining extrapolated productivity series by Szirmai et al. (2005) with new data for labor compensation per person employed for 2002 from Banister (2005).[8]

For India, the most recent study by Erumban (2007) compares India's registered manufacturing sector, using plant-level data from the *Annual Survey of Industries* for 2002–2003. As Erumban chose to compare India to Germany, because of the greater availability of product information to create UVRs, an additional manipulation was needed to transform the

---

[4] For an overview of studies using the ICOP methodology, see http://www.ggdc.net/dseries/icop.shtml.

[5] For China/USA see e.g. Szirmai and Ren (2000), Szirmai et al. (2005) for 1985 and 1995 and Wu (2001) for 1997. For India/USA, see van Ark (1993) for 1973/4 and Timmer (2000) for 1983/4. For India/Germany, see Erumban (2007) for 2002.

[6] A very recent as yet unpublished comparison between China and India for 1995 by Wu et al. (2007) has obtained 98 UVRs.

[7] See Annex A for further detail. The manufacturing UVR obtained by Szirmai et al. (2005) was 4.6 Yuan/US$ as compared to an exchange rate of 8.35 Yuan/US$, suggesting a relative price level for manufacturing production in China at 55% of the US in 1995.

[8] The compensation data related to a weighted average for urban manufacturing firms and large firms at township level, which is seen as roughly comparable to the 'township level and above' data from Szirmai et al. (2005). See van Ark et al. (2006) for a more detailed discussion and presentation of the results.

India/Germany results to a comparison with the United States, for which 1997 ICOP data from Groningen University were used.

Figures 4.1a to 4.1c summarize the results for China and India in comparison with four other emerging economies, of which two East European economies (Hungary and Poland), Mexico and South Korea, from 1990 to 2005. Unfortunately, there are only two data points (1995 and 2002) for China as reliable time series are still lacking, in particular for labor compensation (see also Section 4.4).

Figure 4.1a clearly shows that both China and India are characterized by the lowest levels of labor compensation in manufacturing at between only 2.5–3 percent of the US level in recent years. Since 1995 China has significantly caught up with labor compensation levels in India, which were typically higher than in China. By 2002 China had somewhat higher compensation levels, however.

Figure 4.1b shows that the productivity picture is much closer between various countries, except for Korea. In recent years Hungary and Poland show higher levels, but China, India, and Mexico have similar labor productivity levels of 13–14 percent of the US level. Again China showed a significant catch-up on the other countries and was somewhat ahead of both India and Mexico by 2002.

However, Figure 4.1c shows that small differences in the compensation gap relative to the productivity gap can have large implications for the comparative unit labor cost measure. Because of the relatively high levels of labor productivity compared to labor compensation levels both India and China have the lowest levels of unit labor cost of the six countries in this comparison. Even though China had somewhat superior productivity levels in manufacturing compared to India by 2002, due to its slightly higher compensation level, it was at a slight disadvantage in terms of unit labor cost relative to India.

It is also important to recognize that China's productivity advantage relative to India is only very recent. India clearly had higher-productivity levels for most of the period (as well as in the period before), indicating high levels of capital intensity in India relative to China. When looking at the industry level, however, Table 4.1 shows that by 2002 China has a productivity level advantage over India in most industries, with the major exception of chemicals, basic metals, and metal products, and—perhaps most surprisingly—the aggregate group of office machinery, electrical equipment, and radio, TV, and communication equipment. These numbers therefore suggest a slight comparative advantage for these industries in India.

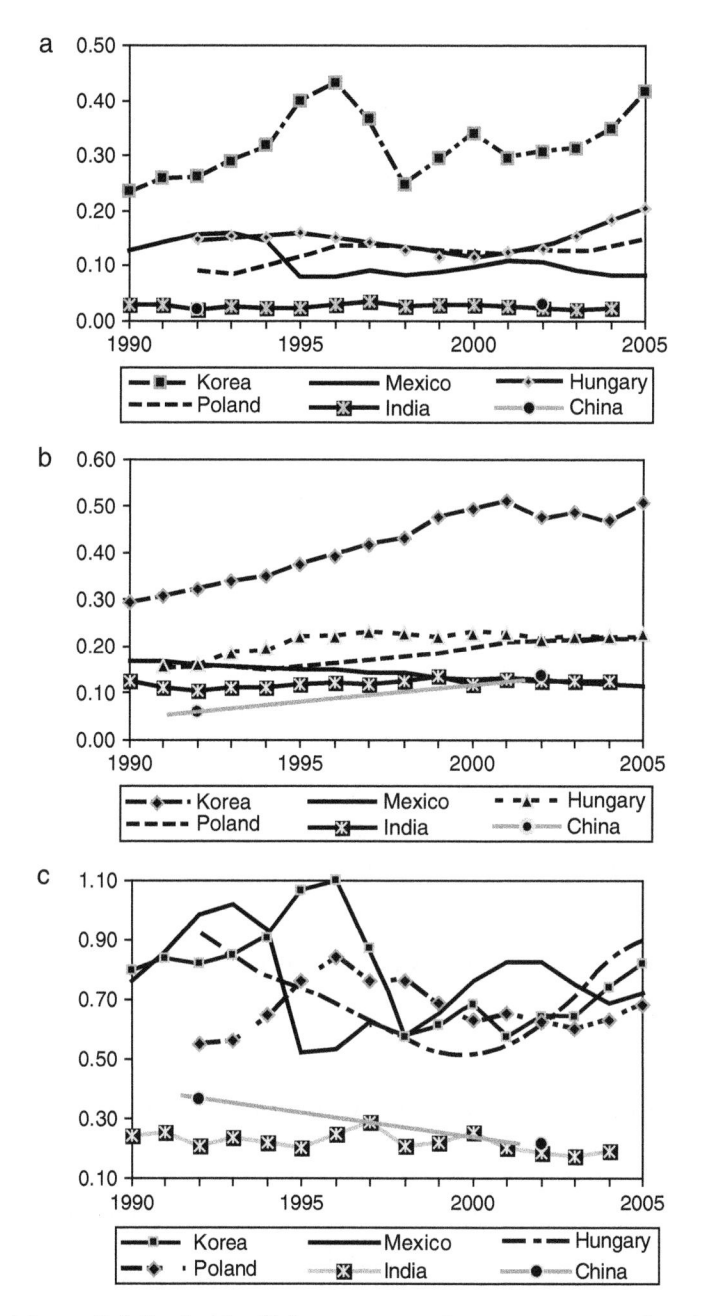

Figure 4.1a.–c. Relative levels of labor compensation per person employed (4.1a), value added per person employed (4.1b) and unit labor cost (4.1c), 1990–2005

Note: labor productivity converted at industry-specific PPPs (see main text); labor compensation converted at exchange rate.

Sources: See Appendix Table 4A.1. India: Erumban (2007, updated); China: Szirmai and Ren (2005) and Banister (2005); other countries from ICOP data, available from ILO, Key Indicators of the Labor Market, 2007 (http://www.ilo.org/public/english/employment/strat/kilm/).

95

Table 4.1. Labor productivity, compensation and unit labor cost, China and India, 2002, PPP converted (US = 100.0)

Industry	China (US = 100) Value Added/ Employee	India Value Added/ Employee	India Compensation/ Employee	India Unit Labor Cost
Food, beverages and tobacco	25.4	7.1	1.6	23.2
Textiles	25.5	11.0	3.0	27.1
Clothing	12.5	8.6	3.0	34.5
Leather and footwear	30.9	13.8	2.0	14.2
Wood, products of wood and cork	26.5	4.5	1.8	40.9
Pulp, paper and paper products	14.8	9.0	2.3	25.3
Coke, petroleum and nuclear fuel	3.6	13.6	3.9	29.0
Chemicals	5.8	15.0	2.4	16.3
Rubber and plastics	13.0	16.8	2.9	17.5
Non-metallic mineral products	24.5	12.7	1.9	15.0
Basic metals	15.9	25.6	4.1	16.1
Fabricated metal products	16.8	19.9	2.9	14.7
Machinery and equipment	40.2	15.3	3.6	23.7
Office machinery		10.3	3.5	34.4
Other elect. machinery	5.9	16.2	3.8	23.6
Radio, TV & comm. equipment		31.4	3.4	10.7
Scientific and other instruments	10.3	11.4	2.9	25.4
Motor vehicles*	40.9	13.0	3.2	24.4
Furniture Other manufacturing	43.7 9.5	21.1	3.4	15.9
Total manufacturing**	13.7	12.6	2.5	19.7

Source: Constructed using data from Erumban (2007) for India; and from Szirmai et al. (2005) for China.
Notes: Labor productivity converted at industry-specific PPPs (see main text); labor compensation converted at exchange rate.
* For China: all transport equipment.
** India excludes printing and publishing and other transport manufacturing.

4.4 Regional comparison of productivity and unit labor cost

While the international comparison of productivity, labor compensation, and unit labor costs provides a useful perspective on global cost competitiveness, it seems desirable for large countries, such as China and India, to look at differences across provinces (in China) and states (in India). Not only does a regional breakdown inform location decisions of investors; it also provides evidence on whether provinces and states show a trend towards greater similarity (convergence) of unit labor cost, for example, under the influence of integrated markets.

The Cost Competitiveness of Manufacturing

Basic data

For China we exploit the information from two major censuses, the *Third Industrial Census* for 1995 and the *First Economic Census* for 2004 to obtain a comprehensive picture on the regional distribution of manufacturing output, labor compensation, and employment, covering thirty provinces and twenty-eight industries. Indeed these two censuses are the only source from which this output and compensation information can be obtained in a consistent way. The downside of using those sources, however, is that we cannot directly obtain a time series that we need to assess the consistency of the two censuses, because of a change in the firm classification in 1998. For 2004, our measure includes the group of 56.67 million employees in 'enterprises of designated size and above', covering approximately 70 percent of total manufacturing employment in China. In Appendix 4A we argue that these measures for 2004 are sufficiently compatible with the measures for 'enterprises at township level and above' for 1995 to make an adequate comparison for those two years feasible.

The primary data for India comes from the *Annual Survey of Industries* (ASI), which is an annual survey of factories registered under Sections 2m(i) and 2m(ii) of the Factories Act (1948) and is the principal source of industrial statistics in India. Registered units are defined as factories employing ten or more workers using power, and those employing twenty or more workers without using power. The entire unregistered manufacturing sector is not covered by the ASI, but over the past twenty-five years the share of unregistered manufacturing in total manufacturing output has shrunk to just over 30 percent. However, the share of unregistered manufacturing in total manufacturing employment is more than 80 percent of total manufacturing employment.

Still there are several reasons for focusing on the larger plants only. These include the difficulties in estimating output and labor compensation for smaller firms, in particular when going down to the regional and industry level. Moreover from a foreign entrepreneur's perspective who is deciding where to locate, for example, China or India, it is the cost competitiveness of these larger firms that is most relevant to the decision making of the entrepreneur.

A related issue is the direct comparability between China's manufacturing firms of designated size and above and India's registered manufacturing factories. This is not a straightforward exercise as China's cutoff criterion in the firm distribution is the level of annual sales, whereas in India it is the number of employees. Moreover, India's distribution is

Table 4.2. Size distribution, China and India: A comparison

Interval	China Designated size and above		India Registered manufacturing	
	% firms	% employment	% factories	% employment
0–49	25.0	3.3	76.8	20.5
50–99	26.2	8.2	10.7	11.7
100–199	23.0	14.2	6.1	12.8
200–499	17.3	23.3	4.0	17.2
500–999	5.3	15.9	1.5	12.2
1000–1999	2.0	12.2	0.6	8.4
2000–4999	0.9	12.1	0.3	8.3
5000 and above	0.2	10.8	0.1	9.0

Sources: Constructed using data from EPWRF-ASI database (2007) for India; and from Industrial Enterprise Statistics for 2004 for China.
Notes: Units in China are firms; units in India are factories.

based on factories, whereas China uses firms which may include multiple factories. Still using the size distribution for India's registered manufacturing sector as reported in the EPWRF-ASI database (2007),[9] we calculated China's distribution using Chinese firm-level data based on China's industrial enterprise statistics for 2004.[10] As can be seen from Table 4.2, the share of employment in higher employment intervals (100 to 199 and above) is far bigger in case of China's manufacturing *firms* of designated size and above as compared with India's registered *factories*. In China among manufacturing firms of designated size and above, only 25 percent of the firms and 3.3 percent of total employment belong to the firms with less than fifty employees, while in India the respective shares in this low interval are 76.8 percent of *factories* and 20.5 percent of employment in those factories.

According to Table 4.2, more than 97 percent of manufacturing firms of designated size and above in China qualify for the definition of the registered manufacturing factories in India. One can even be confident that there are Chinese manufacturing firms below designated size with more than ten or twenty employees in manufacturing, which should be

---

[9] According to the definition of registered manufacturing factories in India, it is preferable to use the cutoff employment size at 10 and 20. However, as we do not have firm-level data from India to calculate the distribution at our desirable employment cutoffs, we have to use the listed cutoffs in India's aggregate table as reported in EPWRF database.

[10] China's industrial enterprise statistics are collected and maintained by NBS. The database is at the individual firm level for 39 industries covering the mining, manufacturing, and utility sectors. In 2004, these firms include all state-owned industrial enterprises and non-state industrial enterprises with annual sales over 5 million yuan (firms of designated size and above).

The Cost Competitiveness of Manufacturing

included in order to make a fully comparable analysis between India and China feasible. Although the unit of observation is the *factory* in India while in China it is the *firm*, which may consist of several factories, it is unlikely that this biases the results much. The large firm scale in China is a result of the favorable policies toward large firms in China, whereas in India, pre-reform policies (such as small-scale industries, labor regulation applying to the registered sector, and licensing) have tended to encourage small factories.

Some descriptive results for Chinese provinces and Indian states

Figures 4.2 and 4.3 show our main results along each of the two dimensions (province/state and industry) in our study. Figure 4.2 provides a comparison of the changes in ALC, ALP, and ULC for total manufacturing across provinces in China (Figure 4.2a) and states in India (Figure 4.2b). In Figures 4.3a and 4.3b we provide a comparison on the same variables by manufacturing industry for each country. The three indicators (ALC, ALP, and ULC) for China are measured for 2004 relative to 1995, and for India in 2002 relative to 1993.

The two figures bring out the stark differences between China and India. Figures 4.2a and 4.3a show a rapid decline in unit labor cost in China across the board, both by province as well as by industry. For the nation

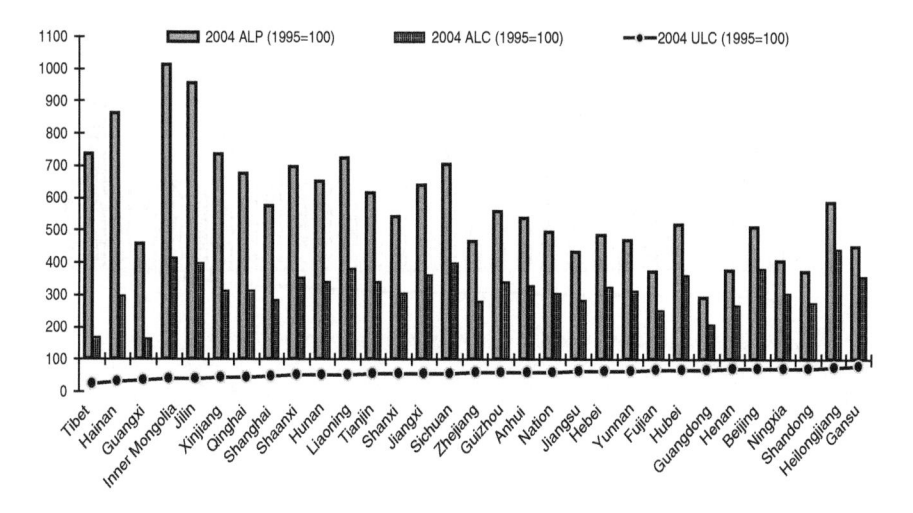

Figure 4.2a. Change in ALC, ALP, and ULC by province for total manufacturing—all China (1995 = 100)

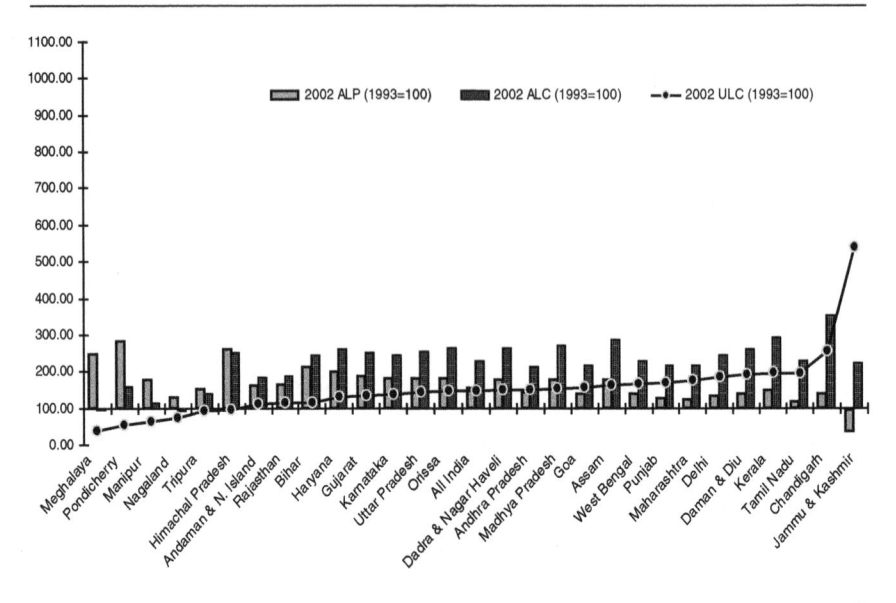

Figure 4.2b. Change in ALC, ALP, and ULC by state for total manufacturing—all India (1995 = 100)

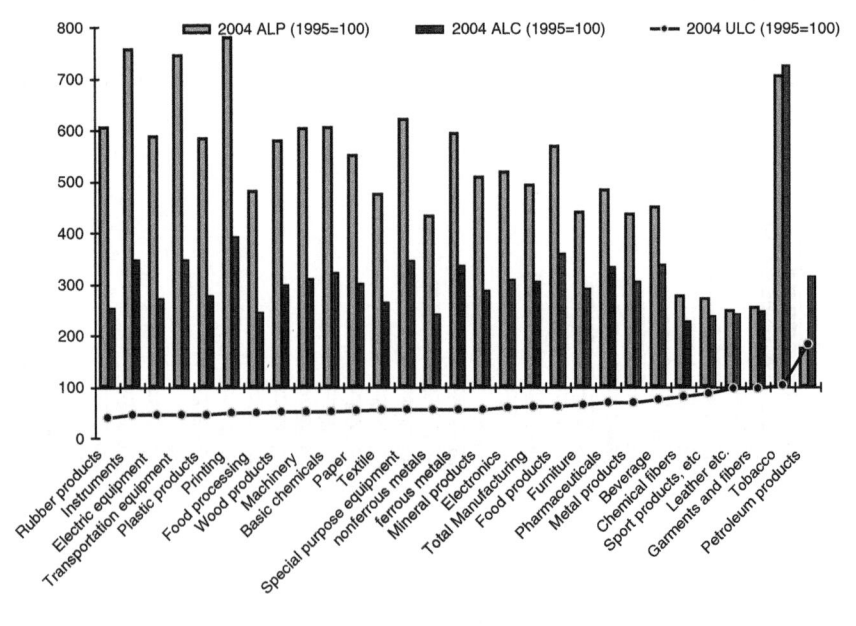

Figure 4.3a. Change in ALC, ALP, and ULC by industry for—all China (1995 = 100)

The Cost Competitiveness of Manufacturing

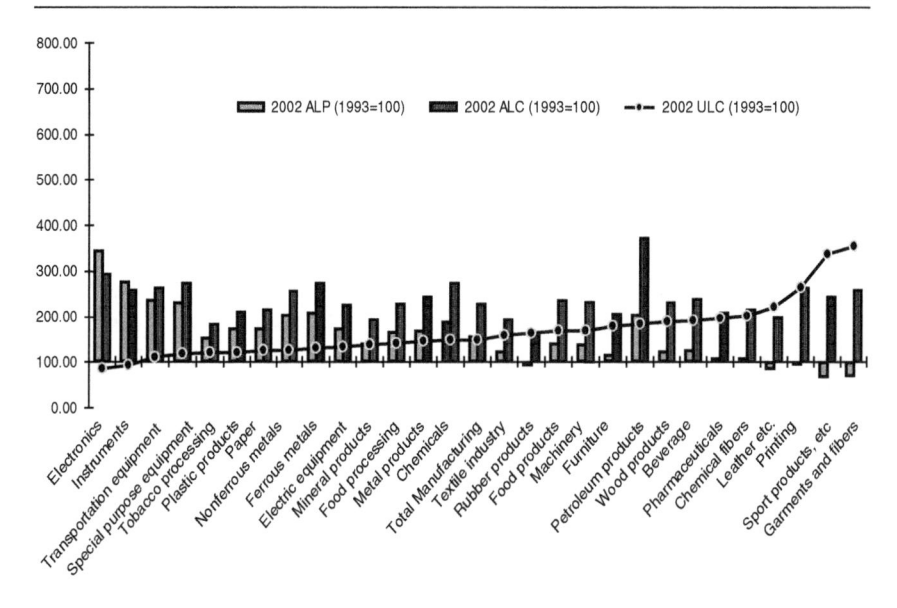

Figure 4.3b. Change in ALC, ALP, and ULC by industry for—all India (1995 = 100)

as a whole, ULC declined by about 40 percent between 1995 and 2004 whereas ALC and ALP increased by three and five times respectively. In contrast, barring a few exceptions, unit labor cost in India increased, both by state as well as by industry (Figures 4.2b and 4.3b). ULC increased by approximately 50 percent reflecting an increase in ALP of 1.5 times which was more than offset by an increase in ALC of 2.25 times over the period 1993–2002.[11]

Looking at changes across provinces within China (Figure 4.2a), some provinces show substantially larger declines in ULC than the national average, but—with the exception of Shanghai—these are all relatively underdeveloped provinces outside the coastal area. While labor compensation grew at a relatively similar rate among provinces (between two and four times) from 1995 to 2004, labor productivity growth differentials were much bigger (between four and ten times). With a few exceptions, the Chinese provinces with the fastest decline in unit labor cost are also typically the ones with the most rapid growth in productivity (between six and eight times). The variation across provinces in the relative ALC, ALP, ULC, as measured by coefficient of variation (CV),

---

[11] The increase in unit labor cost in India contrasts with the flat trend in the international comparison in Section 4.3. However, the present comparison is in national currencies rather than in US$, so that a possible decline in relative price levels in India is not reflected in the national data (see also the concluding section).

101

are 0.21, 0.30, and 0.25 respectively. Hence on the whole, productivity accounted for more of the variation in unit labor cost between provinces than labor compensation.

Looking at India, Figure 4.2b shows that ULC declined for only six states (Meghalaya, Pondicherry, Manipur, Nagaland, Tripura, Himachal Pradesh, Andaman, and Nicobar Island) and dramatically increased for the two states on the right-hand side of the chart (Chandigarh, Jammu and Kashmir). However, it is to be noted that each of these outlier states account for less than 1 percent of gross value added and employment in nationwide gross value added and employment in both benchmark years. If we focus on the *main* states, we find that while ALC changed 2.75 to 3.75 times, which was roughly similar to China, growth in ALP (1–2 times) is far less than the four to ten times increase in China. As a result all the main states in India show an increase in ULC of about 10–100 percent as opposed to a decline in ULC across all the provinces in China. The coefficient of variation in the three indicators (ALC at 0.12, ALP at 0.18, ULC at 0.16) across the main states in India is smaller compared to the respective variation across provinces in China.

Figure 4.3a shows somewhat more variation in ALC (0.29), ALP (0.31), and ULC (0.42) across industries in China than across provinces, in particular for ULC. On the whole, productivity growth and ULC declines are fastest in several capital-intensive industries, including electric equipment and transportation equipment. In contrast, labor-intensive industries, such as sport products, leather, and garments, showed the slowest increases in productivity and the least declines in ULC.

Figure 4.3b shows the results for each of the twenty-eight industries in India. Only two industries (electronics and instruments) show an increase in ALP which offsets an increase in ALC resulting in a decrease in ULC. This is different from China where twenty-six of the twenty-eight industries saw an increase in ALP beyond ALC causing ULC to decline (Figure 4.3a). At the other end, industries such as cultural, educational and sports goods, garments, leather products, and rubber products show the lowest increase in ALP. With little variation in increases in ALC across industries, the first three industries show an increase in ULC which are among the highest. As in China, there is greater variation in the changes in ALC, ALP, and ULC across industries in India than in China. A greater variation in productivity (CV of 0.4), as opposed to labor compensation (CV of 0.18), seems to be accounting for a greater variation in ULC (CV of 0.38) across industries.

The Cost Competitiveness of Manufacturing

Table 4.3a. Change of ALC, ALP & ULC by industry groups and seven regions

	Bohai	South-east	North-east	Central	South-west	North-west	All Nation
			Panel A: ALC Index (04/95)				
Food products	285.4	317.8	459.3	343.7	353.5	370.7	334.3
Textile & clothing	238.2	219.7	331.5	241.7	234.6	250.1	255.4
Wood & paper	283.0	232.6	342.6	309.0	263.7	392.2	298.7
Chemicals	274.5	263.5	384.1	296.4	284.3	317.4	297.7
Metal products	361.0	254.1	393.6	335.1	269.9	325.5	313.2
Machinery	297.8	240.4	364.4	299.8	375.1	341.1	304.7
Transport equipment	314.2	297.1	386.5	390.8	308.4	385.9	346.3
Electronics	371.7	257.1	478.9	379.4	434.0	276.2	322.0
Total manufacturing	302.5	249.8	397.9	320.0	315.6	337.3	304.9
			Panel B: ALP Index (04/95)				
Food products	412.1	626.2	799.2	509.1	488.5	727.0	531.4
Textile & clothing	375.7	279.6	678.5	315.8	642.2	410.5	364.4
Wood & paper	486.3	348.1	658.3	557.7	595.2	739.6	499.1
Chemicals	361.7	406.7	584.0	364.9	598.8	440.5	445.0
Metal products	507.0	428.5	835.7	593.2	536.7	605.6	548.9
Machinery	598.8	462.2	818.3	524.9	796.4	755.6	624.1
Transport equipment	617.6	598.4	866.2	747.6	760.9	910.7	742.6
Electronics	662.9	470.2	749.7	1032.1	−97.9	513.4	592.9
Total manufacturing	439.3	394.9	747.3	504.6	599.4	634.2	494.5
			Panel C: ULC Index (04/95)				
Food products	69.3	50.7	57.5	67.5	72.4	51.0	62.9
Textile & clothing	63.4	78.6	48.9	76.5	36.5	60.9	70.1
Wood & paper	58.2	66.8	52.0	55.4	44.3	53.0	59.9
Chemicals	75.9	64.8	65.8	81.2	47.5	72.0	66.9
Metal products	71.2	59.3	47.1	56.5	50.3	53.8	57.1
Machinery	49.7	52.0	44.5	57.1	47.1	45.1	48.8
Transport equipment	50.9	49.6	44.6	52.3	40.5	42.4	46.6
Electronics	56.1	54.7	63.9	36.8	−443.3	53.8	54.3
Total manufacturing	68.9	63.3	53.2	63.4	52.6	53.2	61.7

Note: Tibet—representing less than 1% of total value added in China—is not separately shown, but included in the total.

A significant contribution of the present analysis is the construction of a full industry by province/state panel for each of the three indicators (ALC, ALP, and ULC) for both China and India. While presentation and discussion of the entire industry by province/state panel for each of the three indicators is not feasible here, we discuss the results in terms of a summarized 5/6-region by 8-industry group panel.[12]

Table 4.3a shows a matrix of the change in ALC, ALP, and ULC by industry group and each of the six regions in China between 1995 and 2004. It shows that the labor compensation increases were the highest

[12] The grouping of 28 industries into 8 industry groups and of provinces (states) into regions is provided in Appendix Tables 4.2 and 4.3 respectively.

Table 4.3b. Change in ALC, ALP & ULC by industry group and region-India

	North	East	Central	West	South	All India
		Panel A: ALC Index (02/93)				
Food products	222.3	195.1	271.6	191.7	230.7	225.4
Textiles & clothing	221.5	222.6	178.3	192.4	193.2	194.5
Wood & paper	230.2	240.7	240.6	206.4	235.5	231.4
Chemicals	229.2	271.0	228.1	213.6	245.8	230.7
Metal products	219.5	246.5	305.0	231.9	208.4	225.8
Machinery	275.7	224.5	272.2	224.4	260.4	245.4
Transport equipment	261.7	286.5	269.7	225.9	287.2	261.3
Electronics	285.2	292.7	292.7	262.4	278.0	278.7
Total manufacturing	238.6	233.5	258.6	214.4	229.1	225.4
		Panel B: ALP Index (02/93)				
Food products	122.4	111.4	137.4	149.4	160.9	142.7
Textiles & clothing	109.9	141.4	138.3	118.1	92.3	109.9
Wood & paper	154.2	66.6	170.4	124.8	113.4	122.5
Chemicals	164.8	192.8	146.5	138.3	138.4	148.7
Metal products	183.6	204.9	209.0	167.4	130.5	167.1
Machinery	180.9	174.7	215.2	151.1	204.5	179.1
Transport equipment	231.9	216.6	230.0	164.7	260.1	233.5
Electronics	272.9	211.2	446.1	412.0	227.4	316.9
Total manufacturing	156.8	166.2	176.1	143.8	139.6	152.8
		Panel C: ULC Index (02/93)				
Food products	181.5	175.2	197.7	128.3	143.3	157.9
Textiles & clothing	201.7	157.4	129.0	162.8	209.3	176.9
Wood & paper	149.3	361.2	141.2	165.4	207.7	189.0
Chemicals	139.1	140.5	155.7	154.4	177.7	155.1
Metal products	119.5	120.3	145.9	138.5	159.7	135.2
Machinery	152.4	128.5	126.5	148.4	127.3	137.0
Transport equipment	112.9	132.3	117.3	137.1	110.4	111.9
Electronics	104.5	138.6	65.6	63.7	122.2	87.9
Total manufacturing	152.2	140.4	146.9	149.1	164.2	147.5

Note: The Northeast—where 4 of the 5 states (except Assam) represent less than 1% of total value added in India—is not separately shown, but included in the total.

in the electronics industry group in the Southwest and Northeast regions. Labor productivity increased fastest in all industry groups in the Northeast region. In contrast productivity growth was slower in the richer provinces in Bohai and the Southeast. ULC declined most rapidly in the Northeast, Southwest, and Northwest regions, and less in the booming regions, such as Bohai, the Southeast, and the Central region.[13] Although the picture is not entirely consistent, there is good reason to argue that the trends in ALP, ALC, and ULC in China are at least in part related to traditional convergence trends. Regions that are characterized by low productivity

---

[13] In this table (as well as in Table 4.4a) we do not separately present the Tibet region, which is very small in terms of its share in total manufacturing (less than 1% of overall manufacturing value added) in China.

The Cost Competitiveness of Manufacturing

Table 4.4a. Relative level of ALC, ALP & ULC by industry groups and seven regions in 1995, All China = 100

	Bohai	South-east	North-east	Central	South-west	North-west	All Nation
			Panel A: ALC				
Food products	98	135	71	82	113	79	100
Textile & clothing	90	130	61	75	81	80	100
Wood & paper	103	139	65	77	108	67	100
Chemicals	104	128	84	76	94	88	100
Metal products	88	127	92	87	104	95	100
Machinery	96	136	79	79	84	84	100
Transport equipment	101	133	91	83	100	78	100
Electronics	113	123	59	69	65	92	100
Total manufacturing	96	129	81	80	96	87	100
			Panel B: ALP				
Food products	93	106	45	99	178	54	100
Textile & clothing	99	141	33	77	38	62	100
Wood & paper	123	143	53	84	83	58	100
Chemicals	127	132	85	75	66	69	100
Metal products	110	138	76	86	80	88	100
Machinery	110	152	60	81	66	56	100
Transport equipment	110	167	89	72	75	45	100
Electronics	153	124	50	47	54	74	100
Total manufacturing	112	132	67	82	91	69	100
			Panel C: ULC				
Food products	105	127	158	83	63	145	100
Textile & clothing	91	92	182	97	210	129	100
Wood & paper	84	98	122	92	130	116	100
Chemicals	82	97	98	102	144	127	100
Metal products	80	92	121	101	130	108	100
Machinery	88	89	131	97	128	149	100
Transport equipment	92	79	102	114	134	173	100
Electronics	74	99	117	149	120	124	100
Total manufacturing	85	98	120	98	106	125	100

Note: Tibet—representing less than 1% of total value added in China—is not separately shown, but included in the total.

levels tended to grow faster in terms of productivity and showed bigger unit labor cost declines than high productivity level regions during this period. This is also clear from Table 4.4a which shows relatively low levels of compensation and productivity in the Northeast, Central, and Northwest regions for the first year in our analysis (1995), whereas the Bohai and Southeast region showed relatively higher levels.

Table 4.3b provides the corresponding 5-region by 8-industry panel of changes in India between 1993 and 2002.[14] It shows that the increase in

---
[14] In this presentation of the India results we do not present or discuss the numbers relating to the Northeast region, where 4 of the 5 states (except Assam) account for less than 1% in All India total manufacturing GVA and employment.

Bart van Ark et al.

ALC exceeded the increase in ALP in all industry groups, with the exception of electronics in West and Central regions. Hence ULC increased between 1993 and 2002 across all regions, industry groups, and their combinations. This is starkly different from China, where the increase in ALP outpaced the increase in ALC causing ULC to decline. Furthermore, the increases in ALP in the case of India were smaller as compared to those in China. Another point that stands out is the similar increase in ALC across regions and industry groups (Panel A), whereas the increase in ALP varies much more (Panel B). Thus, the variation in the changes in ULC across Panel C is largely due to variation in ALP.

Table 4.4b. Relative levels of ALC, ALP & ULC by industry group and region in 1993, All India = 100

	North	East	Central	West	South	All India
		Panel A: ALC				
Food products	121	105	115	154	74	100
Textiles & clothing	94	115	108	116	80	100
Wood & paper	104	89	88	122	91	100
Chemicals	81	103	80	129	69	100
Metal products	65	139	93	92	82	100
Machinery	75	95	99	114	95	100
Transport equipment	78	94	84	135	99	100
Electronics	83	96	99	94	114	100
Total manufacturing	87	122	95	126	77	100
		Panel B: ALP				
Food products	165	114	137	125	65	100
Textiles & clothing	136	49	106	111	98	100
Wood & paper	87	143	65	111	93	100
Chemicals	67	51	90	149	61	100
Metal products	74	111	102	108	89	100
Machinery	76	76	105	124	87	100
Transport equipment	107	53	80	158	96	100
Electronics	100	57	95	95	114	100
Total manufacturing	95	85	99	142	75	100
		Panel C: ULC				
Food products	73	92	84	123	115	100
Textiles & clothing	69	232	102	104	82	100
Wood & paper	119	62	135	109	97	100
Chemicals	120	202	89	87	113	100
Metal products	89	125	90	86	91	100
Machinery	98	124	95	92	109	100
Transport equipment	73	178	105	86	103	100
Electronics	82	168	104	99	100	100
Total manufacturing	92	143	95	89	103	100

Note: The Northeast—where 4 of the 5 states (except Assam) represent less than 1% of total value added in India—is not separately shown, but included in the total.

The Cost Competitiveness of Manufacturing

We also see from Panel B in Table 4.3b that the productivity increase in the electronics and transport equipment industry groups are among the highest for each of the regions. Except for Central and West, these increases are more than offset by an increase in ALC leading to an increase in ULC. These two industry groups also show the largest increase in productivity at the All India level and the lowest increase in ULC. With the exception of Central and East Regions, textiles and clothing showed the lowest increase in ALP and a pattern that carries over to the All India level as well.

From Panels B and C we see that the highest productivity increases and the lowest ULC increases are in the Central and East regions in India. To the extent that these regions have historically been lagging in terms of per capita income, there is some indication of 'catching up' in the sense of traditional convergence trends. Indeed Table 4.4b shows that the North, East, Northeast, and Central (albeit marginally) have lower ALP than All India ALP in 1993. These regions also witness increases in ALP greater than All India increase in ALP.

However, the traditional convergence picture is somewhat distorted by the performance of the South region. First, even though the ALP is 25 percent below the national average and lower than all other regions, it does not show any sign of catching up (ALP increase is the slowest). Second, the South has historically performed above average in terms of per capita income and hence the South's below average ALP is somewhat puzzling and requires further investigation.

4.5 Convergence trends in compensation, productivity, and unit labor cost

Catch-up (beta) convergence

Following the descriptive analysis in the previous section, we verify the convergence trends using conditional and unconditional *beta* convergence analysis, where we relate the growth in the three indicators with their initial levels. We estimate a beta-convergence specification commonly used in the economic growth literature in a cross-country analysis. The general specification takes the following form:

$$Y_{ij} = \alpha_0 + \alpha_1 Z_{ij} + \phi_i + \theta_j + \varepsilon_{ij} \tag{5}$$

where, Y_{ij} is the growth rate (difference of logs) in industry i and province (state) j for one of the three indicators: ALC, ALP, and ULC; Z_{ij} is the log of the initial value of the corresponding indicator; ϕ_i and θ_j are industry and province (state) dummy variables respectively, capturing the industry and province (state) fixed effects. A significant negative coefficient for the initial value of the indicator, i.e. a_1, indicates a convergence trend.

This convergence regression is also tested across states at the aggregate manufacturing level. For example, taking state-level ULC for total manufacturing, the specific regression takes the form of:

$$LnULC_j^t - LnULC_j^{t-1} = a_0 + a_1 LnULC_j^{t-1} + \varepsilon_j \quad (6)$$

Using the industry by province/state panel, we estimate both the unconditional (as above) and a conditional convergence regression:

$$LnULC_{ij}^t - LnULC_{ij}^{t-1} = a_0 + a_1 LnULC_{ij}^{t-1} + \phi_i + \theta_j + \varepsilon_{ij} \quad (7)$$

The results of this analysis are presented in Tables 4.5a and 4.5b for China and India respectively. We perform the analysis at two different levels: Across provinces or states for total manufacturing (Panel A) and for the entire industry by province/state panel (Panel B). For Panel A in each table, we are restricted to examining only the unconditional convergence, whereas in Panel B we examine both unconditional convergence and conditional convergence (taking into account province and industry dummies).

As we see from Table 4.5a, the coefficient on the initial level of ALP, ALC, ULC (in their respective columns) is always negative and statistically significant for China, signaling convergence across provinces, and province-industry pairs.[15] This result is also consistent with the above pattern seen in Tables 4.3a and 4.4a where regions in China with initial lower levels of ALC, ALP, and higher levels of ULC witnessed the biggest changes.

In the case of India, however, the results show a mixed pattern. Results in Panel A in Table 4.5b show no convergence as the coefficients on the initial terms for ALP and ALC are insignificant. Even though the sign on ULC is negative and significant, the high magnitudes are indicative that they are driven by outliers. Indeed if we restrict our sample to main states and do a similar exercise we find the initial ULC is no longer significant. However, in Panel B (unconditional or conditional convergence, all states

[15] Following the common practice in India, we also restrict 30 provinces to those with GVA share more than 1% in the convergence regression analysis for China. The results for those major provinces remain unchanged.

Table 4.5a. Beta convergence, OLS regression results: China

	Dependent variable is the growth of							
	Panel A: By province			Panel B: 28 Industries by 30 provinces				
	ALC	ALP	ULC	ALC	ALP	ULC	ALC	ALP	ULC
Log Initial ALC	−0.618*** (0.147)			−0.370*** (0.048)			−0.848*** (0.055)		
Log Initial ALP		−0.427*** (0.142)			−0.339*** (0.045)			−0.808*** (0.071)	
Log Initial ULC			−0.696*** (0.211)			−0.593*** (0.043)			−0.819*** (0.054)
			−1.282*** (0.211)			−1.099*** (0.042)			−1.508*** (0.094)
Constant	6.488*** (1.258)	5.845*** (1.364)		4.311*** (0.408)	4.908*** (0.430)		8.649*** (0.475)	9.752*** (0.636)	
Industry/province dummies	No	No	No	No	No	No	Yes	Yes	Yes
Observations	30	30	30	805	796	794	805	796	794
R-squared	0.57	0.27	0.44	0.17	0.17	0.38	0.70	0.64	0.67

Robust standard errors in parentheses, * significant at 10%; ** significant at 5%; *** significant at 1%.

Table 4.5b. Beta convergence, OLS regression results: India

Panel A: By state
dependent variable is the growth of

All States

	ALC	ALP	ULC
Log Initial ALC	0.224 (0.17)		
Log Initial ALP		−2.11 (9.5)	
Log Initial ULC			−97.597** (42.1)
Constant	−1.58 (1.8)	77.87 (62.3)	402.97** (162.9)
Industry/State FE	No	No	No
Observations	28	28	28
R-squared	0.06	0.00	0.29

Main States

	ALC	ALP	ULC
Log Initial ALC	−0.104 (0.09)		
Log Initial ALP		21.80 (29.5)	
Log Initial ULC			−20.34 (24.6)
Constant	1.96* (1.0)	−91.63 (200.9)	127.04 (86.6)
Industry/State FE	No	No	No
Observations	16	16	16
R-squared	0.07	0.05	0.03

Panel B: 28 Industries by states
dependent variable is the growth of

All States

	ALC	ALP	ULC	ALC	ALP	ULC
Log Initial ALC	−0.073** (0.035)			−0.361*** (0.055)		
Log Initial ALP		−0.37*** (0.053)			−0.679*** (0.061)	
Log Initial ULC			−0.65*** (0.058)			−0.799*** (0.055)
Constant	1.6*** (0.36)	3.0*** (0.36)	2.71*** (0.20)	4.42*** (0.55)	5.08*** (0.46)	2.90*** (0.22)
Industry/State FE	No	No	No	Yes	Yes	Yes
Observations	543	543	543	543	543	543
R-squared	0.01	0.14	0.31	0.33	0.45	0.54

Main States

	ALC	ALP	ULC	ALC	ALP	ULC
Log Initial ALC	−0.041 (0.038)			−0.304*** (0.061)		
Log Initial ALP		−0.268*** (0.046)			−0.489*** (0.061)	
Log Initial ULC			−0.532*** (0.052)			−0.609*** (0.054)
Constant	1.29*** (0.40)	2.27*** (0.31)	2.34*** (0.19)	3.8*** (0.60)	3.67*** (0.44)	2.34*** (0.20)
Industry/State FE	No	No	No	Yes	Yes	Yes
Observations	412	412	412	412	412	412
R-squared	0.00	0.10	0.27	0.31	0.39	0.48

Robust standard errors in parentheses, * significant at 10%; ** significant at 5%; *** significant at 1%.

The Cost Competitiveness of Manufacturing

or main states) we find strong evidence of convergence across state industry pairs. This contrasts with the lack of any signs of convergence at the aggregate state level. One possible explanation for this could be that while there may be between-state convergence observed at the detailed industry level, large differences in industrial composition across states drive the lack of convergence at the aggregate level. This is an area for further research.

Cross-province/state (sigma) convergence

To obtain a better understanding of the degree of convergence across space, we look at the distribution of the comparative levels of ALP, ALC, and ULC for the two benchmark years across provinces/states in the two countries. This implies we examine *sigma* convergence. In this section we use a simple metric, the coefficient of variation (CV) to understand degree of convergence that has taken place across spatial units (regions and states) for each of the three indicators, ALC, ALP, and ULC. CV, expressed as a ratio of standard deviation to mean, is a standard measure of inequality that helps us gauge the distribution of the variable of interest. Figure 4.4 shows the CV across provinces/states in China and India for each of the three indicators.

Figures 4.4a–f summarize the results for sigma convergence. Figures 4.4a, 4.4c, and 4.4e show that the CVs across seven regions in China[16] for all three variables (ALP, ALC, and ULC) at aggregate manufacturing level ('TOT') exhibit a dramatic decline to well below 0.1. Even though the CVs across provinces (instead of regions) are considerably higher, picking up more variation due to *intra*-regional specialization, the decline in inequality between 1995 and 2004 is still impressive. In particular, the huge decline in the CV for ULC to 0.18 (from 0.30 in 1995) on the basis of the provincial grouping, and even to 0.05 when using the seven region grouping, shows that aggregate unit labor cost levels are now very close between regions. This suggests that provinces (or regions) with high productivity levels relative to the all nation average also have relatively high compensation levels.

This aligning of the ALC and ALP levels across provinces (regions) can essentially be ascribed to the transformation from planning towards a market system. As a result inefficient activities which were carried out at the 'wrong' place due to resource misallocations (given the large differences in gaps for comparative productivity and labor cost levels

---

[16] For this analysis we have included Tibet as the 7th region in our sample.

111

Bart van Ark et al.

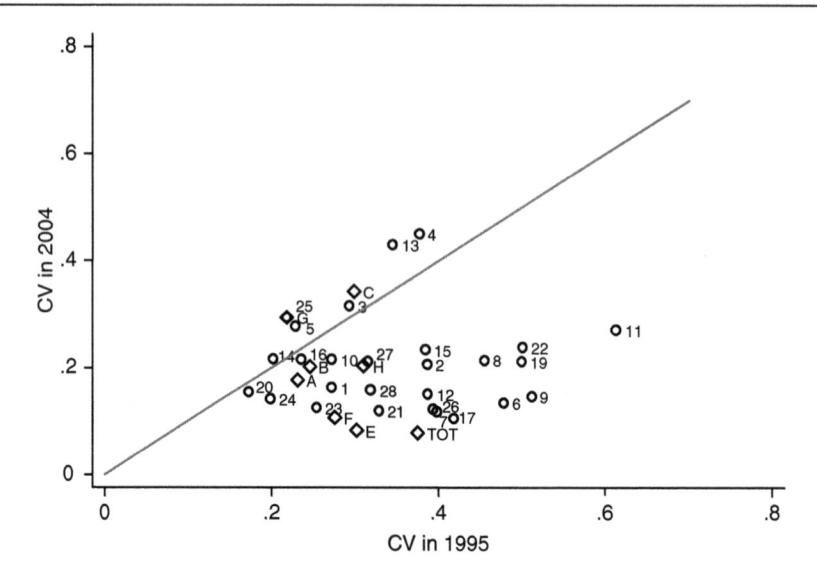

Figure 4.4a. Coefficient of variation for ALC by industry, China

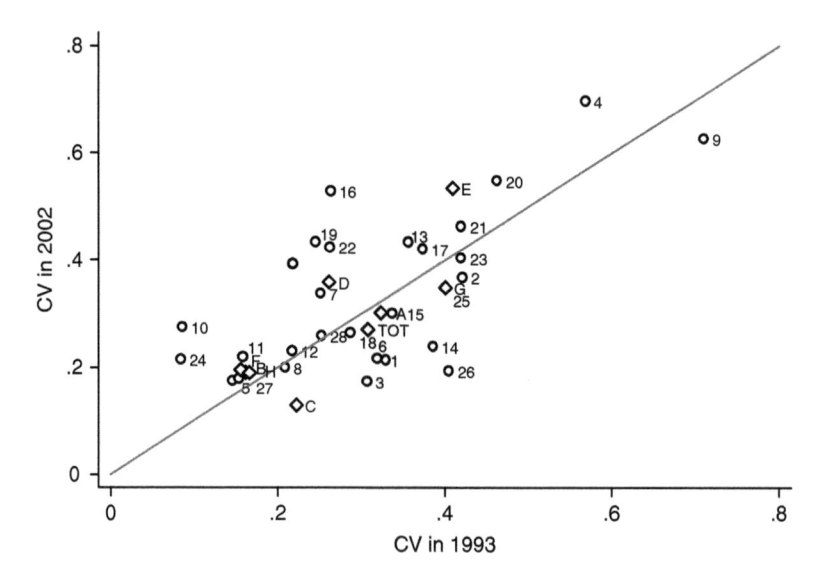

Figure 4.4b. Coefficient of variation for ALC by industry, India

relative to the national average) have been mostly eradicated during this period.

For India, however, even though we see a decline in CV for total manufacturing in ALC and ALP and an increase in the case of ULC across

The Cost Competitiveness of Manufacturing

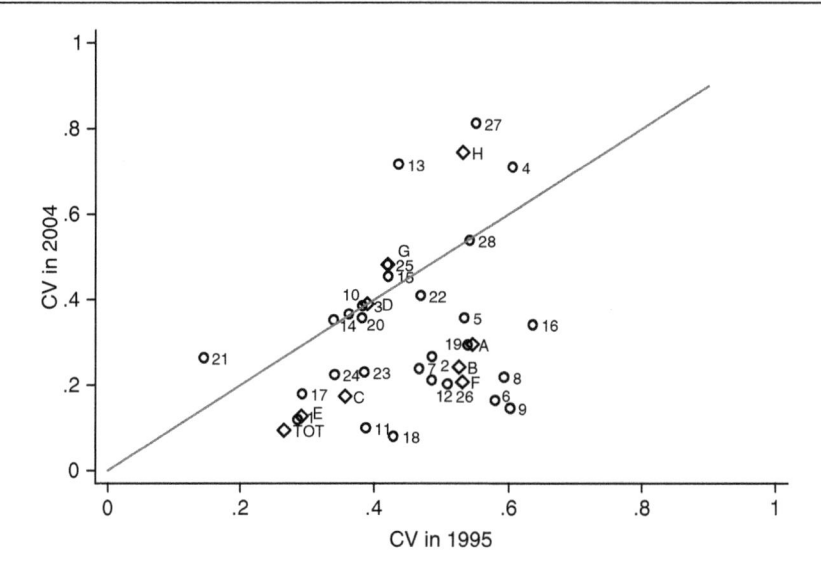

Figure 4.4c. Coefficient of variation for ALP by industry, China

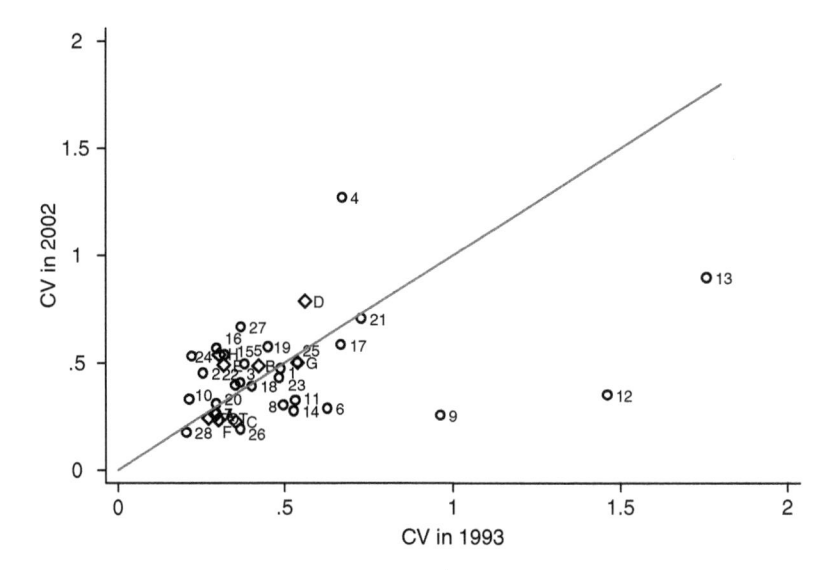

Figure 4.4d. Coefficient of variation for ALP by industry, India

regions, this pattern is not consistent across different spatial groupings even for the total manufacturing. Furthermore, the decline in CV across regions for total manufacturing is not as large as the declines in the case of China. As we see from Figure 4.4b and 4.4d, total manufacturing ('TOT')

113

Bart van Ark et al.

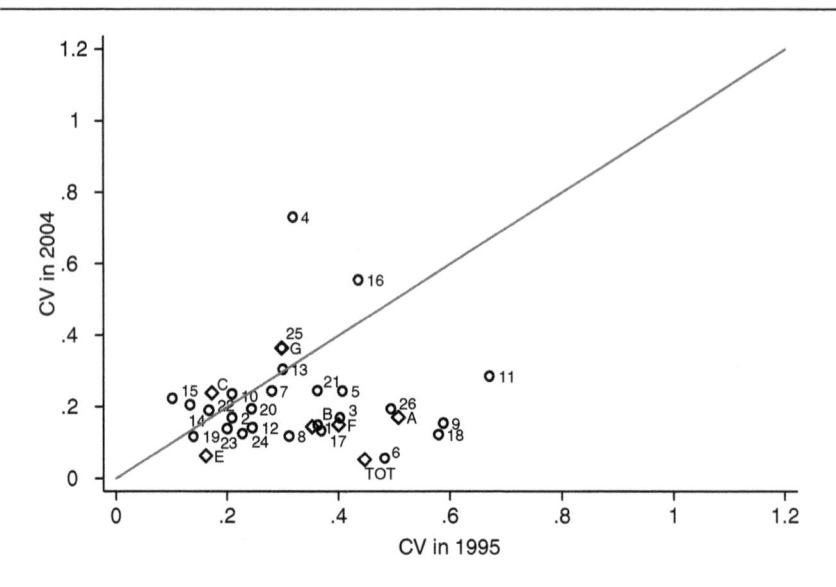

Figure 4.4e. Coefficient of variation for ULC by industry, China

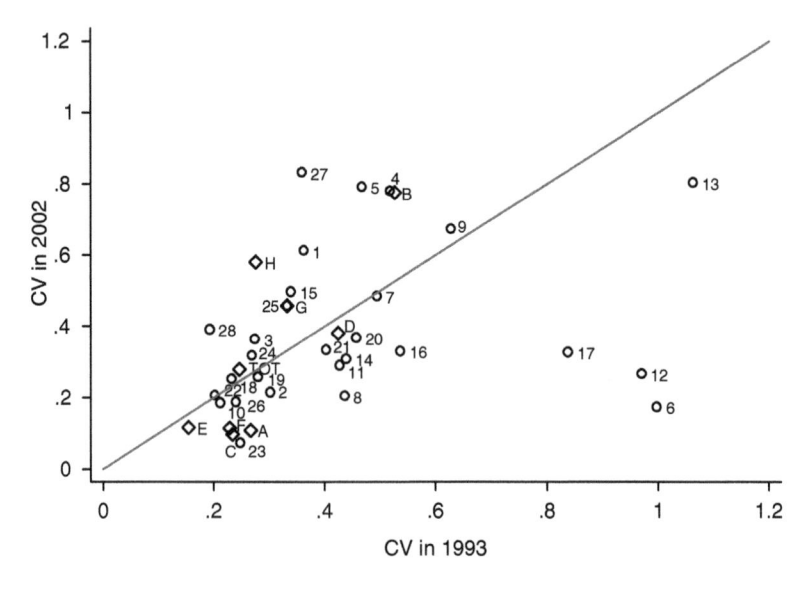

Figure 4.4f. Coefficient of variation for ULC by industry, India

is very close to the 45 degree line indicating only a marginal decline in CVs. This suggests that the kind of market forces that have led to the alignment of ULC across provinces in China are not at play (yet) in the

The Cost Competitiveness of Manufacturing

case of India and points to the immobility of resources across space and industries.

When examining the sigma convergence for individual industries and industry groups, we find that the strong decline in the CV for ALC in aggregate manufacturing, in case of China, is reflected in the decline in regional inequality for six of the eight major industry groups (with the exception of the wood and paper, and transport equipment groups). For labor productivity, the CV for the chemicals group remained constant, but it increased for the last two industry groups, transport equipment and electronics. Indeed transport equipment also exhibited an increase in CV for unit labor cost. In our companion paper for China (Chen et al. 2007), we have linked this observation to the analysis of characteristics of industries that show divergence rather than convergence trends. This points at the possibility that relatively capital- and skill-intensive industries are more likely to show strong spatial concentration effects, so that those are not contributing much to the overall convergence trend.

In India, the results for *sigma* convergence are just the opposite to China. In the case of ALC, only three (food products, wood and paper, and transport equipment) out of eight industry groups show a decline in CV. In addition to these three groups, transport equipment also shows a decline in CV in ALP. For ULC, most industry groups show a decline in CV. However, the extent of these declines are not as big as in the case of China, as the observations stay much closer to the 45 degree line.

Indeed when focusing on the industry level (rather than major industry groups), Figures 4.4a–f show several industries with CVs for 2004 which are larger than for 1995. In China, such divergence cases include, for example, beverages, tobacco, chemicals, and textiles, in addition to transport equipment for average labor compensation (Figure 4.4a). Increased regional inequality for labor productivity (Figure 4.4c) is observed, among others, for tobacco, non-ferrous metals, chemicals, in addition to transport equipment and electronics. Figure 4.4e shows increased inequality for unit labor cost for as many as ten industries between 1995 and 2004, including major industries such as chemical raw materials and fibers and metal products, in addition to transport equipment.

However, in the case of India (Figures 4.4b, 4.4d, and 4.4f), the number of industries showing an increase in inequality is much larger, and of those that show convergence only few show a substantial decline in the CV (i.e. those further to the right and below the 45 degree line in Figures 4.4b, 4.4d, and 4.4f). In most cases, whether there is a decline or an increase in CV, both industries and industry groups are concentrated around the 45 degree line.

Finally, it is striking to see that in China the inequality at the level of industry groups or industries is much higher than for the aggregate manufacturing sector (compare the marker labeled 'TOT' with the industry markers). This trend towards relatively low levels in inequality of ALC, ALP, and ULC at the aggregate level compared to the industry level is also supported by some of the institutional and market reforms that have taken place in China over the past decade. This has allowed regions to specialize in those industries where they have a comparatively high productivity advantage and pay high compensation levels. Standard neoclassical trade theory, however, would predict that these market reforms may also cause an equalization of compensation and productivity levels at industry levels across regions. While this may happen in due time, there is another strand of theory, i.e. that based on New Economic Geography models, that would predict that greater specialization will attract higher paid resources and cause further divergence rather than convergence at industry level, and perhaps even at the aggregate level. In the case of India, however, we do not see any clear trend towards lower inequality at the aggregate level, which suggests that the factor returns are not getting equalized across space and industries due to immobility of resources.

4.6 Conclusion

This chapter focuses on comparisons of productivity, labor cost, and industry-level competitiveness for the manufacturing sector of China and India. The chapter builds on an ongoing research program carried out at The Conference Board and at the University of Groningen. We first provide an international comparison between India and China from a broader international perspective using industry-level output purchasing power parities which convert output into a common currency. We find that in recent years China showed a slightly higher labor productivity level than India in the year 2002, but due to its higher compensation level, China was somewhat at a disadvantage in terms of unit labor cost relative to India. This poses important questions about China's competitiveness relative to other emerging economies, and stresses the need for keeping productivity and compensation levels in line.

In the second half of the chapter, we focus on an analysis of spatial and industry differences in productivity, labor compensation, and unit labor

The Cost Competitiveness of Manufacturing

costs in China and India. Our major findings are summarized as follows. First, labor productivity and labor compensation both increased over the period of this study in China and India. However, in the case of China, labor productivity in 2004 is four to ten times that in 1995 and the labor compensation in 2004 is two to four times relative to its level in 1995. As a result, the unit labor cost declined by 20 to 80 percent. On the other hand, in India, the increase in labor compensation (ALC in 2002 is 1.75 to 2.75 times that in 1993) outpaced the increase in productivity (ALP in 2002 relative to 1993 is between 1 to 2 times), driving up the unit labor cost by 10 to 100 percent. Second, using a simple OLS regression framework, we observe the traditional beta convergence trend—the lagging regions or industries grow faster—in China across provinces as well as for the industry by province panel. However, this convergence trend is confirmed only for the industry by state panel in India, but not at the aggregate state level. Third, there is a clear sigma convergence at the aggregate manufacturing level taking place in China, namely, the spatial dispersion of ALC, ALP, and ULC falls dramatically between 1995 and 2004. This pattern, however, is not unanimously supported by each individual industry and industry group. In India we do not find any consistent reduction in spatial disparity; even for cases that show a fall in inequality, the change is smaller compared to the change in China.

The falling inequality of ULC (as shown by the declining of the CV of ULC) suggests that ALC and ALP are more aligned across regions in China. This trend has most likely been driven by liberalization and the drive towards a market economy. As a result, inefficient activities which were carried out at the wrong place, given the large differences in gaps for comparative productivity and labor cost levels relative to the national average, have been mostly eradicated during the period of study. These transition forces, on the other hand, do not seem to be at work in India, at least not during the time period of this study. The small change in inequality (and in many cases an increase in dispersion) points to the existence of barriers to resource mobility.

Areas for further research

This chapter ties into two major strands of theory in economics predicting the spatial distribution trends during the phase of economic development. Standard neoclassical trade theory would predict that in due time these market reforms may also cause an equalization of compensation and productivity levels at industry levels across regions. However, another strand of theory would predict that greater regional specialization will attract even more highly paid resources and cause further divergence rather than convergence at industry level, and perhaps even at the aggregate level (Krugman 1991; Fujita et al. 1999). To obtain a better understanding of the reasons for the convergence trends in manufacturing compensation, labor productivity, and unit labor cost, in forthcoming work, we need to examine industry-specific features, such as labor intensity, skill intensity, etc. that can potentially contribute to the convergence/divergence patterns in China and India. Preliminary analysis in a companion paper by Chen et al. (2007) points at the possibility that capital- and skill-intensive industries have a greater tendency to concentrate spatially, so that those are not contributing much to the overall convergence trend.

Finally, it is also worthwhile to further reflect on the somewhat different perspectives on the development of comparative productivity and unit labor cost when analyzing China's and India's performance. While the unit labor cost development in India is relatively flat when expressed in US dollars, we observed a significant increase in ULC when measured in national currency. This is mainly due to the fact that relative price levels (the PPP relative to the exchange rate) fell in India relative to the US over this period. As a result productivity in PPP-converted US dollars relative to labor compensation went up faster than when expressed in national currency estimates. In the case of China both international and national estimates show a decline in manufacturing unit labor cost, but the decline in national currency is much faster. Again this suggests a rapid decline in relative price levels in China, and lends some support to current calls for an appreciation of the yuan to other currencies.

Appendix 4A. Basic data for China and India regional comparisons

China

The *First Economic Census of China* was conducted by the National Bureau of Statistics in 2005 with reference to the calendar year 2004.[17] The focus of the census was the nonagricultural and comparatively modern sectors of the economy, in particular industry and services. Using the average numbers of employees in 2004 from the Economic Census, there were 80.8 million employees in China's

---

[17] The reference time for the Economic Census was December 31, 2004, and the flow data covered the whole year of 2004 (China NBS 2005).

established legal manufacturing enterprises, of whom 56.67 million were in the 'manufacturing enterprises of designated size and above'. Enterprises of designated size and above are defined as all state-owned enterprises plus nonstate-owned enterprises that had sales of 5 million yuan (about 600,000 US dollars) or more. The remaining 24.13 million were in manufacturing enterprises below designated size. Moreover the census includes another 23.8 million employees which were self-employed or in household manufacturing firms.

For 2004, we focus exclusively on the group of 56.67 million employees in enterprises of designated size and above, covering approximately 70 percent of total manufacturing employment in China. There are several reasons for focusing on the larger plants only, including the difficulties to estimate output and labor compensation for the other two groups. Moreover, there is no information available on a province by industry basis for enterprises other than those at designated size or above. Finally, from the perspective of competitiveness, the interest in the manufacturing firms of designated size and above (beyond 600,000 US$ sales revenue) only seems justified.

The *1995 Third National Industrial Census* consists of three volumes (by industry, region, and ownership type), plus a summary volume. It differs greatly from the 2004 Economic Census in many aspects. The most notable problem is that there has been a change in the definition of the industrial accounting unit. Up to 1998 the major subset of industries for which the industrial statistics provided extensive information was 'national independent accounting industrial enterprises at and above township level'. Since 1998 this has been replaced by 'all industrial state-owned enterprises (SOEs) with independent accounting system and all industrial non-SOEs with independent accounting system and annual sales revenue in excess of 5 million yuan' (the designated size and above unit). According to Holz and Lin (2001) this change implied that non-SOEs with independent accounting system at or above township level but with sales revenue of no more than 5 million yuan are now excluded from the detailed industrial statistics. On the other hand, village-level enterprises that meet the two requirements are now included (Holz and Lin 2001, 304 n. 2). Even though it is not possible to make a precise assessment of the difference, it appears that 'township level and above' firms covered roughly 60 percent of gross value of output in 1997, whereas 'designated size and above' firms covered 57 percent of gross value of output in 1998 (Holz and Lin 2001, 314, Figure 2), which is a sufficiently small difference to assume that these two categories of firms are reasonably comparable.

Even though both China's *Third Industrial Census* and the *First Economic Census* publish tables at the national, total manufacturing, and industry levels, substantial manipulations to the data were necessary in order to estimate gross value added, labor compensation, and employment because of the incomplete information of these variables in those above tables as well as the comparability in the industry coverage between these two benchmark years. For detailed data construction, see Chen et al. (2007).

India

The primary data used in this study for India comes from the Annual Survey of Industries (ASI). ASI is an annual survey of factories registered under Sections 2m(i) and 2m(ii) of the Factories Act (1948) and is the principal source of industrial statistics in India. Registered units are defined as factories employing ten or more workers using power, and those employing twenty or more workers without using power. ASI frame is based on the list of registered factories/units maintained by the Chief Inspector of Factories in each state/Union Territory (UT). Factory (those falling under the registered manufacturing sector) is the primary unit of enumeration in the survey for the case of manufacturing industries.

ASI covers only on registered units and the unregistered manufacturing sector is not in the ambit of ASI. The survey on the unregistered sector is carried out by the National Sample Survey Organization (NSSO) and the survey is done every five years, the latest one is for July 2005–June 2006. A quick comparison using national accounts data shows that the share of registered manufacturing in total manufacturing value added is approximately 70 percent as of 2005–2006 (the share has increased from a little over 50 percent in 1980–1981) and in terms of employment (using NSSO round 56% and ASI data for 2000–2001) the registered manufacturing accounts for only 17 percent of the total manufacturing employment.

Deflators

Producer price indices (PPIs) by industry at the national level from the CEIC Database are used to deflate labor productivity in China. As the industry classification in CEIC is different from the twenty-eight manufacturing industries in our data set, we could only allocate twelve industry-specific indices from CEIC to the individual twenty-eight industries for the nation as a whole.

In the case of India, the wholesale price index (WPI) at the group/commodity level (base year 1993–1994) from the Ministry of Commerce and Industry (Government of India) are used for the purposes of calculating real values where needed. These deflators are not at the same level of classification as the industries. The concordance from WPI classification to the industrial classification is provided in the Appendix to a forthcoming paper on unit labor cost in India. Wherever the concordance requires aggregating WPI for several groups or commodities, respective weights (weights as used in calculation of the official overall WPI) are used in aggregation. The deflator for total manufacturing used is the weighted average of the deflators for 'manufactured goods', 'coal mining', and 'petroleum processing'.

While we do not have information on price indices for individual provinces (states) by industry, we used price indices by industry at the national level to obtain province/state level deflators, assuming that there is no variation in deflators for each industry across provinces/states. In other words, the deflators used at the All China or All India level for a particular industry are also used at the province or

The Cost Competitiveness of Manufacturing

state level for that corresponding industry. This assumption is made only for the twenty-eight industries and not for the total manufacturing at the state level.

Deflators for province/state at the total manufacturing level are calculated as the weighted average of the deflators for the twenty-eight industries (these deflators, as discussed above, are province/state invariant across industries). Weights used are the respective value added shares of the twenty-eight industries in the corresponding province/state.

Appendix Table 4A.1. Comparative levels of labor compensation, labor productivity and unit labor cost, 1990–2005 (USA = 100)

	Korea	Mexico	Hungary	Poland	India	China
Labor compensation per person employed, USA = 1						
1990	0.236	0.128			0.030	
1991	0.260	0.144			0.029	
1992	0.263	0.159	0.149	0.090	0.021	
1993	0.288	0.161	0.156	0.088	0.027	
1994	0.318	0.146	0.152	0.096	0.025	
1995	0.398	0.080	0.160	0.117	0.024	0.021
1996	0.430	0.081	0.152	0.134	0.031	
1997	0.365	0.091	0.141	0.130	0.034	
1998	0.247	0.083	0.127	0.136	0.026	
1999	0.294	0.088	0.115	0.126	0.030	
2000	0.340	0.099	0.116	0.125	0.030	
2001	0.295	0.110	0.124	0.137	0.026	
2002	0.307	0.106	0.131	0.126	0.024	0.029
2003	0.313	0.093	0.155	0.126	0.022	
2004	0.347	0.083	0.185	0.136	0.024	
2005	0.417	0.084	0.204	0.146		
Labor productivity (Mnf. value added per person employed), USA = 1						
1990	0.296	0.168			0.126	
1991	0.310	0.167	0.158	0.156	0.113	
1992	0.321	0.161	0.163	0.163	0.104	
1993	0.339	0.157	0.185	0.155	0.111	
1994	0.350	0.156	0.198	0.147	0.113	
1995	0.374	0.152	0.220	0.154	0.120	0.059
1996	0.392	0.151	0.220	0.159	0.123	
1997	0.418	0.145	0.231	0.171	0.120	
1998	0.431	0.142	0.230	0.178	0.127	
1999	0.478	0.134	0.220	0.182	0.138	
2000	0.496	0.130	0.228	0.198	0.119	
2001	0.512	0.133	0.228	0.210	0.131	
2002	0.478	0.129	0.215	0.201	0.128	0.137
2003	0.486	0.123	0.221	0.210	0.127	
2004	0.471	0.120	0.220	0.216	0.127	
2005	0.509	0.116	0.229	0.214		
Unit labor cost (labor compensation/labor productivity), USA = 1						
1990	0.797	0.763			0.241	
1991	0.837	0.858			0.255	
1992	0.819	0.985	0.914	0.550	0.207	
1993	0.849	1.023	0.841	0.564	0.240	
1994	0.908	0.934	0.767	0.650	0.222	

(cont.)

Bart van Ark et al.

Appendix Table 4A.1. *(continued)*

	Korea	Mexico	Hungary	Poland	India	China
1995	1.064	0.523	0.728	0.765	0.203	0.365
1996	1.097	0.535	0.689	0.844	0.251	
1997	0.873	0.629	0.612	0.763	0.286	
1998	0.574	0.581	0.555	0.765	0.206	
1999	0.614	0.656	0.522	0.691	0.217	
2000	0.686	0.763	0.508	0.631	0.253	
2001	0.575	0.826	0.544	0.653	0.201	
2002	0.643	0.826	0.610	0.627	0.185	0.213
2003	0.643	0.754	0.704	0.601	0.173	
2004	0.738	0.691	0.842	0.631	0.190	
2005	0.818	0.722	0.893	0.684		

Note: Relative levels for labor compensation are exchange rate converted; relative levels for labor productivity are converted at industry-specific PPPs, using unit value approach as described in text.

Source: Constructed using data for India: Erumban (2007, updated); for China: Szirmai and Ren (2005) and Banister (2005); for other countries from ICOP data, by Groningen Growth and Development Centre, available from ILO, *Key Indicators of the Labor Market*, 2007 (http://www.ilo.org/public/english/employment/strat/kilm/).

Appendix Table 4A.2. Industries and industry groups

28 Sector Code	Description	8 Sector Classification
1	Food processing	
2	Food products manufacturing	
3	Beverage manufacturing	Food products (A)
4	Tobacco processing	
5	Textile industry	
6	Garments and other fiber products	
7	Leather, furs, down and related products	Textiles & Clothing (B)
8	Timber, bamboo, natural fiber & straw products	
9	Furniture manufacturing	
10	Papermaking and paper products	
11	Printing & record medium reproduction	Wood & Paper (C)
12	Cultural, educational, and sport products	
13	Petroleum processing and coking products	
14	Chemical raw materials & products	
15	Medical & pharmaceutical products	
16	Chemical fibers manufacturing	Chemicals (D)
17	Rubber products	
18	Plastic products	
19	Nonmetal mineral products	
20	Smelting & pressing of ferrous metals	
21	Smelting & pressing of nonferrous metals	Metal Products (E)
22	Metal products	
23	Ordinary machinery manufacturing	
24	Special purpose equipment manufacturing	
26	Electric equipment and machinery	Machinery (F)
25	Transportation equipment manufacturing	Transpo-rtation equipme-nt (G)
27	Electronics and telecommunications	Electronics (H)
28	Instruments & stationery machine tools	

Appendix Table 4A.3a. Provinces and Regions—China

Provinces	7 Regions
Beijing Tianjin Hebei Shandong	Bohai
Shanghai Jiangsu Zhejiang Fujian Guangdong	South East
Liaoning Jilin Heilongjiang	North East
Anhui Jiangxi Henan Hubei Hunan	Central
Guangxi Hainan Sichuan Guizhou Yunnan	South West
Shanxi Inner Mongolia Shaanxi Gansu Qinghai Ningxia Xinjiang	North West
Tibet	Tibet

Appendix Table 4A.3b. States and region

New State	Old State	State/UT	Code	Main State	Region
Chandigarh	Chandigarh	UT	CH	No	North (N)
Delhi	Delhi	UT	DL	Yes	
Haryana	Haryana	State	HY	Yes	
Himachal Pradesh	Himachal Pradesh	State	HP	No	
Jammu & Kashmir	Jammu & Kashmir	State	JK	No	
Punjab	Punjab	State	PJ	Yes	
Bihar	> Bihar	State	BH	Yes	East (E)
Jharkhand (JD)		State			
Orissa	Orissa	State	OR	Yes	
West Bengal	West Bengal	State	WB	Yes	
Chattisgarh (CT)	> Madhya Pradesh	State	MP	Yes	Central (C)
Madhya Pradesh		State			
Uttar Pradesh	> Uttar Pradesh	State	UP	Yes	
Uttaranchal (UL)		State			
Dadra & Nagar Haveli	Dadra & Nagar Haveli	UT	DN	No	West (W)
Daman & Diu	Daman & Diu	UT	DU	No	
Goa	Goa	State	GA	No	
Gujarat	Gujarat	State	GJ	Yes	
Maharashtra	Maharashtra	State	MH	Yes	
Rajasthan	Rajasthan	State	RJ	Yes	
Andaman & N. Island	Andaman & N. Island	UT	AN	No	South (S)
Andhra Pradesh	Andhra Pradesh	State	AP	Yes	
Karnataka	Karnataka	State	KK	Yes	
Kerala	Kerala	State	KL	Yes	
Pondicherry	Pondicherry	UT	PY	No	
Tamil Nadu	Tamil Nadu	State	TN	Yes	
Assam	Assam	State	AS	Yes	North East (NE)
Manipur	Manipur	State	MN	No	
Meghalaya	Meghalaya	State	MG	No	
Nagaland	Nagaland	State	NG	No	
Tripura	Tripura	State	TR	No	

5

Law, Institutions, and Finance in China and India

*Franklin Allen, Rajesh Chakrabarti, Sankar De, Jun 'QJ' Qian, and Meijun Qian**

5.1 Introduction

We take a close look at the financial systems of the two largest and fastest growing emerging economies of the world—China and India—to better understand their very impressive growth experience in the presence of legal systems and institutions that would frequently be considered inadequate by developed country standards. The two financial systems differ widely in their nature and evolution. Transiting from a socialist system to a market-based system, China had no formal commercial legal system and associated institutions in place when its economy began to take off in the 1980s. India, on the other hand, has a long history of modern legal institutions and financial markets, and has inherited a set of rich institutions.

---

* We appreciate helpful comments from Reena Aggarwal, Peter Bossaerts, Charles Calomiris, Asli Demirgüç-Kunt, Mihir Desai, Joshua Felman, Nandini Gupta, Ravi Jagannathan, Mudit Kapoor, Raghuram Rajan, Stefano Rossi, Rohan Williamson, and Leslie Young. For assistance with collecting financial data and conducting firm surveys, we wish to thank Sankar De's associates at ISB's Centre for Analytical Finance (CAF). We are grateful to Gaurav Khurana, Narender Khurana, Tridip Ray, and Mausumi Das for their contribution to our surveys in New Delhi, Deepika Luke (CAF) for research assistance, and P. G. Shinde (Centre for Monitoring Indian Economy) for providing data. We wish to acknowledge outstanding research support and other contributions from Leena Kinger Hans (CAF). Sankar De gratefully acknowledges the financial support from the Goldman Sachs and Citi Foundations. We thank our respective institutions and the Wharton Financial Institutions Center for financial support. We would like to thank the Wharton-ISB Joint Research Initiative in India for funding. We are responsible for any remaining errors in the chapter.

Allen et al. 2005 examine three sectors of the Chinese economy: (1) The *state sector* includes all companies such that the Government has ultimate control (state-owned enterprises, or SOEs); (2) the *listed sector* includes all firms that are listed on an exchange and are publicly traded; and, (3) the *private sector* includes all the other firms with various types of private and local Government ownership.[1] They find that the law-finance-growth nexus established by the existing literature works well for the state and listed sectors: With poor legal protection of minority and outside investors, (standard) external markets are weak, and the growth of these firms is slow or negative. However, the size, growth, and importance of these two sectors in the economy are dominated by those of the private sector. In spite of relatively poorer applicable legal protection and standard financing channels, the private sector has been growing much faster than the others and has been contributing to most of the economy's growth. Therefore, there exist effective, alternative financing channels and corporate governance mechanisms, such as those based on reputation and relationships, to support the growth of the private sector.

Using measures from the existing literature, we characterize China's law and institutions, including investor protection systems, corporate governance, accounting standards, and quality of government. China's financial system is dominated by a large but underdeveloped banking system that is mainly controlled by the four largest state-owned banks. Its relatively newly established Shanghai Stock Exchange (SHSE) and ShenZhen Stock Exchange (SZSE) have been growing very fast since their inception in 1990, but their scale and importance are still not comparable to other channels of financing, in particular the banking sector, for the entire economy.

We next examine separately financing channels, corporate governance, and the growth of firms in each of the three sectors. The state sector has been shrinking with the ongoing privatization process, which includes firms going public. Allen et al. notes that equity ownership is concentrated within the state for firms converted from the state sector, and founders' families for nonstate firms (e.g. Claessens et al. 2000; 2002).

---

[1] The private sector includes the following types of firms: (1) collectively and jointly-owned companies, where joint ownership among local Government, communities, and institutions is forged; and, (2) privately-owned companies (but not publicly listed and traded), where controlling owners can be Chinese citizens, investors (or companies) from Taiwan or Hong Kong, or foreign investors (or companies).

Law, Institutions, and Finance

Second, the standard corporate governance mechanisms are weak and ineffective in the listed sector. Finally, both the dividend ratio and firm value of Chinese firms are low compared to similar firms operating in countries with stronger investor protection, consistent with predictions by La Porta et al.

Allen et al. find more interesting results for the private sector. First, the two most important financing channels for these firms during their start-up and subsequent periods are financial intermediaries, including state-owned banks and private credit agencies, and founders' friends and families. Firms have outstanding loans from multiple financial intermediaries, with most of the loans secured by fixed assets or third party guarantees. During a firm's growth period, funds from 'ethnic Chinese' investors (from Hong Kong, Taiwan, and other countries) and trade credits from business partners are also important sources. When asked about the prospect of going public, founders and executives list 'access to large scale of funding' and 'reputation increase' as the most important benefits, and 'disclosure of valuable information to competitors and outsiders' and 'large amount of fees paid' as the most critical disadvantages of going public.

Second, despite the almost nonexistence of formal governance mechanisms, alternative mechanisms have been remarkably effective in the private sector. Perhaps the most important of these is the role of reputation and relationships (Greif 1989; 1993). Without a dominant religion, the most important force shaping China's social values and institutions is the widely held set of beliefs related to Confucius; these beliefs define family and social orders and trust, and are different from western beliefs on the rule of law. Another important mechanism that drives good management and corporate governance is competition. Given the environment of low survivorship during early stages of a firm's development, firms have a strong incentive to gain a comparative advantage. The third important mechanism is the role of local Governments. Within the regions that witnessed the most successful economic growth and improvement in living standards, properly motivated Government officials support and participate in the growth of private sector firms.

India provides a very different setting. Allen et al. (2006) notes that with its English common-law origin, legal protection of investors by the law in India is one of the strongest in the world. For example, India had a perfect score on the Creditor Rights index (4 out

127

of 4),[2] and has a score of five out of six on the Anti-Director Rights index, the highest among more than 100 countries studied in Djankov et al. (2007a). Moreover, India has had a British-style judicial system and a democratic Government for a long time. However, all of our evidence, including aggregate evidence and firm-level evidence from both the Prowess sample and our surveys of the SME sector, uniformly suggests a very different reality. Based on several widely used aggregate measures, the *effective* level of investor protection and the quality of legal institutions in India is far below the average for English-origin countries, though slightly higher than the French-origin countries and other emerging economies.[3] The reasons for the wide gap between investor protection on paper and in practice include a slow and inefficient legal system and corruption within Government in India. Indian firms have much lower dividend payout and valuation (as measured by market-to-book ratios) than similar firms operating in countries with strong investor protection, but are closer to the firms in countries with weak protection judging by the findings in La Porta et al. (2000; 2002b). Equity ownership is highly concentrated within the founder's family and/or the controlling shareholder, more so than even firms in other Asian countries (e.g. Claessens et al. 2000; 2002). Further, smaller firms in India exhibit symptoms of a low investor protection regime (e.g. ownership concentration, dividend ratio, and valuation) more than the large firms. Consistent with these findings, our surveys indicate that the small firms, regardless of age and industry, rely little on the legal system. Over 80 percent of the respondent firms in our survey preferred not to seek legal recourse in any situation, including customer defaults, breaches of contract, or commercial disputes. On the other hand, non-legal sanctions in various forms, such as loss of reputation or future business opportunities or even fear of personal safety, are far more effective deterrents against contract violations and non-payment of dues than legal recourses, and are employed widely. Thus our firm-level evidence for India indicates that strong legal protection is not a necessary condition for conducting business as long as there exist effective, non-legal 'institutional' substitutes.

---

[2] This score was revised from 4/4 in La Porta et al. (1998), based on the Company's Act (1956), to 2/4 in Djankov et al. (2007b), based on the Sick Industrial Companies Act (1985).

[3] Other studies also document this. For example, Djankov et al. (2007a) construct the anti-self-dealing index (control of corporate insiders) for more than 100 countries. India's score of 0.55 (out of 1) is lower than the average (0.67) of English common-law countries.

Second, Allen et al. find that formal financing channels based on stock markets and banks are not essential for corporate operations and investments as long as alternative financing sources pick up the financing slack. In spite of poor investor protection in practice, the Indian economy has grown faster than most others since the early 1990s. Further, firm level evidence indicates that during 1996–2005 (a sufficiently long period for which reliable data is available) the average Indian firm grew at an impressive 10.9 percent compound annual rate. Moreover, as in China, within India too the SME firms grow faster, though they depend little on formal legal channels and use far less formal finance than their larger counterparts. As Allen et al. point out, during 1996–2005, Indian SME firms recorded statistically significantly higher growth rates in sales as well as assets than the larger firms. This finding holds after controlling for all relevant factors (such as age, industry, and assets size in initial years) and correcting for possible survivorship biases due to higher death rates among the smaller firms. It also appears to hold for other sample periods and sizes.

The rest of the chapter is organized as follows. Sections 5.2 and 5.3 present aggregate economy-level evidence on law, finance, and institutions in China and India respectively and other countries and examines the size of formal (external) financing in relation to the level of investor protection and quality of legal institutions. Sections 5.4 and 5.5 focus on firm level evidence in the two countries, but go farther and analyze the magnitude and role of alternative financing sources in corporate investments and growth. Using evidence from our firm level surveys Sections 5.6 and 5.7 present our results—on China and India respectively—that the surveyed firms effectively substitute non-legal mechanisms and alternative financing sources for ineffective legal institutions and inaccessible formal financing sources such as banks. Section 5.8 presents our conclusions.

5.2 Evidence on China's legal and financial systems and growth in the three sectors

In this section we first provide an assessment of China's entire economy, and then of the status of its legal and financial systems. We next compare China to the countries studied in the existing literature, namely, the La Porta et al. sample and the Levine sample. Finally, we compare the growth in the state, listed, and private sectors of China.

Status of China's economy

In July 2007, China had an estimated population of 1.32 billion people, the largest of any country. Table 5.1 Panel A underlines China's status as one of the most important countries in the world. China's GDP ranked fourth in the world using market exchange rates. However, if we use PPP to recalculate GDPs, China's economy is the second largest behind only the US. It may be more useful to compare China's economic growth with other major economies, since China's rapid growth only started in 1979.[4] In terms of PPP-adjusted GDP figures in 2007, China is more than twice the size of India, the second largest emerging economy. In terms of the annual growth rate of PPP-adjusted GDPs during 1990 to 2007, China has been growing much faster than Vietnam, which has the second highest growth rate during the same period. Moreover, China's population growth during the same period was slow, and its per capita PPP-growth rate is also the highest among major economies.

Recently, the PPP estimates produced by the World Bank have undergone a significant revision that reduces the GDP (PPP) estimates of China and India (along with those for many other countries) substantially—to less than a half of the previous estimates. Table 5.1 Panel B provides a comparison of the various PPP measures used by different agencies. Regardless of the change, China's relative size as compared to India and its number 2 ranking the largest economies in the world remain unchanged. India's position slips from third to fifth among the largest economies if one considers the new World Bank figures. The wide range of estimates given by the IMF, World Bank, and CIA underlines how imperfect is the methodology of providing PPP figures.

Legal system

Allen et al. first examine measures of China's legal system and compare them to the average measures of the forty-nine countries studied in La Porta et al. (1998). In terms of overall creditor rights (Table 5.2), China falls in between the English-origin countries that have the highest measures of protection, and French-origin countries that have the poorest protection. China's shareholder protection shows a similar pattern. The

---

[4] Measured by simple exchange rates, China's GDP in 1980 was US$180.6 billion while in 1990 it reached US$368 billion. Also note that the exchange rate between the RMB and US$ changed from US$1 = 4.25 yuan to 8.28 yuan in 1992, which introduced a significant downward bias for China's GDP figure in 1992. This is why using PPP-adjusted figures to measure GDP and its growth is more appropriate.

Law, Institutions, and Finance

Table 5.1. Panel A: The Largest 20 Economies in the World: GDP and Growth

Rank	GDP in 2007 (simple exchange rates) Country/region	US$ billion	GDP in 2007 (PPP) Country/region	Int'l $ billion	GDP growth: 1990–2007 (constant prices) Country/region	Annual growth	Per capita GDP growth: 1990–2007* (constant prices) Country/region	Annual growth
1	US	13,794	US	13,543	China	10.3%	China	9.3%
2	Japan	4,346	China	11,606	Vietnam	7.6%	Vietnam	6.0%
3	Germany	3,259	**India**	**4,727**	**India**	**6.3%**	Korea	4.7%
4	China	3,249	Japan	4,346	Malaysia	6.2%	Taiwan	4.5%
5	UK	2,756	Germany	2,714	Chile	5.6%	**India**	**4.4%**
6	France	2,515	UK	2,271	Korea	5.5%	Chile	4.2%
7	Italy	2,068	France	2,040	Taiwan	5.3%	Poland	3.9%
8	Spain	1,415	Brazil	2,014	Bangladesh	5.2%	Sri Lanka	3.8%
9	Canada	1,406	Russia	1,909	Sri Lanka	5.0%	Malaysia	3.7%
10	Brazil	1,295	Italy	1,888	Yemen, R.	5.0%	Thailand	3.6%
11	Russia	1,224	Spain	1,310	Thailand	4.6%	Bangladesh	3.1%
12	**India**	**1,090**	Korea	1,250	Pakistan	4.6%	Indonesia	3.0%
13	Korea	950	Mexico	1,250	Egypt	4.5%	Peru	2.9%
14	Australia	890	Canada	1,217	Iran	4.5%	Iran	2.9%
15	Mexico	886	Indonesia	1,054	Peru	4.4%	Argentina	2.8%
16	Netherlands	755	Taiwan	750	Indonesia	4.4%	Egypt	2.3%
17	Turkey	482	Australia	731	Turkey	4.0%	Turkey	2.3%
18	Belgium	443	Turkey	723	Argentina	4.0%	Pakistan	2.3%
19	Sweden	432	Argentina	691	Poland	3.9%	Spain	2.2%
20	Switzerland	414	S. Africa	664	Philippines	3.8%	Australia	2.2%

Notes: * Countries with population less than 20 million or GDP less than US$20 billion are excluded from this ranking.
Source: Constructed using data from IMF World Economic Outlook Database 2008.

overall evidence thus suggests that the majority of La Porta et al. sample countries have better creditor and shareholder protection than China.

The table compares legal systems and institutions related to investor protection in India, La Porta et al. country groups (sorted by legal origins) and other large emerging economies. All the emerging economies included in this table are from Table 1 for which information was available. Notation (E), (F), or (G) against a country indicates that the said country belongs to English, French, or German legal origin groups. Creditor rights scores are from Djankov et al. (2007b) and Anti-director rights scores are from Djankov et al. (2007a). Corruption Perception Index values (for 2006) from Transparency International (http://www.transparency.org/policy_research/surveys_indices/cpi/2006), are based on the surveys of firms on whether corruption is prevalent when conducting business in each country and ranges from 0 to 10, with 0 meaning most corrupt and 10 meaning least corrupt. Legal Formalism

131

Table 5.1. Panel B: Comparison of 2007 PPP GDP from different statistical sources

	IMF		World Bank		CIA (US)	
Rank	Country	GDP(PPP) $ billion	Country	GDP(PPP) $ billion	Country	GDP(PPP) $ billion
1	US	13,543	US	12,376	US	13,860
2	China	11,606	China	5,333	China	7,043
3	India	4,727	Japan	3,870	Japan	4,305
4	Japan	4,346	Germany	2,514	India	2,965
5	Germany	2,714	India	2,341	Germany	2,833
6	UK	2,270	UK	1,901	UK	2,147
7	France	2,040	France	1,862	Russian	2,076
8	Brazil	2,014	Russian	1,697	France	2,067
9	Russian	1,909	Italy	1,626	Brazil	1,838
10	Italy	1,888	Brazil	1,585	Italy	1,800
11	Spain	1,310	Spain	1,183	Spain	1,362
12	S. Korea	1,250	Mexico	1,175	Mexico	1,353
13	Mexico	1,250	Canada	1,133	Canada	1,274
14	Canada	1,217	S. Korea	1,027	S. Korea	1,206
15	Indonesia	1,054	Iran	734	Iran	852
16	Taiwan	750	Indonesia	707	Indonesia	845
17	Australia	731	Australia	671	Australia	766
18	Turkey	723	Taiwan	590	Taiwan	690
19	Argentina	691	Netherlands	566	Turkey	667
20	S. Africa	664	Turkey	561	Netherlands	638

Sources: Constructed using data from IMF World Economic Outlook Database 2008, World Bank World Development Indicator 2008, CIA World Fact Book 2008.

Index, from Djankov et al. (2003), measures substantive and procedural statutory intervention in judicial cases at lower-level civil trial courts; the index ranges from 0 to 7, where a higher score means greater formalism or a higher level of intervention in the judicial process. Legality index, from Berkowitz et al. (2003), uses five legality proxies (each range from 0 to 10) from La Porta et al. (1997a, 1998) and principal components analysis to aggregate the individual legality proxies into a single legality index; the index ranges from 0 to 21 with a higher score meaning a better legal environment. Disclosure Requirement index, from La Porta et al. (2006), equals the arithmetic mean of scores (0 or 1; 1 means disclosure required) on six dimensions of disclosure requirements: (1) Prospect; (2) Compensation; (3) Shareholders; (4) Inside Ownership; (5) Contracts Irregular; (6) and Transactions; the overall index ranges from 0 to 1, with 0 meaning no disclosure requirement for anything, and 1 meaning disclosure of everything. Earnings Management index, from Leuz et al. (2003), is the average rank across four measures of earnings management; a higher score implies *more* earnings management.

Table 5.2. Comparing Legal Systems and Institutions

	Creditor rights	Anti-Director rights	Corruption perception index	Legal Formalism index	Legality index	Disclosure requirement	Earnings management score
China	**2**	**1**	**3.3**	**3.4**	**n/a**	**n/a**	**n/a**
India (E)	**2**	**5**	**3.3**	**3.51**	**11.35**	**0.92**	**19.1**
English-origin Ave.	2.28	4.19	5.33	3.02	15.56	0.78	11.69
French-origin Ave.	1.31	2.91	4.39	4.38	13.11	0.45	19.27
German-origin Ave.	2.33	3.04	5.58	3.57	15.53	0.6	23.6
Nordic-origin Ave.	1.75	3.8	9.34	3.32	16.42	0.56	10.15
Sample Ave.	1.8[a]	3.37[b]	5.24	3.58[c]	14.98	0.60[d]	16

Panel B Other Large Emerging Markets (EMs)

Argentina (F)	1	2	2.9	5.49	10.31	0.5	n/a
Brazil (F)	1	5	3.3	3.83	11.43	0.25	n/a
Egypt (F)	2	3	3.3	3.6	10.14	0.5	n/a
Indonesia (F)	2	4	2.4	3.88	8.37	0.5	18.3
Korea (South)(G)	3	4.5	5.1	3.33	12.24	0.75	26.8
Malaysia (E)	3	5	5	3.21	13.82	0.92	14.8
Mexico (F)	0	3	3.3	4.82	10.79	0.58	n/a
Pakistan (E)	1	4	2.2	3.74	8.27	0.58	17.8
Peru (F)	0	3.5	3.3	5.42	9.13	0.33	n/a
Philippines (F)	1	4	2.5	5	7.91	0.83	8.8
S. Africa (E)	3	5	4.6	3.68	11.95	0.83	5.6
Sri Lanka (E)	2	4	3.1	3.89	9.68	0.75	n/a
Taiwan (G)	2	3	5.9	3.04	14.26	0.75	22.5
Thailand (E)	2	4	3.6	4.25	10.7	0.92	18.3
Turkey (F)	2	3	3.8	3.49	9.88	0.5	n/a
Average of EMs	1.67	3.80	3.62	4.04	10.59	0.63	16.61

Notes: [a] Djankov et al. (2007b) average; [b] Djankov et al. (2007a) average; [c] Djankov et al. (2003) average; [d] La Porva et al. (2006) average.

They also compare China's legal system to those of other emerging countries, similar to the growth comparison above. China's corruption index is the fifth worst among the fifteen developing countries. In order to have an effective law enforcement system, a country must have an independent and efficient judicial system with a sufficient supply of qualified legal professionals. First, Djankov et al. (2003) compare the efficiency and formalism of the judicial system across 109 countries including China. The results are based on how two specific types of disputes, the eviction of a tenant and collection of a bounced check, are resolved in a country's judicial system. Since both types of disputes are rare events in China, as the real estate market (including the rental market) and the use of personal checks are underdeveloped and limited to a few large cities, their results are not very meaningful for China.

On the other hand, the Ministry of Justice of China stated that there were 110,000 lawyers and 9,000 law firms as of 2002, while Orts (2001) estimates that there are 150,000 lawyers in China, roughly the same number of licensed attorneys as in the state of California. Lawyers represent only 10 to 25 percent of all clients in civil and business cases, and even in criminal prosecutions, lawyers represent defendants in only half of the cases. Among the approximately five million business enterprises in China, only 4 percent of them currently have regular legal advisers. Moreover, only one-fifth of all lawyers in China have law degrees, and even a lower fraction of judges have formally studied law at a university or college. Needless to say, it will be a long time before China has a strong legal labor force.

Another reason that many new laws are not effectively enforced in China is the intrinsic conflict of interest between 'fair play' in practicing law and the monopoly power of the single ruling party, especially in cases in which Government officials or their affiliates are involved. Consistent with this argument, La Porta et al. (2004) find that China ranks among the worst countries in terms of political freedom as well as the protection of property rights. They also find a positive correlation between political freedom (constitutional rules) and measures of economic freedom (property rights, procedures of start-up firm) across countries, and that judicial independence accounts for the positive effect of common-law legal origin in economic freedom. However, the fact that China scores extremely poorly on both political and economic freedoms and yet enjoyed one of the fastest economic growth rates casts doubt on the importance of political freedom and economic freedom as measured in La Porta et al. (2004).

Law, Institutions, and Finance

Finally, we comment on the current status of China's accounting system. The reform started in 1992, with the enactment of regulations governing enterprises with foreign investment. Since then, the Accounting Standards for Business Enterprises of China, together with the thirteen industry regulation board, have been trying to move China's accounting practice in the listed sector towards the IAS (International Accounting Standards). However, the most glaring problem in China's accounting system is the lack of independent, professional auditors, similar to the situation for legal professionals. This implies that the proposed IAS-based standards may be counterproductive within China's current infrastructure: With few auditors understanding and enforcing the new standards, and given the lack of an effective judicial system, embezzlement of company assets and other forms of fraud may occur more frequently under IAS-based standards, as compared to an alternative system with a much simpler set of accounting standards (e.g. Xiang 1998).

Financial system

We first examine China's financial system at the aggregate level, including both its financial markets and banking system. We then examine its stock exchanges in more detail and briefly discuss its venture capital markets. Finally, we examine problems in the banking sector.

In Table 5.3 we compare China's financial system to those of the La Porta et al.-sample countries (1997a; 1998), using measures from Levine (2002). We first compare the size of a country's equity markets and banks relative to that country's GDP. China's stock markets, which have been growing very rapidly since 1990, are smaller than those of most of the other sample countries, both in terms of market capitalization and the total value traded as a fraction of GDP. Notice that 'total value traded' is a better measure than 'market capitalization' because the latter includes nontradable shares, while the former measures the fraction of total market capitalization traded in the markets, or the 'floating supply' of the market.

The table compares various aspects of financial markets and banking sector of the Indian financial system with those of other emerging countries and La Porta et al. country groups (sorted by legal origins). All the measures are taken from Levine (2002) or calculated from the World Bank Financial Database using the definitions in Levine (2002). We use 2005 figures for all countries.

We compare the development of the entire financial system ('Financial development'), including both banks and markets. Given all other

135

Table 5.3. Comparing financial systems: Banks and markets

Measures	Size of banks and markets					Structure indices: markets vs. banks**					Financial development*** (banking and market sectors)			
	Bank credit/ GDP	Bank Over -head cost/ bank assets	Value traded/ GDP	Market cap./ GDP	Structure activity	Structure size	Structure efficiency	Structure regulatory	Finance activity	Finance size	Finance efficiency
Panel A: China, India and La Porta et al. Country Groups											
China	8	0.01	0.26	0.32	−0.16	0.03	−5.87	16	−2.51	−2.31	3.19
India	0.37	0.02	0.56	0.6	0.43	0.49	−4.44	10	−1.57	−1.51	3.3
English origin*	0.66	0.04	1.53	1.31	0.87	0.76	−3.05	2.26	−0.21	−0.14	3.71
French origin*	0.77	0.04	0.6	0.66	−0.43	−0.05	−4.02	8.5	−1.45	−1.08	2.5
German origin*	1.06	0.02	1.05	0.82	−0.16	−0.37	−4.01	9.65	−0.08	−0.27	3.9
Nordic origin*	1.05	0.02	0.99	0.85	−0.07	−0.2	−3.86	7.74	−0.08	−0.21	3.71
Sample Ave.	0.78	0.03	1.17	1.02	0.28	0.28	−3.55	8.53	−0.5	−0.5	3.48
Panel B other large emerging markets (EMs)											
Argentina (F)	0.1	0.08	0.09	0.3	−0.12	1.07	−4.95	7	−4.7	−3.51	0.13
Brazil (F)	0.29	0.08	0.19	0.51	−0.4	0.56	−4.2	10	−2.88	−1.91	0.93
Egypt (F)	0.45	0.02	0.28	0.66	−0.45	0.39	−5.13	13	−2.06	−1.22	2.61
Indonesia (F)	0.22	0.03	0.15	0.27	−0.4	0.22	−5.48	n/a	−3.45	−2.83	1.63
Korea (G)	n/a	0.02	1.53	0.73	n/a	n/a	−3.73	n/a	n/a	n/a	4.57
Malaysia (E)	1.03	0.01	0.38	1.44	−0.99	0.33	−5.22	10	−0.93	0.39	3.3
Mexico (F)	0.15	n/a	0.07	0.27	−0.75	0.61	n/a	12	−4.6	−3.24	n/a
Pakistan (E)	0.27	0.02	1.27	0.34	1.56	0.24	−3.58	10	−1.08	−2.4	4.06
Peru (F)	0.18	0.07	0.03	0.36	−1.93	0.7	−6.35	8	−5.39	−2.75	−0.98
Philippines (F)	0.26	0.06	0.07	0.35	−1.32	0.29	−5.51	7	−3.98	−2.37	0.21
S. Africa (E)	0.8	0.05	0.84	2.14	0.04	0.98	−3.12	8	−0.4	0.54	2.76
Sri Lanka (E)	0.3	0.04	0.05	0.2	−1.81	−0.4	−6.22	7	−4.24	−2.82	0.16
Taiwan (G)	n/a	0.02	1.79	1.35	n/a	n/a	−3.62	12	n/a	n/a	4.78
Thailand (E)	0.73	0.02	0.51	0.68	−0.37	−0.07	−4.72	9	−0.99	−0.7	3.36
Turkey (F)	0.21	0.06	0.55	0.36	0.96	0.52	−3.4	12	−2.14	−2.57	2.21
Ave. for EMs	0.38	0.04	0.52	0.66	−0.46	0.42	−4.66	9.62	−2.83	−1.95	2.12

Notes: * The numerical results for countries of each legal origin group is calculated based on a value- (GDP of each country) weighted approach.

** Structure indices measure whether a country's financial system is market or bank dominated; the higher the measure, the more the system is dominated by markets. Specifically, 'structure activity' is equal to log(value traded/bank credit) and measures size of bank credit relative to trading volume of markets; 'structure size' is equal to log(market cap/bank credit) and measures the size of markets relative to banks; 'structure efficiency' is equal to log(market cap ratio × overhead cost ratio) and measures the relative efficiency of markets vs. banks; finally, 'structure regulatory' is the sum of the four categories in regulatory restriction, or the degree to which commercial banks are allowed to engage in security, firm operation, insurance, and real estate: 1-unrestricted; 2-permit to conduct through subsidiary; 3-full range not permitted in subsidiaries; and 4-strictly prohibited.

*** Financial development variables measure the entire financial system (banking and market sectors combined), and the higher the measure, the larger or more efficient the financial system is. Specifically, 'finance activity' is equal to log (total value traded ratio × private credit ratio), 'finance size' is equal to log (market cap ratio × bank private credit ratio), and 'finance efficiency' is equal to log (total value traded ratio/bank overhead cost).

Law, Institutions, and Finance

countries' measures are based on private bank credit only, if we only include China's private bank credit, we find that China's overall financial market size ('Finance activity' and 'Finance size') is smaller than the La Porta et al.-sample average level, and each legal-origin group average. In terms of the efficiency of the financial system, China's measure is below all sub-samples of La Porta et al. countries. Based on the above evidence, we can conclude that China's financial system is dominated by a large but inefficient banking sector.

Financial markets. China's Shanghai Stock Exchange, including non-tradable shares, rank fourteenth among the largest stock exchanges in the world at the end of 2006. In addition, the Hong Kong Stock Exchange (HKSE), where selected firms from Mainland China can now be listed and traded, is ranked sixth in the world.

Though China's stock markets have grown fast, these markets are not efficient in that prices and investor behavior do not reflect fundamental values of listed firms.[5] In Table 5.4, 'Concentration' measures the fraction of total turnover of the market in 2006 that is due to the trading and turnover of companies within the largest market capitalization quintile. Large-cap stocks in China are not frequently traded and the concentration ratio, 31 percent, is much lower than in any other major stock exchange in the world except for NYSE. On the other hand, medium- and small-cap stocks are traded extremely frequently in China, as shown by the high 'Turnover Velocity', defined as the total turnover for the year expressed as a percentage of total market cap. China's velocity of 153 percent is even higher than that of NYSE (but lower than NASDAQ).[6]

Consistent with our findings, Morck et al. (2000) find that stock prices are more synchronous in emerging countries, including China, than in developed countries. They contribute this phenomenon to poor minority investor protection and imperfect regulation of markets in emerging markets. One example is the restriction on short sales. Bris et al. (2003) find

---

[5] There is a political economy view, held by some, that the Chinese Government is not particularly concerned with efficiency of financial markets as long as they serve as an easy way of raising funds for the state sector enterprises. While perhaps not wholly without truth, this may be overly simplistic. The inefficiency of the Chinese stock market is due to many reasons: lack of regulation; imbalance between demand and supply; segmentation of shares (A shares, which is floating, and G shares, which was previously not floating). With a relatively short history of equity culture and that too in a high growth period, investors at times view stocks as 'gamble' instruments, dissociated from the underlying fundamental value. Often public information is not sufficient or credible enough to estimate the true fundamental value.

[6] The actual turnover velocity of NASDAQ should be half of the reported figure, 319.5%. This is because unlike NYSE and most other exchanges around the world, NASDAQ dealers report both the buy and sell trades separately, which leads to double counting in the calculation of velocity. See Atkins and Dyl (1997) for more details.

Franklin Allen et al.

Table 5.4. A comparison of the largest stock markets in the world (2006)

Rank	Stock Exchange	Total Market Cap (US$ million)	Concentration (%)	Turnover Velocity (%)
1	NYSE Group	15421167.9	26.6	134.3
2	Tokyo SE	4,614,068.8	58	125.8
3	Nasdaq	3,865,003.6	82.1	269.9
4	London SE	3,794,310.3	84.8	124.8
5	Euronext	3,708,150.1	57	116.4
6	Hong Kong Exchanges	1,714,953.3	68.4	62.1
7	TSX Group	1,700,708.1	67.5	76.4
8	Deutsche Börse	1,637,609.8	77.1	173.7
9	BME Spanish Exchanges	1,322,915.3	—	167
10	Swiss Exchange	1,212,308.4	74.1	130.2
11	OMX	1,122,705.0	79.1	134.5
12	Australian SE	1,095,858.0	—	88.4
13	Borsa Italiana	1,026,504.2	65.6	162.9
14	Shanghai SE	917,507.5	31.5	153.8
15	Korea Exchange	834,404.3	57.6	171.4
16	**Bombay SE**	**818,878.6**	**75.2**	**31.9**
17	**National Stock Exchange India**	**774,115.6**	**68.6**	**67.8**
18	JSE	711,232.3	66.5	48.9
19	Sao Paulo SE	710,247.4	54.6	45.5
20	Taiwan SE Corp.	594,659.4	45.3	141.7
21	Singapore Exchange	384,286.4	41.8	58.2
22	Mexican Exchange	348,345.1	61.7	29.6

Notes: Constructed using data from http//:www.world-exchanges.org, the web site of the international organization of stock exchanges. Concentration is the fraction of total turnover of an exchange within a year coming from the turnover of the companies with the largest market cap (top 5%). Turnover velocity is the total turnover for the year expressed as a percentage of the total market capitalization.

that limiting short-sales contributes to the high co-movement of stock prices, but does not tend to increase the probability of a market crash, as commonly feared by Governments in emerging countries.

The inefficiencies in the Chinese stock markets can be attributed to poor and ineffective regulation. Based on a study of securities laws with the focus on the public issuance of new equity in forty-nine countries (China not included), La Porta et al. (2006) find that private enforcement of laws through disclosure and liability rules is superior to strong regulation by the Government in promoting stock market development. Given China's poor disclosure rules, accounting standards, and judicial systems, the La Porta et al. (2003) result can be used to explain the status of China's stock markets. To improve the quality of Government regulation, Glaeser et al. (2001) argue that regulators must be properly motivated. The concentration and turnover velocity of China's markets (Table 5.4) were actually

Law, Institutions, and Finance

even higher in the late 1990s, and the improvement is in part due to advances in the quality of regulation.

Finally, we briefly discuss China's venture capital markets, which should be regarded as part of the financial markets rather than the intermediation sector (e.g. Allen and Gale 2000a). It is often argued that one of the reasons the US has been so successful in developing new industries in recent years is the existence of a strong venture capital sector (e.g. Kortum and Lerner 2000). Consistent with our previous findings, China's venture capital industry, since its inception in the 1980s, is underdeveloped and its role in supporting the growth of young firms is very limited. Moreover, based on interviews conducted with thirty-six venture capitalists in twenty-four venture companies, Bruton and Ahlstrom (2002) find that the limited formal rules and regulations are often ineffective, while alternative mechanisms based on reputation and relationship are the norm in all stages and phases of the industry.

In summary, the overall evidence on the comparison of external markets for China and other countries' is consistent with La Porta et al. (1997a; 1998) predictions: With an underdeveloped legal system, the fact that China has small external markets comes as no surprise. Figure 5.2 compares China's legal system and external financial markets to those of La Porta et al. countries. The horizontal axis measures overall investor protection in each country, while the vertical axis measures the (relative) size and efficiency of that country's external markets.[7] Countries with English common-law systems (French civil-law systems) lie in the top-right region (bottom-left region) of the graph, while China is placed close to the bottom-left corner of the graph.

Banking sector. China's banking sector is dominated by four large and inefficient state-owned banks. La Porta et al. (2002a) show that the Government owns 99.45 percent of the ten largest commercial banks in China in 1995 (100% in 1970); this ownership level is one of the highest in their sample of ninety-two countries. Moreover, the La Porta et al. result on the negative relation between Government ownership of banks and the growth of a country's economy seems to apply to China's state sector and the status quo of its banking sector. However, high Government ownership has not slowed down the growth of the private sector.

---

[7] Following La Porta et al., the score on the horizontal axis is the sum of (overall) creditor rights, shareholder rights, rule of law, and Government corruption. The score of the vertical axis indicates the distance of a country's overall external markets score (external cap/GNP, domestic firms/Pop, IPOs/Pop, Debt/GNP, and Log GNP) to the mean of all countries, with a positive (negative) figure indicating that this country's overall score is higher (lower) than the mean.

Franklin Allen et al.

Table 5.5a. A comparison of nonperforming loans of banking systems

	1997	1998	1999	2000	2001	2002
China	n/a	**2.0 (2.2)**	**9.5 (10.6)**	**18.9 (24.9)**	**16.9 (22.7)**	**12.6 (15.2)**
Hong Kong	1.3 (3.0)	4.3 (10.2)	6.3 (13.9)	5.2 (12.6)	4.9 (12.9)	3.7 (9.6)
India	n/a	7.8 (1.6)	7.0 (1.6)	6.6 (1.6)	4.6 (1.7)	2.2 (0.8)
Indonesia	0.3 (0.2)	11.8 (4.6)	8.1 (2.0)	13.6 (3.2)	9.9 (2.2)	4.5 (0.9)
Japan	2.7 (5.4)	5.1 (10.8)	5.3 (10.9)	5.8 (11.5)	9.2 (15.3)	7.4 (12.8)
South Korea	2.9 (5.1)	4.8 (6.3)	12.9 (12.9)	8.0 (8.6)	3.4 (3.4)	2.5 (2.6)
Taiwan	2.4 (3.2)	3.0 (3.9)	4.0 (5.7)	5.2 (7.6)	6.2 (9.4)	4.1 (5.2)

Note: NPL is measured as percent of total loans made, and as percent of GDP (numbers in brackets). Both the loan and NPL are the aggregate of all banks in a country.
Source: Constructed using data from the Asian Banker data center 2003, http://www.theasianbanker.com.

The most glaring problem for China's banking sector is the amount of nonperforming loans (NPLs hereafter) within the four largest state-owned banks. A large fraction of these bad loans resulted from poor lending decisions made for SOEs, some of which were due to political or other noneconomic reasons. The additional problem is that data availability on NPLs is limited, which can be viewed as a strategic disclosure decision of the Government. However, this lack of disclosure of NPLs only fuels speculations that the problem must be severe. For example, Lardy (1998) argues that if international standards were used, the existing NPLs within the state-owned banks, as of the mid-1990s, would make these banks' total net worth negative.

Tables 5.5a and 5.5b compare NPLs and banking system profitability in China and six other major Asian economies in recent years. Information on China's NPLs first became available in 1998, but the figures in 1998 and 1999 in Table 5.5a probably significantly underestimate the actual

Table 5.5b. A cross-country comparison of banking system profitability

	1997	1998	1999	2000	2001	2002
China	**6.6 (0.2)**	**4.0 (0.2)**	**3.2 (0.18)**	**3.9 (0.2)**	**3.5 (0.2)**	**4.16 (0.2)**
Hong Kong	18.7 (1.8)	11.0 (1.0)	18.2 (1.6)	18.8 (1.6)	15.7 (1.4)	15.6 (1.4)
India	17.0 (0.9)	9.7 (0.5)	14.2 (0.7)	10.9 (0.5)	19.2 (0.9)	19.6 (1.0)
Indonesia	−3.8 (−0.3)	n/a	n/a	15.9 (0.3)	9.7 (0.6)	21.1 (1.4)
Japan	−18.6 (−0.6)	−19.2 (−0.7)	2.7 (0.1)	−0.7 (0.0)	−10.4 (−0.5)	−14.5 (−0.6)
South Korea	−12.5 (−0.6)	−80.4 (−3.0)	−34.0 (−1.5)	−7.0 (−0.3)	15.8 (0.7)	13.1 (0.6)
Taiwan	11.2 (0.9)	9.5 (0.8)	6.9 (0.6)	5.1 (0.4)	4.0 (0.3)	−5.2 (−0.4)

Note: The profitability is measured as the return on average equity (ROAE), and return on average assets (ROAA). The latter is presented in the brackets.
Source: Constructed using data from the Asian Banker data center 2003, http://www.theasianbanker.com.

size. During the period of 2000 to 2002, China had the largest amount of NPLs among the seven Asian economies, either as a fraction of total new loans made by all banks or as a fraction of GDP in a given year. This comparison includes the period during which Asian countries recovered from the 1997 financial crisis, and the period during which the Japanese banking system was disturbed by the prolonged NPL problem. Moreover, the profitability of China's banking system, measured by the return to equity or assets, is also among the lowest in the same group of economies (Table 5.5b).

In recent years the Chinese Government has taken active measures to resolve this problem. First, four state-owned asset management companies were formed with the goal of assuming these NPLs and liquidating them. Information from the auction data for these companies' shows that the cash recovery on the bad loans ranges from 8 to 60 percent. Second, state-owned banks have improved their loan structure by increasing loans made to individual lenders while being more active in risk management and monitoring of loans made to SOEs. For example, the ratio of consumer lending to total loans made for the four state-owned banks increased from 1 percent in 1998 to 10 percent in 2002.

Third, there has been a boom in the entry and growth of nonstate financial intermediaries, and this trend is expected to continue with more foreign banks entering the domestic credit markets as a result of China's entrance into the WTO. In 1997, total new loans made by the four largest state-owned banks accounted for more than 75 percent of all new loans while new loans made by 'shareholding' banks accounted for less than 7 percent. In 2001, the share of new loans made by state-owned banks dropped to 49 percent while the fraction of new loans made by shareholding banks rose to 23.5 percent. All the above facts taken together can explain why NPLs have been falling in recent years, as reflected in Table 5.5a.

Growth in the state, listed, and private sectors

Table 5.6a compares the growth of industrial output produced in the state and listed sectors vs. that of the private sector from 1996 to 2002. The private sector dominates the state and listed sectors in terms of both the size of the output, and the growth trend: Total output in 1999 is US$1,200 billion for the private sector, while it is around US$400 billion in the state and listed sectors combined; the private sector grew at an annual rate of 14.3 percent between 1996 and 2002, while the combined state

Table 5.6a. Growth rates of the state, listed, and private sectors

Growth rate (%)	Panel A: Industrial output		Panel B: Investment in fixed assets	
Year	State & listed sectors	Private sector	State & listed sectors	Private sector*
1996	15.9	17.4	10.2	17.3
1997	−0.6	18.9	9.0	6.1
1998	−6.5	10.2	17.4	9.0
1999	5.8	6.8	3.8	7.5
2000	14.0	24.2	3.5	11.4
2001	4.6	9.9	6.7	12.6
2002	6.5	12.5	7.2	16.8
Ave. Annual rate (95–02)	5.4	14.3	8.2	11.5

Notes: * includes foreign-owned companies, companies owned by investors from Taiwan and Hong Kong, and TVEs.
Sources: Constructed using data from the China Statistic Yearbooks 2000–2003.

and listed sectors grew at 5.4 percent during the same period (Panel A). In addition, the growth rates for investment in fixed assets of these sectors are comparable (Panel B), which implies that the private sector is more productive than the state and listed sectors. Finally, there has been a fundamental change among the state, listed, and private sectors in terms of their contribution to the entire economy: The state sector contributed 76 percent of China's total industrial output in 1980, but in 1996 it only contributed 28.5 percent; in 1980, individually owned firms, which are a subset of private sector firms, were negligible, but in 1996 they contributed 15.5 percent of total industrial output; the above trend

Table 5.6b. Employment in the state, listed, and private sectors

Year	1995	1996	1997	1998	1999	2000	2001	2002	95–02 annual growth rate (%)
Panel A: Number of employees (million)*									
State & listed sectors	115	116	115	94	89	85	81	77	−5.7
Private sector	221	233	233	235	240	233	245	246	1.5
Panel B: Percentage of total employees belonging to each sector (%)									
State & listed sectors	34.3	33.3	33.0	28.7	27.2	26.8	24.9	23.8	
Private sector	65.7	66.7	67.0	71.3	72.8	73.2	75.1	76.2	

Note: * indicate non-agricultural employees.
Source: China Statistic Yearbooks 2000–2003.

of the private sector replacing the state sector will continue in the near future.

In the table, Panel A displays the growth rate of 'industrial output' for the two sectors in China. The state and listed sectors includes state-owned and publicly traded companies such that the Government holds controlling shares. The private sector consists of firms with all other types of ownership structures. A few things should be made clear here: (1) We are not calling the local Government ownership (e.g. province, county) private. For most SOEs, owners are the local assets bureau or other SOEs. (2) For very small units of 'Government', e.g. a village or a town, we treat them as private, because they are like a community. (3) Local Government plays a crucial role in supporting/impeding the local private sector. For instance in the case of Wenzhou, local Government provides tax reduction, land, and special zone management to encourage enterprises.

The data source for this table is the *Chinese Statistical Yearbook* 2000, 2001, 2002, and 2003. For each sector, we also calculate the weighted-average growth rate across the selected ownership types. Panel B displays the average growth rate of 'investment in fixed assets' for the two sectors.

Table 5.6b presents the number of nonagricultural employees in the three sectors. The private sector is a much more important source for employment opportunities than the other two sectors. Over the period from 1995 to 2002, the private sector employed an average of over 70 percent of all nonagricultural workers, while the Township Village Enterprises (TVEs hereafter), also a subset of private sector firms, are by far the most important employer for workers from the rural areas. Moreover, the number of employees working in the private sector grew at a rate of 1.5 percent per year over this seven-year period, while the labor force in the state and listed sectors retracted. These patterns are particularly important for China, given its vast population and potential problem of unemployment. Botero et al. (2004) compare labor laws and social security systems across eighty-five countries including China, and find that French legal origin, socialist, and poor countries have higher levels of labor regulation than English common law and rich countries. Their evidence on China excludes the labor force in the rural areas. Given the importance of TVEs in terms of employment, this limits the application of their results to China.

5.3 Law, finance, and growth in India: Aggregate evidence

At independence from the British in 1947, India inherited one of the world's poorest economies. The manufacturing sector accounted for only one-tenth of the national product. However, the economy also had arguably the best formal financial markets in the developing world, with four functioning stock exchanges (one of them, the Bombay Stock Exchange (BSE), the oldest in Asia) and clearly defined rules governing listing, trading, and settlements; a well-developed equity culture if only among the urban rich; an old and established banking system with clear lending norms and recovery procedures; and better corporate laws than most other erstwhile colonies. The Company's Act of 1956, as well as other corporate laws and laws protecting the investors' rights, were built on this foundation.

After independence, a decades-long turn towards socialism put in place a regime and culture of licensing, protection, and widespread red tape breeding corruption. In 1990–1991 India faced a severe balance of payments crisis ushering in an era of reforms comprising deregulation, liberalization of the external sector, and partial privatization of some of the state sector enterprises. For about three decades after independence, India grew at an average rate of 3.5 percent (infamously labeled 'the Hindu rate of growth') and then accelerated to an average of about 5.6 percent since the 1980s. Table 5.1 presents information on GDP based on simple exchange rates, GDP based on purchasing power parity (PPP), growth rate in GDP and GDP per capita in constant prices during 1990–2006 for the top twenty countries in *each* category. India's annual GDP growth rate (in constant prices) of 6.1 percent during 1990–2006 was the fourth highest in the world. In 2006, India's PPP-adjusted GDP was also the fourth highest in the world.

In 2004, 52 percent of India's GDP was generated in the services sector, while manufacturing and agriculture accounted for 26 percent and 22 percent respectively. In terms of employment, however, agriculture accounted for about two-thirds of the total labor force (almost half a billion), indicating both poor productivity and widespread underemployment in the sector. Over 90 percent of the labor force works in the 'unorganized sector'.[8]

---

[8] According to the official definition, the unorganized sector comprises: (1) all the enterprises except units registered under Section 2m(i) and 2m(ii) of the Factories Act, 1948, and Bidi and Cigar Workers (condition of employment) Act, 1966; and (2) all enterprises except those run by the Government (central, state, and local bodies) or Public Sector Enterprises.

Law, Institutions, and Finance

Law, institutions, and business environment

The most striking fact about India's legal system is the difference between superior investor protection *under law* as opposed to inferior protection *in practice*. Table 5.2 compares India's scores along several dimensions of law and institutions with those of different country groups based on legal origin (La Porta et al. 1997a; 1998 and others) and sixteen other large emerging economies. These sixteen economies are the subset of the emerging economies included in Table 5.1 for which most of the required information is available (the same countries are also included in Table 5.3). Notice that each of the emerging economies, with the exception of China, is also included in one of the La Porta et al. country groups according to its legal origin (indicated by the letters E, G, and F in the bracket after country name).

As discussed earlier, with the English common-law system, India has strong protection of investors on paper. For example, the scores on both creditor rights (4 on a 0–4 scale in La Porta et al. (1998) based on the Company's Act of 1956, downgraded to 2 in Djankov et al. (2007b) based on the Sick Industrial Companies Act of 1985) and shareholder rights (5 on a 0–6 scale in Djankov et al. 2007a) are the highest of any country in the world. Note from Table 5.2 that even with a revised score of 2 on creditor's rights, India ranks higher than the average for all the country groups (1.8) as well as the average for the emerging economies (1.69) in Djankov et al. (2007b).

To compare law enforcement and the quality of institutions, we employ five sets of widely used measures in Table 5.2 as compared to those used in the original work of La Porta et al. (1998). First, corruption is a major systemic problem in many developing countries and is of particular importance for India. Studies by the World Bank (e.g. World Development Report 2005) have found that corruption was the number one constraint for firms in South Asia and that the two most corrupt public institutions identified by the respondents in India (as well as in most countries in South Asia) were the police and the judiciary. Based on Transparency International's Corruption Perception Index, India had a score of 3.3 on a 0–10 scale in 2006 (a higher score means less corruption), distinctly lower than the average for each country group in Table 5.2 and even lower than the average for the other emerging economies (3.60).

To assess the efficiency and effectiveness of the legal system for contract enforcement, we use two measures. First, by the legal formalism index (Djankov et al. 2003), a measure of the level of intervention in the country's judicial process on a 0–7 scale whereby a lower score is more desirable, India's index, 3.51, is lower than only the average French-origin country among all country groups. However, it is lower than the average for the other emerging economies (4.00). The legality index (Berkowitz et al. 2003), a composite measure of the effectiveness of a country's legal institutions, represents the weighted average of five different estimates of the quality of legal institutions and Government in the country. The index ranges from 0 to 21, with a higher score indicating a more effective legal system. Again, India's score (11.35) is appreciably lower than the average for each country group. However, India's score is marginally higher than the average for the other emerging economies (10.59).

We also compare two measures of the quality of the accounting systems. The disclosure requirements index (La Porta et al. 2006) measures the extent to which listed firms have to disclose their ownership structure, business operations, and corporate governance mechanisms to the legal authorities and the public. The index ranges from 0 to 1, with a higher score indicating more disclosure. Note that India's score of 0.92 is higher than each country group as well as all other emerging economies, suggesting that Indian firms must disclose a large amount of information under law. However, this does not imply the quality of disclosure is good. In terms of the degree of earnings management (Leuz et al. 2003), whereby a higher score means more earnings management, India's score (19.1) is much higher than the average for the country groups (16.00) as well as the average for the other emerging economies (16.61). Clearly, evaluating Indian companies based on publicly available reports is difficult.

As for the business environment in India, a recent World Bank survey found that, among the top ten obstacles to Indian businesses, the three which the surveyed firms considered to be a 'major' or 'very severe' obstacle and which also exceeded the corresponding world averages are corruption (the most important problem), availability of electricity, and labor regulations. Threat of nationalization or direct Government intervention in business is no longer a major issue in India. With rampant tax evasion, the shadow economy in India is significant. It is estimated to be about 23 percent of GDP.[9]

Since the beginning of liberalization in 1991, two major improvements have taken place in the area of creditor rights protection—the establishment of the quasi-legal Debt Recovery Tribunals that have reduced delinquency and consequently lending rates (Visaria 2005) and the passing

---

[9] This figure is 22.4% according to Schneider and Enste (2000), and 23.1% by Schneider (2002) (World Bank). Popular perception, however, would put it significantly larger, particularly given that the corresponding average figure for OECD countries is about 12%.

of the Securitization and Reconstruction of Financial Assets and Enforcement of Security Interest (SARFAESI) Act in 2002 and the subsequent Enforcement of Security Interest and Recovery of Debts Laws (Amendment) Act in 2004. These laws have paved the way for the establishment of Asset Reconstruction Companies and allow banks and financial institutions to act decisively against defaulting borrowers.

To summarize, despite strong protection provided by the law, legal protection is considerably weakened in practice by corruption within the Government and an ineffective legal system. While the need for judicial and legal reforms has long been recognized, little legislative action has actually taken place so far (Debroy 2000). Currently, the Government is trying to emulate the success of China by following the Special Economic Zone approach rather than overhauling the entire legal system.

Formal financial sector: Capital markets and banks

Table 5.3 compares India's capital markets and financial institutions (as of 2005), along several important dimensions, with those of the La Porta et al. country groups and the same sixteen emerging economies (as of 2005) included in Table 5.2.[10] Despite the long history of India's stock exchanges, and the presence of a large number of listed firms (over 10,000), the size and role of the capital markets in allocating resources have been limited in India, as in many other emerging economies. The equity markets were not an important source of funding for the nonstate sector until recently. The ratio of India's market capitalization to GDP rose from about 3.5 percent in the early 1980s to about 34 percent in 2003, but then rose sharply to 60 percent by the end of 2005. However, as shown in Table 5.3, even at this level the ratio for India is still lower than each of the La Porta et al. country groups, and considerably lower than the average for all the country groups (1.02). It is also lower than the average of the other emerging economies (0.65). The situation is very similar in terms of how active stocks are traded in the market, or total value traded in a given year over GDP.[11] The value traded/GDP ratio for India (0.56) is lower than each La Porta et al. country group and significantly lower than the average for all the groups (1.17). It is also marginally lower than the

---

[10] The figures reported in the table use definitions in Levine (2002), but are computed with 2005 numbers for all countries from the World Bank Financial Database.

[11] We estimate that 45% of the total market capitalization of listed firms is actively traded in India, based on our own calculation of free float adjustment factor of about 1,000 large firms listed on the BSE.

emerging economies average (0.62). Finally, the corporate bond market in India is meager, and is viewed as a source of concern by all observers of India's capital markets.

Table 5.3 also indicates that India's banking system has not been effective in providing capital either. The bank credit/GDP ratio for India (0.37) is far below the corresponding figure for every single La Porta et al. country group. Though the average ratio for the other emerging economies (0.32) is marginally lower than India, the leading economies in Southeast Asia, such as Malaysia and Thailand, have much higher ratios. However, the efficiency of the Indian banking sector, measured by the ratio of overhead costs over bank assets, has been superior to most other countries.

'Structure activity' and 'structure size' reported in Table 5.3 indicate whether a financial system is dominated by the capital markets or banks. India's activity and size figures are far lower than the average of English-origin countries, though higher than the average for all La Porta et al. country groups combined, suggesting that India has a more market-dominated system. However, this is mainly due to the small amount of bank credit (relative to GDP) rather than the size of the stock markets. In terms of the relative efficiency of markets vs. banks (measured by 'structure efficiency'), India's banks are more efficient than the markets (largely due to their low overhead costs). Further, the relative efficiency of the banks over markets is stronger in India than in the average of La Porta et al. country groups. Finally, in terms of the development of the financial system, including both banks and markets, India's overall financial market size (measured by 'finance activity' and 'finance size') is much smaller than the average of La Porta et al. country groups. Based on the evidence, we can conclude that India's stock markets as well the banking sector are small relative to the size of its economy, and the financial system is dominated by an efficient (low overhead cost) but significantly underutilized (in terms of providing credit) banking sector.

However, the situation has changed considerably in recent years. Since the middle of 2003 through the end of the third quarter of 2007, Indian stock prices appreciated rapidly, with the popular Sensex index of the BSE rising from about 3,000 to over 16,000 in a period of four years. In fact, as shown in Figure 5.1, the rise of the Indian equity market in this period allowed investors to earn a higher return ('buy and hold return') from investing in the Sensex index than from the S&P 500 index and other major indices in the UK and Japan, and marginally lower than the SSE index in China, during 1992–2006. Many credit the continuing reforms

Law, Institutions, and Finance

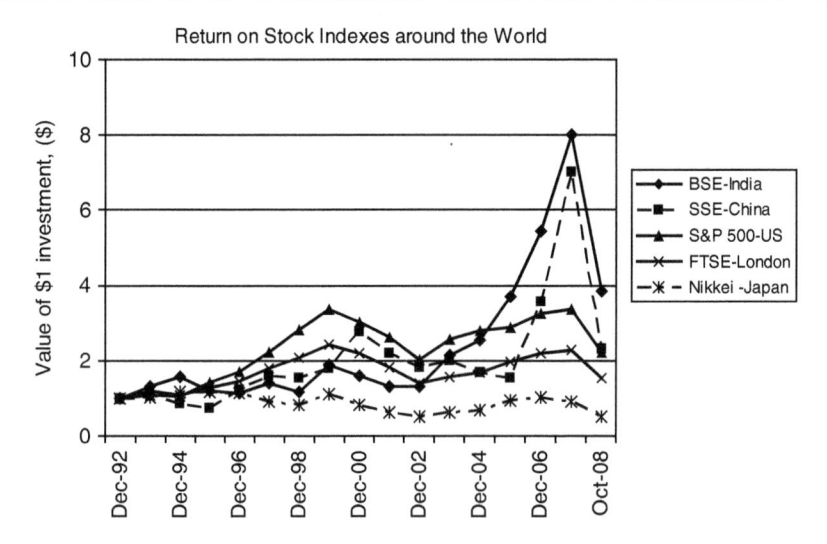

Figure 5.1. A comparison of performance of stock indexes ('buy and hold' returns during December 1992 and September 2007)

and more or less steady growth as well as increasing foreign direct and portfolio investment in the country for the recent explosion in share prices.[12] At the end of 2006, the BSE was the sixteenth largest stock market in the world in terms of market capitalization, while the National Stock Exchange (NSE) ranked seventeenth. However, trading in BSE is one of the most concentrated among the largest exchanges in the world, with the top 5 percent (in terms of market capitalization) of the listed companies accounting for over 75 percent of all trades.

Over the decades, India's banking sector has grown steadily in size (in terms of total deposits) at an average annual growth rate of 18 percent. There are about 100 commercial banks in operation with 30 of them state owned, 30 private sector banks, and the rest 40 foreign banks. Still dominated by state-owned banks (they account for over 80 percent of deposits and assets), the years since liberalization have seen the emergence of new private sector banks as well as the entry of several new foreign banks. This has resulted in a much lower concentration ratio in India than in other emerging economies (Demirgüç-Kunt and Levine 2002). Competition has clearly increased with the Herfindahl index (a measure

---

[12] According to the Reserve Bank of India's *Handbook of Indian Statistics*, both foreign direct investment and portfolio investment (mostly in stocks) have been growing fast during the past 15 years, with portfolio investment accounting for two-thirds of the total investment. The cumulative foreign investment inflows equaled 12% of GDP in 2005, as compared to only 0.03% in 1990.

Franklin Allen et al.

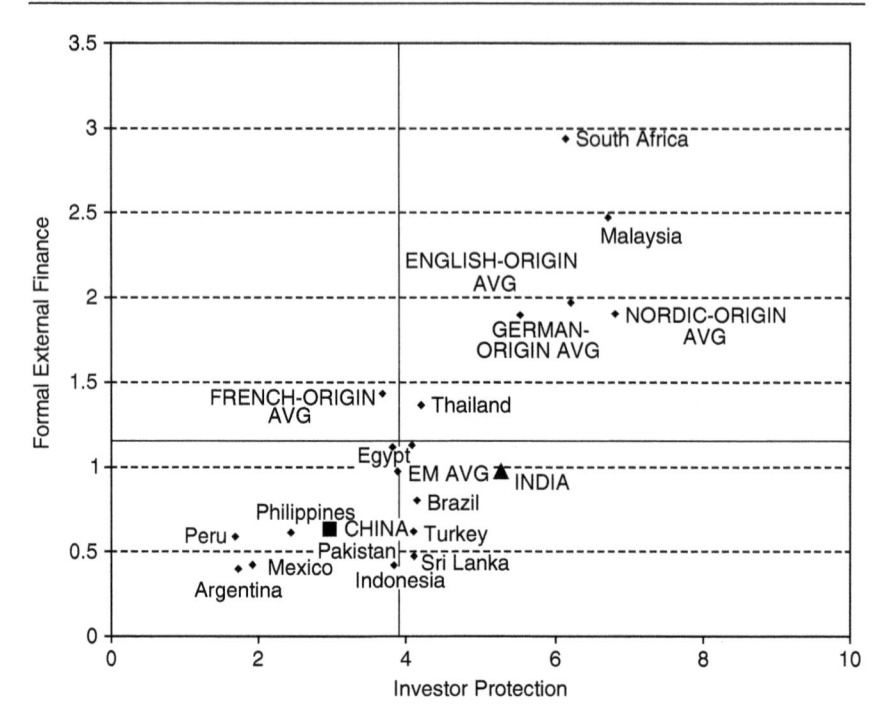

Figure 5.2. Investor protection and external financing: International comparison

Notes: The figure compares India's legal system and external financial markets to those of La Porta et al. country groups and the other emerging markets (as of 2005) as well as various legal origin country groups. The score on the horizontal axis measures overall investor protection in a country. It is the sum of creditor rights, anti-director rights, corruption perception index, and legality index *minus* the legal formalism index from Table 5.2. For China, the score on the legality index was not available. Hence, we have used the Rule of Law score from International Country Risk Guide instead. Each score is rescaled on a 0 to 10 scale before being included in the final sum. The final sum is then rescaled on a 0 to 10 scale also. The vertical axis measures the (relative) size of that country's external markets and is given by the sum of the ratios of (private) bank credit and market capitalization to GDP from Table 5.3. The solid horizontal and vertical lines represent the simple (unweighted) sample means of all the data points shown in the graph.

of concentration) for advances and assets dropping by over 28 percent and about 20 percent respectively between 1991 and 2001 (Koeva 2003). Within a decade of its formation, a private bank, the ICICI Bank has become the second largest in India. Compared to most Asian countries the Indian banking system has done better in managing its NPL problem. The 'healthy' status of the Indian banking system is in part due to stringent requirements for commercial loans. In terms of profitability, Indian banks have also performed well compared to the banking sector in other Asian economies.

5.4 Firms' financing sources in China: Aggregate evidence and cross-country comparisons

In this section we compare, at the aggregate level, how firms raise funds in China and in La Porta et al.-sample countries with the emphasis on emerging economies. It is then worthwhile to study what other channels of financing are playing the role of substituting for external capital markets and standard, textbook financing channels.

China's most important financing channels

The four most important financing sources for all firms in China, in terms of fixed asset investments, are: (Domestic) bank loans; firms' self-fundraising; state budget; and foreign direct investment. By far the two most important sources of financing channels are self-fundraising and bank loans. Consistent with previous evidence on China's banking sector, bank loans, including loans from the nonstate banks, provide a large amount of funds to firms, and constitute a large fraction of firms' total financing needs. For example, firms in the state sector rely on bank loans to raise more than 25 percent of their total financing needs. A similar pattern holds for jointly and collectively owned companies, both of which belong to the private sector. Our survey evidence below (Section 5.5) also indicates that bank loans are important financing sources for the private sector, especially during the firms' start-up period. Self-fundraising includes proceeds from capital raised from local Governments (beyond the state budget), communities, other investors, internal financing channels, such as retained earnings, and all other funds raised domestically by the firms. Since the data source used, the *China Statistical Yearbook* (2000–2002), does not provide the breakdowns of 'self-fundraising', we only have the total figures in subsequent tables and graphs.

The size of total self-fundraising of all firms grew at an average annual rate of 14 percent over the period of 1994 to 2002. At the end of 2002, total self-fundraising (for fixed asset investment) reached US$275.5 billion, compared to a total of US$106.6 billion for domestic bank loans for the same year. It is important to point out that equity and bond issuance, which are included in self-fundraising, apply only to the listed sector, and account for a small fraction of this category. Moreover, self-fundraising is the most important source of financing for many types of firms. For example, individually owned firms (private sector), not surprisingly, rely mostly on self-fundraising (about 90 percent of total financing). Interestingly, even for state-owned or quasi-state-owned companies, self-fundraising is also important in that it captures somewhere between 45 percent and 65 percent of total financing.

State budget and foreign (direct) investment are the other two important financing sources. As was the case for all socialist countries, China used to rely on a central planning system to allocate the state budget to most of the companies in the country. But the state budget now only contributes 10 percent of state-owned companies' total funding. On the other hand, foreign investment is comparable to the state budget, both in terms of aggregate size and in terms of the relative importance in firms' financing. This evidence confirms that China has evolved from a centrally planned, closed economy toward an open market economy.

With the knowledge on the four financing channels at the aggregate level, we now focus on different types of firms' financing decisions. The results are presented in Figures 5.3a, 5.3b, and 5.3c. In all of these figures, each of the four connected lines represents the importance of a particular financing channel over the time period 1994 to 2002, measured by the percentage of firms' total financing coming from this channel.

First, Figure 5.3a (5.3b) illustrates how firms in the listed sector (state sector) finance their investment (for fixed assets). While the listed sector

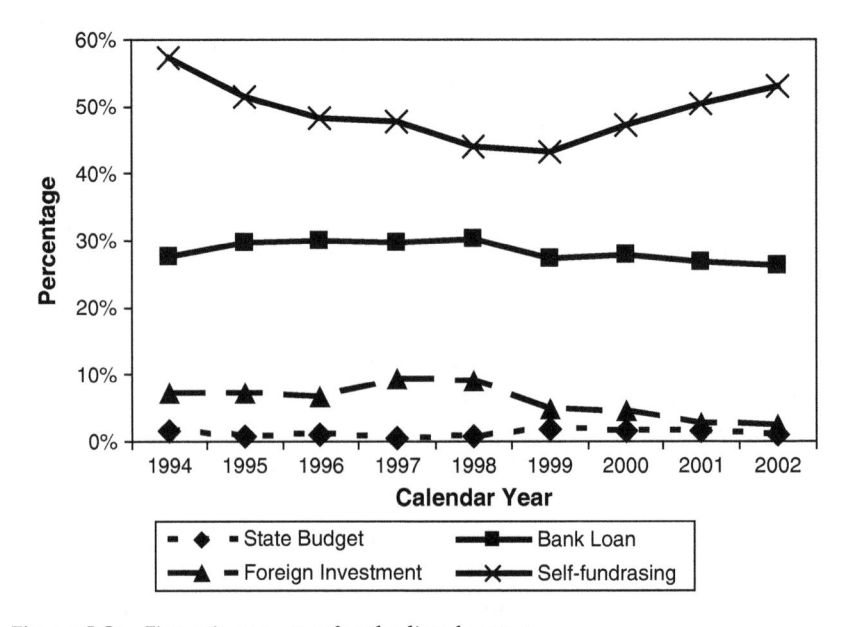

Figure 5.3a. Financing sources for the listed sector

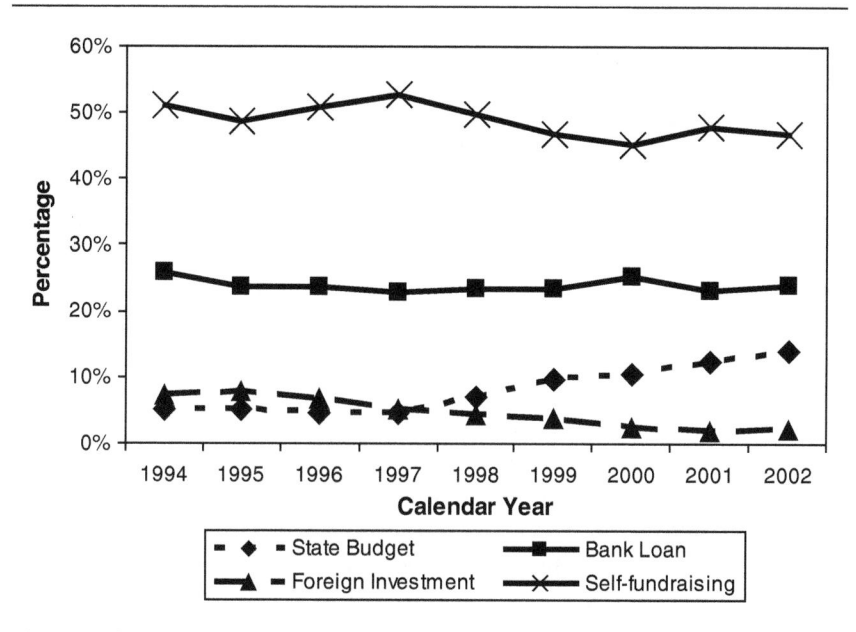

Figure 5.3b. Financing sources for the state sector

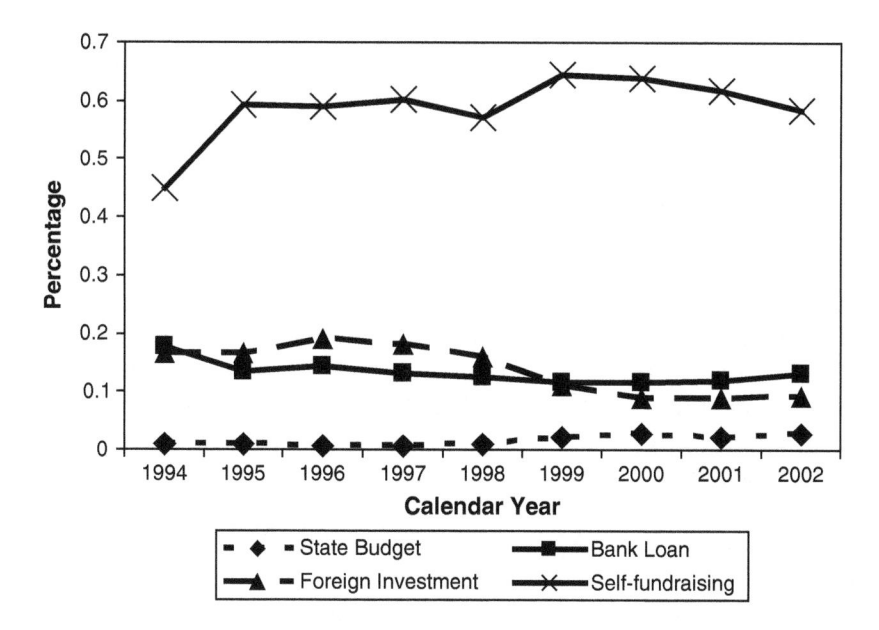

Figure 5.3c. Financing sources for the private sector

has been growing fast, SOEs are on a downward trend as privatization of these firms is still in progress. Around 30 percent of publicly traded companies' funding comes from bank loans, and this ratio has been very stable despite the fast growth of the stock markets (Figure 5.2a). Around 45 percent of the listed sector's total funding comes from self-fundraising, including internal financing and proceeds from equity and bond issuance. Moreover, equity and bond sales, which rely on the use of external markets, only constitute a small fraction of total funds raised, compared to internal financing and other forms of fundraising. Combined with the fact that self-fundraising is also the most important source of financing for the state sector (Figure 5.3b), we can conclude that alternative channels of financing are important even for the state and listed sectors.

Next, we consider how firms in the private sector raise funds (Figure 5.3c). Self-fundraising here includes all forms of internal finance, capital raised from family and friends of the founders and managers, and funds raised in the form of private equity and loans. Clearly, this category is by far the most important source of financing, accounting for close to 60 percent of total funds raised. Moreover, since firms in this sector operate in an environment with poorer legal and financial mechanisms and regulations than those firms in the state and listed sectors, all financing sources probably work differently from how they work in the state and listed sectors, and those in developed countries. In Section 5.5 below, we present detailed evidence on how different types of self-fundraising help private sector firms at various stages.

Evidence on the listed sector

In this section, we focus on publicly traded companies and examine their financing and investment decisions. As stated in the Introduction, we want to draw general conclusions on whether there are fundamental differences between the Chinese firms and firms studied in previous papers (La Porta et al. 1999b; 1997a; 2000; 2002b). Before doing so, we first look at the unique ownership structure and corporate governance mechanisms in Chinese firms.

TYPES OF STOCKS, OWNERSHIP STRUCTURE, AND CORPORATE GOVERNANCE

Listed firms in China issue both tradable and nontradable shares (Table 5.7a). The nontradable shares are either held by the state/Government or by other legal entities (i.e. other listed or nonlisted firms or organizations).

Table 5.7a. Types of common stock issued in China

Tradable on the exchanges?	Definition
No (Private block transfer possible)	
State-owned shares**	Shares that are controlled by the central Government during the process in which firms are converted into a limited liability incorporation but before they are listed. All these shares are managed and represented by the Bureau of National Assets Management, which also appoints board members on firms' boards.
Entrepreneur's shares	Shares reserved for firms' founders during the same process described above; different from shares that founders can purchase and sell in the markets.
Foreign owners	Shares owned by foreign industrial investors during the same process.
Legal entity holders	Shares sold to legal identities (such as other companies, listed or nonlisted) during the same process.
Employee shares	Shares sold to firm's employees during the same process.
Yes (New issued shares)	
A shares	Chinese companies listed in Shanghai or Shenzhen Stock Exchanges, and shares sold to Chinese (citizen) investors.
B shares	Chinese Company listed in SHSZ or SZSE, but shares are sold to foreign investors.
H shares	Chinese Company listed in Hong Kong (shares can only be traded on the HK Exchange but can be held by anyone).

Note: ** There are subcategories under this definition.

Among the tradable shares, Class A and B shares are listed and traded in either the SHSE or SZSE, while Class A (B) shares are issued to Chinese investors (foreign investors including those from Taiwan and Hong Kong). Finally, Class H shares can be listed and traded on the HKSE and are issued by selected 'Red Chip' Chinese companies.

Table 5.7b demonstrates that nontradable shares constitute a majority of all shares and most of these shares are held by the state, while the majority of tradable shares are A shares. Table 5.7c provides some evidence on the relation between ownership and control of the Board of Directors. Information provided here is based on a survey of corporate governance practices among 257 companies listed on the SHSE conducted in 2000 by the Research Center of SHSE. Consistent with Tables 5.7a and 5.7b and the 'one-share, one-vote' scheme adopted by firms in the listed sector, state and legal person shareholders appoint most of the board members, while the other directors are appointed by the Government.

The standard corporate governance mechanisms are limited and weak in the listed sector (e.g. Schipani and Liu 2002). First, listed firms in China have a two-tier board structure: The Board of Directors and the Board of Supervisors. The supervisors of a listed firm, ranking above the

Franklin Allen et al.

Table 5.7b. Tradable vs. nontradable shares for China's listed companies

Year	State/ total shares	Nontradable^/ total shares	Tradable/ total shares	A/total shares	A/tradable shares*
1992	0.41	0.69	0.31	0.16	0.52
1993	0.49	0.72	0.28	0.16	0.57
1994	0.43	0.67	0.33	0.21	0.64
1995	0.39	0.64	0.36	0.21	0.60
1996	0.35	0.65	0.35	0.22	0.62
1997	0.32	0.65	0.35	0.23	0.66
1998	0.34	0.66	0.34	0.24	0.71
1999	0.36	0.65	0.35	0.26	0.75
2000	0.39	0.64	0.36	0.28	0.80
2001	0.39	0.64	0.36	0.29	0.80
2002	n/a	0.65	0.35	0.26	0.74
2003	n/a	0.64	0.35	0.27	0.76

Notes: ^ = Nontradable shares include 'state owned' and 'shares owned by legal entities'. * = tradable shares include A, B, and H shares. Source: Constructed using data from China Security Regulation Committee Reports (2000) and http://www.csrc.gov.cn.

directors, are usually either officials chosen from Government branches or executives from the parent companies, while the Board of Directors is controlled by the firm's parent companies. Not all directors are elected by the shareholders, and the rest are nominated and appointed by the firm's parent companies and the nomination process is usually kept secret (Table 5.7c). Incentive pay is rarely explicitly specified in the directors' compensation packages, while the consumption of perks, such as company cars, is prevalent.

The external governance mechanisms are also weak. First, the existing ownership structure, characterized by cross-holdings of shares among listed companies and institutions, makes hostile takeovers virtually

Table 5.7c. Ownership and control in listed firms of China

	Company ownership and control (%)	
Shareholder type	Ownership	Control (board seats)
State	24	21
Legal person	44	48
Employees	2	3
Tradable Shares	30	4
Total	100	76

Source: Constructed using data from Table 4.6 p.83, 'Corporate Governance and Enterprise Reform in China, Building the institutions of Modern Market,' 2002, World Bank publication.

impossible. Second, institutional investors do not have a strong influence on management or on the stock market, as they are a very recent addition to the set of financial institutions in China. Moreover, ineffective bankruptcy implementation makes the threat and penalty for bad firm performance noncredible. The World Bank's cross-country information on the efficiency of bankruptcy procedures, which is based on surveys of lawyers and bankruptcy judges around the world, indicates that China's 'goals of insolvency' index is equal to the median of the sample of 108 countries.

Finally, the Government plays the dual roles of regulator and blockholder of many listed firms. The China Securities Regulation Committee (CSRC) is the counterpart of the SEC in the US, and its main role is to monitor and regulate stock exchanges and listed companies, while the Government exercises shareholder control rights in listed firms mainly through state-owned asset management companies, which hold large fractions of the state shares. However, since the top officials of these asset management companies are elected by the Government, it is doubtful that they diligently pursue their fiduciary role as control shareholders. Moreover, the Government's dual roles can lead to conflicting goals in dealing with listed firms, which in turn weakens the effectiveness of both of its roles.

EVIDENCE ON OWNERSHIP, FINANCING, DIVIDEND, AND VALUATION

In this section, we examine and compare various characteristics of listed firms in China with those of other countries. Our results on China's listed sector are based on a sample (panel data) of more than 1,100 listed firms that we collect from SHSE, SZSE, and the 'Asia Emerging Market Database' of the *Taiwan Economic Journal*, for the period 1992 to 2000. Table 5.8a presents the summary statistics for a 'snapshot' of the sample firms at the end of 2000. From Panel A, the average market cap is US$448 million (median is US$355 million), and the average leverage ratio, measured by the ratio of long-term debt and common equity, is 32 percent (median is 9%). In short, these are large firms operating in virtually all industries. Panel B compares listed firms converted from the state sector to those nonstate firms. First, 80 percent of the sample of listed firms used to be state owned (921 out of 1,163 firms). Second, the two groups of firms are similar in terms of most of the financial ratios except for leverage: Firms that used to be state owned have much higher leverage than the other

Table 5.8a. Summary statistics of Chinese listed firms (in US$ millions)

Panel A: Key financial items and ratios (whole sample)

	Mean	Median	Min	Max	Std. Dev	Number of obs
Market cap. (US$ mil)	448.2	354.9	0.0	8,190.2	513.9	1174
LT debt/Common equity	0.3	0.1	0.0	6.9	0.6	981
Net income	99.6	502.0	−1,215.9	21,718.6	721.0	979
EPS	0.2	0.2	−3.2	1.6	0.4	979
Proceeds from stock sales	163.6	0.0	−290.8	29,379.2	987.0	975 (272)
Dividend	50.8	18.4	0.0	8,106.0	270.2	979 (617)
Retained earnings	26.4	33.2	−2,125.7	2,210.18	234.4	979 (951)
Bonds issue	0.8	0.0	0.0	521.0	17.3	975 (6)
Long term borrowing	634.9	233.1	0.0	157,053.1	5,073.7	974 (895)

Panel B: Listed firms converted from SOEs vs. nonstate firms

Types of listed firms and sample size	Market Cap. (US$ mil.)	Tobin's Q	Dividend/ Earnings	Dividend/ Net sales	L-T Debt/ Book Equity	Return on Assets
Previously SOEs (921)	490.62	0.50	0.48	0.06	0.35	0.028
Previously non-SOEs (242)	454.94	0.51	0.11	0.06	0.24	0.028
Difference in means (t-test)	1.03	−0.19	0.85	−0.08	3.00*	0.004

Notes: Firms are listed in SHSE and SZSE (as of December 2000). Constructed using data from Taiwan Economic Journal's 'Asia Emerging Market Database' (http://www.tei.com.tw/).

group, partially due to the large amount of bank loans accumulated in these firms prior to their IPO.

Table 5.8b compares the ownership structure of these firms to those from the La Porta et al. (1999b) sample, which includes over 1,000 listed companies from 33 countries. The main result of La Porta et al. (1999b) is that countries that protect minority shareholders poorly (strongly) tend to have more concentrated (dispersed) ownership, as shown in the first two panels of Table 5.8b. The ownership structure of listed firms in China, shown in Panel C of Table 5.8b, is consistent with the prediction of Burkart et al. (2003), and closer to that of other Asian firms documented in Claessens et al. (2000) than to the La Porta et al. (1999b) results. The dominant owner of 60 percent of our sample firms is the (central) Government, while for 13.6 percent of firms, the dominant owner is founders' families. We also find that for 24.17 percent (1.83 percent) of firms, the dominant shareholder is a financial company

Table 5.8b. Ownership structures of Indian firms vis-à-vis other country groups

Controlling Shareholder*	Foreign	Widely-held (%)	State (%)	Family/Indiv. (%)	Financial Corp. (%)	Non-Fin. Corp. (%)
	Panel A: LLS (1999b) Sample of Large Firms					
High-antidirector average		34.2	15.8	30.4	5.0	5.8
Low-antidirector average		16.0	23.7	38.3	11.0	2.0
Sample average		24.0	20.2	34.8	8.3	3.7
	Panel B: LLS (1999b) Sample of Medium Firms					
High-antidirector average		16.7	10.3	50.9	5.8	1.7
Low-antidirector average		6.0	20.9	53.8	6.7	2.7
Sample average		10.7	16.2	52.5	6.3	2.2
	Panel C: Asian Firms					
Asia (no Japan, Claessens et al. 2000)		3.1	9.4	59.4	9.7	18.6
China (Allen, Qian, Qian 2005)		**0.4**	**60.0**	**13.6**	**1.8**	**24.2**
	Panel D: Indian Firms					
	NRI/OCB**			a	b	c
Full Sample	10.7	1.9	0.4	77.6	1.0	8.8
All SMEs	3.5	1.6	0.0	80.4	0.1	14.4
All Large Enterprises	12.8	1.9	0.5	76.7	1.3	7.2
BSE 500[d]	18.1	1.8	0.3	73.0	2.1	5.1

Notes: * We list these 'controlling shareholders' (% indicate fraction of sample firms having a particular type of controlling shareholder): (1) 'Widely-held' firms are defined as no single large shareholder owns more than 10 percent of shares; (2) 'State' firms are those with the controlling shareholder being the state/Government; (3) 'Family' firms are those with the controlling shareholder being the founder's family; (4) 'Financial' ('Non-financial') are firms with a widely-held financial (non-financial) corporation as the controlling shareholder.
** Non-Resident Indians (NRIs) are individuals of Indian nationality or Indian origin resident outside India. Overseas Corporate Bodies (OCBs) include overseas companies, partnership firms, societies and other corporate bodies which are owned predominantly (at least 60%) by individuals of Indian nationality or Indian origin resident outside India.
a: For these Indian firms, we identify the dominant shareholder to be private block-holders, but we are not sure how many blockholders there are and whether they are related or not.
b: For these Indian firms, we identify the dominant shareholder to be a financial company, but we are not sure whether the financial company is widely held or not.
c: For these Indian firms, we identify the dominant shareholder to be another listed and traded corporation, but we are not sure whether this corporation is widely held or not.
d: Based on 317 non-financial large firms included in the BSE 500 index.

(another listed firm). Since we do not have ownership data for this financial company (listed firm), we do not know whether this company (listed firm) is widely held or not. But given the fact that state ownership is prevalent in listed firms and banks, it is reasonable to assume that they

Table 5.8c. Comparing external financing, dividend, and valuation

Country	English origin average	French origin average	German origin average	Nordic origin average	Sample average	China	India Large Enterprises	India SMEs
			Panel A: External financing					
Market cap/sales	1.52	0.72	1.39	0.98	0.81	0.06	0.25	0.49
Market cap/cash flow	15.3	−2.96	13.94	−41.52	1.05	0.52	2.54	2.43
Debt**/sales	0.38	0.11	0.8	0.24	0.12	0.67	0.27	0.06
Debt/cash flow	0.99	2.15	−0.5	−39.76	0.04	5.34	1.68	0
			Panel B: Dividend and valuation					
Dividend/Earnings	0.21	0.17	0	0.35	0.128	0.21	0.07	0
Dividend/Sales	0.017	0.055	0	0.02	0.008	0.017	0.003	0
Tobin's Q	1.56	1.06	1.51	1.77	1.04	1.56	0.94	0.85
# of observations	10,192	2,969	5,133	523	42	10,192	1,761	992

Notes: In La Porta et al. (1997a), a ratio (e.g., market cap/sales) for a given country is the median ratio in 1994 for all the firms from that country in their sample. The average ratio for a country group based on legal origin is the arithmetic average of the country ratios. La Porta et al. use Worldscope data.
** Debt includes long-term debt only (as in La Porta et al. 1997a)

are not widely held. Finally, only 0.44 percent of all firms are widely held so that no shareholder owns more than 10 percent of stocks.

Table 5.8c provides some evidence on financing sources at the firm level. The ratios for all the countries (except for China) in the table are taken from La Porta et al. (1997a).[13] The evidence in Table 5.8c is consistent with previous evidence at the aggregate level: In terms of total equity, the listed Chinese companies do not rely on external markets as much as their counterparts in La Porta et al. countries, but they do rely more heavily on debt, and in particular bank debt, than firms in La Porta et al.-sample countries.

Finally, we examine dividend policies and valuations of listed firms in China, and compare these to firms studied by La Porta et al. (2000, 2002b). Making the most out of the available data,[14] we perform three different sets of empirical tests and find similar results. First, La Porta et al. (2000)

---

[13] In La Porta et al. (1997a), a ratio (e.g. market cap/sales) for a country is obtained by first finding the median of this ratio across firms within various industries, and then by taking the average of the medians across industries. A similar procedure is taken to find the ratios for China using our data set of listed firms. Finally, we take the average (median) ratios across groups of countries according to their legal origins, and compare them to those of China.

[14] The data sets that we employ include: (1) accounting and financial information for 1,100+ listed firms from China (1990–2000); and, (2) La Porta et al. (2000, 2002b) results are based on information for over 4,100 firms from 33 countries (1989–1994), while detailed firm-level data for La Porta et al.-sample firms are not available to us; however, we do have their cross-sectional summary statistics by country, as well as the regression results across countries.

find that firms in countries with poorer protection of outside shareholders tend to have lower dividend ratios due to more severe agency problems. Using the dividend-to-earnings ratio as a proxy for dividend policy, we find that on average Chinese firms tend to underpay dividends to their shareholders compared to firms in countries studied in La Porta et al. (2000). Second, La Porta et al. (2002b) find that firms in countries with poorer protection of outside shareholders tend to have a lower Tobin's Q, measured by the market-to-book asset ratios. When we examine the Tobin's Q of listed firms in China, we cannot reject the hypothesis that on average their Tobin's Q is lower compared to countries with better shareholder protection (La Porta et al. 2002b).

Overall, because investor protection is weak (and the agency problem is severe) in the listed sector in China, both the dividend ratio and Tobin's Q are low compared to similar firms operating in countries with stronger investor protection. These results confirm that La Porta et al. predictions work well for China's listed sector, which includes many firms converted from the state sector, and is also consistent with evidence presented in Figure 5.2.

5.5 Law, finance, and growth in the Indian corporate sectors: Firm level evidence

The organized sector of the Indian economy consists of the state and the nonstate (private) sectors. The state sector comprises Public Sector Undertakings (PSUs), in which the Government has majority (at least 50%) ownership and effective control. Almost all the PSUs are 'public companies' as defined by the Indian Company's Act of 1956 (a company that has a minimum paid-up capital of Indian rupees 500,000, or US$11,100, and more than fifty shareholders). The nonstate sector includes over 76,000 public companies and numerous smaller 'private' companies (with less than fifty shareholders). Over 10,000 of the 'public' companies are listed on one or more of the stock exchanges, though a small fraction of them actually trade. Finally, there is an unorganized sector that consists of smaller businesses that do not belong to any of the above categories. Verifiable data about the unorganized sector is scarce. The figures and analysis we present in this chapter cover only the organized sector.

Table 5.9 presents comparisons of state and nonstate sectors during the period 1990–2003. In terms of contribution to GDP, the size of the state sector (excluding Government spending) during 1990–2003 has

Table 5.9. Comparing the state and nonstate sectors in India: 1990–2003 (in US$ billions)

	GDP from State and nonstate sectors		State sector—public sector undertakings (PSUs)			Registered nonstate corporations* (listed and unlisted)		
Year	State sector GDP[a,b]	GDP from all nonstate sectors[a,c]	Number of units ('000)	Paid-up capital[d]	Employment (million)[e]	Number of units ('000)	Paid-up capital[d]	Employment (million)[e]
1990–91	20.03	96.19	1.16	15.26	19.06	200.97	5.53	7.68
1991–92	24.94	156.26	1.17	17.45	19.21	223.29	6.51	7.85
1992–93	28.10	126.56	1.18	18.90	19.33	249.18	8.72	7.85
1993–94	33.25	140.84	1.19	19.28	19.45	274.47	10.49	7.93
1994–95	35.85	169.13	—	—	19.47	304.42	14.79	8.06
1995–96	39.16	194.04	1.20	21.91	19.43	352.09	18.75	8.51
1996–97	37.75	210.40	1.22	21.68	19.56	407.93	24.54	8.69
1997–98	41.11	222.72	1.22	22.69	19.42	449.73	28.58	8.75
1998–99	43.88	223.54	1.22	21.15	19.41	483.28	30.59	8.70
1999–00	43.15	248.86	1.23	22.14	19.31	510.76	38.64	8.65
2000–01	43.55	265.68	1.24	21.43	19.14	541.19	42.90	8.65
2001–02	51.22	276.50	1.27	21.87	18.77	567.83	49.67	8.43
2002–03	64.41	302.94	1.26	22.71	18.58	587.99	57.26	8.42
CAGR	10.22	10.03	0.70	3.37	−0.21	9.36	21.51	0.77

Notes: * These include all listed and unlisted (but registered) companies.
[a]: Output and GDP figures exclude agriculture; [b]: Total (nonagriculture) GDP generated from all nonstate sector firms; [c]: Includes GDP from non-corporate nonstate sector as well; [d]: Paid-up capital for a company is the number of shares outstanding times the face value or par value per share; [e]: Employment figures only include registered firms, and excluding SSI firms and non-registered firms.
Source: Constructed using data from the India-Stat, Central Statistical Organization and the Reserve Bank of India.

been around one-fifth of the nonstate sectors (including unorganized sectors but excluding agriculture).[15] In terms of capital base, (organized) nonstate sectors have been growing faster than the state sector. During 1990–2003, paid-up capital in the state sector grew at an annual rate of 3.37 percent, with its share in the economy-wide total corporate paid-up capital declining from 73 to 28 percent.[16] By contrast, paid-up capital in nonstate corporations has been growing at an annual rate of 21.5 percent.

Firms in the SME sector constitute an important segment of the Indian economy, contributing to over 40 percent of the value added in manufacturing (according to O. S. Kanwar, the President of FICCI, a national

---

[15] Among nonstate sectors, firms operating in the services industries (e.g. commerce and hotels, community and business services) had surpassed traditional manufacturing industries in terms of number of units and size of investments.

[16] Paid-up capital for a company is the number of shares outstanding multiplied by the face value of the shares; it does not include reserves and surpluses.

chamber of commerce in India).[17] The official definition of an SME is different for manufacturing and services sectors. Under the 'Micro, Small and Medium Enterprises Development Act 2006' of the Government of India, a manufacturing firm that has investments in fixed assets of plant and machinery below Rs.100 million (US$2.22 million) qualifies as an SME; for firms in the services sector, the ceiling is Rs.50 million (US$1.11 million) in fixed assets.

In the remainder of this section, we analyze the patterns of ownership, financing, and growth of public companies in manufacturing and services. While public companies under the Indian Company's Act of 1956 are required to make their financial statements publicly available, verifiable financial data for private companies are not available from organized sources.

Evidence from the World Bank's Business Environment Survey data

In this section we supplement the above analysis using evidence of the World Bank's Investment Climate Survey data. These surveys cover a very large number of firms across different size groups in various countries and covers issues on which it is difficult to get secondary data. We show the basic information and regression analysis based on this data from China and India in Tables 5.10a–h.

SUMMARY STATISTICS

Our sample from the World Bank survey includes two countries: China and India. For China, we have observations of surveys conducted in 2002 and 2003. For India, 2002 and 2005. There are 3,948 firm*year observations for China, 1,548 firms in 2002 and 2,400 firms in 2003. There are 4,114 firm*year observations for India, 1,827 firms in 2002 and 2,287 firms in 2005. We don't know which firms are surveyed in both years.

REGRESSION ANALYSIS

(1) The first group of regressions addresses the determinants of financing sources of firms.

---

[17] The importance of small and medium firms is hardly unique to India—high-growth economies are typically marked by a vibrant SME sector. Using a sample of 76 countries (India not included), Beck et al. (2005) find a strong association between the importance of SMEs and GDP per capita growth. However, they are not able to establish that SMEs exert a causal impact on growth or poverty reduction.

Table 5.10a. Evidence from the World Bank's Investment Climate Survey data: Basic Information

		China 2002	China 2003	India 2002	India 2005
Types of firms					
(1)	% of Domestic firms	70.6	87.6	98.1	98.2
	% of foreign firms	29.4	12.4	1.9	1.8
(2)	% of Listed firms	1.7	2.3	15.0	0
(3)	% of Private sector[a]	79.8	77.8	98.6	98.2
	% of Government sector[b]	19.4	21.7	1.3	0.5
	% of Others	0.7	0.4	0.1	1.3
(4)	% of Manufacturing firms	65.9	67.1	99.8	99.9
	% of Services firms[b]	34.1	32.9	0.2	0.1
(5) Age of firms operated in the country (mean)					
	Full sample	14.5	16.0	16.8	16.8
	Domestic firms	16.9	17.0	16.7	16.7
	foreign firms	8.9	9.1	20.1	18.1
	Listed firms	11.5	11.5	25.3	n/a
	Private sector	11.5	12.8	16.6	16.7
	Government sector	26.8	27.4	34.3	24.3
	Manufacturing firms	16.3	16.6	16.8	16.8
	Services firms	11.0	14.8	8.0	17.0
Firm size (mean)					
(6) Employment	Full sample	502	482	95	n/a
(no. of people)	Domestic firms	494	480	86	n/a
	foreign firms	522	500	566	n/a
	Listed firms	2,461	1,801	327	n/a
	Private sector	359	285	90	n/a
	Government sector	1,082	1,192	451	n/a
	Manufacturing firms	499	374	94	n/a
	Services firms	508	706	205	n/a
(7) Total sales	Full sample	25.9	25.3	17.3	15.9
(end of last year)	Domestic firms	12.9	20.1	16.8	14.5
(in US$ million)	foreign firms	55.7	62.1	43.5	104.7
	Listed firms	190.1	126.5	107.5	n/a
	Private sector	25.6	26.2	17.2	16.2
	Government sector	24.4	21.4	27.0	8.17
	Manufacturing firms	30.6	21.5	17.3	16.0
	Services firms	16.5	33.0	7.3	0.02

Note: [a] We define a firm to be in private sector if the firm's ownership by private sector is more than 50 percent. The same is for state-owned firms.
[b] Observation number for this type of firms in India survey is extremely small (= <10).

The *dependent variables* used are (a1). Internal Financing: Likelihood of usage; (a2). Internal Financing: Amount of usage given usage>0; (b1). Trade credits: Likelihood of usage; (b2). Trade credits: Amount of usage given usage>0; (c1). Family, friends borrowing: Likelihood of usage; (c2). Family, friends borrowing: Amount of usage given usage>0; (d1).

Law, Institutions, and Finance

Table 5.10b. Financing sources and efficiency

(1) Financing sources (Observations are in only 2003 for China, 2005 for India)

(Percent of firms who used the source in the last year and among them, the average % of finance from this source)	China Working Capital		China New Investments		India Working Capital		India New Investments	
Internal funds or retained earnings	24.9	52.6	23.8	64.1	83.6	56.0	80.7	64.5
Local Commercial banks	38.2	68.6	28.6	70.7	61.7	49.3	52.9	59.1
Foreign-owned banks	0.6	27.9	0.4	33.0	2.2	42.1	2.0	44.0
Lease arrangement	n/a	n/a	n/a	n/a	3.8	18.1	3.4	27.3
Funds from states	0.7	51.9	1.1	48.9	n/a	n/a	n/a	n/a
Trade credits	4.7	47.9	2.2	47.7	27.8	31.5	12.7	35.4
Credit cards	n/a	n/a	n/a	n/a	3.2	21.9	2.4	35.5
Equity sales	17.9	65.2	16.1	77.0	5.0	30.0	3.7	30.0
Family, friends	10.5	54.6	9.1	64.7	28.0	31.6	16.4	42.3
Informal money lenders	4.6	40.7	3.2	57.6	2.4	23.8	1.6	36.9
Others	49.0	78.7	49.4	86.4	1.6	48.7	1.3	70.0

(2) Financing Efficiency (Observations are in only 2002 for both countries)

(mean of non-zero answers, except fee on check[a])	China Days it takes	China Fee as % of transaction	India Days takes	India Fee as % of transaction
Clear a check	4.7	0.6	11.1	1.6
A domestic wire	5.5	0.7	7.9	2.5
A foreign wire	8.9	2.3	12.5	3.6

[a] It is common that there is no fee charge on clear a check, but not for wiring. For check, the mean for non-zeros are (1.02 and 2.2 respectively in China and India).

Table 5.10c. Growth

Average Annualized %	China 1999–2001	China 2000–2002	India 1999–2001	India 2002–2004
(1) Growth of sales	34.7	21.1	14.5	n/a
(2) Growth of salary, bonus, and benefits paid out	23.4	16.1	9.8	n/a

Informal financing: Likelihood of usage; (d2). Informal financing: Amount of usage given usage>0.

Notes

(i) The usage and amount have summed obs. from working capital and new investments.

165

(ii) Informal financing is the sum of trade credits, family friends borrowing, money lender, and others. We keep internal source independent here since it is important in every country.

(iii) Given the large number of zero, regression results by using amount measure including zeros is very similar to the likelihood measure with more significant t-stats.

The *explanatory variables* include (a). log(firm size): Use total sales in 2000; (b). log(firm age): 2003—the starting year of operation in the country; (c). the largest shareholder: For Indian firms, there are four dummies: The largest shareholder is Government; individuals/family, foreign, bank/investment funds. For Chinese firms, such differentiation is not available, hence we use private sector vs. state-owned sector; (d). exporter: Dummy; (e). perception on judicial efficiency and fairness: A rank as surveyed; (f). Perception on Government efficiency: A rank as surveyed; (g). perception on official influence rule implementation; a rank. (h). country dummy, or year dummy, or interactive variables.

Note: Financing sources are observation in 2003 China and 2005 India survey data, but many of the explanatory variables are observed in 2002 survey only.

THE RELATION BETWEEN FIRM GROWTH AND FIRM CHARACTERISTICS

The *dependent variables* used: (a). Growth of firm's total sales; (b). Growth of salary, wage, bonus, and other benefits paid out. Both are in annualized percent 1999–2001.

The *explanatory variables* used: (a). log(firm size): Use total sales in 2000; (b). log(firm age): 2003—the starting year of operation in the country; (c). the largest shareholder: For Indian firms, there are four dummies: The largest shareholder is Government; individuals/family, foreign, bank/investment funds. For Chinese firms, such differentiation is not available, hence we use private sector vs. state-owned sector; (d). exporter: Dummy; (e). perception on judicial efficiency and fairness: A rank as surveyed; (f). Perception on Government efficiency: A rank as surveyed; (g). perception on official influence rule implementation; a rank. (h). country dummy, or year dummy, or interactive variables. Financing sources: internal, vs. informal, vs. formal used for Working capital financing. Use dummies as well as amounts (without excluding zeros).

Law, Institutions, and Finance

Table 5.10d. Internal (observations are in only 2003 survey for china, 2005 for India)

	Chinese firms		Indian firms		Chinese & Indian firms	
	Likelihood	Amount	Likelihood	Amount	Likelihood	Amount
Constants	−3.60	171.18	2.11	133.31	−0.69	151.98
	(−8.59)	(7.46)	(3.45)	(12.03)	(−2.55)	(19.40)
Log(firm size)	**0.26**	**−4.68**	−0.04	**−3.22**	**0.11**	**−4.00**
	(8.78)	**(−2.66)**	(−1.06)	**(−3.66)**	**(4.62)**	**(−3.39)**
Log(firm age)	−0.10	**−8.47**	0.02	−3.13	**−0.48**	−6.08
	(−1.18)	**(−1.73)**	(0.18)	(−1.35)	**(−6.11)**	(−1.39)
Exporters	**−0.36**	−9.89	**0.59**	**17.89**	−0.16	−10.81
	(−1.75)	(−0.97)	**(2.17)**	**(4.01)**	(−0.85)	(−1.08)
Judicial environment			−0.03	1.67		
			(−0.36)	(1.22)		
Government efficiency			0.07	**2.55**		
			(0.91)	**(1.74)**		
Official Impact Private Sector	**0.70**	−7.50				
	(3.88)	(−0.77)				
India Log(firm size)					0.06	0.55
					(1.63)	(0.46)
India Log(firm age)					**0.91**	2.94
					(7.69)	(0.62)
India Exporters					0.39	**27.26**
					(1.15)	**(2.50)**
# of observations	1,337	412	1,216	1,073	2,629	1,556
Adjusted/Psuedo R^2	0.06	0.03	0.01	0.03	0.28	0.04

Notes: Unfortunately, we cannot do this at this time because of the missing match in the observation period. But we can do it later when a better sample becomes available.

Caveat for this group of regressions. Constrained with the observation availability, our growth rate is measured for period 1999–2002 and other variables are measured in 2002 (financing source is 2002 for China and 2004 for India). There is a look-ahead bias. Therefore any causality should not be inferred from here.

5.6 Survey evidence on the Chinese private sector

Allen et al. focus on how firms in the private sector raise funds, their various growth paths, and the alternative mechanisms employed by owners that can substitute for formal corporate governance mechanisms.

Table 5.10e. Trade credit (observations are in only 2003 survey for china, 2005 for India)

	Chinese firms		Indian firms		Chinese & Indian firms	
	Likelihood	Amount	Likelihood	Amount	Likelihood	Amount
Constants	−6.01	18.41	−0.49	98.00	−1.28	97.11
	(−6.88)	(0.63)	(−1.21)	(8.18)	(−4.75)	(11.35)
Log(firm size)	**0.23**	−2.72	−0.03	−1.25	0.03	**−4.58**
	(4.46)	(−1.20)	(−1.16)	(−1.35)	(0.70)	**(−2.70)**
Log(firm age)	−0.16	13.76	−0.04	**−14.55**	**−0.81**	7.63
	(−1.01)	(1.73)	(−0.54)	**(−5.65)**	**(−5.44)**	(0.94)
Exporters	**0.73**	−12.13	**−0.77**	**−21.01**	**1.01**	−4.53
	(2.58)	(−0.90)	**(−3.64)**	**(−5.06)**	**(3.52)**	(−0.36)
Judicial environment			−0.05	−1.16		
			(−0.94)	(−0.87)		
Government efficiency			0.01	1.54		
			(0.27)	(1.03)		
Official Impact Private Sector	**1.37**	**49.54**				
	(2.74)	**(4.40)**				
India Log(firm size)					−0.02	**3.11**
					(−0.49)	**(1.84)**
India Log(firm age)					**0.89**	**−20.35**
					(5.64)	**(−2.46)**
India Exporters					**−1.85**	−16.67
					(−5.26)	(−1.29)
# of observations	1,337	79	1,216	290	2,629	394
Adjusted/Psuedo R²	0.08	0.12	0.02	0.23	0.10	0.17

Anecdotal evidence in two successful regions

WENZHOU

Wenzhou, a city in the Zhejiang province, is the home of some of the earliest and most successful firms of the private sector. Entrepreneurs in the region are known for their keen business sense and innovation, as well as sharp management skills (e.g. Johnson et al. 2002). They usually start their family-run businesses in townships with a similar product emphasis, in order to have easy access to the necessary technology, human capital, and potential clients and partners. Thus we observe specialization by regions (e.g. Town A produces shoes, Town B radio parts, etc.). This specialization can be a result of the attempt of firms to signal to potential customers that they are competitive by locating the firm in a region filled with other firms producing and selling similar products. During recent years, certain developed areas have shifted product emphasis from labor-intensive products, such as clothes, to more high-tech products, such as computer parts.

Law, Institutions, and Finance

Table 5.10f. Family/friend borrowing (observations are in only 2003 survey for china, 2005 for India)

	Chinese firms		Indian firms		Chinese & Indian firms	
	Likelihood	Amount	Likelihood	Amount	Likelihood	Amount
Constants	−0.24	248.91	−1.09	79.24	0.18	144.22
	(−0.38)	(7.60)	(−2.55)	(4.36)	(0.72)	(10.35)
Log(firm size)	**−0.27**	**−13.98**	−0.04	−1.89	**−0.17**	**−5.63**
	(−6.67)	**(−5.45)**	(−1.46)	(−1.42)	**(−5.84)**	**(−2.60)**
Log(firm age)	**−0.36**	−13.28	0.01	**−10.13**	**−0.33**	3.69
	(−2.59)	(−1.58)	(0.14)	**(−2.23)**	**(−3.31)**	(0.48)
Exporters	−0.06	**−29.11**	**−0.58**	**−26.98**	−0.05	**−27.71**
	(−0.19)	**(−1.70)**	**(−2.90)**	**(−3.74)**	(−0.15)	**(−1.79)**
Judicial environment			**0.10**	1.70		
			(1.80)	(0.79)		
Government efficiency			0.02	**4.22**		
			(0.42)	**(2.00)**		
Official Impact Private Sector	**1.58**	4.76				
	(3.87)	(0.24)				
India Log(firm size)					**0.07**	0.69
					(2.18)	(0.32)
India Log(firm age)					**0.23**	**−19.32**
					(1.94)	**(−2.36)**
India Exporters					−0.52	6.90
					(−1.37)	(0.40)
# of observations	1,337	149	1,216	306	2,629	471
Adjusted/Psuedo R^2	0.10	0.18	0.02	0.10	0.06	0.20

The failure rate for start-ups in most industries is high. New product strategies often start with mimicking successful or popular products. Patent laws are difficult to implement, and often disputes are settled among the entrepreneurs themselves, similar to the evidence found in Vietnam by McMillan and Woodruff (1999b). To better overcome this problem, some entrepreneurs expend effort and money to ensure that the key parts of their new products are difficult to disassemble and copy. Another product strategy for many entrepreneurs is that they often aim at 'exporting' their products to other regions, including foreign countries, instead of selling them locally.

KUNSHAN

Kunshan County, which is in Jiangsu province and is close to Shanghai, is famous for attracting foreign direct investment, especially from Taiwanese investors. Some of the most effective Government policies have

Table 5.10g. Total informal financing (observations are in only 2003 survey for china, 2005 for India)

	Chinese firms		Indian firms		Chinese & Indian firms	
	Likelihood	Amount	Likelihood	Amount	Likelihood	Amount
Constants	1.25	252.68	−0.10	97.64	0.79	182.70
	(3.37)	(20.59)	(−0.29)	(7.79)	(3.89)	(23.33)
Log(firm size)	**−0.09**	**−8.87**	−0.03	−1.25	**−0.06**	**−5.65**
	(−3.52)	**(−9.88)**	(−1.14)	(−1.21)	**(−2.82)**	**(−7.22)**
Log(firm age)	0.11	−2.94	−0.04	**−12.20**	**0.17**	**7.28**
	(1.36)	(−1.03)	(−0.57)	**(−3.61)**	**(2.51)**	**(2.96)**
Exporters	0.19	5.42	−0.88	−31.68	0.17	0.37
	(0.98)	(0.77)	(−5.17)	(−6.21)	(0.90)	(0.05)
Judicial environment			0.05	0.55		
			(1.14)	(0.35)		
Government efficiency			0.05	**3.12**		
			(1.07)	**(1.97)**		
Official Impact Private Sector	0.01	**−17.78**				
	(0.09)	**(−3.39)**				
India Log(firm size)					−0.01	−0.65
					(−0.41)	(−0.65)
India Log(firm age)					**−0.27**	**−28.64**
					(−3.01)	**(−8.14)**
India Exporters					**−1.02**	**−21.50**
					(−4.01)	**(−2.48)**
# of observations	1,337	884	1,216	514	2,629	1,441
Adjusted/Psuedo R^2	0.01	0.11	0.03	0.12	0.05	0.37

Note: * Means multiplication where 'India' is a 0–1 binary dummy.

included setting up special development zones with favorable land and tax policies. In 1997, Kunshan set up a high-tech development zone, in which enterprises, in the ownership form of joint ventures, cooperatives, and ventures solely owned by foreign investors, can take full advantage of a tax waiver and tax reduction for initial periods. Firms whose high-tech products are export-oriented can enjoy even more tax advantages. There is also a center in a special zone established by the local Government; this center acts as the liaison between the local Government, entrepreneurs, and foreign investors, and as the regulator as well as service provider for enterprises operating in the zone. Enterprises in the zone are required to report their operating and financial information to, and are regulated by the center, but they understand that the center will almost never interfere with their internal decisions. The center's officials are mainly from the local Government. The high-tech development zone has grown very fast since its inception in 1997.

Table 5.10h. Growth of firms (observations are in only 2002 survey).

	Chinese firms		Indian firms		Chinese & Indian firms	
	Growth of sales	Growth of benefits paid out	Growth of sales	Growth of benefits paid out	Growth of sales	Growth of benefits paid out
Constants	−26.76	69.59	39.83	12.43	1.84	40.28
	(−0.59)	(3.06)	(2.20)	(1.04)	(0.08)	(3.41)
Log(firm size)	**15.55**	**4.02**	1.78	2.20	**14.31**	**4.82**
	(2.79)	**(2.45)**	(1.03)	(1.76)	**(2.87)**	**(3.14)**
Log(firm age)	**−41.22**	**−29.19**	**−9.36**	**−4.74**	**−42.66**	**−26.46**
	(−2.46)	**(−3.86)**	**(−2.34)**	**(−2.02)**	**(−2.67)**	**(−3.97)**
Exporters	21.67	16.74	−3.31	3.92	21.87	15.81
	(0.63)	(1.20)	(−0.97)	(1.02)	(0.65)	(1.16)
Judicial environment	5.60	0.91	0.38	−0.32	4.27	1.66
	(0.71)	(0.25)	(0.24)	(−0.52)	(0.56)	(0.47)
Government efficiency	−13.19	−6.51	−2.96	−0.44	−14.78	−5.45
	(−1.06)	(−1.26)	(−1.35)	(−0.73)	(−1.17)	(−1.04)
Official Impact	9.53	2.42	−1.89	**−2.08**	8.74	3.02
	(1.07)	(0.64)	(−0.99)	**(−2.39)**	(0.99)	(0.81)
Private Sector	−4.07	−5.96				
	(−0.40)	(−0.74)				
Individual/family as the major shareholder			6.11	−12.24		
			(1.10)	(−1.04)		
Financial firms as the major shareholder			−4.88	−1.81		
			(−1.49)	(−0.67)		
India Log(firm size)					**−10.51**	**−4.32**
					(−2.46)	**(−2.50)**
India Log(firm age)					**35.69**	**20.04**
					(2.11)	**(2.83)**
India Exporters					−27.93	−9.94
					(−0.82)	(−0.70)
India* Judicial environment					−2.73	−2.77
					(−0.35)	(−0.79)
India* Government efficiency					12.98	4.27
					(1.00)	(0.80)
India* Official Impact					−9.83	−5.61
					(−1.10)	(−1.50)
# of observations	1,259	1,233	1,099	991	2,358	2,224
Adjusted R-square	0.02	0.02	0.03	0.03	0.03	0.04

Note: For Judicial, Government efficiency, and official impact, we also interact them with size and age respectively. The robust tstats of those interactive variables are not significant. (Non-robust ones are significant.)
* Means multiplication where 'India' is a 0–1 binary dummy.

During the early stage of the above special zone, investors from Taiwan were willing to commit their capital to these start-ups and refinance them when necessary. The reason that many investors are from Taiwan is no coincidence: Many people in Kunshan have relatives in Taiwan and through them investors obtained information on the investment opportunities. The Taiwanese investors also came to understand that although there were almost no formal investor protections, local Government officials have an incentive to cooperate with the development of the special zone and try to create an economic boom in the local economy. This is the case because a booming economy can greatly enhance the chance of an official being promoted, in addition to participating in profit-sharing. During the early stage of development, Taiwanese investors did not stay in the area as they often do now. As a result, there was virtually no monitoring of the entrepreneurs, and there was complete separation of ownership and control.

Survey evidence

Among the seventeen firms that we surveyed and which provided us detailed answers to our questions, one firm is from suburban Shanghai, three are from Jiangsu province, and the remaining thirteen are from Zhejiang province. These firms operate in a wide range of industries. The average age of the firm is over eleven years, and they employ an average of over 1,600 employees. The average size of (book) assets is US$55 million, with average return on assets being 10 percent. Finally, on average firms are highly levered, with the average (private and bank) debt to (private) equity ratio reaching 2.1.

Figure 5.4a provides more background information for the survey firms. There are significant variations in the past performance and the expected future performance (top two histograms) of firms. In terms of ownership structure (second panel of histograms), both at start-up and at the present time, the two dominant forms are 'founder and family', and 'shareholding', which resembles a private equity structure. Around 35 percent of the founders of our sample firms worked in TVEs prior to starting up their own firms (bottom histogram), while 23 percent (18%) of the founders worked in SOEs (Government agencies). The experience from the state sector or other private sector firms is valuable for the entrepreneurs, as they not only gained knowledge on how to run a private firm, but also learned how to deal with Government officials.

FINANCING CHANNELS

Figure 5.4b presents evidence of the financing channels of the firms. First, it is not surprising that during the start-up stage, funds from founders' family and friends are an important source of financing (top-left histogram). Moreover, funds from friends, in the form of private loans and equity, are also very important during the firm's subsequent growth

Law, Institutions, and Finance

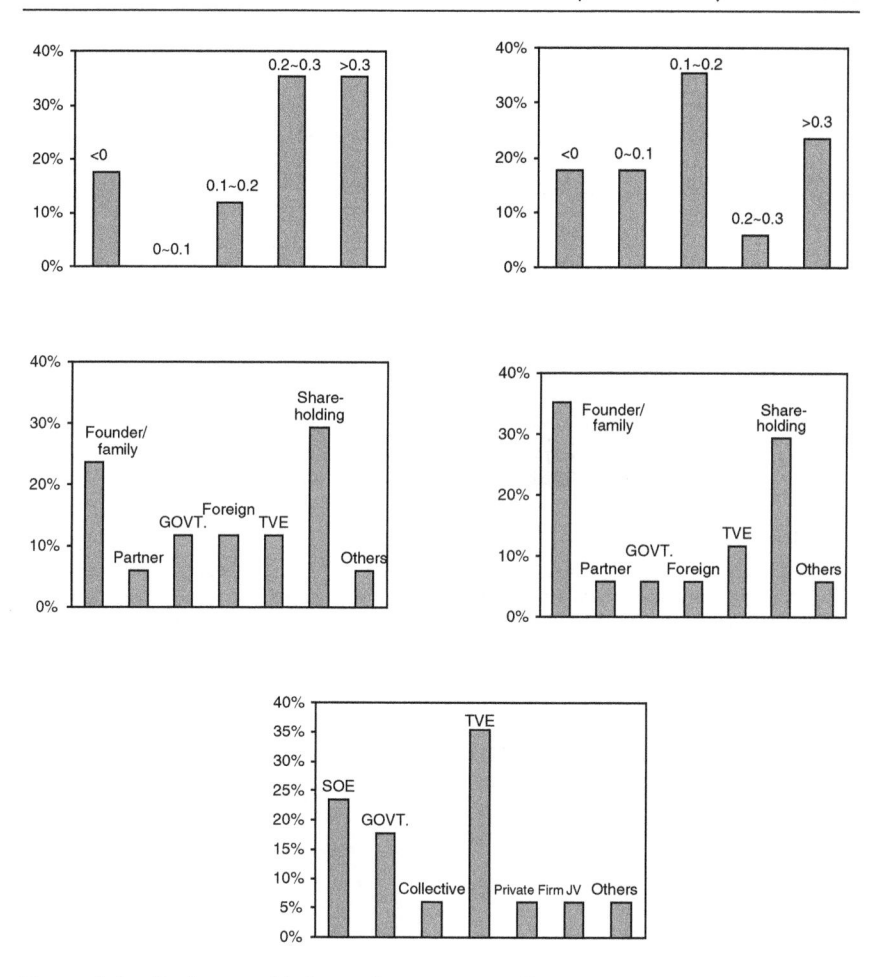

Figure 5.4a. Background information on survey firms

period (top-right histogram). In some cases there are no formal written contracts between the friends/investors and the entrepreneurs, implying that reputation- and relationship-based implicit contractual agreements have worked effectively. Second, internal financing, in the form of retained earnings, is also important (not reported in Figure 5.4b): Survey firms retained an average of 55 to 65 percent of their net income for reinvestment during the initial two to three years of existence.

Third, funding from financial intermediaries is one of the most important sources for the surveyed firms. In terms of start-up financing, over 40 percent of firms surveyed regard 'banks' as either a 'very important'

173

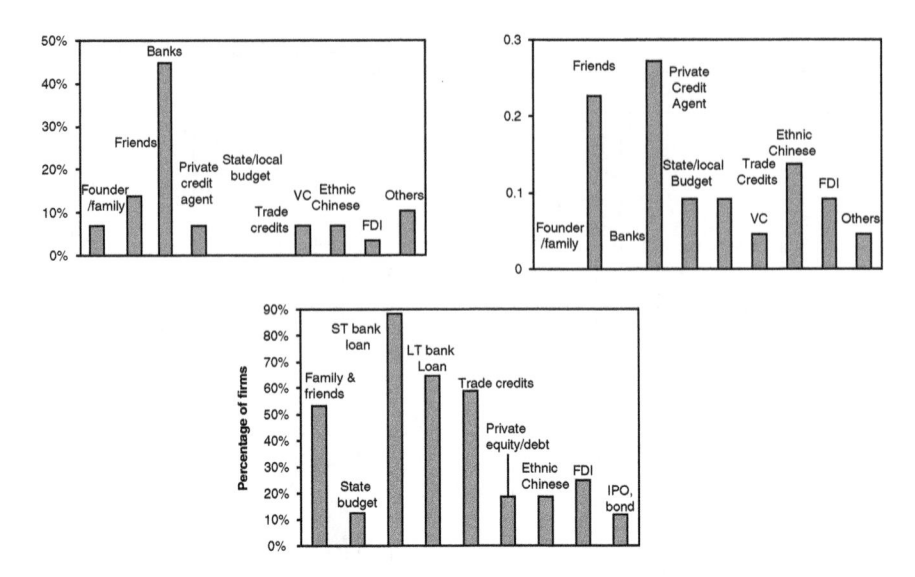

Figure 5.4b. Financing channels of survey firms

Note: Figure 5.4b presents survey results on firms' financing channels: Each bar represents the percentage of firms that regard a financing source as very important (25–50%) or extremely important (>50%) during their start-up and growth periods. PCA = private credit agencies; Budget = state/local budget, and VC = venture capital. Figure 5.4c presents results on selected governance mechanisms among these firms.

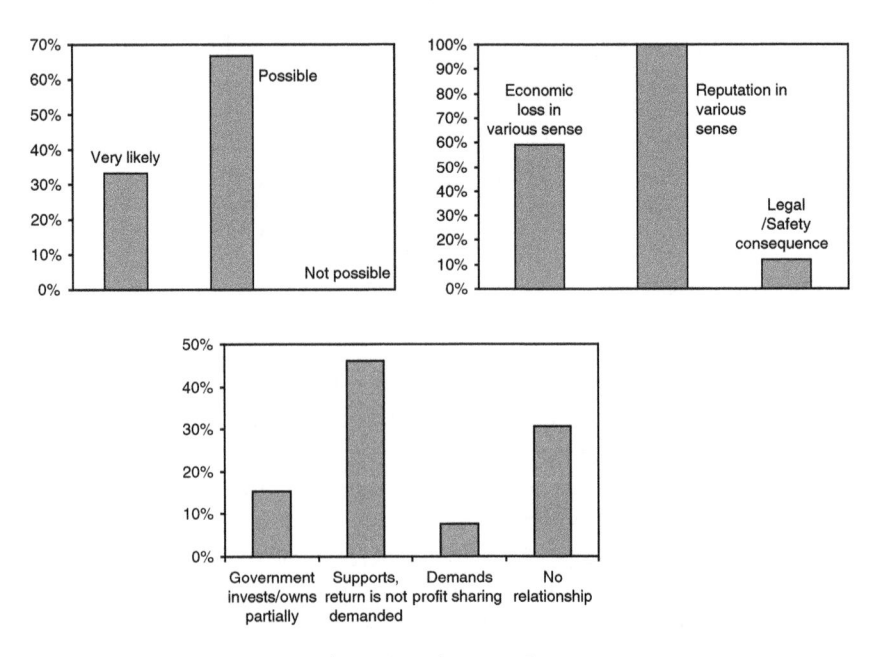

Figure 5.4c. Governance mechanisms of survey firms

(25–50% of total funding needs) or an 'extremely important' (more than 50% of total funding needs) financing source. The four largest state-owned banks are ranked the highest in terms of providing funds, while other state-owned banks are ranked second. However, it is not clear that state-owned banks provide the cheapest start-up financing channel for all private sector firms. The caveat is that almost all the surveyed firms that received start-up financing from state-owned banks had already established close relationships with those banks before their inception as shown in Figure 5.5. In fact, not a single firm rates banks as very important or extremely important during their growth period. Financing from private credit agencies (PCAs), instead of banks, is the most important channel during a firm's growth period. These nonstate lenders usually charge very high interest rates and/or require a large amount of collateral on loans, and can force liquidation should the entrepreneurs default; the associated loan contracts resemble junk bonds to a certain degree.

On average, each surveyed firm currently has a loan relationship with 4.3 banks or other financial intermediaries, with the maximum (minimum) being 12 (1). Collateral value counts for 82.6 percent of the loan value on average with a maximum (minimum) of 120 percent (20%). Fixed assets are the most popular form of collateral, with third-party guarantees being the second-most popular form. These facts imply that financial institutions, state or private, seem to understand the risk of start-up firms and try to 'price' this risk in their loan contracts. In a few cases the local Government provides the third-party guarantee, indicating an active role played by Government officials in supporting the growth of firms.

During a firm's growth period (Figure 5.4b), there are a few other channels that are important sources of financing, in particular, investment from 'ethnic Chinese' (investors from Hong Kong, Taiwan, and overseas Chinese), mostly in the form of private loans and equity. This financing source, as compared to investment from non-Chinese foreign direct investment (FDI), relies on the relationship between the investors and the entrepreneurs. Other sources include trade credits among business partners, state and local budgets, and FDIs, while investment from venture capitalists (VCs) is not widely used during either the start-up stage or the growth period. When asked about which financing channels are least costly (bottom histogram in Figure 5.4b), while most of the surveyed firms point to short- and long-term bank loans, almost 60 percent of

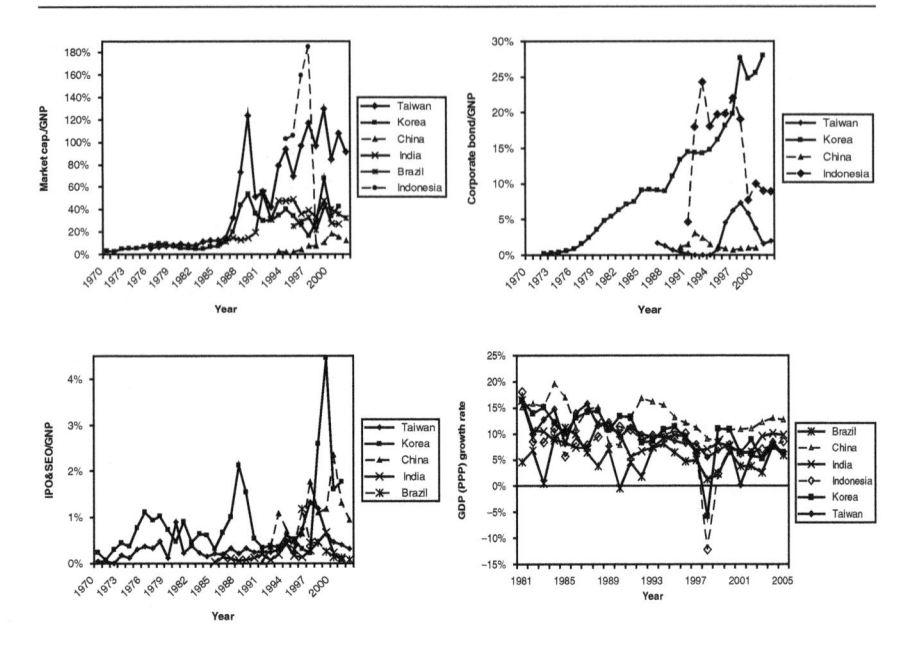

Figure 5.5. Comparing financing channels in emerging economies

Note: Figure 5.5 compares the time series of stock market capitalization/GNP ratios across six emerging economies in the top-left pane, the time series of the ratios of the amount of corporate bonds outstanding/GNP in top-right pane, while in the bottom-left pane the figure presents the time series of IPO and SEO issuance (in a given year)/GNP. The calculations for all the ratios in these three panels are based on local currencies of a country in a given year. In the bottom-right pane the figure compares time series of the growth rates of GDP, and the growth rates are calculated using PPP-adjusted GDP figures in order to avoid biases caused by different currency policies.

firms indicate trade credits among business partners (e.g. McMillan and Woodruff 1999a).

For start-up firms, securing land and other fixed assets is important for their survival. While not reported in the figures, more than half of the surveyed firms purchase the long-term 'operation-rights' of the land (20–50 years) from the Government, which has the ultimate control. With operation rights, a firm has more control over the land than under a 'land rental' contract. For example, firms can rent the land to another party once obtaining the operation rights from the Government. Land rental contracts have shorter terms on average (5–10 years). In terms of fixed assets, sixteen out of the seventeen firms purchased and own all of their fixed assets. Among them, nine firms purchased their fixed assets from the state sector, and seven out of the nine firms considered the price they paid to be the same as the market value of the assets. One firm's executive

Law, Institutions, and Finance

indicated that for the rental portion of fixed assets from SOE, there are no formal contracts between the firm and the SOE.

Finally, when asked about the prospects of going public, founders and executives list 'access to large scale funding' and 'reputation increase' as the most important benefits, and the 'disclosure of valuable information to competitors and outsiders' and 'large amount of fees paid' to the Government, investment banks, and consulting firms as the most critical disadvantages of going public.

CORPORATE GOVERNANCE

Figure 5.4c provides some information on governance mechanisms. First, over 60 percent (30%) of firms believe that if their own firm were not run efficiently and were to find itself in financial distress, it is 'possible' ('very likely') its assets would be purchased by another firm or investor; no one answered it is 'not possible' for this to occur. Not reported in the figure, we also asked firms about product market competition: 40 percent of surveyed firms believe that if their firm were not operating efficiently, within three to six months 20 percent of its market share would be taken away, while 80 percent of firms' founders/executives believe the entire market share of the firm would be taken away in two years. When asked about what type of losses concern them the most if the firm were to fail (top-right histogram in Figure 5.5c), every firm's founders/executives (100%) said reputation loss is a major concern, while only 60 percent of them said economic losses are of major concern.

The success of a firm in the private sector depends crucially on the support from local Government. Over 40 percent of survey firms state the local Government 'supports' the growth of the firm without demanding profit sharing, while for some other firms, the Government is either a partial owner or demands profit sharing without investing in the firm (bottom histogram in Figure 5.4c). The supportive attitude of the local Government toward firms in the private sector is remarkable considering the fact that the Chinese Government is widely regarded as corrupt and disrespectful of property rights (e.g. Le Porta et al. 2004).

Discussion

In this section we discuss mechanisms supporting the growth of the private sector. We believe the most important reason for the growth is the work of alternative financing and governance mechanisms. Perhaps the most important mechanism is reputation and relationships.

These have been of particular relevance and importance to China's institutional development. Without a dominant religion, one can argue that the most important force shaping China's social values and institutions is the set of beliefs first developed and formalized by Kong Zi (Confucius). This set of beliefs clearly defines family and social orders, and are very different from western beliefs on how legal codes should be formulated and how individuals and businesses negotiate (e.g. Pye 1982; Chow 2002). Using the World Values Survey conducted in the early 1990s, Le Porta et al. (1997b) find that China has one of the highest levels of social trust among a group of forty developed and developing countries. We interpret high social trust in China as being influenced by Confucian beliefs. Interestingly, the same survey, used in Le Porta et al. (1997b), finds that Chinese citizens have a low tendency to participate in civil activities. However, our evidence shows that with effective alternative mechanisms in place, citizens in the developed regions of China have a strong incentive to participate in business/economic activities.

The second most important mechanism is competition in product and input markets, which has worked well in both developed and developing countries (e.g. McMillan 1995; 1997; Allen and Gale 2000b). What we see from the success of private sector firms in Wenzhou and other surveyed firms suggests that it is only those firms that have the strongest comparative advantage in an industry (of the area) that survive and thrive. Djankov et al. (2002) examine entry barriers across eighty-five countries including China. Entry barriers are a relevant factor for the growth of China's private sector, as lower entry barriers foster competition. Djankov et al. find that countries with heavier (lighter) regulation of entry have higher Government corruption (more democratic and limited Governments) and larger unofficial economies.

With much lower barriers to entry compared to other countries with similar (low) per capita GDP, China is once again an 'outlier' in the Djankov et al. sample. The outlier status is even stronger considering that China is one of the least democratic countries, and such countries tend to have high barriers to entry. Based on our survey evidence, we conclude that there exist non-standard methods to remove entry barriers in China: First, sixteen out of the seventeen firms applied for a license (required) before the business started, with 50 percent of them indicating that it takes two weeks to one month to go through the procedure and 37.5 percent say it takes one to two months. The main problem for the application for a license seems to be dealing with Government bureaucracy. To ease this problem, most of the firms' founders/executives ask the friends of Government officials to negotiate on their behalf, or the firms can offer profit sharing to Government officials. But these methods are consistent with our results that alternative mechanisms based on reputation and relationships provide the most important support for the growth of the private sector.

There are other effective corporate governance mechanisms. First, Burkart et al. (2003) link the degree of separation of ownership and control to different legal environments, and show that family-run firms will emerge as the dominant form of ownership structure in countries with weak minority shareholder protection, whereas professionally managed firms must be the optimal form in countries with strong investor protection. Our survey evidence on the private sector and empirical results on the listed sector, along with evidence in Claessens et al. (2000; 2002), suggests that family firms are a norm in China and other Asian countries, and these firms have performed well. Second, Allen and Gale (2000a) show that if cooperation among different suppliers of inputs is necessary and all suppliers benefit from the firm doing well, then a good equilibrium with no external governance is possible, as internal, mutual monitoring can ensure the optimal outcome. We have shown trade credits are an important form of financing for firms during their growth period. Third, the common goal of sharing high prospective profits can align interests of local and foreign investors with entrepreneurs and managers to overcome numerous obstacles and achieve their common goal. Under this common goal in a multiperiod setting, implicit contractual agreements and reputation can act as enforcement mechanisms to ensure that all parties fulfill their roles to make the firm successful. Profit sharing also makes it incentive compatible for officials at various levels to support the growth of the firm.

Finally, there is a strand of literature studying transitional economies, such as Russia, China, Vietnam, and Eastern European countries, from Socialist systems to market systems. It is important to point out why China differs from other transitional economies. First, with the exception of Russia, China's economy is much larger and more diversified than other transitional economies. With a small and homogeneous economy, a country can adjust its legal and financial systems to the strengths of its economy much easier than a large country can. The recent economic struggle in Russia illustrates this point (e.g. Shleifer and Treisman 2000). The success of China's private sector demonstrates that alternative mechanisms can work wonders even in large and diversified economies.

Second, it is probably easier for other countries to adopt drastic reform measures in the short run. China, under the influence of Confucius' views, is different in that people hold the belief that fundamental changes in society should be gradual and should be fully implemented only after they are proven correct. This view, however, does not prevent regional experiments conducted at a smaller scale. Accordingly, China adopted a gradual, 'dual track' path in its economic reform, where the continued enforcement of the existing planning system goes alongside with the fast-paced development of financial markets, as compared to the 'big bang' approach taken by some other countries (e.g. Lau et al. 2000).

Third, the role played by the Government during the reform process is very different in China than in most other transition economies, and in particular, Russia (e.g. Blanchard and Shleifer 2001). In a broader context, Le Porta et al. (1999a) find that Governments in countries with French or socialist origins have lower quality (in terms of supporting economic growth) than those with English common laws and richer countries. However, China is a counter example to La Porta et al.'s argument on Government: While the Chinese Communist Party largely remains autocratic, Government officials, especially those in the most developed areas (e.g. Jiangsu and Zhejiang provinces), played an active supporting role in promoting the growth of the private sector. This is different from the 'grabbing hand' role played by Government officials in other countries (Frye and Shleifer 1997). The reason for this supporting role is threefold. First, starting in the early 1980s, the central Government of China implemented a mandatory retirement age for almost all bureaucrats at various levels, which made the officials younger and more familiar with capitalist ideas. In Russia, officials from the old regime were entrenched and able to extract rents from the new economy without any contribution. Next, during early stages of China's reform, TVEs, in which local Governments are partial owners, provided the most important source of growth in the private sector. The enormous success of TVEs and the promotion of the associated officials provided examples and incentives to other officials to follow suit. Finally, as discussed above, profit sharing with firms in

Law, Institutions, and Finance

a multiperiod setting also makes it incentive compatible for officials at various levels to support the growth of the firm.

5.7 Conclusions

In this chapter we examine and compare the formal systems of law and finance in China and India and the alternative institutional arrangements and governing mechanisms in the two countries, and the relation between the development of these systems and their economic growth.

With one of the largest and fastest growing economies in the world, China differs from most of the countries studied in the law, institutions, finance, and growth literature, and is an important counter example to the existing findings: Its legal and financial systems as well as institutions are all underdeveloped, but its economy has been growing at a very fast rate. More importantly, the growth in the private sector, where applicable legal and financial mechanisms are arguably poorer than those in the state and listed sectors, is much faster than that of the other sectors. The system of alternative mechanisms and institutions plays an important role in supporting the growth in the private sector, and they are good substitutes for standard corporate governance mechanisms and financing channels.

India too has a special place among the countries studied in the law, institutions, finance, and growth literature. Despite its English common-law origin and British-style judicial system and democratic Government, there is enough documented evidence to suggest that the effective level of investor protection and the quality of legal institutions in India are quite weak. We examine the legal and business environment in which Indian firms operate and compare our results to those from other countries. We conduct our analysis using extensive and rich datasets, including aggregate country-level data, large firm-level samples, and our own surveys of small and medium Indian firms. We also employ a broader framework of analysis than in most existing law and finance studies. The framework includes not only formal legal options (courts) and formal financial channels (stock markets and banks) but also their institutional substitutes, including non-legal methods based on reputation, trust, and relationships to settle commercial disputes and enforce contracts, and alternative financial channels, such as friends and family financing and trade credit.

Going forward, our results pose an important question for both researchers and policymakers: Should China also transform the private sector toward the 'standard form' like it has been doing for the state sector? Given the success of the private sector and the deficiency in the state and listed sectors in China, much more research is required in order to better understand how alternative mechanisms work where standard mechanisms are not available or not suitable. These effective substitutes worked well in China, and similar substitutes based on relationship and reputation may have also worked well in other economies including developed economies. Our results thus have general implications: There are important factors connecting law, institutions, finance, and growth that are not well understood. A better understanding of how these nonstandard mechanisms work to promote growth can shed light on optimal development paths not only for China, but also many other countries.

As for India we find that Indian firms in general, and the smaller firms in particular, show symptoms of poor investor protection, including concentrated ownership, low dividend payout, and low valuation. Our empirical tests show that firms in the SME sector in India effectively substitute non-legal deterrents, such as loss of business and reputation, for legal penalties and alternative finance for funds from markets and financial institutions. Interestingly, our results also establish that the small firms grow faster than large-scale firms which operate in environments with stronger legal protection and easier access to formal finance. We find that to a large extent Indian firms too conduct business outside the formal legal system and do not rely on formal financing channels from markets and banks for most of their financing needs. Instead, firms across the board, and in particular, small and medium firms, use non-legal methods based on reputation, trust, and relationships to settle disputes and enforce contracts, and rely on alternative financing channels such as trade credits to finance their growth.

The results of this chapter have important implications for future research. It will be interesting and important to examine whether substitute mechanisms similar to those that have worked well in India and China have also supported the growth of firms in other economies where formal mechanisms are ineffective. At the end of 2005, China and India together accounted for 40 percent of the world population and 19 percent of the world GDP in PPP terms. Given the status of the two countries, the findings call for more single-country studies to understand better how the *effective* level of investor protection as opposed to the nominal level affects corporate financing and growth, and leads to wide use of substitute legal and financing mechanisms.

Finally, given all other things equal, formal mechanisms by their nature should be more rigid and slower to work. Hence, informal mechanisms are perhaps more suitable for dynamic economies (India, China), dynamic corporate sectors (SME), and industries (software). The law and finance literature has identified an important determinant of formal external finance, namely quality of legal protection. Perhaps history, culture, and economic growth at the country level and corporate growth rate and size at the firm level are other possible candidates. New and imaginative research is necessary to understand these complex but important issues.

6

China and India: A Tale of Two Trade Integration Approaches

*Przemyslaw Kowalski**

6.1 Introduction

China and India's GDP growth rates have outperformed world average growth rates and, indeed, those of other lower- and middle-income countries for the most part of the last fifteen years. According to official statistics China has grown at an average rate of close to 10 percent annually during 1990–2006; a rate at which income more than doubles every seven years. Although regarded as a success, India's performance was less spectacular than China's with an approximate rate of growth of 6 percent annually though in reality the difference in growth rates between the two countries may be smaller. Heston (2007), for example, points out that, according to recent purchasing power studies, officially reported national growth rates may overstate China's actual growth, which is not so much the case in India.[1] The growth of world economy in the corresponding period amounted to approximately 3 percent annually (Figure 6.1).

As pointed out by the World Bank (2007), the two countries now account for approximately 37.5 percent of world population and

---

* The material presented here draws on the author's work carried out within the OECD Secretariat, in particular on Greene et al. (2006) and Kowalski and Dihel (2009). The views presented are strictly those of the author and do not necessarily represent the views of the OECD or its member countries or co-authors of the two aforementioned reports. Useful comments by Ralph Lattimore, Matthieu Bussière, participants of the Conference on India and China's Role in International Trade and Finance and Global Economic Governance in New Delhi and excellent statistical assistance by Clarisse Legendre are gratefully acknowledged.

[1] Heston (2007) cites Maddison and Wu (2007), who have estimated lower growth rates than official rates (7.85% p.a. vs. 9.6% for total GDP).

A Tale of Two Trade Integration Approaches

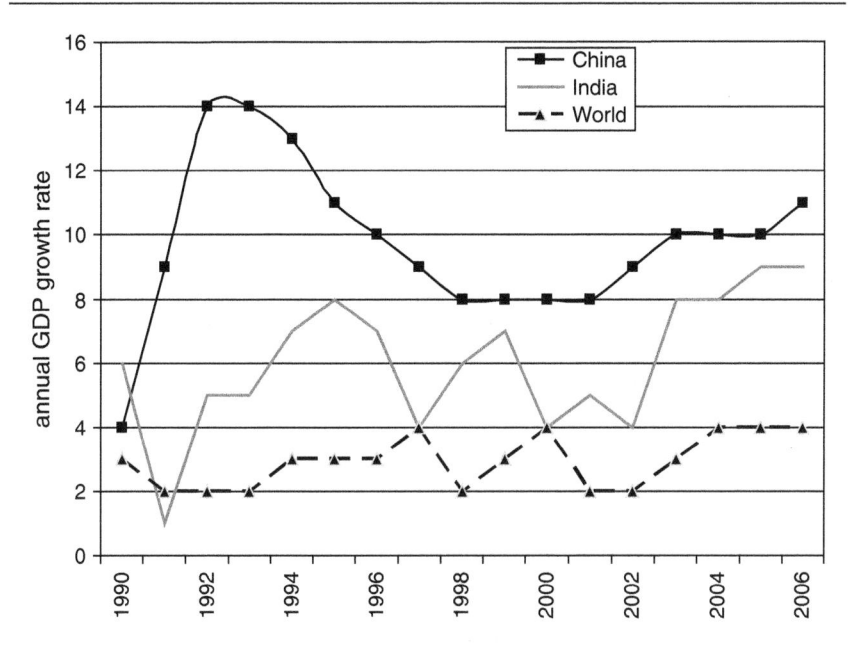

Figure 6.1. Annual GDP growth rate 1990–2006
Source: Constructed using data in the World Bank's World Development Indicators.

6.4 percent of the value of world output and income at current prices and exchange rates; as their per capita production and consumption approach levels similar to those of today's developed economies, as they are indeed already doing (see Figure 6.2), major effects on global markets and resources can be expected. Indeed, this has already been happening for some time with the great influence of China's demand and supply on the world markets observed since the beginning of the 1990s. India's overall influence on world markets, despite the several successful stories of individual companies or sectors, has been more limited so far (see Figure 6.3) but the potential is clearly there (Lehman Brothers 2007; OECD 2007a). In fact, one could argue that because the economic growth is being achieved in India with less intervention by the authorities and within a democratic political system, it may be in some respects more sustainable than the growth achieved in China (Huang 2008).

While China and India are both very populous, both have a history of central planning and inward oriented policies and both are poorer as compared to the OECD area, they are in fact two very different countries with diverging development opportunities and challenges. Some of these broad differences are revealed in Table 6.1, which compares a list of

185

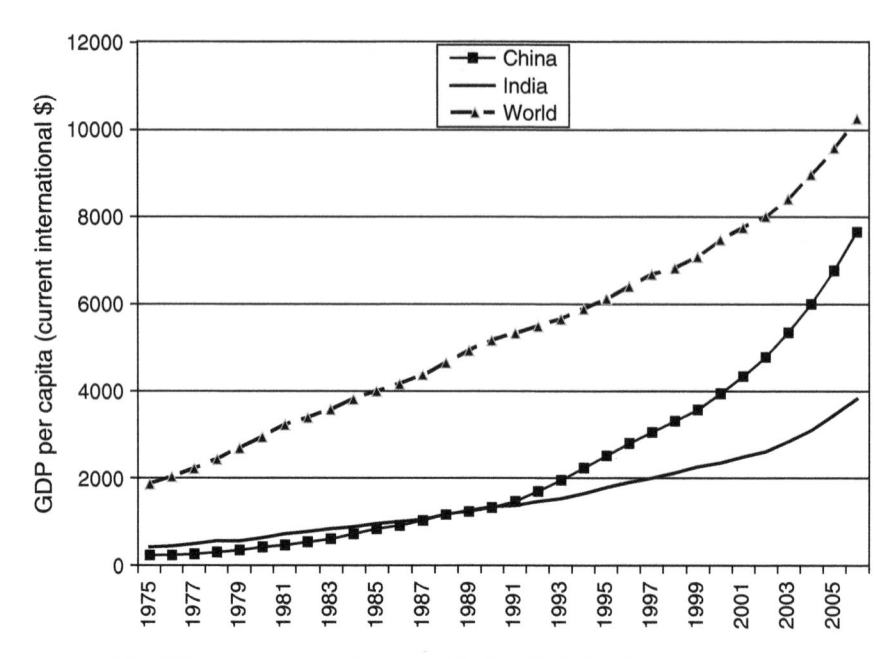

Figure 6.2. GDP per capita in China and India 1975–2006
Source: Constructed using data in the World Bank's World Development Indicators.

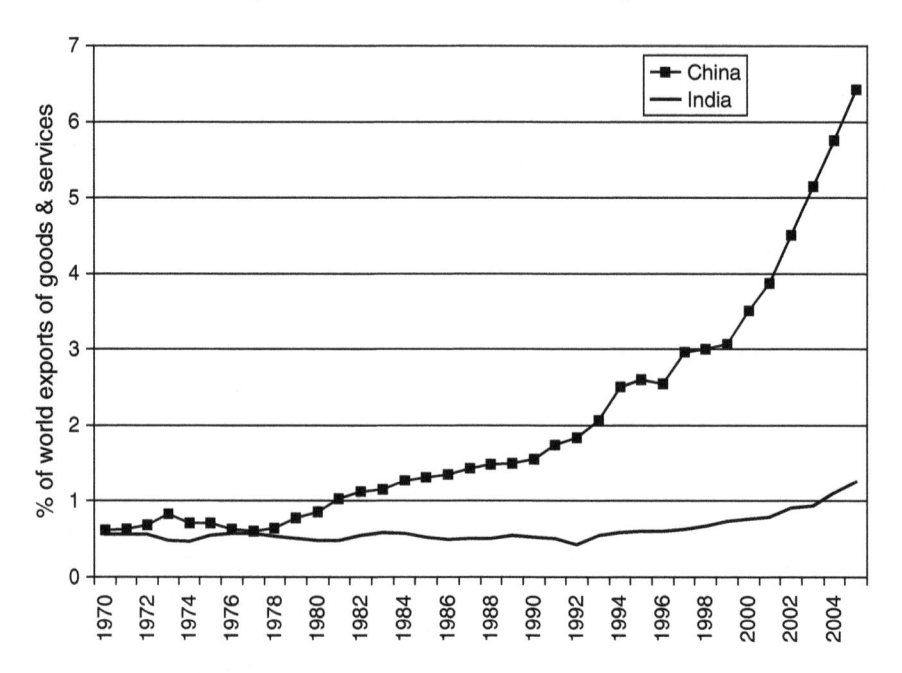

Figure 6.3. Shares in world exports
Source: Constructed using data in the World Bank's World Development Indicators.

A Tale of Two Trade Integration Approaches

Table 6.1. Selected indicators

	China	India	Germany	Japan	United States	World
Agricultural land (000' sq. km)	5,549	1,800	170	47	4,169	49,377
Arable land (hectares, million)	103.4	159.4	11.8	4.4	176.7	n/a
Population, total (million)	1,312	1,110	82	128	299	6,518
Birth rate, crude (per 1,000 people) in 2005	12	24	8	8	14	20
Death rate, crude (per 1,000 people) in 2005	6	8	10	9	8	9
GDP (current US$ billion) in 2006	2,668	906	2,907	4,340	13,202	48,245
GDP per capita, PPP (current international $) in 2006	7,660	3,827	31,744	32,385	44,155	10,252
GINI index in 2004	47	37	28	n/a	41	n/a
Goods exports (BoP, current US$ billion) in 2003	438	59	745	449	717	7,498
Goods imports (BoP, current US$ billion) in 2003	394	68	600	343	1,261	7,406
Service exports (BoP, current US$ billion) in 2003	47	26	124	78	299	1,921
Service imports (BoP, current US$ billion) in 2003	55	26	173	112	250	1,881
Distance from EU (in km)	7,971	6,420				
Distance from US (in km)	10,994	11,762				
Distance from Japan (in km)	2,098	5,848				

Note: Gini coefficients for China and India correspond to 2004, for Germany and United States to 2000.
Source: Constructed using data from WDI, CEPII.

selected resource, geographical, and economic indicators. Taking a bird's-eye view at the two economies India is closer to Europe in terms of geographical distance by some 1,500 kilometers (and yet closer if a sea distance is considered) while China is closer to the United States by some 700 kilometers and to Japan by some 3,750 kilometers. Culturally, because of the past colonial links with the British Empire and the widespread use of the English language, India is much closer culturally to both the EU and the US, while China can be considered closer to Japan. Both countries are very large in terms of surface and population and are quite diverse geographically and ethnically. China has almost three times as much agricultural land as India does but India's arable land resources are larger than those of China by almost 60 percent. India's population and labor force are growing much faster than China's, including the skilled segment of the labor force. Despite relatively similar populations, according to the World Development Indicators database China's economy is almost three times bigger than India's (at current prices and exchange rates) and the Chinese GDP per capita in purchasing power parity terms is double that of India. According to the first results of the 2005 UN International Comparison Program (ICP) of purchasing power parities reported by Heston (2007) China's and India's total outputs in 2005 amounted to respectively 73 and 30 percent of the US level. Corresponding price levels were 35 and 30 percent of the US level.

These and many other differences, including the scale, scope, and timing of already undertaken economic policy reforms, are reflected in the rather distinctive development paths that the two economies have been following as well as in their distinctive trade profiles. While in both China and India the share of agriculture in GDP has been declining,[2] its place has been taken primarily by manufacturing in China and by services in India. As a result in 2006 services accounted for 56 percent of India's GDP compared to 41 percent in China.[3] This is also reflected in the recent trade developments. India quite clearly has not been able to match China's conquest of the world's goods markets, even though recently more dynamism has been observed in certain segments of the Indian manufacturing sector (Lehman Brothers 2007). Yet, for some time now, the developments in India's services sector have generated trade flows that are more comparable to those of China in absolute terms and are much higher than in China if we account for the economy size. Evidence is also mounting that the product composition of these two economies' trade is quite different and that, for the moment, the two enormous economies are not competing directly in the world markets (Dimaranan et al. 2007).[4]

The reminder of this chapter goes deeper into the trade and trade policy developments in China and India in order to hypothesize about the implications for their own economies and the world economy as

---

[2] This is notwithstanding the fact that close to 40% and 60% of respectively China and India's population live in the rural areas.

[3] Heston (2007) points out that international price comparisons suggest that in both China and India capital goods for example are relatively expensive as compared to prices of consumption and that capital stocks estimated in local currencies probably overestimate the contribution of fixed capital formation and capital-intensive activities to growth. These discrepancies may also be reflected in sector shares and structural composition of recent growth in both countries, likely overestimating the contribution to output of manufacturing. In fact, differences in relative prices across countries have serious implications for all sorts of international comparisons, including comparisons of trade performance.

[4] This chapter deals predominantly with external trade developments and national trade policies of China and India and as such does not go into much detail in discussion of regions. Nevertheless, it must be born in mind that in both China and India economic activity is very unevenly distributed and that there are major differences in product specialization and incomes in individual regions. Discussion of economic performance across China's regions can be found in OECD (2005) and across India's regions in OECD (2007a).

A Tale of Two Trade Integration Approaches

a whole. In particular it aims to shed light on the following set of questions:

- What has been the role of international trade in China and India's recent economic growth?
- What has been the role of trade policy in China and India's recent economic growth?
- What is the remaining potential for improving economic outcomes by reforming trade policy?
- What are other policies that could help these countries to further improve their integration with the world markets?

6.2 Main trade developments

General trade trends

China's economic transformation and integration with world markets is one of the most remarkable economic developments of recent decades: China's share in world goods trade has increased from less than 1 percent in 1970 to close to 8 percent in 2006 (see Figure 6.3). The expansion of international trade has been the key feature of the country's rising prominence in the world economy with average annual growth rates of trade at three times the world rates. Already in 2005 China became the third largest trading nation after the United States and Germany and its contribution to the growth of world merchandise trade over the period 1996–2006 amounted to 20 percent. Looking forward, it is estimated that China will become the world's top exporter by the beginning of the next decade owing to attractiveness to FDI, a high domestic saving rate, improvements in productivity spurred by reduced internal and external barriers to trade, and a significant surplus of labor (OECD 2005).

The considerable expansion of China's trade in recent years concerns both goods and services. However, as compared with its goods trade, services exports remain at lower levels and are growing more slowly. Indeed, while goods trade surplus reached US$134 billion in 2005, services saw a gradually deepening deficit that appeared at the beginning of the 1990s and reached US$9 billion in 2005. Overall, Chinese goods exports account for approximately 90 percent of its total exports, which is substantially higher than the world average at a little over 80 percent (Table 6.2). This is clearly visible in the breakdown of China's current account in period 2000–2006 (Figure 6.4) which is characterized

Table 6.2. Trade in goods and services, world and China (percentage)

	Goods World	Goods China	Services World	Services China
Exports				
1994	80	86	20	14
2001	80	89	20	11
2004	80	90	20	10
Imports				
1994	79	85	21	15
2001	80	85	20	15
2004	80	88	20	12

Source: Constructed using data from IMF Balance of Payments Statistics (2006).

by a relatively stable negative balance on services (app. 0.5% of GDP), gradually improving income and current transfers balance (counted together, from –0.7% of GDP in 2000 to 1.4% in 2007) and a rocketing surplus on trade in goods (from 2.9% to 7.7% of GDP).

All this suggests that China's exceptional integration into the world economy was mainly driven by goods trade. As we discuss below, among other things, this reflects a certain duality in China's economic policy: The opening up of trade and FDI in manufactured goods that resulted in

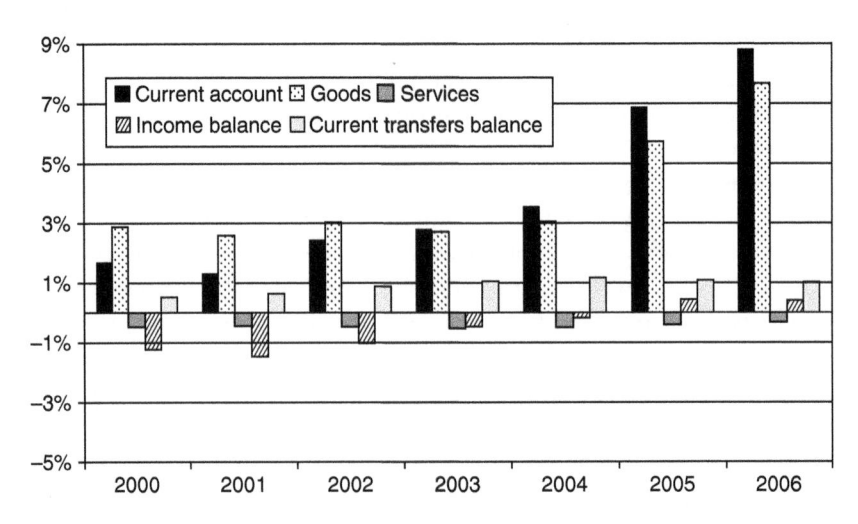

Figure 6.4. China's current account structure (as % of GDP)

Source: Constructed using data in the IMF's Balance of Payments Statistics.

A Tale of Two Trade Integration Approaches

the emergence of a largely private sector[5] and the high level of public ownership and important regulatory barriers in services sectors.

The product composition of China's merchandise trade has undergone a major change since the beginning of reforms with the large rise in the value of manufacturing exports and the significant increase over the years in imports of fuel, energy, and capital goods (Greene et al. 2006). To illustrate more recent changes Table 6.3 presents the top twenty-five products (at the 6-digit level of the harmonized system) exported by China in 1996 and 2006. First of all, the comparison reveals that China's exports were less concentrated in 1996 than they were in 2006; for instance the top twenty-five products accounted for 20 percent and 33 percent of total merchandise exports, respectively. Furthermore, a clear diversification is observed away from lower-technology products, such as footwear, toys, apparel, and petroleum products, towards ICT sector products, such as automatic data processing machines, transmission apparatus and parts and inputs into electronic products, amongst others. Both the growing specialization and the going up the value chain are manifestations of the raising sophistication of China's manufacturing sector. In the services sector, too, China has for some time already been diversifying away from transportation and financial and insurance services toward the exports of other business services (mainly professional services) as well as travel (Table 6.4).

China's major trading partners are on the export side the European Union followed by the United States and Japan (Figure 6.5). Together, these three trading partners provided markets for just below 50 percent of China's total exports in 2006, and made up 34 percent of China's import bill. On the imports side Japan and ASEAN countries are very important and, indeed, while China has positive trade balance with the EU and the US it has negative trade balance with the ASEAN group. It is quite clear that this reflects in part greater specialization in production in the Asia region. As Greene et al. (2006) describe China has emerged as the final processing and assembly platform for a large volume of exports originating from its Asian OECD neighbours but destined for markets in Europe and North America. With time the sourcing increasingly involves other fast growing Asian economies.

---

[5] In terms of sectoral policies, emphasis was placed on investment in export-oriented manufacturing determining a more rapid development of these sectors.

Table 6.3. Changing structure of China's trade: 25 top exports and their share in total exports

Product name	1996 value ($ '000)	1996 share % of total exports	Product name	2006 value ($ '000)	2006 share % of total exports
Petroleum oils and oils obtained from bituminous minerals (crude)	2,789,285	1.9	Digital automatic data processing machines	43,383,744	4.5
Input or output units	1,984,923	1.3	Transmission apparatus incorporating reception apparatus	35,753,598	3.7
Other footwear with uppers of leather	1,901,782	1.3	Parts and accessories of the automatic data processing machines	32,618,566	3.4
Other footwear with outer soles and uppers of rubber or plastics	1,831,672	1.2	Input or output units	25,676,922	2.7
Other toys	1,653,536	1.1	Other parts of transmission apparatus, radar apparatus or television receivers	23,969,022	2.5
Parts and accessories of the automatic data processing machines	1,626,778	1.1	Monolithic integrated circuits, digital	18,410,882	1.9
Articles of apparel, of leather or of composition leather	1,440,980	1.0	Other devices, appliances and instruments	13,231,578	1.4
Travel goods, similar containers of plastics or of textile materials	1,397,615	0.9	Colour television receivers	12,837,204	1.3
Other radio-broadcast receiver, with recording or reproducing apparatus	1,301,715	0.9	Storage units	11,917,080	1.2
Other articles of plastics	1,254,054	0.8	Other video recording or reproducing apparatus	7,699,542	0.8
T-shirts, singlets, other vests, knitted or crocheted, of cotton	1,136,873	0.8	Printed circuits	7,649,519	0.8
Storage units	1,113,778	0.7	Petroleum oils, oils obtained from bituminous minerals, preparations thereof	7,048,166	0.7
Men's or boys' trousers, overalls, breeches, of cotton	1,067,967	0.7	Video recording or reproducing apparatus, magnetic tape-type	6,994,314	0.7

A Tale of Two Trade Integration Approaches

Containers (including containers for the transport of fluids) specially designed and equipped for carriage by one or more modes of transport	1,062,390	0.7	Digital processing units	6,940,671	0.7
Bituminous coal	933,028	0.6	Static converters	6,870,148	0.7
Prepared or preserved other fish	926,594	0.6	Sweaters, pullovers, sweatshirts, waistcoats (vests), knitted or crocheted, of manmade fibers	6,010,093	0.6
Other parts and accessories of apparatus of recording or reproducing	907,436	0.6	Containers (including containers for the transport of fluids) specially designed and equipped for carriage by one or more modes of transport	5,983,954	0.6
Toys Representing Animals, Stuffed	894,411	0.6	Other sound reproducing apparatus	5,899,948	0.6
Other vessels for the transport of goods and other vessels for the transport of both persons and goods	886,313	0.6	Other footwear with uppers of leather	5,642,838	0.6
Telephone sets	864,714	0.6	Other apparatus, for carrier-current line systems	5,354,160	0.6
Cigarettes (containing tobacco)	832,530	0.6	Other footwear with outer soles and uppers of rubber or plastics	5,308,018	0.5
Table, floor, wall, window, ceiling or roof fans	794,176	0.5	T-shirts, singlets, other vests, knitted or crocheted, of cotton	5,312,081	0.5
Other parts of transmission apparatus, radar apparatus or television receivers	792,810	0.5	Other data processing machines	5,091,647	0.5
Other footwear with outer soles of rubber or plastics	788,533	0.5	Video games of a kind used with a television receiver	5,077,359	0.5
Men's or boys' anoraks, wind-cheaters, wind-jackets, of man-made fibres	781,899	0.5	Other vessels for the transport of goods and other vessels for the transport of both persons and goods	5,070,829	0.5
Total	30,965,793	20.6		315,571,880	32.6

Source: Constructed using data from COMTRADE, author's calculations.

Table 6.4. China: Services trade composition (US$ million and %)

	1990	1994	2001	2004
SERVICES—Total trade	1,503	321	−5,933	−9,699
Services exports	5,855	16,620	33,334	62,434
Transportation services	46.2	18.5	13.9	19.3
Travel	29.7	44.1	53.4	41.2
Other services	24.1	37.4	32.7	39.4
Communications	2.7	4.2	0.8	0.7
Construction	n/a	n/a	2.5	2.4
Insurance	3.9	10.2	0.7	0.6
Financial	n/a	n/a	0.3	0.2
Computer and information	n/a	n/a	1.4	2.6
Royalties and license fees	n/a	n/a	0.3	0.4
Other business services	15.7	21.3	25.3	32.0
Personal, cultural, and recreational	n/a	n/a	0.1	0.1
Government, n.i.e.	1.8	1.6	1.3	0.6
Services imports	4,352	16,299	39,267	72,133
Transportation services	74.6	46.8	28.8	34.0
Travel	10.8	18.6	35.4	26.5
Other services	14.6	34.6	35.7	39.4
Communications	0.3	0.9	0.8	0.7
Construction	n/a	n/a	2.2	1.9
Insurance	2.2	11.5	6.9	8.5
Financial	n/a	n/a	0.2	0.2
Computer and information	n/a	n/a	0.9	1.7
Royalties and license fees	n/a	n/a	4.9	6.2
Other business services	6.7	19.0	19.1	19.3
Personal, cultural, and recreational	n/a	n/a	0.1	0.2
Government, n.i.e.	5.5	3.2	0.6	0.7

Source: Constructed using data from IMF Balance of Payments Statistics (2006).

According to some crude approximations almost half of China's exports are the subject of such 'triangular' trade though this share is higher in certain high-technology products trade (see section 'Importance of trade in China and India's growth' for more on processing trade). This has resulted in a shift in China's bilateral trade relationships that now show increasing trade surpluses with Europe and North America, and rising deficits with many Asian countries.

China's trade and investment liberalization has created an attractive business environment and has had a significant impact on FDI inflows.[6] FDI grew from essentially zero in 1979 to US$636 million in 1983, to US$60.3 billion in 2005 (Greene et al. 2006). China has been the largest FDI recipient among all developing countries since 1993 and ranked the first in the world in terms of FDI inflows in 2002. Currently, China is the

---

[6] For a detailed analysis of China's investment policy, see OECD (2003; 2006c).

A Tale of Two Trade Integration Approaches

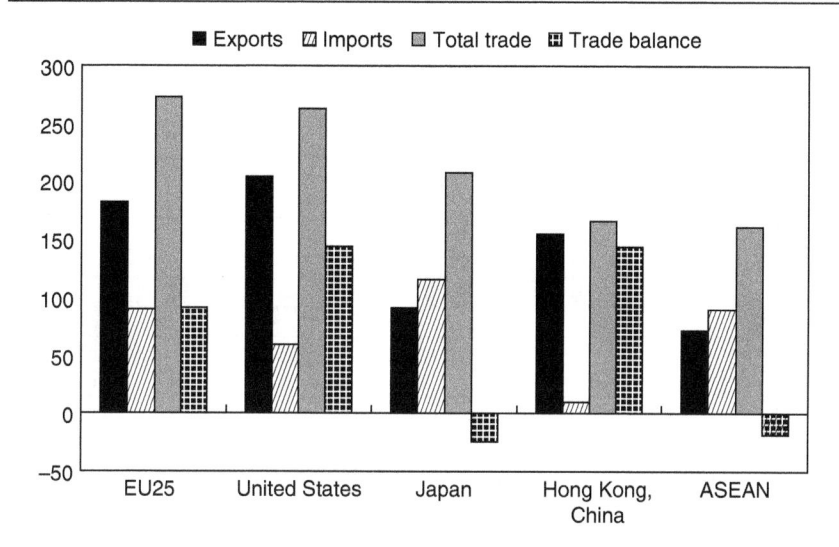

Figure 6.5. China's top trading partners (in billions US$)

Note: ASEAN corresponds to Brunei, Cambodia, Indonesia, Laos, Malaysia, Myanmar, Philippines, Singapore, Thailand, and Vietnam.

Source: Constructed using data in UN's COMTRADE, and World Bank's WDI databases.

third largest recipient of FDI after the US and the UK (UNCTAD 2005). It is important to note however that China's FDI performance must be viewed in an international perspective. In terms of FDI inflows per capita, China ranks lower than all OECD countries save for one, and even ranks relatively low among developing countries.[7] Additionally, there are some concerns about the quality of these investment flows; much of China's FDI is relatively short-term, in labor-intensive manufacturing, with foreign investment in high-tech and the services sectors lagging behind (Greene et al. 2006).

India's recent economic dynamism has led many to compare it with China and to expect a similar dramatic insertion in world markets. However, India's trade expansion is much less impressive and its nature is quite different from that of China. Its share in world trade of goods and services has first declined steadily since the beginning of the 1970s to around 0.5 percent at the beginning of 1990s and then rose steadily to just above 1 percent currently. The compound annual growth rate of India's exports of goods and services for the 1990–2005 period was 14 percent—well above the world average growth of 6 percent. In particular, in the last five

---

[7] OECD (2003, 37–40).

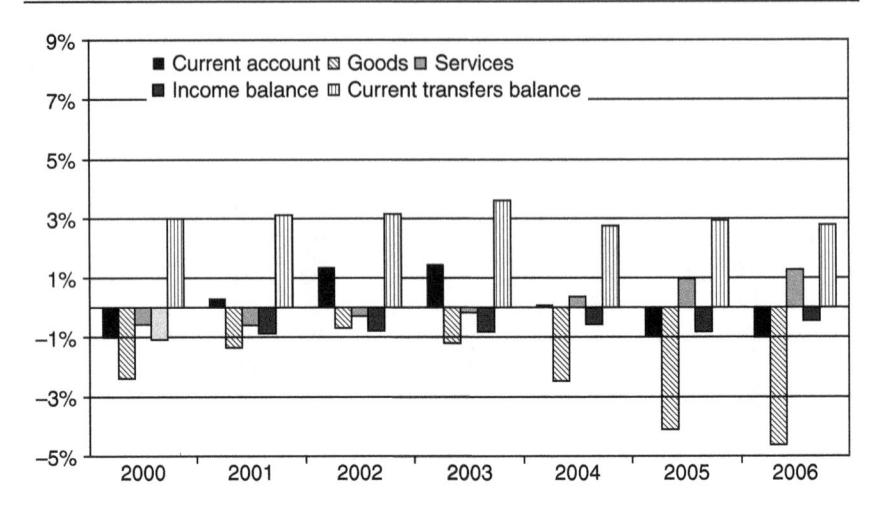

Figure 6.6. India's current account structure (as % of GDP)
Source: Constructed using data in the IMF's International Finance Statistics.

years Indian exports have increased at around 18–20 percent per annum—three times the rate of world trade growth. Yet, these significant increases reflect to a large extent a relatively low base; India's contribution to the growth of world trade over the period 1996–2006 amounted to a mere 2 percent, as compared to 20 percent in the case of China.

Remarkably, the recent growth in India's trade has been led by services rather than manufacturing. This is illustrated by the evolution of the structure of India's current account (Figure 6.6) which shows a deepening negative balance on trade in goods (from –2.4% of GDP in 2000 to –4.6% of GDP in 2006) and a gradually improving balance on services trade (from –0.6% of GDP in 2000 to 1.3% in 2006)—broadly speaking a reverse of the situation in China (see Figure 6.4 and discussion above). A distinctive feature of India's current account is the large and consistently positive current transfers balance, driven mainly by remittances.

The deteriorating balance on goods trade reflects deepening deficits in trade of capital and intermediate goods (and raw materials to some extent) which apparently cannot be adequately satisfied by the Indian manufacturing sector. Balance on consumer goods was actually positive and growing over the period 2003–2006. Deficiencies of the manufacturing sector are also reflected in the export performance. Despite the fact that India is relatively abundant in skilled labor and capital, its manufacturing exports are highly concentrated in low-technology goods and the share of high-

A Tale of Two Trade Integration Approaches

Table 6.5. Changing structure of India's trade: 25 top exports and their share in total exports

Product name	1996 value ($ '000)	1996 share % of total exports	Product name	2006 value ($ '000)	2006 share % of total exports
Other nonindustrial diamonds	4,028,039	12.3	Petroleum oils, oils obtained from bituminous minerals, preparations thereof	11,439,920	11.2
Semi-milled or wholly milled rice, whether or not polished or glazed: Parboiled:	891,755	2.7	Other Nonindustrial Diamonds	11,214,411	11.0
Oil-cake, solid residues resulting from extraction of soya-bean oil	769,332	2.3	Iron ores and concentrates (non-agglomerated)	3,519,748	3.4
Men's or boys' shirts, of cotton	748,712	2.3	Articles of jewelry and parts thereof, of other precious metal, whether or not plated or clad with precious metal	3,357,736	3.3
Frozen shrimps and prawns	725,340	2.2	Other organic compounds	1,690,186	1.7
Cotton yarn (combed cotton 85% or more; 714.29 Decitex or more)	557,561	1.7	Other medicaments (put up in packings for retail sale)	1,424,499	1.4
Women's or girls' blouses, shirts, of cotton	526,754	1.6	Semi-milled or wholly milled rice, whether or not polished or glazed: Parboiled:	1,364,245	1.3
Articles of jewelry and parts thereof, Of other precious metal, whether or not plated or clad with precious metal	517,244	1.6	T-shirts, Singlets, Other Vests, Knitted or Crocheted, of Cotton	1,107,091	1.1
Petroleum oils, oils obtained from bituminous minerals, preparations thereof	482,013	1.5	Other flat-rolled products, electrolytically plated or coated with zinc	1,059,096	1.0
Iron ores and concentrates (non-agglomerated)	428,364	1.3	Women's or girls' blouses, shirts, of cotton	1,018,038	1.0
Articles of apparel, of leather or of composition leather	424,351	1.3	Oil-cake, solid residues resulting from extraction of soya-bean oil	968,327	0.9
Cotton (not carded or combed)	413,215	1.3	Frozen shrimps and prawns	853,041	0.8
Cashew nuts	362,095	1.1	Other furnishing articles, not knitted or crocheted, of cotton	800,439	0.8

(continued)

Table 6.5. Continued

Product name	1996 value ($ '000)	1996 share % of total exports	Product name	2006 value ($ '000)	2006 share % of total exports
Other furnishing articles, not knitted or crocheted, of cotton	353, 989	1.1	Other parts and accessories	780, 573	0.8
Coffee (not roasted, not decaffeinated)	307, 810	0.9	Men's or boys' shirts, of cotton	688, 108	0.7
Cotton yarn (uncombed cotton 85% or more; 714.29 Decitex or more)	304, 175	0.9	Refined copper: Cathodes and sections of cathodes	677, 377	0.7
Other medicaments (put up in packings for retail sale)	303, 013	0.9	Cotton (not carded or combed)	639, 447	0.6
T-shirts, singlets, other vests, knitted or crocheted, of cotton	284, 767	0.9	Women's or girls' skirts, divided skirts, of wool or fine animal hair	620, 452	0.6
			Women's or girls' skirts, divided skirts, of cotton	619, 769	0.6
Uppers and parts thereof, other than stiffeners	218, 913	0.7	Cashew nuts	586, 046	0.6
Men's or boys' shirts of cotton, knitted or crocheted	216, 426	0.7	Frozen boneless bovine meat, processed	559, 829	0.5
Carpets and floor coverings of wool, of pile construction, not made up	216, 382	0.7	Other made up textile articles	517, 458	0.5
Tilapia (Tilapiinae), Mullet, Monkfish (Lophius spp), Butterfish, Sablefish (Anoplopoma fimbria)	205, 101	0.6	Insecticides	496, 891	0.5
Women's or girls' dresses, of cotton	194, 191	0.6	Other vehicles, spark-ignition engine of a cylinder capacity exceeding 1,000 cc but not exceeding 1,500 cc	485, 405	0.5
Insecticides	185, 512	0.6	Other Flat-rolled products of iron or nonalloy steel, hot-rolled, of a thickness of less than 3 mm (0.118 inch)	455, 084	0.4
New pneumatic tyres of rubber, of a kind used on buses or lorries	185, 445	0.6	P-xylene	440, 296	0.4
Total	13, 850, 499	42.1	total	46, 763, 060	45.7

Source: Constructed using data from COMTRADE, author's calculations.

technology manufactured goods in its total exports has barely changed since the mid-1990s and remains under 5 percent, as compared to 30 percent for China (see Table 6.5). Indeed, India's current merchandise export structure is still heavily skewed towards petrol products, jewellery, furniture, chemical products and textiles and wearing apparel, a structure that resembles to a certain extent the structure of China's exports at the beginning of the 1990s (Table 6.3). Superficially, the structure of exports seems a little more concentrated in 2006 than in 1996 but this is largely driven by the emergence of exports of petroleum oils.[8] Additionally, it is not easy to classify the direction of changes in the structure of top India's exports. On the one hand, a few more sophisticated products, such as motor vehicle parts, made it to the top twenty-five products in 2006. On the other hand, several traditional manufacturing products, such as gems and jewellery, wearing apparel and certain food products that already dominated India's exports in 1996 have yet gained in importance in 2006. This suggests that India has not integrated into the global production networks of high technology products to the extent China did.

The still very traditional profile of India's merchandise trade is also confirmed by a more detailed analysis of its revealed comparative advantage indices and growth rates conducted by Kowalski and Dihel (2009). Most of the products in which India is estimated to have a revealed comparative advantage belong to the primary and labor-intensive sectors. During the last ten years, India has developed a revealed comparative advantage only in chemical and metal manufacturing. In fact, in high-technology segments, such as *office, accounting and computing machinery* and *radio, television and communication equipment* RCA indices have actually deteriorated over time.

In addition to the analysis of revealed comparative advantage indices Kowalski and Dihel (2009) reported on two different analytical assessments that capture the skill intensity evolution of India's export mix. The methodology based on the skill intensity classification developed by UNCTAD[9] revealed that despite the rapid growth in trade flows, India has not managed to develop a high-technology export sector

---

[8] As argued in Kowalski and Dihel (2009), this is due to the rapid development of domestic refining capacity. In 1996, India imported both crude and refined petrol (around 2/3 crude and 1/3 refined) and exported only negligible quantities. In 2005 its imports of crude petrol have more than tripled (in quantity), its imports of refined petrol have considerably declined, and refined petrol has become a key export. It is yet unclear whether this export boom is sustainable or it was due to an incipient excess domestic refining capacity.

[9] Source: UNCTAD 2002. The original categories are supplemented with the category of primary.

Table 6.6. High technology exports

	2000	2002	2004
Brazil	18.61	16.83	11.59
China	18.58	23.31	29.81
India	5.01	4.76	4.88

Source: Constructed using data from WDI.

and that its export mix in terms of skills requirements remained stable in period (1996–2005) (Figure 6.7). Another classification developed by the Hamburg Institute of International Economics based on the ISIC-classification revealed that the share of high-technology manufactured goods (such as pharmaceuticals, radio and telecommunication equipment, office and computer equipment) in India's total exports has barely changed since 1996 and remains under 5 percent. Even the share of medium-technology products which include the whole of the chemical sector and motor vehicles has increased by less than 5 percentage points and stood at 19 percent in 2005. Table 6.6 complements these findings by presenting the World Development Indicators classification of high-technology exports; they provide higher estimates of shares of high-technology trade but a similar flat trend and performance inferior to that of Brazil and China.[10]

Services appear to have done much better and India has emerged as a global player in information technology and business process outsourcing, as well as services related to pharmaceuticals. Mode 4-related trade has also been important amounting in value terms to over 90 percent of total cross-border services exports (Kowalski and Dihel 2009). A process of export reorientation is clearly underway and a significant shift has taken place towards more advanced, in some cases high-skill intensive, services. Moreover, new services, such as computer and selected professional services, have emerged in India's exports to a greater extent than in other developing and emerging countries. A closer look at the sectoral composition of services trade in Table 6.7 reveals *Other services* being the top export category during the period 1994–2004. *Computer and information services* have experienced the largest increases, while transport and travel services registered a considerable drop between 1994 and 2003. In 1994 three types of services (*travel, transportation,* and *other business services*) accounted for almost 100 percent of all services exports; in 2000

---

[10] The figures are in percentage of manufactured exports and not total exports.

A Tale of Two Trade Integration Approaches

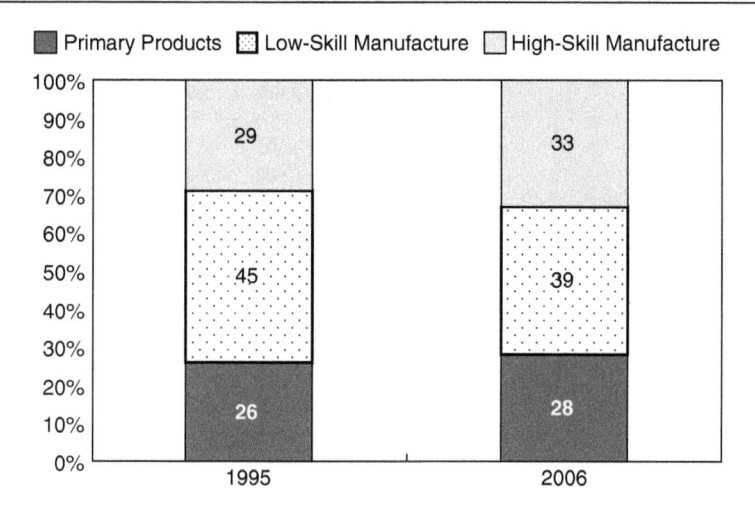

■ Primary Products ▨ Low-Skill Manufacture ☐ High-Skill Manufacture

	1995	2006
High-Skill Manufacture	29	33
Low-Skill Manufacture	45	39
Primary Products	26	28

Figure 6.7. Evolution of India's export mix according to skill intensity (1996 and 2005)

Source: Constructed using data in the UN's COMTRADE database.

they represented 57 percent and in 2003 only 42 percent. The most spectacular evolution was recorded by *computer and information services* whose share in India's services exports almost doubled between 2000 and 2003 to reach almost half of India's services exports.

A more detailed analysis of India's services export performance based on selected trade indicators such as sectoral revealed comparative advantage and intra-industry trade indices performed by Kowalski and Dihel (2009) confirms that India has a strong revealed comparative advantage in *computer and communication services. Travel, financial* and *communication services* feature high levels of intra-industry trade, indicating India's integration into the global service supply chain. Interestingly, trade in *computer services* in India seem to be entirely an inter-industry phenomenon.

In terms of geographical orientation of goods and services exports in recent years, India has increased its shares in all partner countries' markets but these shares remain relatively small and concern a few low-technology products. Since 2000, India's orientation towards OECD markets has been slowly decreasing, from 55 percent of its merchandise exports to only 43 percent in 2004. The EU remains the top destination but has seen its share of Indian exports reduced by 3 percentage points in five years. In merchandise trade, the rise of China as a key export destination is particularly noticeable. Exports to China increased from less than 2 percent

Table 6.7. India: Composition of services and trade (US$ millions and percentages)

	1990	1994	2000	2001	2002	2003
SERVICES	−1,465	−2,162	−2,503	−2,763	−1,563	−2,313
Total Credit	4,625	6,038	16,684	17,337	19,478	23,397
Transportation services, credit	20.7	28.4	11.9	11.8	12.7	13.1
Travel credit	33.7	37.6	20.7	18.4	15.9	16.6
Other services, credit	45.6	34	67.4	69.7	71.4	70.3
Communications			3.6	6.4	4.0	4.6
Construction			3.0	0.4	1.2	1.2
Insurance	2.7	2.4	1.5	1.6	1.7	1.7
Financial			1.7	1.8	3.1	1.7
Computer and information			28.3	42.7	45.6	48.6
Royalties and license fees	0.0	0.0	0.5	0.2	0.1	0.1
Other business services	42.5	31.5	24.9	13.5	13.9	11.1
Govt. n.i.e.	0.3	0.1	3.9	3.1	1.8	1.3
Total Debit	6,090	8,200	19,187	20,099	21,041	25,710
Transportation services, debit	56.1	55.7	45.4	42.3	40.5	36.4
Travel debit	6.5	9.4	14.0	15.0	14.2	13.7
Other services, debit	37.4	35.0	40.6	42.8	45.3	50.0
Communication			0.5	1.3	4.8	2.4
Construction			0.7	2.3	2.9	4.7
Insurance	5.6	6.0	4.2	4.0	4.2	4.5
Financial			6.7	8.9	6.8	1.9
Computer and information			3.0	4.5	4.3	2.6
Royalties and license fees	1.2	1.1	1.5	1.6	1.6	1.6
Other business services	28.2	25.8	22.5	18.6	19.4	31.5
Government, n.i.e.	2.4	2.1	1.5	1.5	1.2	0.8

Source: Constructed using data from IMF BOP (2006).

of total India's exports (rank 14) in 2000 to more than 6.6 percent in 2004 (rank 3) and are still growing at the rate of 58 percent per annum. Exports to Singapore have also grown and now represent around 5 percent of India's total. However, apart from the phenomenal rise of exports to Singapore, which was heavily influenced by exports of refined petroleum, there are few signs that India is fully integrating into the south and Southeast Asia trading hub. A similar trend can be identified in terms of India's services trade with OECD countries: The OECD countries' group share in India's services exports decreased from approximately 33 percent in 1999 to about 26 percent in 2003.

India's inward FDI has increased considerably since 1991 and the annual FDI inflows grew from US$3.1 billion in 2002/03, to US$5.6 billion in 2005/06.[11] As in many other parts of the world, but perhaps for

---

[11] Based on data from UNCTAD and the Indian Secretariat for Industrial Assistance. There is a discrepancy in FDI numbers in certain cases. The RBI calculates FDI inclusive of reinvested earnings. However, the numbers used here, which were provided by the Department of

different reasons, FDI inflows into India are shifting increasingly away from manufacturing towards services sectors. In fact, in India, FDI is heavily concentrated in services. The share of services sector in total FDI inflows rose from 5 percent in 1990 to more than 50 percent during the post-reform period (1991–2005). However, likely reflecting the structure of services trade barriers (see below), the inflow of services FDI has been restricted to a few of the most deregulated sectors, such as transport and financial services. Between 1991 and 2005, the top six recipients of FDI have been electrical equipment (14.5%), transportation industry (11%), telecom (11%), power and oil refinery (10%), and other services sector (8.45%).[12] When it comes to FDI outflows from India, a similar concentration in services sectors is observed. The share of services in total FDI outflows increased to around 45 percent in the period 1999–2003. Non-financial services constitute around 36 percent and trade approximately 5 percent of total FDI outflows.

Importance of trade in China and India's growth

The remarkable parallel growth and trade performance in both China and India prompts the classic 'chicken and egg question', namely, whether the opening up to trade drove the growth of GDP or whether trade increased simply as a consequence of GDP growth and expansion of their shares in the world GDP. To gauge the influence of trade on GDP several analysts consider the evolution of exports to GDP or exports and imports to GDP ratios. Yet, the use of such ratios can be criticized as meaningless or even misleading since exports or imports are turnover measures while GDP is a valued added concept. Still, as long as we remember this important distinction these measures can give us a feeling of the extent of exporting activity as compared to economy's income.

In China, clearly, the observed trade expansion reflects at least in part greater specialization in production in the Asia region where China engages in the final processing and assembly of large volume of exports originating from its Asian neighbours that are destined for markets in Europe and North America. As mentioned above, according to certain rough approximations almost half of China's exports are the subject of such 'triangular' trade though this share is higher in certain

---

Industrial Policy and Promotion, look only at investment made through the automatic or approval route.

[12] Monthly Reports by the Indian Secretariat for Industrial Assistance.

high-technology products trade. Certainly, existence of such a processing activity would be reflected in relatively high exports to GDP ratios.

In this context some commentators have suggested that that the claim that China is an export-led economy might be a myth (UBS 2007). Processing activity is not nearly as present in India but a similar question about the actual contribution of exports to its GDP can be asked. UBS (2007) argues that despite the fact that imports and exports are rising in absolute terms when expressed as ratios of GDP, the estimate of actual value added contribution of exports to GDP is barely rising over time. Yet, the UBS (2007) analysis is itself not free of limitations; the value added contribution is calculated by using very broad assumptions about the domestic content and the shares of valued added in domestic content.[13] When this is done, unsurprisingly, the actual exports value added share for most Asian economies is far less than the exports/GDP ratio; for China this ratio is 10 percent and is not increasing over time as rapidly as the exports to GDP ratio does. We have taken the same approach as the UBS (2007) with the improvement that the actual data from social accounting matrices was used to measure the value added content in the final value of production by broad sector.[14] These were then multiplied by corresponding exports data from the UN COMTRADE database to obtain an estimate of the export value added. The results of this exercise for China and India are presented in Figures 6.8 and 6.9.

It is evident that both for China and India a simple export to GDP ratio statistic overestimates the actual contribution of exports to GDP. For China the simple ratio of exports to GDP is four times larger than the estimated export value added to GDP ratio (36% in 2005 compared to 8% in 1996). For India the simple ratio is 3.25 times larger (13% in 2005 compared to 4% in 1996). More importantly, however, both the simple and the more sophisticated ratios are much lower for India (e.g. 4% of exports value added in GDP as compared to 8% for China) suggesting that international trade likely plays currently a less important role in India's growth as compared to China. Moreover, this ratio has clearly been increasing for China, especially since 2000, while for India it has been lingering around the 3 percent level. From these figures we can conclude that trade has played a lesser role in India's recent economic expansion. This conclusion is also consistent with the fact that India's share in world

---

[13] They assume a 50% domestic content share for light manufacturing, a range from 20% to 50% for electronics and 70% for heavy industry and resource exports. Next a constant value added to total domestic content of 50% is assumed.

[14] The data comes from the Global Trade Analysis Project database.

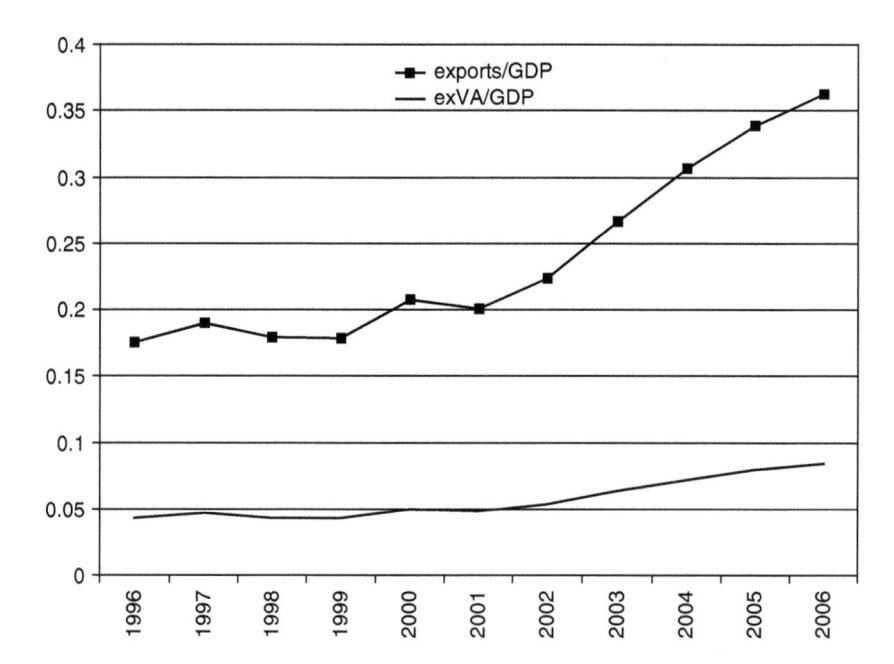

Figure 6.8. China: Exports to GDP and exports value added to GDP ratio
Source: Constructed using data in the GTAP, COMTRADE databases.

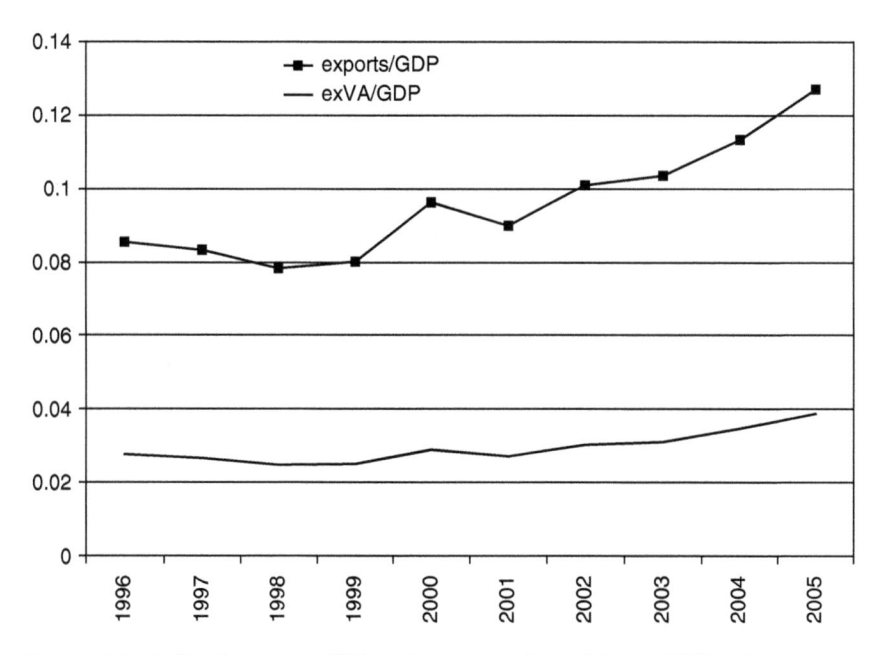

Figure 6.9. India: Exports to GDP and exports value added to GDP ratio
Source: Constructed using data in the GTAP, COMTRADE databases.

trade is still currently lower than its share in world output, which is not the case for China (Bussière and Mehl 2008).

6.3 Trade policy developments

China initiated gradual and incremental economic reforms over twenty-five years ago, beginning the transition from central planning to a more market-based economy. Access to foreign markets, capital, and advanced technology through greater integration into the multilateral trading system were important ways in which this process was meant to be facilitated. The resulting opening to world trade over the past quarter of a century is one of the more impressive aspects of China's economic reform and structural change and its accession to the WTO in 2001 can be seen as a coronation of the integration process.

As already foreshadowed, China's transition to a more open economy was a gradual and highly managed transition. It began with export processing in a few authorized special export processing zones (EPZs) along China's southern coast. By the mid-1980s export processing was more widely spread and China was increasingly characterized by a two-tiered export regime: A very open export processing segment benefiting from duty-free imports and a domestic export sector that was afforded high levels of protection through tariffs and multilayered non-tariff barriers (Greene et al. 2006).

In 1992 China declared its intention to establish a 'socialist market economy' and began to make substantial tariff cuts. This process was greatly strengthened by the extensive reforms that China agreed to implement as a part of its WTO accession. These included lowering of trade barriers in almost all sectors of its economy, providing national treatment, protecting intellectual property rights, improving transparency and eliminating non-tariff barriers among others. Some of these commitments are still being implemented and this ongoing process is likely to further deepen China's integration with the world economy.

Upon accession to the WTO, China agreed to bind all its import tariffs. After implementing all the commitments China's average bound tariff on agricultural products will decrease to 15 percent, ranging from 0 to 65 percent, with the highest rates applied to cereals. For industrial goods this average will decrease to 8.9 percent with a range from 0 to 47 percent, with the highest rates applied to photographic film and automobiles and related products (WTO 2001b). The two panels of Table 6.8 present

Table 6.8. China's average trade-weighted tariffs by trading partner and product at the time of accession to the WTO in 2001

	Australia	New Zealand	China	Hong Kong-China	Russia	Japan	Korea	Canada	United States	Mexico	EU15	Rest of western Europe	Rest of World	Average for product category
Agriculture and fishing	19.3	12.9	0.0	27.1	23.9	9.0	14.5	20.7	68.4	4.5	21.0	11.9	65.1	50.4
Natural resources	0.0	0.0	0.0	3.0	0.3	2.9	2.8	1.2	2.3	0.1	1.5	2.8	0.5	0.6
Coal	4.5	4.5	0.0	0.0	4.3	3.5	0.0	0.0	4.5	0.0	3.6	0.0	4.1	4.3
Oil	0.0	0.0	0.0	0.0	0.0	0.0	0.0	0.0	0.0	0.0	0.0	0.0	0.0	0.0
Food products and beverages	17.1	20.3	0.0	33.5	16.7	24.3	22.2	19.5	18.5	9.6	24.5	17.4	15.4	18.3
Textiles, clothing and leather	18.6	10.8	0.0	21.7	19.3	21.7	18.8	10.5	17.0	13.0	16.7	17.5	18.0	19.4
Chemicals and chemical products	15.6	10.6	0.0	14.5	9.1	12.6	11.6	8.7	10.9	14.2	11.4	10.1	15.7	12.9
Other manufacturing	14.7	8.0	0.0	14.1	3.3	14.6	16.0	2.3	10.4	18.5	14.5	14.3	9.9	11.7
Metal products	11.4	7.2	0.0	4.7	5.5	8.0	9.4	4.2	5.3	7.1	9.0	4.2	6.4	7.5
Motor vehicles and parts	22.5	14.9	0.0	17.8	17.6	42.3	47.7	32.5	30.3	23.9	36.2	43.9	35.4	38.1
Machinery and equipment	13.4	12.4	0.0	13.8	6.0	13.0	12.9	8.0	10.3	14.5	12.1	12.8	13.5	12.1
Electronic equipment	11.6	10.9	0.0	10.0	12.8	10.5	11.3	11.4	10.2	9.2	10.8	11.3	8.9	10.1
Average for partner country	10.8	11.9	0.0	4.7	6.3	13.6	13.4	10.0	13.6	7.6	10.9	8.4	12.2	
	After implementation of WTO accession commitments													
Agriculture and fishing	18.9	8.3	0.0	10.0	15.3	8.1	10.8	19.6	4.7	6.3	20.2	9.3	6.3	9.7
Natural resources	0.0	0.0	0.0	3.0	0.2	2.9	2.8	1.2	2.2	0.1	1.5	2.7	0.6	0.5
Coal	4.5	4.5	0.0	3.5	4.3	3.5	4.1	5.0	4.5	3.7	4.8	4.4	4.2	4.4
Oil	0.0	0.0	0.0	0.0	0.0	3.0	0.0	6.0	0.2	3.0	0.1	0.0	0.0	0.0
Food products and beverages	11.5	10.0	0.0	17.5	9.8	13.8	14.8	9.6	11.2	5.3	12.0	11.1	10.9	11.2
Textiles, clothing and leather	16.0	10.1	0.0	13.7	12.0	9.2	9.4	5.3	8.9	6.8	9.5	9.4	8.6	9.6
Chemicals and chemical products	8.6	6.9	0.0	7.2	6.0	7.2	6.4	5.1	6.6	7.7	7.1	6.7	11.4	8.2
Other manufacturing	7.2	3.5	0.0	7.5	1.4	10.9	9.8	0.8	6.2	9.9	8.6	8.7	5.9	7.2
Metal products	6.0	3.8	0.0	3.7	4.4	5.4	6.0	3.1	3.6	4.3	5.9	3.6	4.9	5.1
Motor vehicles and parts	12.2	10.3	0.0	9.2	11.9	15.9	18.3	11.4	13.8	8.9	14.6	16.3	13.9	15.0
Machinery and equipment	6.9	6.4	0.0	7.5	5.0	6.7	6.7	4.9	5.2	7.8	6.9	7.7	7.4	6.6
Electronic equipment	1.1	0.8	0.0	2.0	4.0	2.4	4.2	1.0	0.6	0.9	1.4	1.9	1.2	1.8
Average for partner country	8.0	6.5	0.0	2.6	4.4	6.2	6.8	6.1	4.0	2.0	5.3	4.8	5.1	

Source: Constructed using data from CEPII MacMap data accessed through GTAP database.

Table 6.9. China's tariff structure

	Agricultural products			Non Agricultural products			Maximum tariff
	Simple mean tariff	Weighted mean tariff	Std dev	Simple mean tariff	Weighted mean tariff	Std dev	
1992	46.6	19.2	26.5	41.4	33.0	33.1	220.0
2001	24.5	54.3	21.0	14.5	12.6	9.3	121.6
2004	16.5	22.8	12.0	9.6	5.2	6.8	68.0
2005	15.0	11.8	10.6	9.0	4.6	6.2	65.0

Source: Constructed using data from UN TRAINS.

bilateral trade-weighted tariffs imposed by China in year 2001 and after implementation of its WTO commitments which were scheduled mostly for 2004 but in no case later than 2010 (WTO 2001a or b). China has also committed to a further phased reduction and removal of non-tariff barriers, for the most part by 2005, but no later than 2010. Subsidies for agricultural production are to be limited to 8.5 percent of the value of farm output (Greene et al. 2006).

As Table 6.9 shows, the reduction of tariffs during the 1990s has resulted in China being perhaps one of the most open developing countries with tariff levels close to OECD levels. The simple average Chinese tariff rate on non-agricultural products was reduced from 41 percent in 1992 to 14 percent in 2001 and further to 9 percent in 2005. The simple average tariff on agricultural imports was reduced from 47 percent in 1992 to 24 percent in 2001 and 15 percent in 2005.

The trade reforms that China has embraced as a result of its WTO accession are a continuation of a long-standing trend that saw a sustained reduction in non-tariff barriers and in levels and dispersion of tariffs. However, in the area of services, China's WTO commitments represent milestones (Greene et al. 2006). They include opening of key services sectors to foreign participation, elimination of geographical limitations, forms of establishment, and scope of business activities among others. Additionally, China agreed to allow foreign services suppliers to engage in the retailing of all products by the end of 2003. Since the end of 2004, all firms have the right to import and export all goods except those subject to state trading monopolies (such as oil or fertilizers). Foreign firms have been allowed to distribute virtually all goods domestically since the end of 2006. Foreign financial institutions are permitted to provide services without client restrictions for foreign currency business upon accession;

A Tale of Two Trade Integration Approaches

local currency services to Chinese companies (since December 2003); and services to all Chinese clients (since December 2006). China promised to eliminate by the end of 2006 most restrictions on foreign entry and ownership, as well as most forms of discrimination against foreign firms. Access is likely to be improved further with the planned introduction of transparent and automatic licensing procedures.

Greene et al. (2006) provide a detailed quantitative analysis of China's services liberalization commitments as specified in its GATS schedule. Indices of trade restrictiveness are calculated to describe the consequences of implementation of China's commitments in five services sectors (banking, insurance, telecommunication, distribution and engineering services).[15] It is estimated that implementation of WTO commitments in banking would lower the restrictiveness of this sector to below the OECD average. By contrast, in all other sectors, despite significant liberalization measures, the restrictiveness indices remain above the OECD average but are lower than in most developing countries covered in the analysis (see Greene et al. 2006). Greene et al. (2006) also estimate welfare implications of China's implementation of WTO commitments in goods and services with a use of a multi-country, multi-sector computable general equilibrium model of the world economy that features increasing returns to scale and large-group monopolistic competition. Importantly, the model includes a treatment of foreign direct investment on a bilateral basis which, given the importance of foreign presence in the Chinese economy, is essential for understanding the impacts of its liberalization. The results indicate that China itself clearly stands to gain substantially from its liberalization. Implementation of the WTO commitments by China in goods and services sectors is estimated to increase its real income by almost 2 percent, while a scenario with full liberalization is expected to yield a 3 percent increase in its real income, the estimates that are considered as quite high in this type of analysis.[16]

---

[15] The approach is described in OECD (2007c).

[16] The estimated impact on OECD economies is limited and heterogeneous across the group. This is because of the still limited extent of trade integration with the OECD area and the structure of bilateral trade flows between China and individual OECD economies which reflect divergent patterns of comparative advantage as well as differences in structure of trade barriers and geographical location. The most direct impact is expected through improved export performance of OECD countries that are already trading with or investing intensively in China but still face significant market access barriers. The observed trade patterns suggest that the impact through the market access channel is likely to be more important for Korea, Japan, Australia, and New Zealand, while the impact on other OECD economies is likely to be limited.

Table 6.10. FDI regulatory restrictiveness scores by country and sector (0 = open, 1 = closed)

	China	India	OECD Average
Business services			
Legal	0.300	1.000	0.221
Accounting	0.425	1.000	0.196
Architecture	0.100	1.000	0.094
Engineering	0.100	0.050	0.094
Total	0.231	0.863	0.152
Telecoms			
Fixed	0.550	0.350	0.198
Mobile	0.450	0.350	0.143
Total	0.525	0.350	0.184
Construction	0.150	0.250	0.074
Distribution	0.450	0.600	0.072
Finance			
Insurance	0.350	0.450	0.135
Banking	0.550	0.350	0.157
Total	0.504	0.373	0.152
Hotel & Restaurants	0.150	0.050	0.072
Transport			
Air	0.550	0.550	0.443
Maritime	0.550	0.050	0.280
Road	0.150	0.050	0.106
Total	0.466	0.215	0.299
Electricity	0.750	0.150	0.326
Manufacturing	0.400	0.200	0.076
Total	0.405	0.401	0.148

Source: Constructed using data from OECD (2006a, b or c).

Despite the ambitious GATS commitments and the fact that more than a half of China's merchandise exports are generated by foreign-invested companies there is some indication that China's FDI policies may be more restrictive than trade or investment data suggest. OECD's FDI regulatory restrictiveness index which aims to measure deviations from national treatment, i.e. discrimination against foreign investment (OECD 2006b), suggests that China's FDI policies were somewhat more restrictive than those in India in 2006, including in the manufacturing sector (see Table 6.10). Analysis of components of the total index for China in OECD (2006b) reveals that the gap between China and India is largely due to cumbersome screening and operational restrictions rather than limitations on foreign ownership.

A Tale of Two Trade Integration Approaches

Overall, the available evidence suggests that China's integration process so far is characterized by a certain duality. On the one hand, the opening up of trade and, perhaps to a lower extent FDI, in manufactured goods has spurred the emergence of a large private sector. On the other hand, the high level of public ownership and important regulatory barriers seem to dominate the services sectors. Services activities continue to be constrained by high entry barriers, excessive state involvement, opaque regulatory process, and overly burdensome licensing and operating requirements. The full implementation of GATS commitments would imply significant reforms and liberalization measures with important gains for China and many of its trading partners. The need for additional measures supporting the development of the sector is fully appreciated by China's authorities: The Eleventh Five-Year Plan for the first time emphasizes development of the services sector with a view to alleviate the potential negative impact on the overall structure of industry, job opportunities, and comprehensive competitiveness.

2005 has marked India's tenth anniversary as a member of the WTO and more than fifteen years of sustained reductions in trade protection. The extent of India's tariff liberalization is well illustrated by the fall in collected customs duties expressed as a percentage of the value of imports (from more than 60% in 1990 to around 10% currently) as well as the reduction of the share of customs duties in Government revenue (from above 40% in 1990 to less than 10% currently, Figure 6.10). The decreasing reliance on trade taxes reflects continuing commitment to trade liberalization but also the shifting of revenue collection from tariffs to more efficient ways of collecting taxes by broadening the tax base and movements towards a value added tax.

Table 6.11. India's tariff structure

	Agricultural products			Non Agricultural products			Maximum tariff
	Simple mean tariff	Weighted mean tariff	Std dev	Simple mean tariff	Weighted mean tariff	Std dev	
1990	82.9	50.3	46.3	82.2	49.6	38.5	355.0
2001	40.6	49.1	26.8	31.0	24.8	8.6	210.0
2004	37.4	60.9	30.1	27.8	21.0	8.5	182.0
2005	37.6	52.3	33.5	15.0	12.0	7.4	182.0

Source: Constructed using data from UN TRAINS.

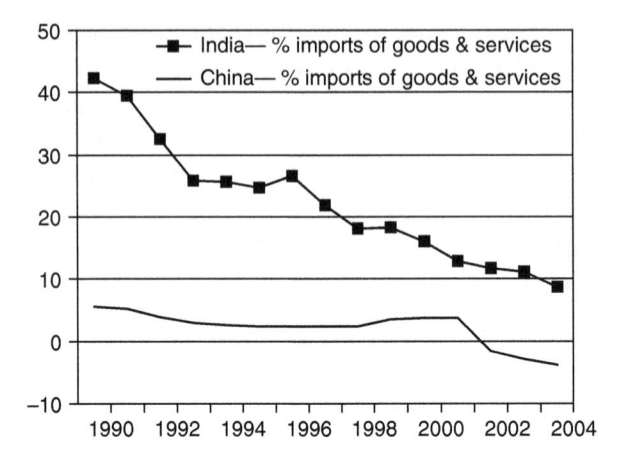

Figure 6.10a. Taxation of international trade: Duties as % of value of imports of goods and services

Source: Constructed using data in the IMF's Government Finance Statistic Database.

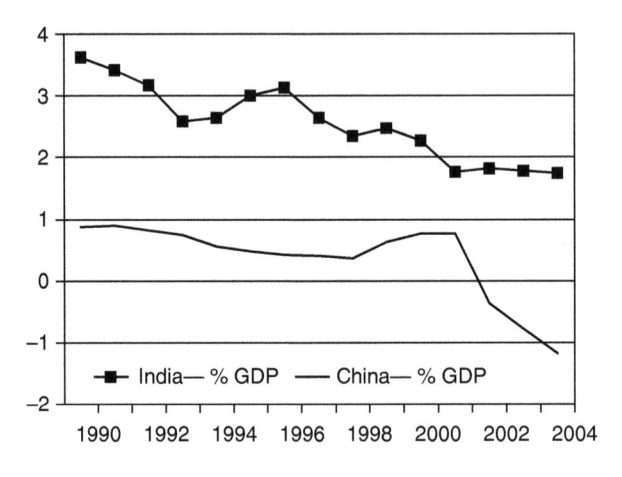

Figure 6.10b. Taxation of international trade: Duties as % of GDP

Source: Constructed using data in the IMF's Government Finance Statistic Database.

Tariff reductions have been implemented across the board generating market access improvements but also entailing the added benefit of reducing tariff dispersion, and thus economic distortions and complexity (Table 6.11). Over the period 1990–2005 (for which we have consistent data) the proportional tariff reductions on imports of manufacturing merchandise have gone deeper than corresponding cuts in the agricultural sector. In fact, for agricultural products the reduction in tariffs calculated

A Tale of Two Trade Integration Approaches

on trade-weighted basis is negative with tariffs actually increasing by 2 percentage points over the period while that for manufacturing (38) suggests considerable liberalization effort in the past. The corresponding proportional tariff cuts for agriculture and manufacturing are respectively −4 and 75 percent. Tariff peaks for non-agricultural products have continued falling from 30 percent in 2003 to 12.5 percent in 2006 while tariffs peaks on agricultural products have remained unchanged. By focusing non-agricultural tariff reduction on tariff peaks, India has been narrowing protection differentials between raw materials, capital goods, and consumer goods.

These statistics point to a significant liberalization effort, especially in manufacturing. Yet, it has to be remembered that at the beginning of reforms India's tariffs were among the highest in the world and that the current trade-weighted average tariffs of close to 52 percent in agriculture and 12 percent in manufacturing still imply a significant wedge between domestic and world prices, and act as an indirect tax on exports through imports. This puts Indian producers that rely on imported inputs at a competitive disadvantage (capital and intermediate goods constitute the bulk of India's imports), and holds inefficient producers in the domestic market. The lowered but still high tariff barriers certainly do not improve the situation of low growth in the industrial sector (Figure 6.11) which is one of the factors impeding reallocation of labor force from the agricultural sector.[17]

Statistics presented in Tables 6.12 and 6.13 are even more revealing and show that the overwhelming majority (between 72% and 100%) of India's imports are not imported for domestic consumption but, rather, are used as intermediate inputs by the domestic manufacturing and services sectors. Table 6.12 presents the ten top India's imports and shows that over 60 percent of India's imports on average face applied tariffs higher than 10 percent and bound tariffs of around 30 percent. Within a number of these product categories the maximum tariffs are as high as 100 percent and there are a number of national and international tariff peaks.[18]

---

[17] Employment in the agricultural sector persists despite its decreasing contribution to India's GDP.

[18] Taking the example of imports of machinery and equipment, the simple average tariff of almost 15% is entirely a production cost increasing measure—99% of imports machinery and equipment imports are used as intermediate inputs in production. Another example is 10% tariff on imports of crude oil—the biggest India's import (26% of the total). 100% of these imports are an intermediate input into the production of the petroleum products a part of which are successfully exported (9% in 2003). Other similar examples include inputs into the production of the chemical, rubber, and plastic products and services sectors, such as

213

Przemyslaw Kowalski

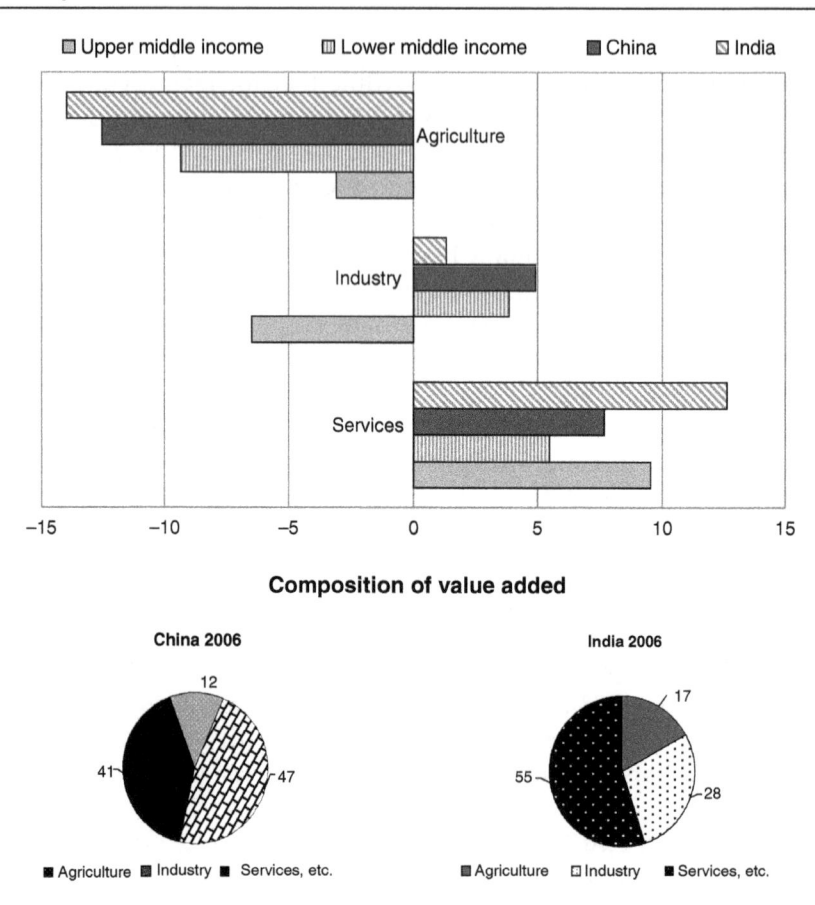

Figure 6.11. Percentage change in sectoral value added, 1991–2006, % of GDP
Source: Constructed using data in the World Bank's World Development Indicators.

In an effort to offset the high taxation of intermediate products and barriers to services trade, India has opted to cultivate an extremely complex system of duty exemption schemes, special investment and establishment rules, and special economic zones (SEZs) that provide incentives particularly to exporting firms. There are more than a hundred duty exemption acts in place covering all types of activities from restaurants to agriculture, handlooms, leather and footwear, or gems and jewellery. The majority of special initiatives involve some type of import duty exemption, in general between 2.5 and 5 percent of the FOB value of exports. For

construction, transport, and electricity generation. All in all, in an alarming majority of cases, moderate to high tariff hurt mostly domestic firms that rely on imported inputs.

sectors dominated by very small players, specific instruments are in place to channel duty-free imports through trade associations. Other schemes, such as the export promotion of capital goods scheme (EPCG), promises a 5 percent duty for imports of capital goods subject to an export obligation equivalent to eight times the duty saved over a period of eight years. Agri-export zones grant duty-free imports of capital goods. In the last few years, each financial bill has added to the number of special focus initiatives and other promotional measures undermining parallel efforts to simplify export procedures, such as efforts to launch an automated electronic environment for all exports.

There are currently no signs that the system will be simplified in the near future but it appears that the Indian Government is planning to alleviate the burden on domestic industry. Indeed, in 2006 the Trade Minister, Kamal Nath announced two new schemes *Focus Products* and *Focus Markets* aimed at providing a thrust to employment generation, particularly in semi-urban and rural areas. The objective of the Focus Products scheme is to promote exports of labor-intensive industrial products by allowing a duty credit facility at 2.5 percent of the FOB value of exports on 50 percent of the export turnover of notified products, such as value-added fish and leather products, stationery items, fireworks, sports goods and handloom, and handicraft items. The Focus Markets scheme aims at promoting exports to specified markets and allows duty credit facility at 2.5 percent of the FOB value of exports of all products to the notified countries.

Various reports dealing with India's services sectors highlight particular problems related to market access in financial, telecommunication, and distribution services. The OECD (2007c) assessed barriers in banking, insurance, telecom (fixed and mobile), and distribution service and liberalization effects in many countries, including India.[19] The study employs various alternative weighting methods and improved econometric specifications that include barriers affecting each mode of services supply and additional sector-specific regulatory variables and draws conclusions that India is quite restrictive in banking, insurance, mobile telecom, and distribution, as compared to both OECD and selected emerging markets (Figures 6.12 through 6.14).[20] The TRIs are well above the OECD average and

---

[19] See OECD (2007c).

[20] The OECD (2007c) attempted to include a large number of measures that can impede trade in services via various modes of supply. It is important to note that, at this stage, the study considers a combination of formal and actual barriers. A country can have regulatory measures in place which restrict trade, but these may not be applied in practice. Moreover, even if restrictions are applied, their effect depends on how they are applied in practice. Given

Table 6.12. Top ten Indian imports

Product name	Value of imports	% of total imports	Simple average Applied	Simple average Bound	Weighted average Applied	Weighted average Bound	Standard deviation	Maxi-mum	Domestic peaks	International peaks
OIL-Oil	3,9101,473	26.36	10		10		0	10	0	0
OME-Machinery and equipment	1,6895,653	11.39	14.57	31.19	13.77	27.07	2.46	15	0	0
CRP-Chemical, rubber, plastic	1,5427,099	10.4	15.38	42.72	14.43	37.59	4.62	100	4	127
NFM-Metals n.e.c.	1,4129,823	9.53	14.68	39.39	15	39.65	1.47	15	0	0
ELE-Electronic equipment	1,1071,414	7.46	7.55	9.86	2	0.91	7.47	15	0	0
OMN-Minerals n.e.c	8650,334	5.83	12.04	36.28	12.91	38.86	4.39	15	0	0
OTN-Transport equipment n.e.c	8130,431	5.48	20.21	29.96	7.71	8.45	30.05	100	20	20
P_C-Petroleum,coal products	7101,582	4.79	13.61	25	13.9	25	1.64	15	0	0
I_S-Ferrous metals	6150,379	4.15	18.9	39.59	19.45	39.94	2.08	20	0	511
COA-Coal	3380,848	2.28	21.67	31.25	15	25	12.57	55	0	1

Source: Constructed using data from UN TRAINS.

Table 6.13. Disposition of top ten Indian imports

Product Name	Disposition of imported goods (%) Production	Disposition of imported goods (%) Consumption	Main importing sector	% of imports	Disposition of output of main importing sector Domestic	Disposition of output of main importing sector Exports
OIL-Oil	100	0	P_C-Petroleum,coal products	100	94	6
OME-Machinery and equipment	99	1	CDGS-investment in capital goods	42	100	0
CRP-Chemical, rubber, plastic	90	10	CRP-Chemical, rubber, plastic	56	87	13
NFM-Metals n.e.c.	100	0	OME-Machinery and equipment	30	89	11
ELE-Electronic equipment	86	14	CDGS-investment in capital goods	80	100	0
OMN-Minerals n.e.c	100	0	CNS-constructio	66	100	0
OTN-Transport equipment n.e.c	96	4	CDGS-investment in capital goods	73	100	0
P_C-Petroleum,coal products	72	28	OTP-transport n.e.c.	41	96	3
I_S-Ferrous metals	100	0	I_S-Ferrous metals	48	93	7
COA-Coal	88	12	ELY-electricity	68	100	0

Source: Constructed using data from GTAP and UN TRAINS databases.

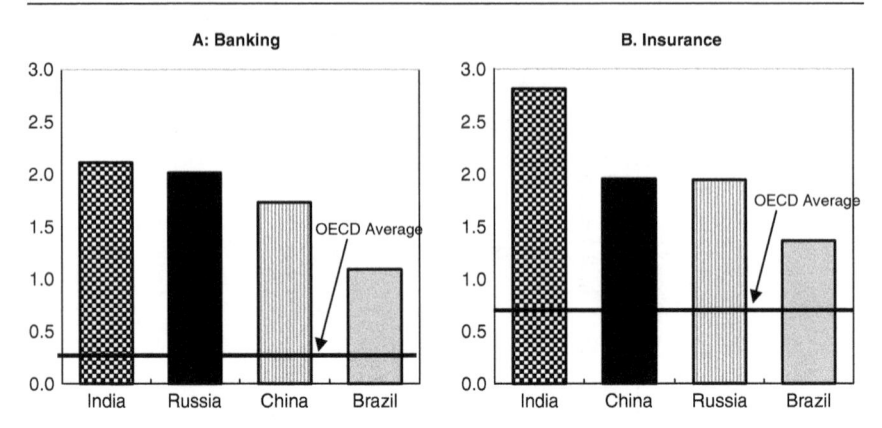

Figure 6.12. Banking and insurance TRIs—India and selected emerging economies
Source: Calculations based on the methodology described in OECD (2007c).

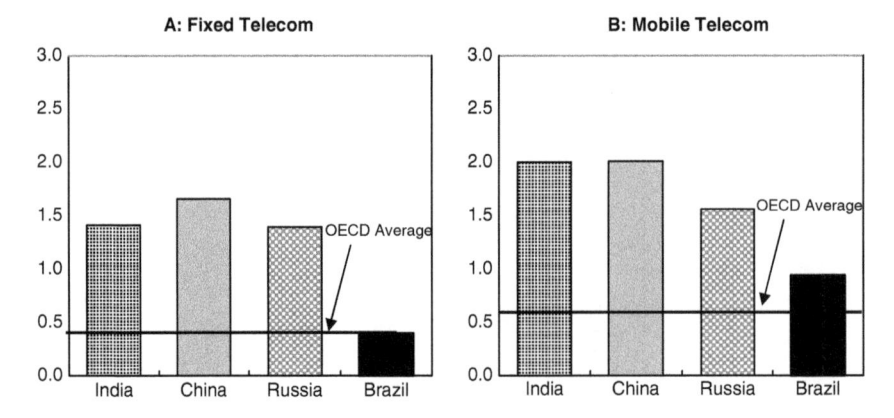

Figure 6.13. Telecom TRIs—India and selected emerging economies
Source: Calculations based on the methodology described in OECD (2007c).

most of the selected emerging economies, including China. Moreover, most of these services sectors have for a long time been in the public domain and they suffer not only from high barriers to trade, but also from domestic constraints in terms of burdensome regulatory measures and state monopolies. These services consequently suffer from inefficiencies and low growth. The negative impact of restrictions on the performance of banking and distribution services is elaborated on in more detail in Kowalski and Dihel (2009).

these caveats, the proposed lists of restrictions and the results should be treated with caution. Where possible, this analysis indicates how results may change if the practical application on regulatory measures is taken into account.

A Tale of Two Trade Integration Approaches

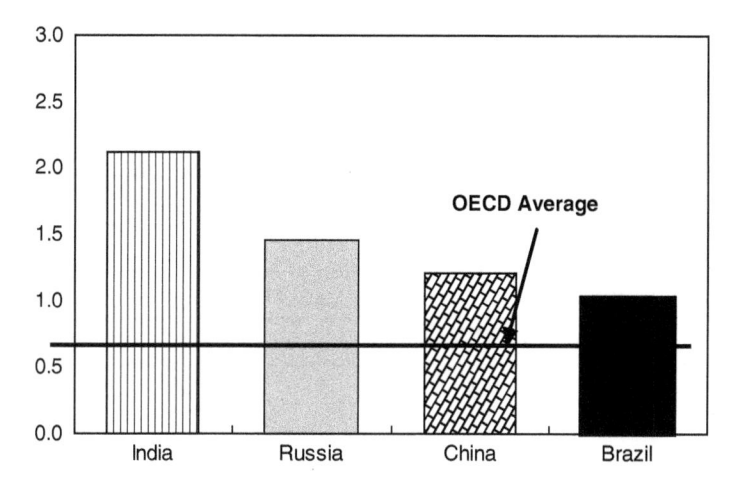

Figure 6.14. Distribution TRIs—India and selected emerging countries
Source: Calculations based on the methodology described in OECD (2007c).

The goal of the *New Foreign Trade Policy* is to double India's percentage share of global merchandise trade within the next five years. In 2004 when the Government announced the new policy this was interpreted as achieving a 20 percent growth per annum in exports and increasing India's share in world trade from 0.8 to 1.5 percent by 2009. As far as means are concerned, the New Foreign Trade Policy[21] appears to be based on: Continuing liberalization efforts by reducing tariffs, unshackling controls, simplifying procedures and bringing down transaction costs; extensive use of duty rebates and exemptions to neutralize the incidence of all levies and duties on inputs used in export products; establishing export processing zones, so-called special economic zones, to boost exports and harness FDI into infrastructure building.

The objective set for the New Foreign Trade Policy must be seen as quite ambitious. Figure 6.15 traces the historical trend in exports growth and the projected, much higher, growth that would be implied by the New Foreign Trade Policy. Whether the means the Government envisages will be sufficient to achieve such an ambitious outcome is unclear. In particular it is unsure whether export-related duty exemptions and preferential treatment of economic agents operating in the SEZs are the best way to promote economic efficiency and growth. While strong exports are the sign of an economy's competitiveness and the source of foreign currency

---

[21] Foreign Trade Policy 2004–2009, Directorate General of Foreign Trade, Ministry of Commerce and Industry, Government of India, 2004.

Przemyslaw Kowalski

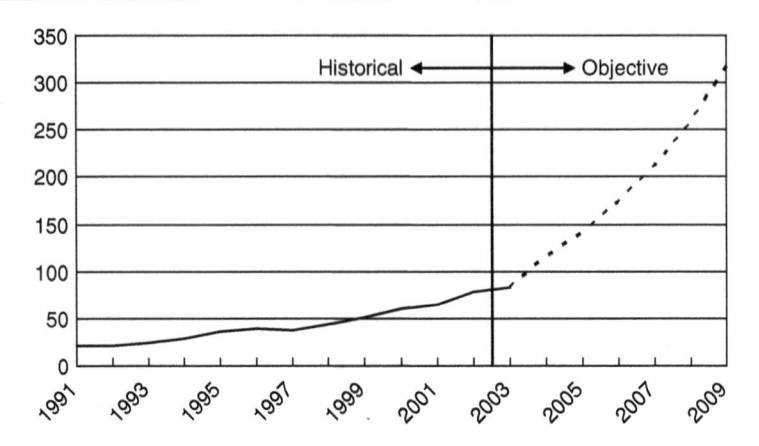

Figure 6.15. Doubling India's share of world trade: The size of the challenge exports in billions US$

Source: Authors' projection based on assumption of 6.5% world trade and WDI data on Indian exports.

earnings, exporting firms do not operate in a vacuum and discriminatory exports-oriented policies may in some circumstances produce more harm than good. At a very general macroeconomic level, maintaining moderately high import tariffs with a system of export-oriented duty exemptions can be called a system of 'negative incentives'; costs of production are higher than in less protected transition countries except for those Indian producers which are already capable of exporting (Kowalski and Dihel 2009). This is bound to have a negative impact on the Indian economy in general and perhaps even on exports since this activity is also carried out within an inefficient national economy. Indeed, as much as 75 percent of the capital in the SEZs originates from domestic sources. Is it plausible to expect increased investment in exporting activity with policies that do not encourage the efficient domestic production?

It is also uncertain that the Indian SEZs can develop and generate economic benefits to the extent those in China do. This is because they tend to be suboptimally sized, which prevents realization of scale economies, and are usually located in the vicinity of already large cities magnifying the already existing diseconomies of Indian agglomerations (Mitra 2008). All these elements suggest that the net economic benefits of the current web of SEZs for India as a country are uncertain, notwithstanding the private sector or Government support. More generally, SEZs are always a suboptimal policy from an economic point of view (Engman et al. 2007). They can merely provide an interim solution to countries with poor business environments where bridging deficiencies at a national level is temporarily impossible. This may indeed be the case in India—a large, low-income country with enormous population, poor infrastructure, and fiscal problems—but it would not be rational to treat this as a sustainable long-term solution that can substitute for reforms aimed at making business easier for everyone. Even as a temporary solution, the benefits are not guaranteed especially if the rents associated with operating within SEZs create perverse economic incentives.

In this context the two main elements of India's New Foreign Trade Policy seem somewhat contradictory. On the one hand, the across-the-board liberalization efforts are to be continued. On the other hand, duty exemptions and other privileges geared mainly towards export promotion are to be enhanced. In fact, if the first objective is realized, the second, at least when it comes to import duty exemptions, becomes redundant. It seems that across-the-board import duty reduction could have more beneficial economy-wide and export effects than selective duty exemptions in export sectors, especially because this is the only logical end point. We therefore argue that, if SEZs are to stay as an interim policy in India, a proper cost-benefit analysis of the current SEZs system and across-the-board liberalization is warranted to minimize any potential inefficiency.

In addition, a number of studies point out several other factors that impede the development of the tradable sectors in India as well as that of the economy as a whole (OECD 2007a). One of the key hurdles to Indian productivity growth has been a lack of infrastructure support from the Government. In 2005, infrastructure spending was US$28 billion in India (3.6% of GDP), compared with US$201 billion in China (9.0% of GDP). It is estimated that poor and poorly used infrastructure cuts India's growth rate by about 1 to 1.5 percentage points a year[22] and without change the desired double-digit growth seems highly unlikely.

India-based enterprises still face significant challenges in terms of the ease of doing business despite the dismantling of the License Raj[23] in 1990. For example, the cost for a start-up is much greater than in China. Despite significant reforms in the area of licensing systems, much more time to obtain the necessary licenses is needed in India than in China or other countries in South Asia. Furthermore, the time required for

---

[22] 'Analysis—India's politics block much-needed economic reform', Reuters 2006.

[23] The term 'License Permit Raj' refers to the elaborate licenses, regulations, and the accompanying red tape that were required to set up business in India between 1947 and 1990. The License Raj was accorded on a selective basis to selected companies.

Table 6.14. Doing business in China and India—selected indicators, 2006

		India	China	South Asia	OECD
Overall indicator	Rank	134	93		
Starting a business	Cost (% GNI per capita)	73.7	9.3	46.6	5.3
Dealing with licenses	Procedures (number)	29.0	20.0	16.1	14.0
	Time (days)	367.0	270.0	226.6	149.5
	Cost (% of income per capita)	84.0	606.0	375.7	72.0
Trading across borders	Time for exports (days)	27.0	18.0	34.4	10.5
	Cost to exports (US$ per container)	864	335.0	1,236.0	811
	Time for import (days)	41.0	22.0	41.5	12.2
	Cost to imports (US$ per container)	1,244.0	375.0	1,494.9	882.6
Registering property	Procedures (number)	6.0	3.0	5.8	4.7
	Time (days)	62.0	32.0	118.6	31.8
	Cost (% of property value)	7.8	3.1	5.3	4.3
Enforcing a contract	Procedures (number)	56.0	31.0	38.7	22.2
	Time (days)	1,420.0	292.0	968.9	351.2
	Cost (% of debt)	35.7	26.8	26.4	11.2
Employing workers	Difficulty of hiring index	33.0	11.0	41.8	27.0
	Difficulty of firing index	70.0	40.0	37.5	27.4
	Rigidity of employment index	41.0	24.0	34.8	33.3
	Non-wage labor cost (% of salary)	16.8	44.0	5.8	21.4
Closing a business	Time (years)	10.0	2.4	3.6	1.4
	Cost (% of estate)	9.0	22.0	6.3	7.1
	Recovery rate (cents on the dollar)	13.0	31.5	19.5	74.0

Source: Constructed using data from The World Bank (2007) Doing Business Comparing Regulations—http://www.doingbusiness.org/.

exporting and importing and its cost to export and import remain much higher than in China. The enforcement of contracts remains inefficient and extremely difficult. Last but not least, labor regulations are inflexible, as reflected by the rigidity of the employment index that is much higher than in China or other South Asian economies (Table 6.14). Finally, somewhat similarly to China, India is confronted with skill problems due to low educational standards though, as opposed to China, it will have increasing working population for another generation (Lehman Brothers 2007).

Overall, the remaining protection in both goods and services sectors is still much higher in India as compared to China or other large emerging economies. First, this means that intermediate inputs and capital goods—the bulk of India's imports—remain expensive. Second, the remaining trade barriers and the complexity of the system combine with the high levels of domestic red tape restricting new entry and competition to keep India's competitiveness at low levels, particularly in agriculture and manufacturing sectors. As a result, pro-competitive effects in the tradable sector—the main driver of growth in most transition countries—are not as common as they could be.

6.4 Conclusion

The comparison of the key features of trade integration processes and the economic outcomes of China and India reveals that while much has already been achieved in both these economies in terms of opening up, the Chinese reforms, especially with respect to manufacturing trade, have gone further and that this is likely one of the key determinants of the better economic performance of China. The evidence gathered suggests also that international trade will likely remain a crucial factor that can allow China and India to continue, or perhaps even speed up, the growth enjoyed in the last decades.

Of the two countries, China is probably a better example to be followed as far as trade policy is concerned but China's integration process so far remains characterized by a certain duality. On the one hand, the opening up of trade and FDI in manufactured goods has spurred the emergence of a largely private and dynamically growing sector. On the other hand, the high level of public ownership and important regulatory barriers continue to dominate the services sectors. The full implementation of China's GATS commitments would likely imply significant reforms and liberalization measures with important gains for China and many of its trading partners.

India has gone a long way in reducing its tariffs on non-agricultural products as well as certain non-tariff barriers but moderate protection still persists which likely adds to the costs of intermediate inputs and, thus, to the hurdles faced by the Indian manufacturing sector. India has revealed a comparative advantage in certain segments of the services sector but its services trade policy is still very restrictive, even as compared to China. The extent of liberalization achieved so far and the outcomes it brought about suggest that the remaining goods and services trade barriers are just one item on the list of reforms that India needs to tackle in order to promote trade-led expansion of labor-intensive activities. Other important priorities analysed elsewhere (OECD 2007a; Kowalski and Dihel 2009) include, for example: Reforming small-scale industry policies that prevent realization of economies of scale and productivity increases in the sector; relaxing of labor market rigidities that hinder the inter-industry and interstate labor mobility and underpin misallocation of resources across industries and states; tackling infrastructure bottlenecks; and reducing regulatory differences across states.

Part III

Challenges to Sustaining Growth

7

China's Growth Model: Choices and Consequences

Eswar S. Prasad

7.1 Introduction

China has maintained a phenomenal rate of growth over the last two decades, with annual GDP growth averaging about 10 percent. What accounts for this impressive growth performance? How long is it likely to last and what are the risks? This chapter attempts to address these questions by providing a critical evaluation of the combination of macroeconomic and structural policies that has generated this growth. While it is hard to argue with success, I will argue that the choice of policies has led to unbalanced growth and portends serious risks for the future.

I will also provide a brief contrast between the Chinese and Indian growth models. While India has had a much lower average rate of growth over the last two decades, India's economy has picked up pace since 2005, growing at an average rate of over 8 percent per annum. Unlike in the case of China, this growth has been more balanced, with private consumption and investment contributing significantly to this growth.

One concern of Chinese policymakers is about the sustainability of high growth. But sustainability is not the only issue. There are many costs associated with the current growth model that deserve attention. For instance, tight management of the exchange rate has been facilitated by financial repression and a relatively closed capital account. These policies have curtailed financial sector development (which the authorities have declared to be a major policy priority), leading to inefficient intermediation of domestic capital. There are clearly large welfare costs associated with these constraints.

Indeed, rapid growth can mask, or in some cases even exacerbate, a number of deeper problems. The financial sector is in poor shape and has distorted domestic demand; the patterns of investment financing could lead to a resurgence of nonperforming loans (NPLs) in the future and, by fueling a buildup of excess capacity in some sectors, could generate deflationary risks in the medium term. Meanwhile, in the short term, some of the pressures are becoming evident in other forms, such as asset price booms (in the equity markets, in particular).

Another aspect of the growth strategy is that it has involved a number of policy distortions and constraints that have greatly reduced the room for policy maneuver in case any big shocks, either internal or external, should hit the economy. Monetary policy is typically the first line of defense against such shocks but monetary policy is constrained by the objective of maintaining a tightly managed exchange rate. Fiscal policy could play a role in buffering the economy against shocks, especially since the explicit levels of the fiscal deficit and Government debt are quite low, but this may be deceptive as there are large contingent liabilities in the state-owned banking system and huge unfunded pension liabilities. The financial system is still dysfunctional in many ways and may not be deep or robust enough to withstand a significant shock.

What sorts of shocks is the Chinese economy likely to be vulnerable to? Possible internal shocks include loss of confidence in the banking system, social instability generated by rising inequality, and the bursting of the stock price bubble. External shocks include international capital market crises, a collapse of external demand, US trade sanctions, flaring-up of tensions over Taiwan, etc.

To deal with such shocks and to make growth more balanced and sustainable, reforms to the financial system, the state-owned enterprise sector, and the social safety net will all be needed. Many of these reforms are interrelated and trying to implement these reforms in isolation may not be an effective way to proceed. For instance, stable macroeconomic policies and a well-developed and efficient financial sector are essential ingredients for balanced and sustainable growth. In turn, these two intermediate objectives would be helped by effective monetary policy and further capital account liberalization. A flexible exchange rate is a prerequisite for both of these. Thus, a broader approach to policy reforms will be essential to make growth more balanced and less vulnerable to shocks.

India's growth may also be hitting some constraints, although ones quite different from those of China. The financial system in India is in better shape than that of China, although it, too, has a long way to go in becoming an efficient intermediary of savings into productive investment. The real constraints to growth in India are likely to come from the low levels of investment in infrastructure and human capital, as well as weak public institutions and governance.

7.2 The composition of growth in China and India

Investment in physical capital has been a major contributor to growth in China during this decade, in some recent years accounting for nearly two-thirds of nominal GDP growth (see Figure 7.1). Private consumption, by contrast, has made a much smaller contribution to growth (Aziz 2006; Lardy 2006). It is only very recently that net exports have made a significant contribution to growth, despite the widely held view that China is an 'export-led' economy. In India, private consumption has been an important contributor to growth, with investment playing a significant but not dominant role. In sharp contrast to the composition of growth in China, net exports have not made a positive contribution to growth as the trade balance has been consistently negative in recent years.

Why has investment growth in China been so strong? A substantial fraction of this investment in China has been financed by credit provided by state-owned banks at low interest rates. Indeed, cheap capital has played a big part in skewing the capital–labor ratio and holding down employment growth (Aziz 2006). Recent increases in the base lending rate have been far too small to raise the real price of capital to a meaningful level for an economy that is experiencing annual real growth of over 10 percent (Figures 7.2a and 7.2b). In addition, local Governments provide subsidized land in order to encourage investment. And energy prices continue to be administered and made available to enterprises at prices below international levels.

Much of the recent investment has also been financed through retained earnings of profitable firms, which ought to be more defensible on the basis of economic criteria. However, even here the picture is not clear. Profitable state enterprises were not, until very recently, required to pay dividends to the state. This suggests that such investment may have been spurred by the minimal rates of return on bank deposits which made even marginal investment projects seem in the money. The risk, of course, is that such high rates of investment in industries with favorable demand conditions may be leading to a buildup of excess capacity in those very

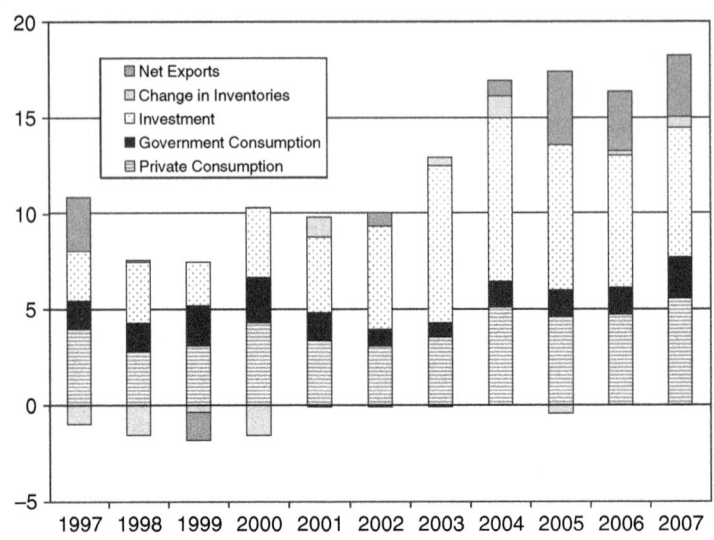

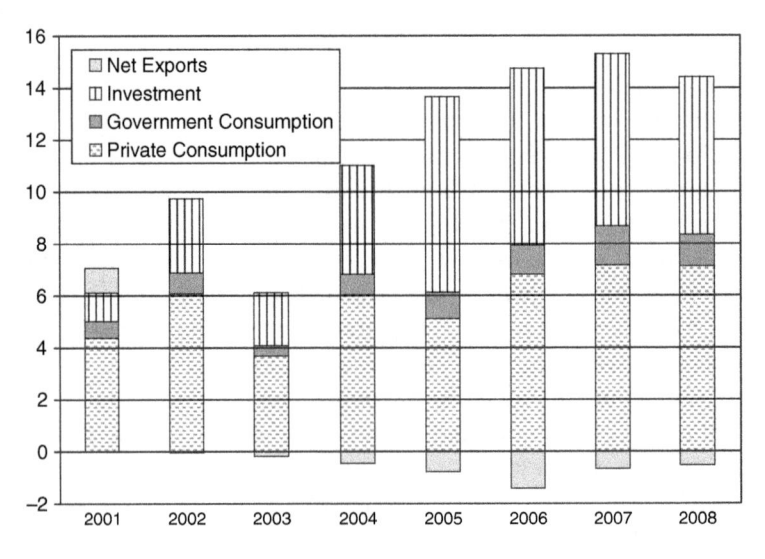

Figure 7.1. GDP growth

Source: Constructed using data in the CEIC database.

Note: The growth rate is of nominal GDP.

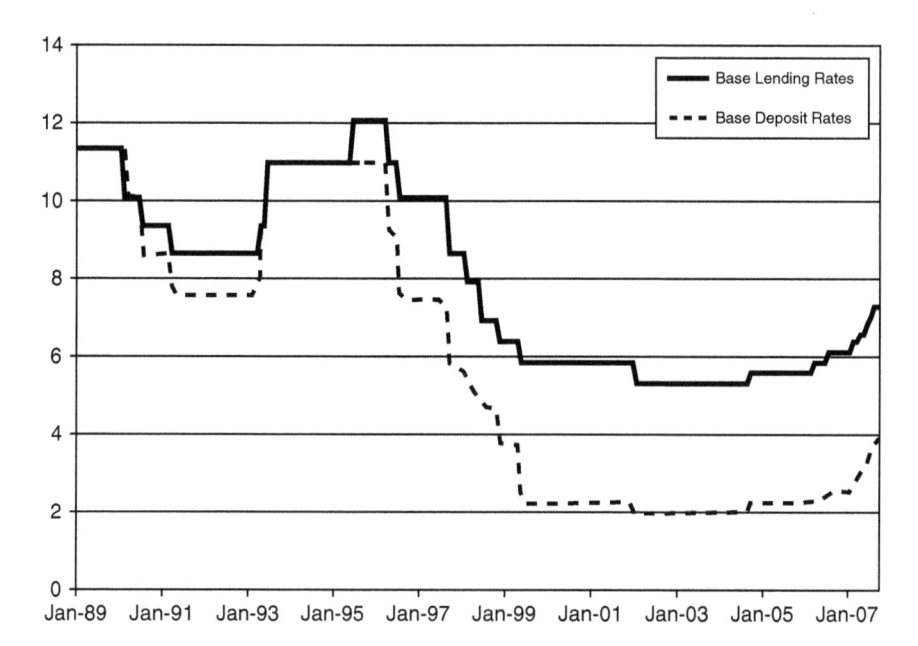

Figure 7.2a. Base lending and deposit rates (one-year rates %)

Figure 7.2b. Real lending and deposit rates (one-year rates, %)

Source: Constructed using data in the CEIC database.

Note: Real rates calculated by deflating the nominal rates by twelve-month trailing CPI or PPI inflation.

industries; this could become evident if there were to be adverse demand shocks in the future (Goldstein and Lardy 2005).

While investment has been high, national savings have been even higher, with both household and corporate savings rising in recent years. The uncertainties engendered by the transition to a market economy, the limited availability of instruments to borrow against future income to finance purchases (major durable goods, housing, etc.), and the lack of international portfolio diversification opportunities have all contributed to high household savings (Chamon and Prasad 2007). Financial system repression has meant that there are few alternatives to funneling these savings into deposits in the state-owned banking system.

Households willingly hold bank deposits despite the weaknesses of the banking system because of implicit deposit insurance provided by the Government. This provides abundant liquidity for banks to expand credit which, because of the distorted incentives faced by lenders, largely finances investment by state enterprises. State enterprises that do make profits are not required to pay dividends, encouraging them to plow retained earnings (which are counted as enterprise savings) back into investment. Thus, the investment boom in recent years has been fueled by cheap credit and overoptimistic expectations of future demand growth in sectors that are doing well at present.

7.3 Policy choices

China has kept its exchange rate fixed relative to the US dollar since 1995. China's strong productivity growth relative to its trading partners has generated pressures for currency appreciation during this decade. This pressure has been held back only by massive intervention in the exchange market. The current account surplus is likely to hit 12 percent of GDP in 2007, another indication of a substantially undervalued currency. Figure 7.3 shows that, despite an appreciation of the renminbi vs. the US dollar since June 2005, the real effective exchange rate of the renminbi is now *below* its recent peak in 2002 (largely due to the US dollar's depreciation against other major currencies).

In contrast to the tightly managed exchange rate regime of China, India's exchange rate regime has allowed for a great deal more flexibility (see Figure 7.4), although the Reserve Bank of India did undertake substantial exchange market intervention since the beginning of this decade in order to temper the appreciation of the rupee.

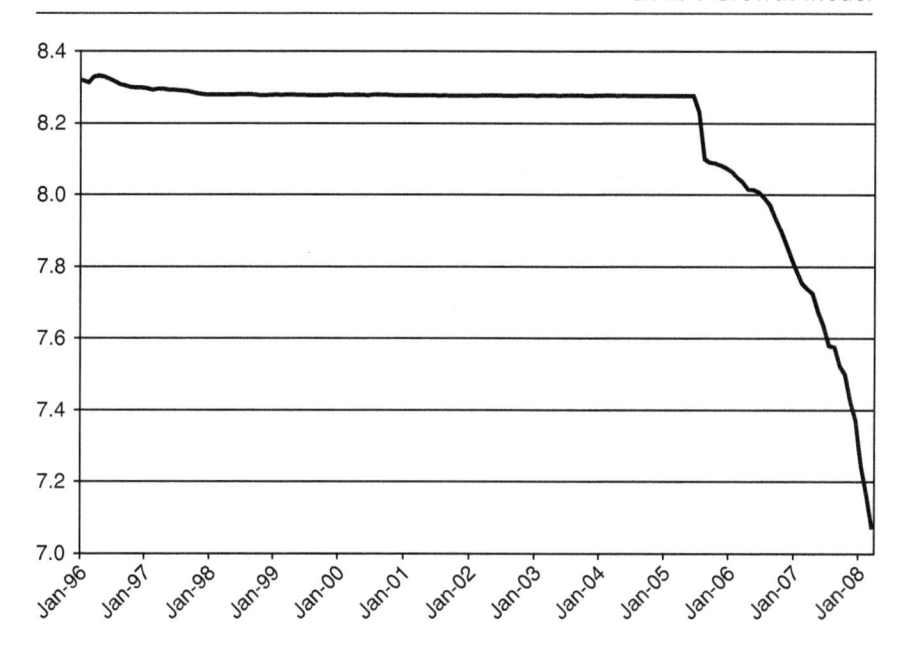

Figure 7.3a. RMB-US$ exchange rate

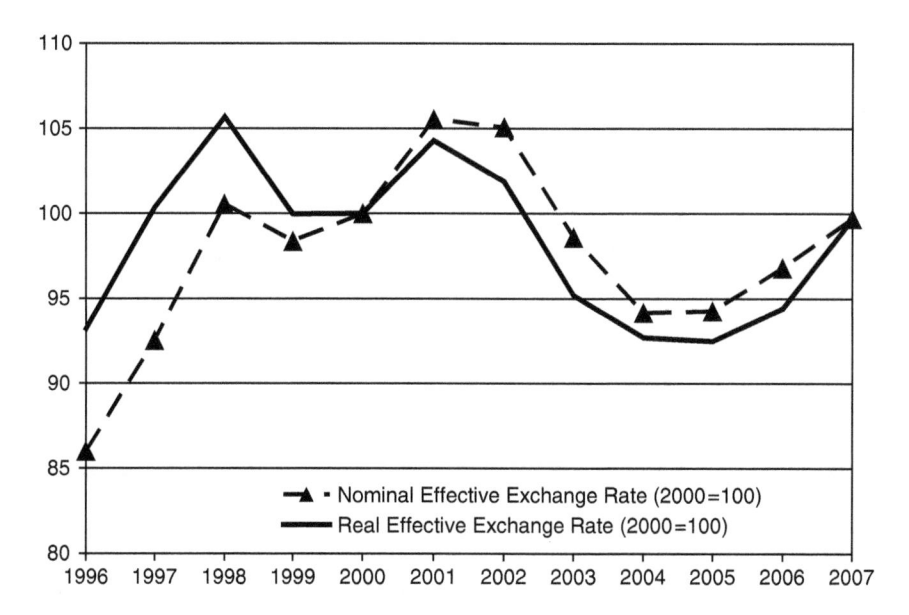

Figure 7.3b. Real and nominal effective exchange rate for China

Note: Constructed using data in the IMF's International Finance Statistics database.
Source: Data for 2007 are up to July 2007.

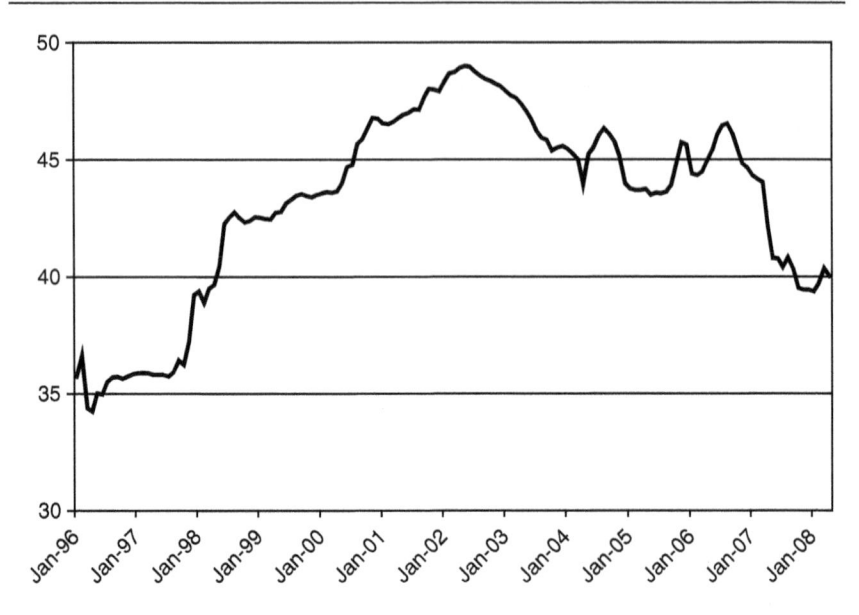

Figure 7.4a. Rupee-US$ exchange rate
Source: Constructed using data in the IMF's International Finance Statistics database.

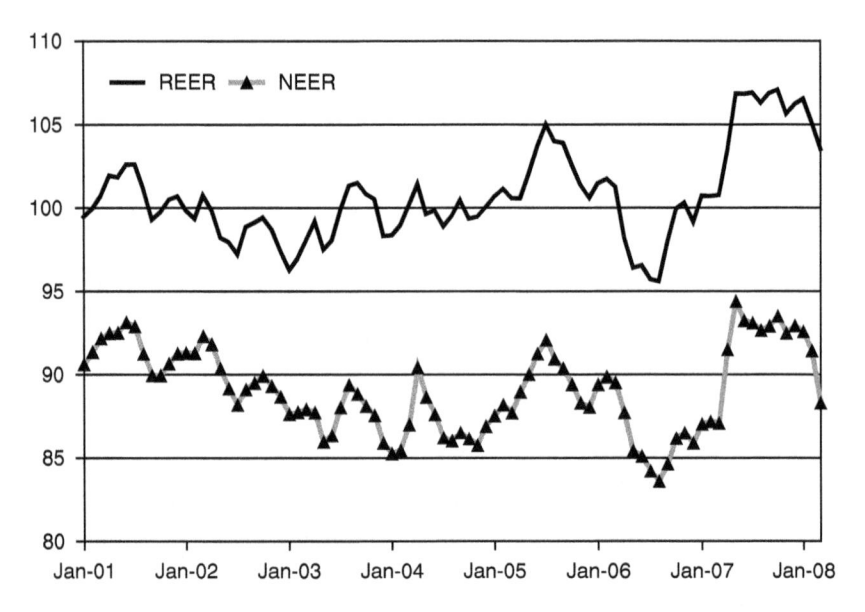

Figure 7.4b. Real and nominal effective exchange rate for India
Source: Constructed using data in the Reserve Bank's of India's website.

China's exchange rate policy has resulted in a massive accumulation of international reserves since 2001 (Figure 7.5). During the period 2001–2004, inflows of speculative capital (in anticipation of eventual renminbi appreciation) accounted for most of the pickup in the pace of reserve accumulation relative to the period 1998–2000. During 2005–2006, speculative inflows shrank but the slack was more than taken up by a dramatic surge in the trade balance, which doubled the rate of reserve accumulation that had been seen during 2001–2004. The inflows resulting from these factors have added to the liquidity in the banking system and further complicated the control of credit growth.

Why have these inflows not led to rampant inflation in China? The answer lies in the ability of the People's Bank of China (PBC) to sterilize these inflows. Such sterilization usually quickly runs into limits in most emerging market economies. Government bonds that are used to soak up liquidity have to offer increasingly high yields to convince domestic economic agents to hold them, leading to ever increasing costs to the budget.

In China, private saving rates (both household and corporate) continue to be very high; most of these savings invariably flow into the banking system since there are few alternatives. This has made the banks flush with liquidity, particularly at a time when they are under pressure to hold down growth in credit. Moreover, banks have an incentive to hold PBC bills rather than increase their lending since corporate lending, for instance, carries a capital requirement of 100 percent while no capital needs to be put aside for lending to the Government. So there is a great deal of demand for PBC bills even at relatively low interest rates. This means that, at the margin, sterilization is essentially a moneymaking operation for the PBC (abstracting from the effects of changes in the exchange rate).

But such a cost–benefit calculation can be deceptive. The lack of exchange rate flexibility not only reduces monetary policy independence, it also hampers banking sector reforms. The inability of the PBC to use interest rates as a primary tool of monetary policy implies that credit growth has to be controlled by blunter and non-market-oriented tools, including targets/ceilings for credit growth as well as 'non-prudential administrative measures' (which effectively amount to moral suasion). This vitiates the process of banking reform by keeping banks' lending growth under the administrative guidance of the PBC rather than letting it be guided by market signals. This constraint has also perpetuated large efficiency costs via provision of cheap credit to inefficient state enterprises (Dollar and Wei 2007). The incidence of these and other costs of banking

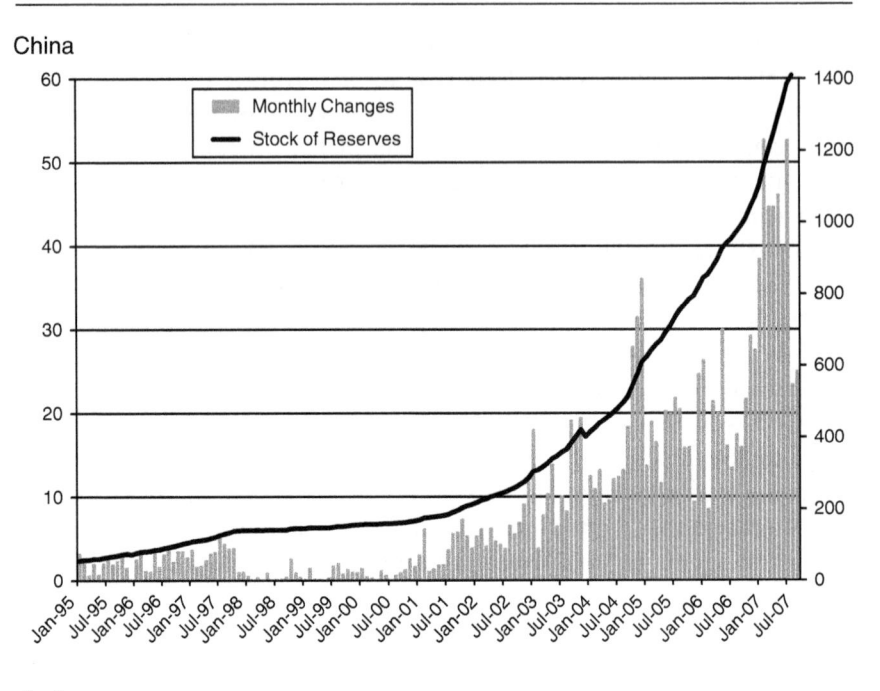

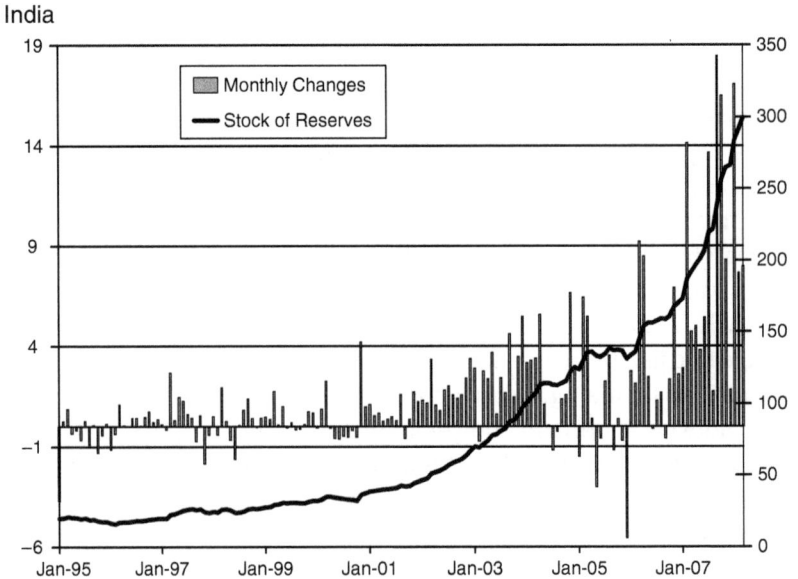

Figure 7.5. Foreign exchange reserves: Flows and stocks (in billions of US$)
Source: Constructed using data in the CEIC database.

system inefficiency are not obvious, but they may ultimately be borne by depositors in the form of low (or negative) real returns on their saving.[1]

The management of capital flows has been another crucial component of macroeconomic policy. Extensive capital controls, along with tax benefits and other incentives, have been used to promote inward FDI while other forms of inflows, especially portfolio debt, have been discouraged (Prasad and Wei 2007). Capital controls have also played an important role in protecting the banking system from external competition by restricting the entry of foreign banks and by making it harder to take capital out of the country. The limited development of debt and equity markets means that the state-owned banking system is effectively the only major game in town, for both borrowers and savers.

7.4 The reform agenda

The complexity of the macroeconomic problems facing China makes it difficult to isolate specific policy solutions. The traditional approach of undertaking incremental reforms in a limited and experimental manner may not work well anymore.[2] Given the prominence of China's exchange rate regime in discussions about China–US bilateral relations as well as the issue of global current account imbalances, currency policy provides a good illustration about the interconnectedness of various reforms.

Let us begin by analyzing the costs of having a tightly managed, rather than flexible, exchange rate. An inflexible exchange rate, while not the root cause of imbalances in the economy, requires a large set of distortionary policies for its maintenance over long periods. It is these distortions that—through multiple channels—hurt economic welfare and could, over time, shift the balance of risks in the economy.

Indeed, exchange rate flexibility matters for China, but not necessarily because it will directly have a large or lasting impact on problems such as the US–China trade imbalance.[3] Rather, the case for a flexible

---

[1] In July 2007, the benchmark one-year deposit rate was raised to 3.33% and the tax rate on bank interest income was cut from 20% to 5%. The effective after-tax deposit rate is now 3.16%, which is still below the current rate of CPI inflation.
[2] See Blanchard and Giavazzi (2005) and Prasad and Rajan (2006) for more on this point.
[3] While Chinese currency appreciation by itself may not have much of an impact on global current account imbalances, it would be an important step towards resolving those

exchange rate rests on a deeper set of policy priorities, with the ultimate objective being balanced and sustainable growth in the longer term.

An independent interest rate policy is a key tool for improving domestic macroeconomic management and promoting stable growth and low inflation. Monetary policy independence is, however, a mirage if the central bank is mandated to attain an exchange rate objective. Capital controls do insulate monetary policy to some extent, but they are notoriously leaky and tend to become increasingly less effective over time.[4] Thus, a flexible exchange rate is a prerequisite for an independent monetary policy.

Independent interest rate policy, in turn, is a key input into financial sector reforms. Using interest rate policy, rather than Government directives, to guide credit expansion is essential to encourage banks to become more robust financial institutions. Trying to foster the commercial orientation of the banking sector in the absence of monetary policy tools to guide credit and money growth vitiates banking reforms.

The argument that the financial system needs to be fully modernized before allowing currency flexibility therefore has it backwards. Indeed, durable banking reforms are likely to be stymied if the PBC's ability to manage interest rates is constrained by the exchange rate objective. The PBC then has to revert to its old practice of telling state banks how much to lend and to whom, which hardly gives banks the right incentives to assess and price risk carefully in their loan portfolios. This makes banking reforms even more complicated than they already are.

Another requirement for broader financial development is a stable macroeconomic environment, for which again good macroeconomic policies, including effective monetary policy, are necessary. On the flip side, the lack of effective macroeconomic management could generate risks via the financial sector. In the absence of room for maneuver on interest rates, liquidity flows into the economy could result in asset price bubbles, including in the real estate and stock markets. These markets

---

imbalances since other Asian economies may be emboldened to allow their currencies to appreciate as well if China made the first move.

[4] A crude way of measuring *net* flows through unofficial channels is to look at the errors and payments category of the balance of payments. Prasad and Wei (2007) document that, during periods of downward (depreciation) pressures on the renminbi—e.g. the Asian crisis period—errors and omissions were negative and large, suggesting significant capital flight. During 2003–2005, the errors and omissions turned into large positive numbers, reflecting speculative inflows in anticipation of renminbi appreciation. *Gross* unofficial flows could of course be much larger.

could become vulnerable to sudden and unpredictable shifts in investor sentiment that could send them tumbling at the slightest provocation, with broader ripple effects through the economy.

For developing the domestic financial sector, opening up of the capital account—to inflows as well as to outflows—could also serve as an important catalyst.[5] Inflows can bring in technical expertise on developing new financial instruments, creating and managing risk assessment systems, and improving corporate governance. Indeed, the approach of using foreign strategic investors to improve the efficiency of domestic banks is a strategy the Chinese authorities see as playing a useful role in their overall reform effort. Allowing outflows would help increase efficiency by creating competition for the domestic banking system and limiting the captive source of funds (bank deposits) that now keep domestic banks flush with liquidity. However, opening the capital account ahead of introducing greater flexibility in the exchange rate could pose serious problems in the future.[6]

Ultimately, stable macroeconomic policies and a well-developed and efficient financial sector are crucial ingredients for balanced and sustainable growth. Exchange rate policy is clearly not an end in itself but has an important role to play in achieving these deeper policy reforms and also the ultimate objectives in terms of growth and welfare.

7.5 Monetary policy

There are good reasons why China should move away from using the exchange rate as an anchor for inflation expectations. It should, instead, adopt an explicit inflation objective—a long-run range for the inflation rate and an explicit acknowledgement that low inflation is the priority for monetary policy—as a new anchor for monetary policy (Goodfriend and Prasad 2007). An inflation objective, coupled with exchange rate flexibility, would work best to stabilize domestic demand in response to internal and external macroeconomic shocks. Indeed, focusing on inflation stability is the best way for monetary policy to achieve broader objectives such as financial stability and high employment growth. Over time, the inflation objective would provide a basis for currency flexibility.

[5] See Kose et al. (2006).
[6] See Eichengreen (2004); Prasad et al. (2005); and Yu (2007).

The time is right for making the switch—economic growth is strong and headline inflation is low. At an operational level, the PBC could continue its current approach to monetary policy, which includes setting targets for money and credit growth. The crucial difference would be to switch the strategic focus from the exchange rate to the inflation objective, which means that the currency could appreciate or depreciate in response to more fundamental economic forces, such as productivity growth. This framework would subsume monitoring of monetary aggregates, such as M2 and private credit, but directly targeting these aggregates is increasingly inappropriate for an economy that is undergoing rapid structural transformation and changes in the structure of its financial markets.

A full-fledged inflation targeting regime could serve as a useful long-term goal, but the approach I have outlined above is more practical for the foreseeable future and should deliver most of the benefits of formal inflation targeting.

Two related points are worth noting. Independent interest rate policy requires a flexible exchange rate, not a one-off revaluation or a sequence of revaluations. A flexible exchange rate buffers some of the effects of interest rate changes, especially in terms of offsetting the temptation for capital to flow in or out in response to such changes. A one-off revaluation can solve this problem temporarily, but could create even more problems subsequently if interest rate actions in a different direction become necessary, or if investor sentiment and the pressures for capital inflows or outflows shift.

Another crucial point is that exchange rate flexibility should not be confused with full opening of the capital account. An open capital account would allow the currency to float freely and be market determined. But the exchange rate can be made flexible and the objective of monetary policy independence achieved even if the capital account is not fully open.

A concern often expressed by Chinese policymakers is that, given the fragility of the domestic banking system, exchange rate flexibility could be disastrous. There are two possible factors behind this concern. One is that sharp changes in the value of the currency could destroy bank balance sheets. There is little evidence, however, that Chinese banks have large exposures to foreign currency assets (and/or external liabilities denominated in renminbi) that would hurt their balance sheets greatly if the renminbi were to appreciate in the short run.

A more serious concern is that outflows of capital could starve the domestic banking system of liquidity by allowing domestic savers to take their money abroad. This is where the difference between exchange rate flexibility and capital account liberalization becomes especially important. There is no reason why, with even the moderately effective capital controls that are in place now, China could not allow for more exchange rate flexibility. A flexible exchange rate, even if it does not yield a 'true' market equilibrium rate because capital flows are constrained, can allow for an independent monetary policy. And this flexibility does not by itself generate channels for evading controls on capital flows. In short, as a reason for not moving more quickly towards a flexible exchange rate, banking system weaknesses constitute a red herring.

As noted earlier, India has amore flexible exchange rate and, hence, a more independent monetary policy than China. Nevertheless, the maintenance of an implicit exchange rate objective has often acted as a constraint on monetary policy, created unrealistic expectations about the central bank's ability to control both inflation and the nominal exchange rate, and made it harder to anchor inflationary expectations. Thus, even in the case of India, a move to an inflation objective as the primary goal of monetary policy could have beneficial effects.

7.6 Concluding remarks

China and India have both made tremendous strides on the road to economic prosperity. But there remains a large agenda for reforms to ensure the sustainability of their growth and make both economies resilient to shocks.

China's rising integration with the world economy makes it increasingly vulnerable to external shocks, and there are many sources of internal pressures as well. Some difficult policy reforms will have to be put in place to meet the challenges that lie ahead. External pressure from the international community can play a helpful role, if pitched in the right way, by reorienting the discussion in a fashion that brings into sharper focus the linkages between currency reform and other core reforms on which there is broad consensus within China.

In India's case, further reforms to the financial system and to the monetary policy framework are important, as are more substantial investments in physical infrastructure and human capital. This would allow India to take advantage of two strengths that it has relative to many other middle-income economies including China—a broader financial system (notwithstanding all its lacunae, it still looks good in relative terms) and a young labor force.

Ultimately, it is deep and enduring reforms that promote sustained and balanced growth in China and India that are in the best interests of these economies as well as the world economy.

8
Deconstructing China's and India's Growth: The Role of Financial Policies

Jahangir Aziz

8.1 Introduction

Much has been written about China and India's recent economic performance. And why not? With a third of the world's population and nearly two-thirds of the world's poor, the sustained high growth of these two countries over the last decade is unprecedented. How these two countries have managed to sustain such high growth rates clearly hold important lessons for both development theorists and practitioners.

This chapter looks into the role played by the financial sector in the growth process of China and India. The role of the financial sector in growth is an old topic and, by and large, the theoretical literature considers well-developed financial intermediation, by matching investors with savers better, to be an essential driver of growth (beginning with Schumpeter 1911).[1] The most well-known formalization is the McKinnon–Shaw hypothesis that Government restriction by repressing financial development adversely affects both the level of investment and productivity and thus overall growth. This argument has been reformalized in various ways (Greenwood and Jovanovic 1990; Bencivenga and Smith 1991; Pagano 1993), but the overall theme is the same. Another strand of this literature emphasizes the role played by financial development in reducing the cost of external financing by firms.

---

[1] This view is not unchallenged. Economic development could lead to higher demand for financial services that shows up as positive correlation between the two variables or even that financial sector development could impede growth if it leads to higher volatility discouraging risk-averse investors (Mauro 1995; Singh 1997).

243

Informational asymmetry or transaction costs make internal financing cheaper than external funds (Myers and Majluf 1984). Financial development reduces these informational asymmetries and transactions costs.

The empirical side of the literature is, however, not that persuasive. Lack of sufficient data and the inability to measure the nature of financial development with available measurable indicators has been a major drawback. However, there is some (and growing) evidence to suggest that at least when variations across countries are considered then financial development appears to play a role in economic development (Beck et al. 2000; King and Levine 1993; Rajan and Zingales 1998). Subject to a number of qualifications, this literature finds that financial systems directly influence growth and that well-functioning systems need stable macroeconomic policies, strong legal and information systems, a contestable environment, and regulations that empower markets through better information disclosure and increases access to markets (Demirgüç-Kunt and Levine 2008).

Supporting country-specific evidence is far harder to find as variations in financial development and institutions is typically not very dramatic for the short time period data typically available in most countries (Athukorala and Sen 2002). Indeed in the case of China, Aziz and Duenwald (2003) fail to find any evidence that financial development had helped growth along the channels considered important in the theoretical literature using province-level panel data. In fact, they find that most of the increased financial intermediation, proxied by higher bank deposit and lending, was used to finance the less efficient public sector that did not play a major positive role in China's growth over the period 1978–2002. However, they argue that keeping such enterprises afloat was important for preserving social stability, which may have indirectly helped growth. Bank loans were used to fund social transfers to the vast public sector employees that could not be easily re-employed in the fast growing private sector. By doing so, social stability was maintained that helped investment and growth. However, using later (survey) data, Aziz and Cui (2007) find that financial constraints impeded employment growth of small and medium-scale firms, i.e. constraints on external finances affected working capital that is typically used for current expenses, such as wages, although investment, which was made largely from internal savings, was not affected. Thus, while overall growth may not have been affected by the lack of financial sector development, job creation was slowed. The lack of access to external finances also appears to have played a large role in impeding the growth of firms in other countries (Ayyagari et al. 2005; Beck et al. 2005).

In the context of India, where the financial system is usually considered to be more developed than that in China and data is more easily available, there is some evidence that financial sector development (both in terms of access and in terms of instruments available) have had a positive impact on growth (Allen et al. 2007; Oura and Kohli 2008). Much of the evidence supporting the positive role of financial development in India rests on the negative impact financing constraints have on firm growth and the extent to which financial sector reforms have eased these constraints. Indeed, Ghosh (2006) using data from 1995 to 2004 for 1,141 firms finds that for both small- and large-sized firms, financial liberalization in India in the post-1992 period eased firms' financial constraint in funding investment.

This chapter revisits this issue as the connection between growth and financial development in fast changing economies like China's and India's could be more deep rooted and complicated than what can be captured by simply looking at the relationship between available proxies for financial development and that for economic growth. The basic argument being that links between financial development and growth depend crucially on the nature of financial institutions and financial policies pursued in a country that are not well captured available proxies, such as deposit or credit growth. Instead, financial policies and institutions change the way investment and saving decisions are made, such that looking at these decisions explicitly may provide a better sense of the connection between the financial sector and economic performance of a country.

To explore this idea within a reasonably parsimonious framework, this chapter turns to a seemingly unrelated strand in the literature, namely business cycle accounting (BCA), following Chari et al. (2007). Early examples of this approach are the studies by Bergeoing et al. (2002); Chari et al. (2002a; 2002b); Hayashi and Prescott (2002); and Kydland and Zarazaga (2002), who analyzed the Great Depression and protracted downturns in the Japanese, Mexican, Chilean, and the Argentine economies in the 1980s and 1990s.

In broad terms, the BCA literature extends the conventional one-sector Solow growth model to include various types of market imperfections or wedges that distort decisions of agents operating in otherwise competitive markets. Typically, these wedges look like simple productivity shocks, time varying labor income and capital income taxes, and Government consumption and are labeled as efficiency, labor, investment, and Government wedges. However, it turns out that equilibria of a large variety of commonly used paradigms, including those that depend on asymmetric information, financial distortions, and heterogeneity across firms and households, are found to be equivalent to those of a one-sector Solow growth model with one or more of these wedges. Thus, these wedges, despite their apparent simplicity, can reflect rich and complex economic environments and contractual arrangements among firms and households.

Data is then used to estimate the size and temporal behavior of these wedges based on explicitly derived equilibrium conditions of a neoclassical growth model embedded with simple market frictions. The estimated frictions act as a guide for the types of market distortions that are quantitatively more important than others in explaining the comovement of output, labor, consumption, and investment in the actual data. The quantitatively more important wedges are then mapped into more complex market environments that could be plausible explanations for such frictions. Once such a mapping is achieved, one has a framework to assess which structural features or institutional arrangement, policies, or reforms are relatively more important than others in explaining growth.

In deriving the wedges, preference and technology parameters in this chapter were chosen to be as close as possible to the ones that are typically assumed in the literature for most countries. This is in contrast to some studies such as by Fehr et al. (2005) who choose preference parameters to match Chinese savings behavior or Bosworth and Collins (2008) and Bosworth et al. (2007), who choose technology parameters to match income shares of capital and labor in China and India. Fine tuning these parameters to better match the data is unappealing since it leaves little room for policy changes or reforms to play any role. Put differently, to a large extent these studies appear to be saying that the Chinese and Indian economies have performed the way they have because to a large extent households and firms in these two countries are Chinese and Indian. Instead by assuming that Chinese and Indian households have the same preferences and technological choices (as do agents in other countries), differences in economic performance are entirely due to differences in market structures, policies, and efficiency. The approach in this chapter is to find China- and India-specific market distortions that may have constrained optimizing households and firms to behave in such a way that the comovements of growth, consumption, and investment in the model economies mimic those in the China and India data.

Deconstructing China's and India's Growth

The results from this exercise suggest that in both China and India distortions to the cost of capital may be quantitatively important in understanding their growth experience. In China, the cost of capital has been persistently lower than what would have been the case in a standard one-sector Solow growth model without any frictions—the optimal cost of capital. In India, the cost of capital has been persistently higher than this optimal level. In China, the high growth, which has been largely driven by rapid investment, coincides with a negative wedge between the actual and optimal cost of capital, while in India, where growth has also been driven by investment, the wedge, while still high and positive has declined. In the case of China, the suppression of the cost of capital below its optimal level is a reflection of continued financial repression that has implied a large implicit tax on household's investment income. In India, the falling wedge is a sign of reduced financial repression following the reforms undertaken in the 1980s and 1990s.

The chapter puts forward a number of reasons why the cost of capital has been distorted in the two countries. In China, it has been the use of the banking sector to provide cheap financing by tolerating a large level of nonperforming loans in the past and in the present the large retention of corporate profits because of weak corporate governance (especially by the state) and the need for firms to self-insure themselves against state-directed credit constraints imposed on bank lending. In India, the cost of outside financing has been high because of lack of competition until recently, high retention of resources by the state (directly and indirectly) to finance fiscal deficits, and directed lending. As reforms have increased competition and financial repression has declined as the state has reduced deficits, the cost of capital has also fallen.

In terms of policies, reducing financial distortions in both countries turns out to be key. In China, allowing the cost of capital to reflect the true resource costs is important not only to reduce investment, but also to raise household income and consumption, both of which are needed if China is to sustain its high growth without relying on exports. The Government has embarked on this rebalancing exercise to keep the economy on a sustained high-growth path. The concern is that the capacity created by the continued rapid investment could potentially lead to declining prices and profits, and spark another round of bank loan defaults; or the needed continued expansion in international market share, given that domestic consumption is not rising fast enough, could run up against stiffer price competition or rising protectionist pressures, especially if the global economy slows at the same time. In India, the concern is that infrastructure bottlenecks could slow down growth or prevent it from increasing. Given the size of such infrastructure needs, it is likely that private sector financing will be needed such that the cost of long-term capital has to come down further. While the model here does not differentiate between different capital types, it shows that investment in India is lower than optimal (again defined with respect to the model). If India is to raise its investment rate, cost of capital needs to be lowered through greater efficiency gains in financial intermediation. This calls for further liberalization of the financial sector. In contrast and in what might be termed as a return to economic fundamentalism, this chapter asks the question: How far can the neoclassical growth model be used to explain China and India's growth? Why is this question important? The neoclassical model provides a framework where the explanatory power of any particular factor can be quantitatively assessed and compared across other countries in a general equilibrium environment (unlike most econometrics-based studies), and because policies developed in this framework are among the most researched in the literature and thus their implications better understood.

8.2 China and India's recent growth experience

Since the 1990s, China's real growth rate has averaged around 9 percent while that of India around 6 percent. India, however, went through a balance of payments crisis in 1992–1993 and in recent years its growth rate has edged up closer to that of China's. Indeed, by some measures the growth drivers also appear to be very similar. Since 1990, growth in both China and India has been driven by rapid investment. The investment-to-GDP ratio in China increased by 8.2 percentage points between 2000 and 2005, while that in India by 9.8 percentage points. Against this rise in investment, in both China and India private and Government consumption fell. In China, private consumption-to-GDP ratio fell by nearly 12.2 percentage points, while in India by 10.8 percentage points. The large difference is in net exports. In China net exports rose by 5.8 percentage points of GDP, while in India by 2.4 percentage points.

Notwithstanding these similarities, these variables in levels are very different between the two economies. By 2005, China's gross investment-to-GDP ratio had reached 43 percent, while that of India's was around 30 percent. Private consumption's share in GDP in China had fallen to 38

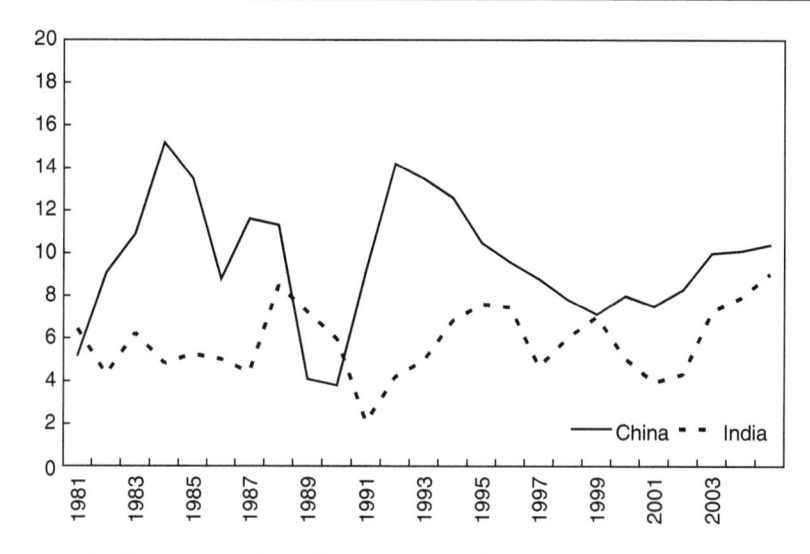

Figure 8.1. China and India: GDP growth rate (%)

percent—one of the lowest in the world, while that in India was around 58 percent.

8.3 China and India's economy as a neoclassical growth model

Against this background, this chapter asks the question whether the standard one-sector neoclassical growth model can explain the behavior of macroeconomic variables in China and India. The answer should be no. The exercise, however, should serve as a benchmark and helps to understand the specific ways in which the two economies deviate from the standard model and thus help to pin down the market structure, institutions, and policies that may have been important.

In this one-sector economy, a representative household lives infinitely in a world of certainty, each period choosing consumption and investment to maximize lifetime utility. As is customary, households own capital and rent it out to firms and, in turn, own these firms.

Typically, in such models, the household also chooses its working hours, and for industrial countries, this choice typically turns out to be important. In the case of both China and India, data on hours worked is hard to come by and although the International Labor Organization has some survey information, it is patchy and covers only a few manufacturing industries. Acknowledging this drawback of the model, we drop labor

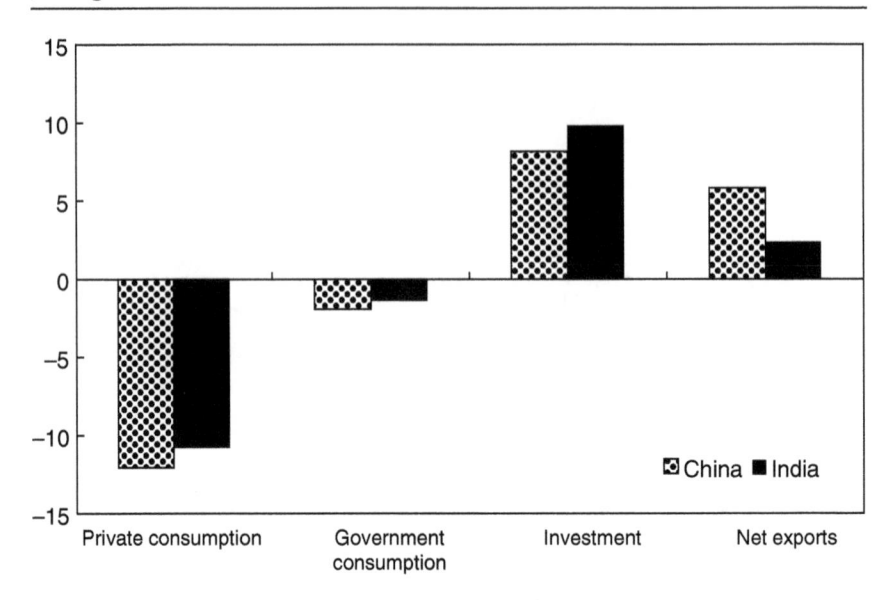

Figure 8.2. Changes in GDP components: 1990–2005 (in percentage points of GDP)

choice from the household's maximization problem. This simplifies the household's problem to maximizing:

$$\sum_{t=0}^{\infty} \beta^t N_t \log(c_t)$$

subject to the budget constraint:

$$N_t c_t + X_t \leq w_t + r_t K_t + \Pi_t \tag{1}$$

where N is the size of working-age population, c is per capita consumption $\frac{C}{N}$, X is investment, K is capital, and Π is total transfers (including Government transfers net of taxes and corporate profits). There are two relative prices—w the real wage rate and r the real return from renting capital.

On the production side, a representative firm operates a Cobb–Douglas technology given by $Y = A_t K_t^\alpha L_t^{1-\alpha}$, where Y is aggregate output, A measures the level of total factor productivity (TFP), and L is the number of workers employed. Using these notations, the firm's problem is to maximize profit given by:

$$\sum_{t=0}^{\infty} \lambda_t \left(A_t K_t^\alpha L_t^{1-\alpha} - w_t L_t - r K_t \right) \tag{2}$$

There are two feasibility constraints in this model economy, which are the national income identity:

$$C_t + X_t + G_t = Y_t \qquad (3)$$

where G is Government purchases, and the law of capital accumulation given by:

$$K_{t+1} = (1 - \delta)K_t + X_t \qquad (4)$$

where δ is the depreciation rate. To derive the policy functions and the steady-state of the system, all aggregate variables are detrended as follows:

$$k_t = \frac{K_t}{A_t^{\frac{1}{1-a}} N_t}, \; c_t = \frac{C_t}{A_t^{\frac{1}{1-a}} N_t}, \; y_t = \frac{Y_t}{A_t^{\frac{1}{1-a}} N_t}, \; \gamma_{t+1} = \left(\frac{A_{t+1}}{A_t}\right)^{\frac{1}{1-a}},$$

$$g_t = \frac{G_t}{Y_t}, \; n_{t+1} = \frac{N_{t+1}}{N_t}, \; e_t = \frac{L_t}{N_t}$$

Using these notations, one arrives at:

Aggregate production function: $\quad y_t = k_t^a e_t^{1-a}$ \hfill (5)

Marginal product of capital: $\quad r_t = a k_t^{a-1} e_t^{1-a}$ \hfill (6)

Marginal product of labor: $\quad w_t = (1-a) k_t^a e_t^{1-a}$ \hfill (7)

Resource constraint: $\quad c_t + \gamma_{t+1} n_{t+1} k_{t+1} - (1-\delta)k_t = (1-g_t)y_t$ \hfill (8)

Substituting and rearranging the terms (5)–(8) lead to the following three relationships:

$$\lambda_t = \frac{\beta^t}{c_t A_t^{\frac{1}{1-a}}}$$

$$c_{t+1} = \frac{c_t}{\gamma_{t+1}} \beta \left[1 - \delta + a \left(\frac{e_{t+1}}{k_{t+1}}\right)^{1-a}\right] \qquad (9)$$

$$k_{t+1} = \frac{1}{\gamma_{t+1} n_{t+1}} \left[\left\{(1-\delta) + (1-g_t)\left(\frac{e_t}{k_t}\right)^{1-a}\right\} k_t - c_t\right] \qquad (10)$$

where, λ_t, is the multiplier associated with the household's budget constraint. The solutions to (9) and (10) constitute equilibrium for this economy.

Jahangir Aziz

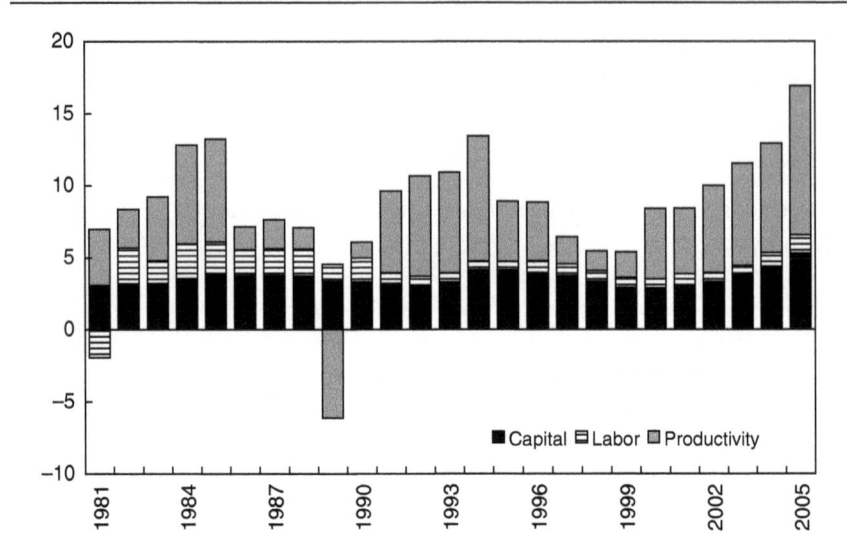

Figure 8.3. China: Growth accounting (%)

The balanced growth path of the model is given by:

$$\frac{k_s}{e_s} = \left(\frac{\frac{\gamma}{\beta} - (1-\delta)}{\alpha}\right)^{-\frac{1}{1-\alpha}}$$

$$c_s = k_s \left(1 - \delta + (1-g_s)\left(\frac{e_s}{k_s}\right)^{1-\alpha} - \gamma n\right)$$

$$y_s = k_s^\alpha e_s^{1-\alpha}$$

where the variables with subscript 's' denote their respective steady-state levels. In terms of the language in the BCA literature, the sequence of 'Solow' residuals, $\{A_t\}$ given by $A_t = \frac{Y_t}{K_t^\alpha E_t^{1-\alpha}}$, is the *efficiency wedge*, while the sequence of $\{g_t\}$ is the *Government wedge*.

8.4 Calibrating the growth model

For both China and India, GNP and its components are constructed using official expenditure side data.[2] Turning to the parameters of the growth model, we assume that $\alpha = 0.35$, as is standard. The share of labor

[2] For details on how the China expenditure side data is constructed, see Aziz (2006); Barnett and Brooks (2006); Aziz and Cui (2007).

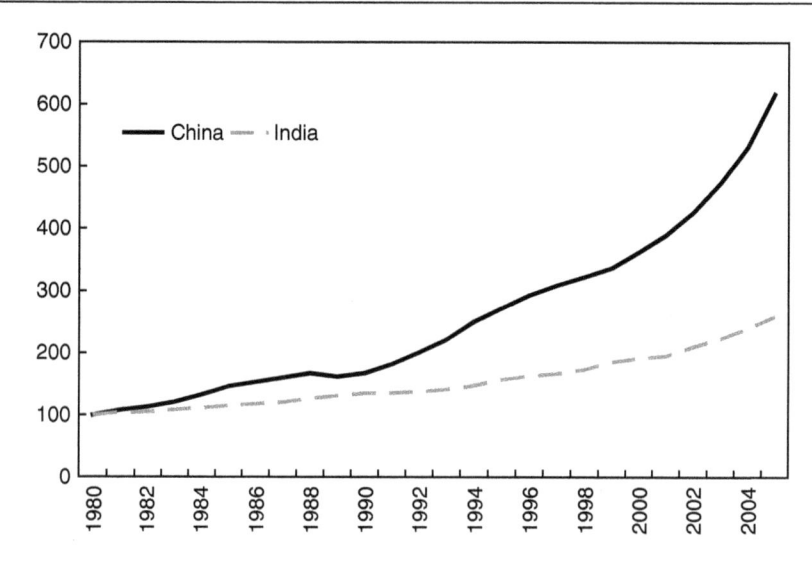

Figure 8.4. China and India: Labor productivity

income in both China's and India's national income is less than 0.65 and this is also the case in several other countries especially in many of the fast-growing Asian economies. However, weak statistical coverage and institutional factors—such as high markups enjoyed by firms—are often cited as the causes. As a recent study shows, in most countries once such data issues are accounted for, the share of labor is around two-thirds (Gollin 2002). Acknowledging this weakness and noting that statistical adjustments as undertaken in Gollin may reduce these discrepancies, we proceed with the growth accounting.[3]

For China, the capital stock series is constructed using the perpetual inventory method. Real gross fixed domestic investment is augmented with the real current account deficit or surplus to arrive at gross national investment, which is then used to construct the capital stock series. The initial capital stock for 1979 is chosen to be such that the capital–output ratio is 2.1 as in Nehru et al. (1993), who used PPP-adjusted national accounts. The depreciation rate was chosen to be 0.06 using available breakdown in fixed asset investment and assuming that structures last for twenty-five years and equipment for ten years.

---

[3] Interestingly, studies that have estimated production functions directly for China, such as Chow (1993), Chow and Li (2002), and Heytens and Zebregs (2003), have found similar values for capital's share in national income.

Jahangir Aziz

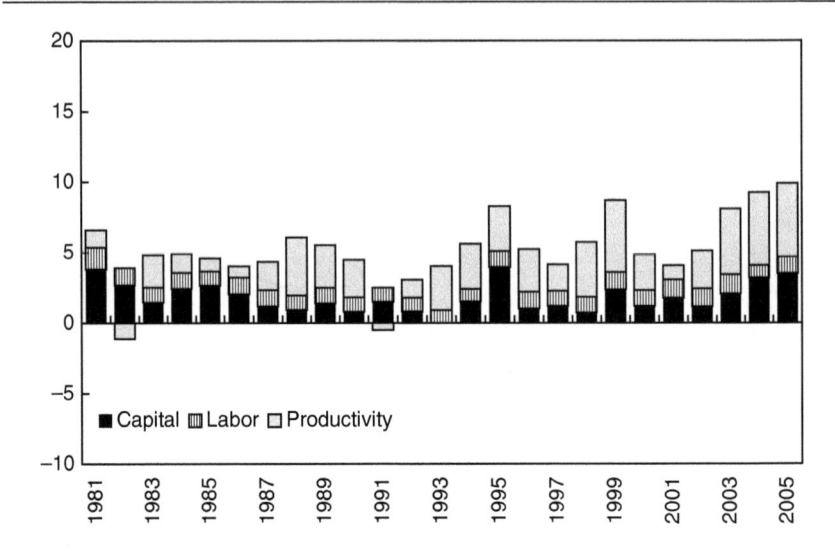

Figure 8.5. India: Growth accounting (%)

In the case of India, the official capital stock series is used (and augmented using investment data beyond 2003), which has an implied average depreciation rate of around 4 percent possibly reflecting the larger share of equipment investment. Data on employment is taken from published labor statistics and includes employment in the agricultural sector for both China and India. The share of employment, e, is derived by deflating total employment by the working-age population, as is standard.

Using the calibrated parameters as a starting point, we first derive the sequence of the technology parameter, $\{A_t\}$. As can be seen from the above figure, much of China's remarkable increase in labor productivity since the 1980s has been due to efficiency gains with substantial contribution from rising capital per worker. On the other hand, the capital–output ratio, after falling through the 1980s, rose sharply in the late 1980s and early 1990s before contracting by the mid-1990s. Since then it has risen steadily. While differing in absolute levels, the story is very similar in the case of India. Increases in labor productivity, especially in recent years, have been due to significant improvement in efficiency and in capital use per worker. In both countries, but especially in China the contribution of labor to growth has been remarkably small. Some of this could be due to poor quality of labor statistics, such that the efficiency gains may be overstated.

Deconstructing China's and India's Growth

8.5 Simulating the Solow growth model

The model is next simulated for the period 1980–2005. The sequence of technological shocks is treated as exogenous with $\{A_t\}_{t=1980}^{2004}$ set equal to its derived value in the growth accounting exercise of the previous section, while from 2004 onwards the growth rate in TFP is set equal to its average over 1990–2004. The discount factor $\beta = 0.97$, such that the long-term real interest rate is around 3 percent. As discussed earlier, $\alpha = 0.35$ and the initial stock of capital set at its derived value in $\tilde{K}_{1979}$. The simulation is carried out using the 'shooting algorithm' discussed in Hayashi and Prescott (2002) such that the economy reaches a balanced growth path by 2015. The algorithm requires simulating equations (9) and (10) forward for a given initial level of consumption and then solving for this initial level such that the economy is in a steady state in 2015 and beyond. Changing the terminal date does not affect the results.

In the case of both China and India, the standard Solow model fails to mimic the actual data. With $\{A_t\}$ as the only exogenous shock, the simulated output path closely traces the actual path until around the late 1980s, after which they deviate and the former ends up about 17–18 percent below the latter by 2005. Consumption's share of GNP

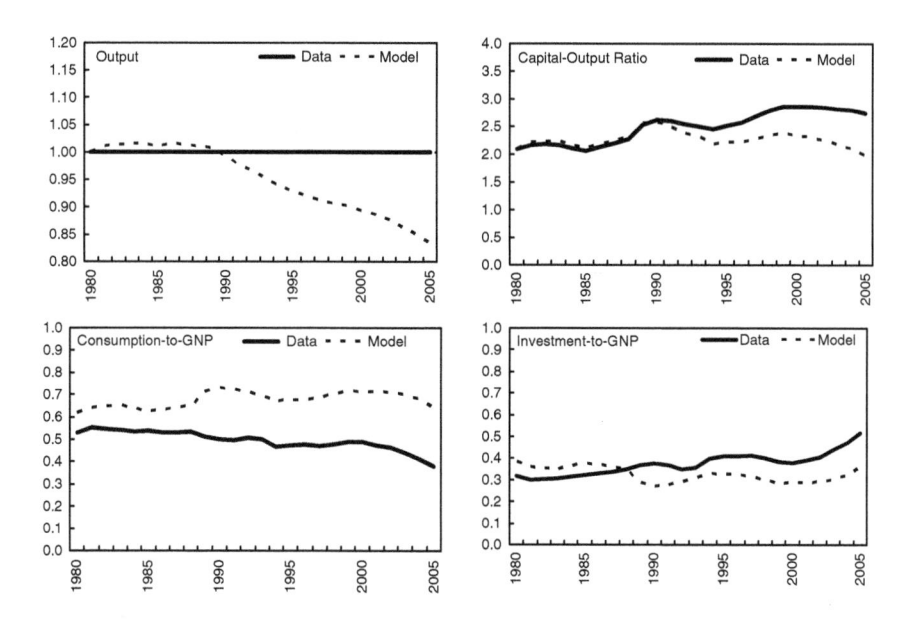

Figure 8.6. China: Simulation with efficiency wedge

Jahangir Aziz

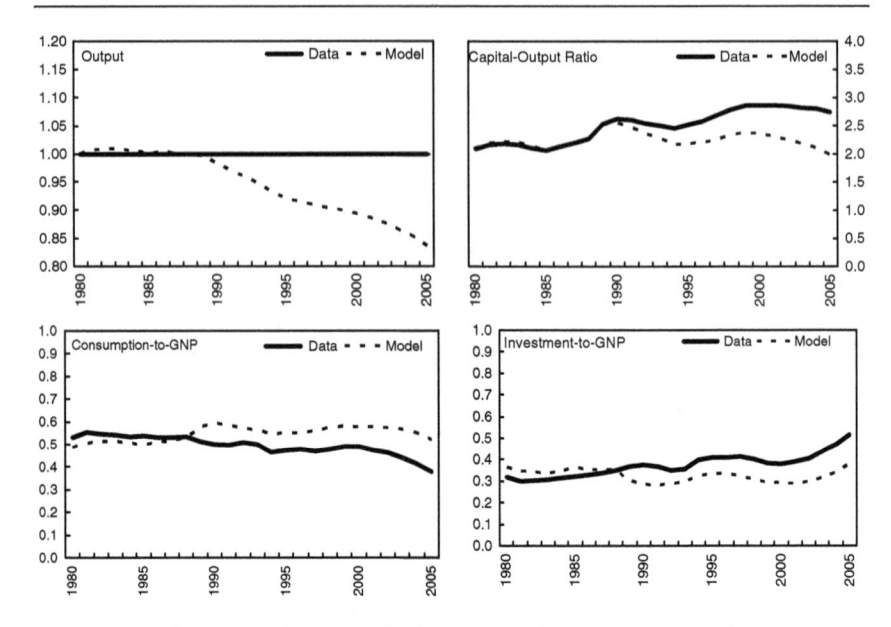

Figure 8.7. China: Simulation with efficiency and Government wedges

is much higher than in the data (nearly 20 percentage points), while the investment-to-GNP ratio is that much lower. As a result, the capital-output ratio does not increase as much as it does in the data and labor productivity is lower. This in a sense underlies the current concern over China's growth pattern, namely, 'too much' dependence on investment and too little on consumption. Put differently, Chinese consumers are not consuming as much as the high growth rate of the economy would imply.

Adding the Government wedge improves the model's fit somewhat. The sequence of Government consumption $\{g_t\}_{t=1980}^{2004}$, is set equal to its value in the data derived above and is assumed to remain at its 1990–2005 average level beyond 2005. Simulated output is 15 percent lower than the actual by 2005. Consumption as a share of GNP is still higher than in the data, but the gap closes to around 15 percentage points.

In the case of India, the model fails more spectacularly even after adding the Government wedge. By 2005, simulated GNP is about 15 percent higher and throughout the simulation period, simulated consumption is lower and investment higher than in the data. However, the model begins to better track the data in later years. Initially, simulated consumption is

Deconstructing China's and India's Growth

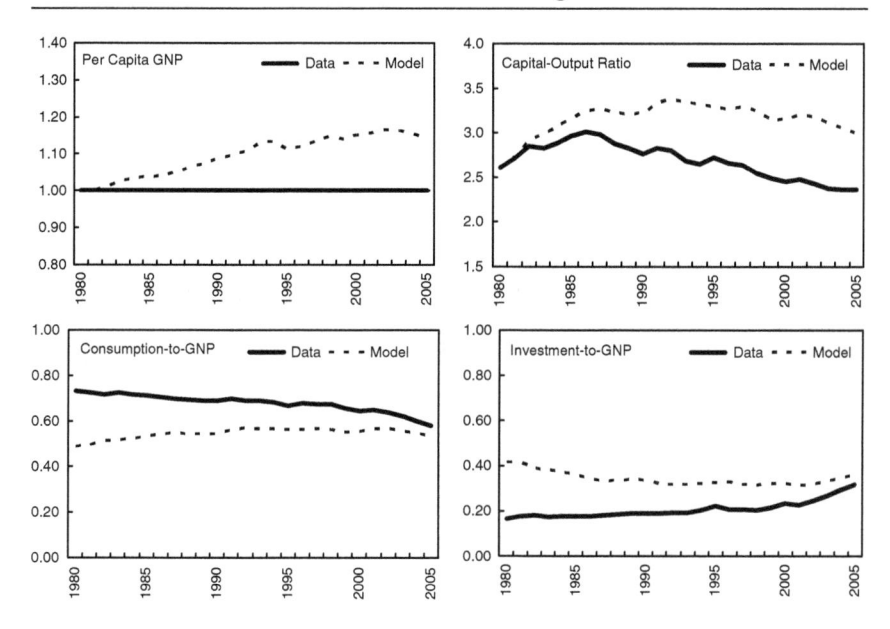

Figure 8.8. India: Simulation with efficiency and Government wedges

about 25 percentage points of GDP lower than in the data, but the gap narrows to around 5 percentage points of GDP by 2005. However, the continuous higher simulated investment results in the modeled capital-output ratio to be close to 3 as against 2.4 in the data by 2005.

8.6 Investment wedge

An investment wedge is introduced in the model in the form of a time-varying tax on gross capital income, τ_t following Hayashi and Prescott (2002); Chari et al. (2004). As a result, the household's budget constraint changes to:

$$C_t + X_t \leq w_t + (1 - \tau_t)r_t K_t + \Pi_t \qquad (11)$$

and the intertemporal equilibrium condition becomes:

$$c_{t+1} = \frac{c_t}{\gamma_{t+1}}\beta\big((1-\delta) + (1 - \tau_{t+1})ak_{t+1}^{a-1}\big) \qquad (12)$$

As can be easily seen from equation (12), the investment wedge is essentially the difference between the marginal rate of intertemporal

257

Jahangir Aziz

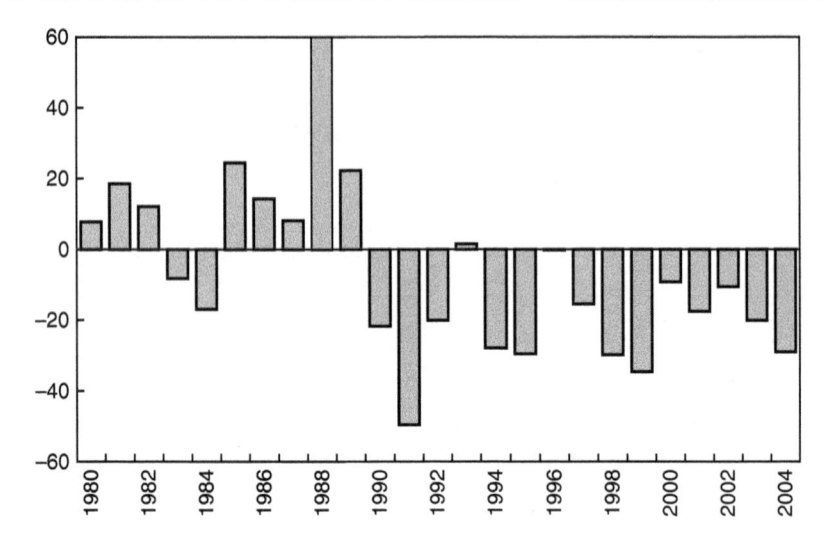

Figure 8.9. China: Derived investment wedge (%)

substitution in consumption (given the log utility function, this is just the growth rate of consumption) and the marginal product of capital. The sequence of investment wedge $\{\tau_t\}_{1980}^{2004}$ is computed using the growth rate of real consumption in the data, the derived sequence of capital stock $\{k_t\}_{1980}^{2004}$ and the calibrated parameters, β and δ.

The result is striking. Virtually all through the last two decades, the investment wedge in China has been negative. (The sharp increase in capital income tax in 1988 is an artifact of the way the wedge has been constructed and is due to a significant fall in real consumption growth in a year of very high inflation.) While in the 1980s the wedge, on average, was positive at around 9 percent, it turned negative in the 1990s to around 25 percent, before easing modestly to 15 percent in the 2000s. In terms of return to capital, while in the 1980s, the wedge reduced the return on capital by 2.6 percentage points, while it added, in the 1990s and 2000s, 3.1 and 2.2 percentage points, respectively.

This is in sharp contrast to the investment wedge in India, where it has been positive through out the simulation period. However, after falling sharply between 1993 and 1995, the period immediately following the balance of payments crisis when India embarked on substantial opening of the economy and liberalization of its financial sector, the wedge increased in the late 1990s before coming down again since 2002. The

Deconstructing China's and India's Growth

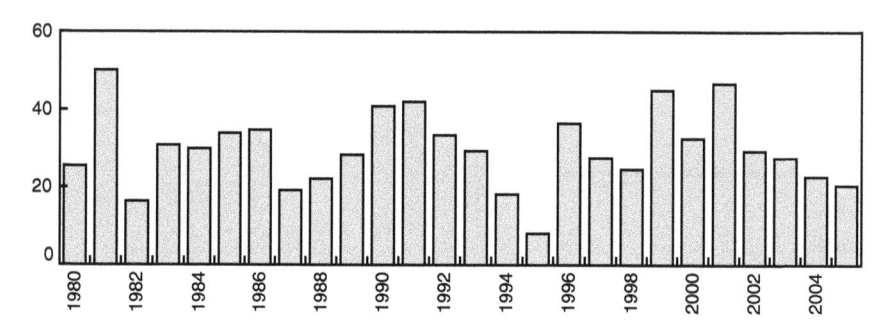

Figure 8.10. India: Derived investment wedge (%)

positive investment wedge found in India is similar to that derived for other countries, including Mexico, Chile, and Japan. In these countries, the wedge is positive, reflecting not only high income tax rates, but also a variety of frictions that increase the cost of capital, although they are not explicitly captured in the sparse environment of the one-sector Solow growth model. In Japan, this wedge is broadly equivalent to the effective marginal income tax rate (Hayashi and Prescott 2002), while in Mexico and Chile the wedges are greater than the effective tax rates suggesting other significant costs of capital (Bergeoing et al. 2002).

Once the investment wedge is included in the simulation, the gap between the simulated and actual data is virtually closed in the case of China. Comparing the gap when only the efficiency and Government wedges were used, the cumulative effects of the investment wedge explains about 12–13 percent of 2005 GNP, and lowers the consumption-to-GNP ratio (increases the investment-to-GDP ratio) by 12–13 percentage points. These are large numbers and they underscore the role played by the distortion to the cost of capital in inducing such large investment rates. Put differently, one can construct a counterfactual scenario where an economy identical to China, except for a zero investment wedge, would reach a level of GNP in 2004, which is 5 percent lower than China's actual output, but with consumption's share of GNP 13 percentage points higher or investment's share about 13 percentage points lower.

In the case of India, similar results hold. The investment wedge explains about 13–14 percent of 2005 GNP, increases consumption-to-GNP share by 5 percentage points and lowers that of investment by the same amount. Although for earlier years the fit is not as good, the distortion explains about 17 percentage points of the lower investment-to-GDP

Jahangir Aziz

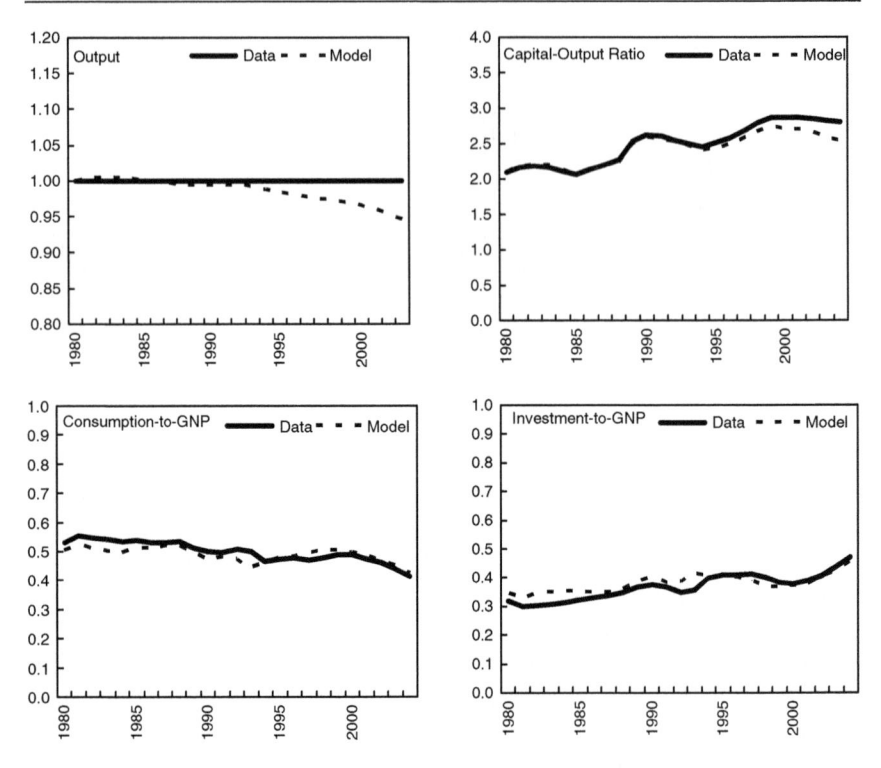

Figure 8.11. China: Simulation with efficiency, Government and investment wedges

(higher consumption-to-GDP) in the data. While the results are not as dramatic for the later years as is the case in China, the investment wedge is a significant explanatory variable. To be sure, much of the rise in investment-to-GDP ratio in the later years appears to be driven by the higher efficiency gains, such that much less was left for the decline in the investment wedge to explain. In contrast, the efficiency gains in the later years could not explain a large part of the rise in investment in China.

8.7 Interpreting investment wedges as financial frictions

China's nonperforming loans

In the case of China, as shown in Aziz (2006) these wedges can be interpreted as financial frictions brought about by state-owned banks in China

Deconstructing China's and India's Growth

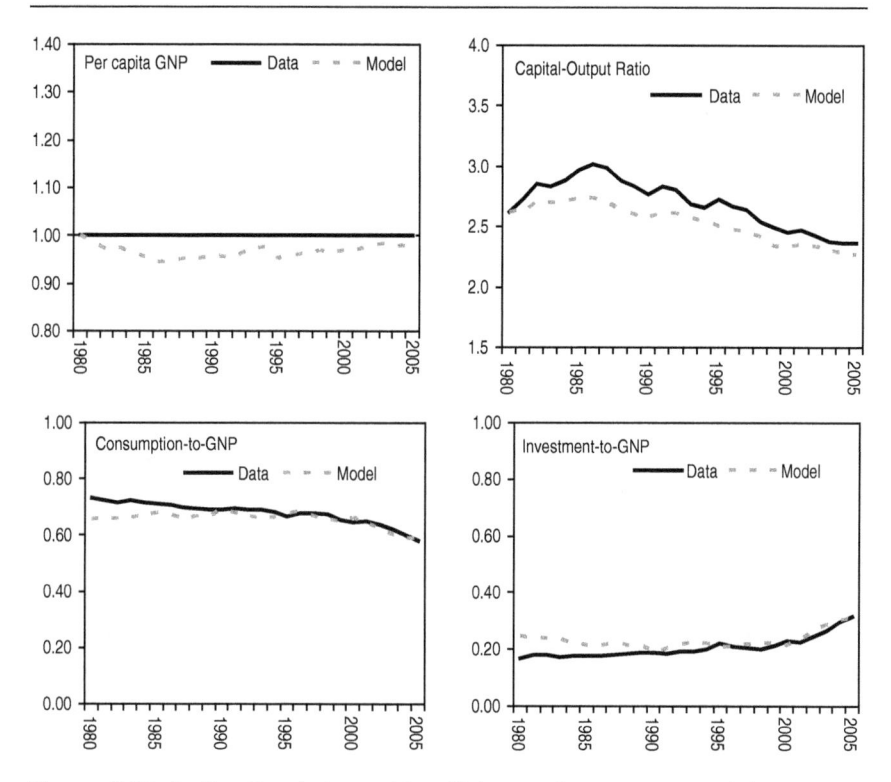

Figure 8.12. India: Simulation with efficiency, Government and investment wedges

tolerating large nonperforming loans that were later (from 1999 to 2006) recapitalized with Government funds.[4] To see how this would happen, suppose the 'average' or representative firm in China is one that faces a lower cost of capital because it can default on part of its loan without facing sanctions. Let μ_t be the proportion of loans that a firm does not repay, either because the firm does not fear effective punitive actions or the banks have been implicitly allowed to do so (what is generally called 'legacy' loans) under Government directives. The firm's profit, under these conditions, is given by

$$\sum_{t=0}^{\infty} \lambda_t \left(k_t^a e_t^{1-a} - w_t e_t - r_t (1 - \mu_t) k_t \right)$$

[4] In addition, Lardy (1998); Karacadag (2003); Anderson (2006); and Dobson and Kashyap (2006) among others provide descriptions of how nonperforming loans were accumulated in China's banking system.

261

with the associated necessary profit maximization condition $(1 - \mu_t)r_t = a(\frac{e_{t+1}}{k_{t+1}})^{1-a}$.

Consumers still receive r_t which is equal to $(\frac{1}{1-\mu_t})a(\frac{e_{t+1}}{k_{t+1}})^{1-a}$. It is easy to see that if one defines $\hat{\tau}_t = (\frac{\mu_t}{1-\mu_t})$ then $r_t = (1+\hat{\tau}_t)a (\frac{e_{t+1}}{k_{t+1}})^{1-a}$ and consumption is given by

$$c_{t+1} = \frac{c_t}{\gamma_{t+1}}\beta\left[(1-\delta) + (1+\hat{\tau}_{t+1})a\left(\frac{e_{t+1}}{k_{t+1}}\right)^{1-a}\right],$$

which is the same as equation (12).

The household's budget constraint becomes $c_t + x_t \leq w_t e_t + (1-\hat{\tau}_t)r_t k_t + \hat{\pi}_t$, where $\hat{\pi}_t = \pi_t - \hat{\tau}_t r_t k_t$. As a result, the two economies—the one with the investment wedge and the one with NPLs—yield identical allocations. In the steady state of such an economy, $\frac{k_s}{e_s} = (\frac{\frac{\gamma}{\beta}-(1-\delta)}{a(1+\hat{\tau})})^{-\frac{1}{1-a}}$ as opposed to $(\frac{\frac{\gamma}{\beta}-(1-\delta)}{a})^{-\frac{1}{1-a}}$ when there is no distortion. As is easily evident a higher $\hat{\tau}$ leads to a higher capital stock in the steady state.

The question, of course, is whether this effect was large enough to matter at the macroeconomic level. Based on official estimates, the stock of NPLs that was created in the last ten to fifteen years would, at the end of 2004 amount to around 26 percent of GNP. In addition, banks in China also carry 'special mention' loans, which are loans that are not being fully serviced at present, but for legal reasons or because the corporate client is undergoing restructuring, they are not classified as nonperforming. It is possible that some or a substantial portion of these loans could turn out to be nonperforming. The fourth large bank, Agricultural Bank of China, is the second largest in terms of deposits and is still without a formal restructuring plan. It is possible that when such a plan is put in place the bank's recorded NPLs will increase. In the prototype economy with the investment wedge, the accumulated stock of net negative wedge at the end of 2004 stood at around 60 percent of 2004 GNP (assuming a zero starting stock in 1990). However, it is typically the case that there is a time lag between when a loan becomes nonperforming in the economic sense and when it gets classified as such in the accounting sense. If this time lag were about two years, which is not atypical of Chinese banking practice, then the reported NPLs in 2004 would be reflecting NPLs created in 2002.

Taking into account the time lag in reporting, the 2002 negative wedge in terms of the 2004 GNP of the prototype economy stands at around 46 percent. However, one needs to add to this capital income tax received by the Government. In China, the flat income tax rate

Deconstructing China's and India's Growth

Reported NPLs on balance sheet	1,575
NPLs transferred to AMCs	1,770
Original transfer in 1999–2000	1,420
Additional BOC and COB transfer	350
Write-offs	324
Total	3,668
(In percent of 2004 GNP)	25.8
Special mention loans	1,140
(In percent of 2004 GNP)	8.0

Figure 8.13. China: Official estimates of NPLs created (end 2004) (in billions of renminbi)

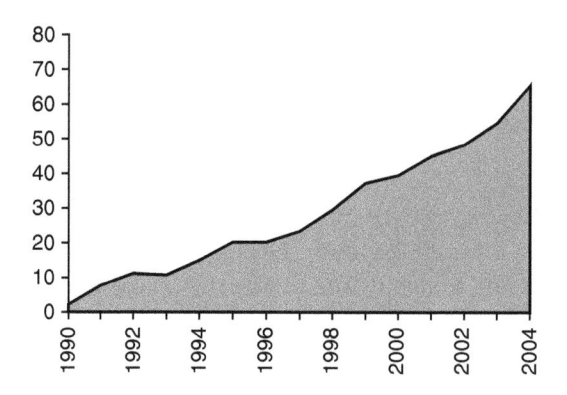

Figure 8.14. Derived cumulative capital income wedge (% of 2004 GNP)

is currently 33 percent for domestic firms and 15 percent for foreign firms. However, the effective average income tax rate has been around 4–5 percent (on gross capital income), on average, since the early 1990s, and is around 6–7 percent.[5] This reflects a wide range of general and specific concessions awarded to firms. Using the above corporate tax rates and adding the derived capital income tax to the net wedge raises the gross wedge that would be reported in 2004 in the prototype economy to around 48 percent of GNP. This is still higher than the created NPLs reported by Chinese banks, but closer to estimates by outside analysts, such as Anderson (2006). While an exact mapping of the reported NPLs

---

[5] The rate is somewhat higher around 9–10 percent on capital income net of depreciation. Note that these are the average effective tax rates, and not the marginal tax rates. Given the lack of adequate information, it is difficult to compute the marginal rate. In addition, data on capital income tax is available only from 1992 as published in the *Chinese Statistical Yearbook*, prior to this period separate income tax data is not available.

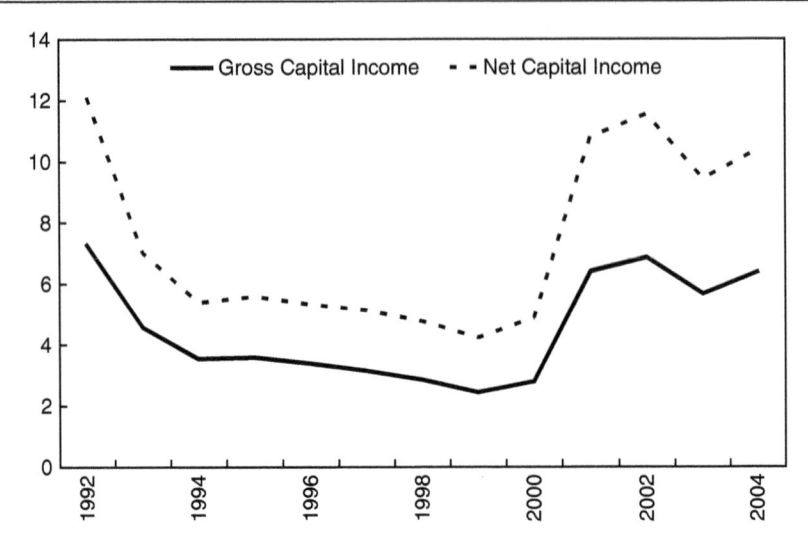

Figure 8.15. China: Average effective tax rate (%)

and the model-based wedges cannot be established, it is clear that NPLs may have been a major conduit through which investment was supported and that the wedge derived from the Solow growth model is not unrealistic.

Borrowing constraints and bank reform in China

However, in the last few years significant progress has been made in reforming China's banking sector. And although it may be too early to evaluate the impact of these reforms on bank behavior (Podpiera 2006), it appears that at least the three big banks (BOC, CCB, and ICBC) may have put in place internal controls which could have potentially slowed the creation of new NPLs. Yet the estimated investment wedge appears to have increased in the last few years, although, on average, it is lower than in the 1990s.

To address this issue, one needs to look into a particularly striking feature of the Chinese economy, namely, that corporate savings is the largest source of financing investment. A cursory look at the breakdown of savings across sectors shows that while household savings has fallen from around 21 percent of GDP in the early 1990s to 19 percent of GDP in 2004, corporate and Government savings, on the other hand, have steadily increased. In fact, during the past five years, enterprise and Government

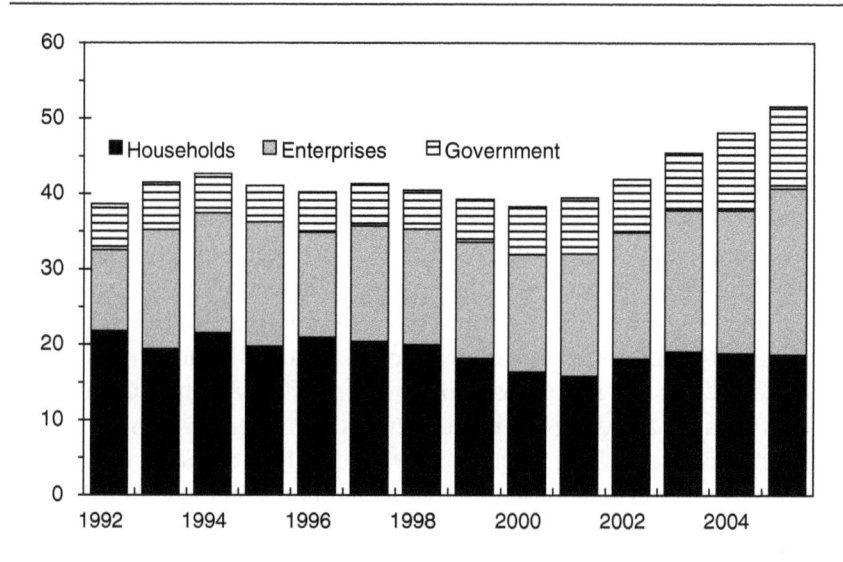

Figure 8.16. China: Domestic savings by sectors

saving each rose by around 4 percentage points of GDP, and they now represent around 19 and 10 percent of GDP, respectively.

The dominance of internal savings in financing investment is in a large part due to the structure of firm ownership and China's poor financial intermediation, i.e. due to an underdeveloped banking system, which has been unable to meet the investment needs, particularly of the vast number of small and medium-scale enterprises, many of whom are in the private sector. Surveys and studies show that the private Chinese firms are constrained in their access to credit. Such constraints reflect the lending practices and regulatory framework that favor the state-owned enterprises over the private firms (Huang 2003), the lengthy bank restructuring since the late 1990s, which discouraged lending until recently, and the underdeveloped bond and equity markets, which provide few channels of indirect financing. Indeed, according to the business environment survey conducted by the World Bank, the share of Chinese firms that complain about access to financing as a key obstacle to their business is significantly higher than other East Asian economies. The smaller the firms, the more constrained they are.[6] This of course does not preclude many other firms, especially the large SOEs, from borrowing from banks without facing any

---

[6] The World Bank survey taken in 1999 showed that 80% of private firms face financial constraints in China, and Chinese firms' reliance on retained earnings is higher than in other countries.

Jahangir Aziz

constraints. Aziz (2006) shows that characterizing the representative firm as being credit constrained leads to a distortion that is quantitatively large enough to explain the observed aggregate behavior of consumption and investment.

To illustrate the nature of this problem, assume that due to firms' limited commitment households (or banks) are not willing to lend without collateral and the capital owned by entrepreneurs (the owners of firms) can only be used for this purpose. However, in the presence of the borrowing constraint, a firm's return to saving an additional unit of capital is not only the marginal product of capital it receives next period but also the 'return' from loosening the borrowing constraint. Thus, the return to internal savings of entrepreneurs is higher than the marginal product of capital as long as the borrowing constraint is binding, and this could lead to higher accumulation of capital than otherwise. The detailed microeconomic environment where such borrowing constraints appear as optimal arrangements is not discussed in Bernanke and Gertler (1989) and Carlstrom and Fuerst (1997).

Assume that wages are paid in advance of production each period and therefore firms need to borrow funds to do so. Since there is no uncertainty in the model, the setup is difficult to justify and should be seen only as a device to introduce the use of working capital. In particular, it is also assumed that all working capital is borrowed and all investment is undertaken from internal savings of firms. This is clearly an extreme assumption as firms borrow both for working capital and for investment purposes. The assumption, however, keeps the model simple and helps to highlight the issue.

The household's budget constraint: Changes to $c_t + \gamma_{t+1} n_{t+1} l_{t+1} - l_t \leq w_t e_t + r_t l_t + \pi_t$, where l_t is the household's savings. Firms maximize

$$\sum_{t=0}^{\infty} \lambda_t (k_t^a e_t^{1-a} - (1+r_t)w_t e_t - (\gamma_{t+1} n_{t+1} k_{t+1} - (1-\delta)k_t)),$$

subject to

$$(1+r_t)w_t e_t \leq \theta_t k_t$$

As noted earlier, wages need to be paid before production so that firms need to borrow $w_t e_t$. However, the funds that a firm can borrow are subject to a collateral constraint. The only collateral is the capital the firm owns. And this is the key institutional set up that drives the result. In other papers that have used a similar set up, such as Chakraborty (2005) and

Kobayashi and Inaba (2005) in the case of Japan during the 1990s, the collateral is either land or equity, both of which are difficult to pledge as collateral given China's private property rules. In addition, until 2006–2007 the stock market was not a significant source of financing. How representative is this stylization of the Chinese economy? Using the World Bank survey of firms, Aziz and Cui (2007) show that 40 percent of all firms and 80 percent of privately owned firms are financially constrained in meeting their working capital needs and that this constraint adversely affects the number of workers firms employ. The average employment growth for firms that are not financially constrained is about 5.5 percent annually, while in firms that reported facing financial constraints employment growth was less than 0.8 percent per year. In contrast, financial constraint had no impact on firm investment, i.e. the investment growth was statistically the same for firms that were financially constrained and those that were not. This evidence and the fact that neither land nor equity can be pledged as collateral given China's private property rules (only after the 2007 reforms is urban land treated as private property) suggests that assuming that firm capital is the only source of collateral is not an unrealistic stylized representation. Banks lend to a firm such that its debt service, $(1+r_t)w_t e_t$, does not exceed, $0 < \theta_t < 1$, fraction of the firm's capital stock.

After some substitutions, when the borrowing constraint is binding the equilibrium conditions for this economy become:

$$c_{t+1} = \frac{c_t}{\gamma_{t+1}} \beta \left(1 - \delta + \left(\frac{e_{t+1}}{k_{t+1}} \right)^{1-a} - \theta_{t+1} \right) \quad (13)$$

$$r_t = a \left(\frac{e_t}{k_t} \right)^{1-a} - \theta_t - \delta$$

$$k_{t+1} = \frac{1 + r_{t+1}}{(1 + r_{t+1} + \theta_{t+1})\gamma_{t+1} n_{t+1}} \left((1 - g_t) y_t + (1 - \delta) k_t - c_t + \frac{\theta_t k_t}{(1 + r_t)} \right)$$

And in steady state, $\frac{k_s}{e_s} = (\frac{\gamma}{\beta} - (1-\delta) + \theta_s)^{-\frac{1}{1-a}}$

Comparing this steady state with that of the standard model, it is clear that capital will be higher as long as θ_s is appropriately small.

As before, define $\hat{\tau}_t = \frac{(1-a)(\frac{e_t}{k_t})^{1-a} - \theta_t}{a(\frac{e_t}{k_t})^{1-a}}$, then the household savings function (13), becomes $c_{t+1} = \beta \frac{c_t}{\gamma_{t+1}}((1-\delta) + (1+\hat{\tau}_{t+1})a(\frac{e_{t+1}}{k_{t+1}})^{1-a})$, which is equivalent to equation (12) and the borrowing constraint looks identical to an investment wedge. This wedge will be positive, i.e. the implicit rate of return to capital will be higher than in the standard model as the borrowing constraint is binding. To see this note that when the borrowing

267

constraint is binding $(1-a)(\frac{e_t}{k_t})^{-a} - (1+r_t)w_t > 0$ and $\theta_t \frac{k_t}{e_t} = (1+r_t)w_t$, and thus $(1-a)(\frac{e_t}{k_t})^{1-a} - \theta_t > 0$. Consequently, the equilibrium of such an economy will look the same as one where there is negative tax on capital income equivalent to $\hat{\tau}$. In a period when banks are restructuring, such as in recent years in China, banks become more cautious about their lending. This intensified the borrowing constraints faced by firms, increasing the returns from loosening the constraint and encouraging firms to increase internal savings.

It is difficult to pin down the value of θ_t from Chinese banking data as working capital is not separately recorded. While prudential norms related to maximum loan-to-value ratios exist, it is unclear how extensively these have been implemented and to what extent they have been binding. Approximating working capital as short-term loans (less than one-year maturity) less trade credits, data from 1999–2005 reveals that the ratio of such loans to capital stock has been declining and on average over this period the ratio stood around 0.25. For simulation purposes, two experiments were conducted. In the first, θ_t was set to 0.25 for the entire period 1980–2004, and in the second experiment it was raised to 0.4 for 1980–1989 and lowered to 0.25 from 1990 to 2004.

With $\theta_t = 0.25$ for the entire period, the simulated consumption and investment path tracked well the data for the period 1990–2004, but did rather poorly in the 1980s, when simulated consumption was too low and investment too high compared to the data. This suggests that the borrowing constraint may not have been that severe in the 1980s. Easing the constraint by increasing θ_t to 0.4 in the 1980s improves the fit of the simulation better (Figure 8.18). Indeed, for this path of $\{\theta_t\}$ the simulated consumption and investment path tracks the data on consumption and investment quite well. However, the implied path for output tracks the data less well. By 2005, simulated GNP is about 10 percent below that in the data. In the absence of firm evidence on θ_t, it is

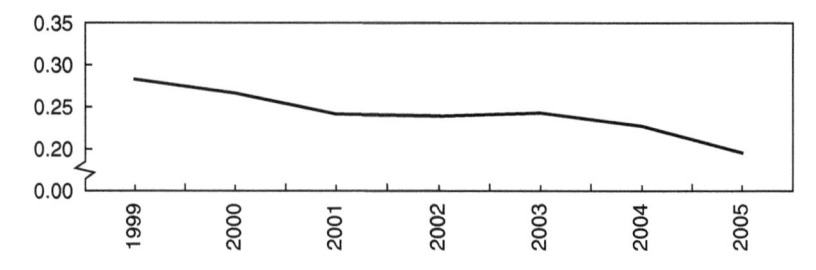

Figure 8.17. Short-term bank loan to capital ratio

Deconstructing China's and India's Growth

difficult to ascertain the contribution of this factor. What the exercise shows is that such borrowing constraints can potentially explain some part of the consumption-investment comovement in the Chinese data and that it is possible that the recent bank reforms have led to a tightening of the constraint that may have induced higher internal savings by firms.

Self-insurance against administrative controls

Another reason why firms have been increasing internal saving may have to do with the way Government has tended to guide lending. While Government has steadily removed itself from intervening directly in the economy, one of the indirect ways it has retained its intervention is by guiding lending to specific sectors depending on what it has viewed as being priority areas for investment. Much of this has been on allocating

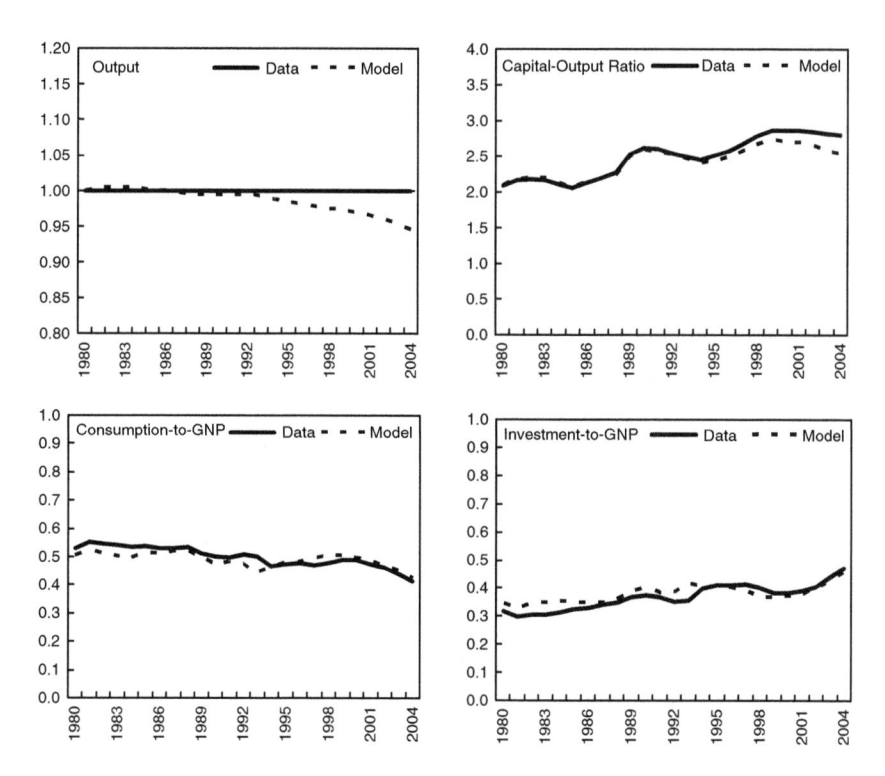

Figure 8.18. China: Simulation with borrowing constraint (theta = 0.35 for 1980–94 and theta = 0.25 thereafter)

269

Jahangir Aziz

resources sectorally, but to some extent this practice has also been a tool to control overall investment. In general, the Government has tried to control investment from going to sectors with overcapacity through administrative orders. Depending on its reading of the economic situation, the Government has made changes to the sectors in the guidance list. While the objective of this guidance has been to influence the sectoral allocation of investment funds, the practice may have had a general impact on firm behavior. Given that the Government could change the status of a sector in the guidance list, all firms are faced with uncertainty over whether banks would provide loans or not. As this type of uncertainty is uninsurable, firms have sought to self-insure through retaining profits as internal savings, and a rise in this uncertainty would lead to high corporate savings.

To see the impact of such Government policy more clearly, the standard model is altered in the following way. At the end of each period, a firm applies to a bank for a loan. Bank loans are in the form of contracts that specify the interest rate and the amount, i.e. $\{r_t, x_t\}$. With probability ε_t the loan is approved and with probability $1 - \varepsilon_t$ the loan is rejected. If the loan is rejected, the firm carries out production only with the capital stock it owns, otherwise it borrows the amount that it needs. Labor decisions by the firm are taken before the loan is approved. This assumption is needed to make the loan approval matter in equilibrium. To see this suppose a firm decides on its hiring decision after the bank loan is approved. In this case, firms with higher capital will hire more workers than firms with lower capital. Given that the technology follows constant returns to scale, aggregate output will not be affected by this contractual change. As Government policy in China is used to channel funds to certain sectors and away from others, the probability of approval is sector-specific with some sectors facing a lower probability of rejection than others. However, to keep the analysis tractable here, it is assumed that all firms face the same risk and π_t is drawn independently each period, i.e. it is the risk faced by the representative firm. The firm's problem now becomes:

$$\text{Max} \sum_{t=0}^{\infty} \lambda_t \left(k_t^a e_t^{1-a} - (\gamma_{t+1} n_{t+1} m_{t+1} - (1-\delta) m_t) - w_t e_t - r_t x_t \right) \quad (14)$$

subject to $x_t > 0$ with probability ε_t and $x_t = 0$ with probability $1 - \varepsilon_t$.

As shown in Aziz (2006), letting $\rho_t = \frac{m_t}{k_t}$ be the share of firms' own capital to total capital the equilibrium condition in this economy can be written

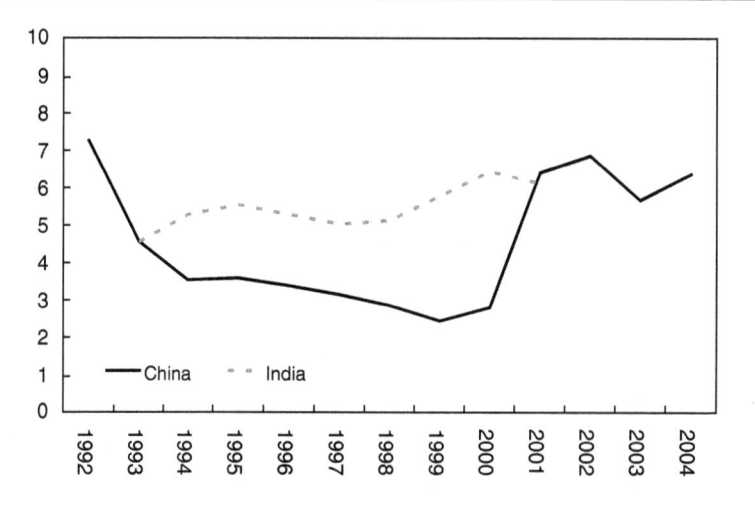

Figure 8.19. Effective gross capital income tax rate (%)

as

$$c_{t+1} = \beta \frac{c_t}{\gamma_{t+1}} \left((1-\delta) + (1+\hat{\tau}_{t+1})a \left(\frac{e_{t+1}}{k_{t+1}}\right)^{1-a} \right), \tag{15}$$

where

$$\hat{\tau}_t = \varepsilon_{t+1} \left(\frac{\varepsilon_{t+1}}{1 - \rho_{t+1}(1 - \varepsilon_{t+1})} \right)^{1-a} + (1 - \varepsilon_{t+1}) \left(\frac{1}{\rho_{t+1}} \right)^{1-a} - 1$$

This is again equivalent to equation (12). This expression for $\hat{\tau}_t$ is strictly positive as long as $0 < \varepsilon_t < 1$ and $0 < \rho_t < 1$ and thus $\hat{\tau}_t$ appears as a negative tax, raising the return on internal savings by firms above the marginal product of capital because of its self-insurance value. In addition, as ε_t falls, i.e. the probability of being credit constrained increases, the wedge, $\hat{\tau}_t$, also increases. This provides greater incentive to save. While China's state planning commission (NDRC) lists industries that are not in a priority sector or where there maybe overcapacity to banks and this list changes over time, it is difficult to use this information to estimate $\{\varepsilon_t\}$. Although quantitative estimates are difficult to come by, it is possible that this factor also played a significant role in the rise in China's corporate savings in recent years.

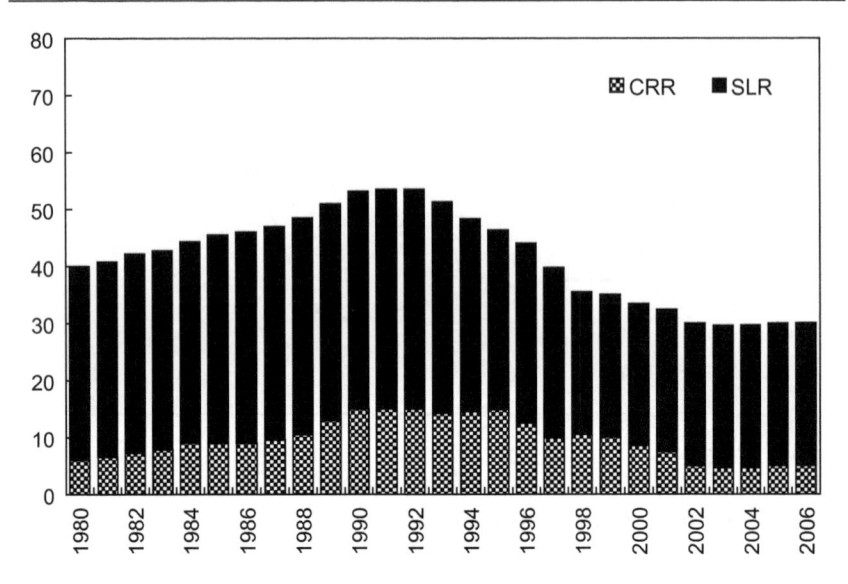

Figure 8.20. India: CRR and SLR (% of deposit)

8.8 Financial sector reforms in India

Turning to India, as the investment wedge is positive and large, a natural place to start is with capital income tax. As in China, the statutory capital income tax rate is high—40 percent in earlier years and 35 percent in later years. However, the average effective tax rate is not. As shown in Poirson (2006) the average effective tax rate in the 1990s and the early 2000s was around 5.2 percent. (Data limitations prevent extending the effective rate calculation beyond 2003.) While the marginal tax rate is likely to be higher, typically $1\frac{1}{2}$–2 times that of the average rate, it is unlikely to be a big explanatory variable given that the investment wedge averaged around 25 percent fluctuating between 40 and 10 percent.

This brings up financial sector reforms as a candidate explanation. In the case of China, financial repression in the form of high tolerance for nonperforming loans and the use of firm capital as collateral for bank financing depressed the effective cost of capital, thereby leading to overinvestment (compared to the level predicted by the standard Solow growth model). In the case of India, financial repression in the form of preemption of loanable funds by the state to finance its deficits and over-regulation of the banking sector and capital markets kept the cost of capital for the private sector at elevated levels until recent reforms. While financial sector reforms began in 1985, quantitative controls on bank loans remained strong with high cash reserve ratio (CRR) and statutory liquidity ratio (SLR), the latter used as a tool for captive fiscal deficit financing. By 1991, the CRR (15.5%) and SLR (38.5%) together preempted more than half of bank deposits. Since 1992, as part of a wider reform package in response to the balance of payments crisis, wide-ranging banking and capital market reforms have been implemented.

These reforms are well described in several papers including Panagariya (2004); Singh (2004); Bery and Singh (2005); Mohan (2005). No attempt is made here to list them exhaustively; instead some of the main ones are pointed out. Clearly among the most important was the end of administered interest rates.[7] As a result of these changes, both deposit rates and lending rates have on average fallen since 1992. At the same time, both the CRR and the SLR were cut significantly, although the SLR remains around 25 percent. In addition, entry and branch expansion requirements for domestic private banks were eased and from 2003 for foreign banks. Moreover, prudential norms were rationalized and public sector banks recapitalized both through the budget and the market. Alongside banking reforms, the Government also undertook major capital market changes, in particular through the repealing of the 1947 Capital Issues Act and the enactment of the SEBI Act of 1992 that paved the way for firms to raise capital through fully market-determined rates. Subsequent laws expanded the use of credit derivatives and in 1999 the ban on forward trading was lifted. In addition, the stock exchanges were modernized and demutualized, while payments systems were upgraded. Importantly, bankruptcy and insolvency procedures were liberalized in 2002.

While these infrastructural reforms were lowering financial intermediation costs, a more market-oriented management of public debt also improved the efficiency of the financial system. Abandoning a long tradition, in 1992 the Government began issuing debt at market-determined interest rates and in 1997 abolished automatic monetization of fiscal deficit through the issuance of treasury bills. This expanded the set of debt instruments very rapidly, as well as hedging tools such as interest swaps, forward and futures trading. The management of market liquidity was also made more efficient through the establishment of the repo market. While it is difficult to match the impact of these changes with the derived investment wedge, it is clear that the wedge, after remaining virtually

---

[7] Only the rate on savings deposit and that on interest charged on export credits are controlled by the Reserve Bank of India. In addition, banks are not allowed to exceed their declared prime rate for small loans. There are caps on margins for foreign borrowing and deposits from non-resident Indians.

constant through the 1980s, fell sharply after the first round of reforms in 1992 and then in the 2000s. Compared to China, nonperforming loans were not a major problem in India, and while their reduction and the recapitalization of state-owned banks may have been helpful, they are unlikely to be a major driver of the investment wedge.

This brings us to the role of borrowing constraints. Several firm-level studies have pointed to access to external finance as a major factor determining the growth of firms in India (Ghosh 2006; Allen et al. 2007; Oura and Kohli 2008). While there are tentative similarities between China and India in the rise in internal savings as a source of financing this is unlikely to be driven by a tightening in borrowing constraints in India. Recall that in China, firms responded to the tightening of borrowing constraints by increasing savings as that was the only source of collateral for bank loans. This is not the case in India given the vastly better developed private property rights and even if that were to be the case the rise in internal savings has so far been rather modest. Instead in the case of India, borrowing constraints were likely to have been eased by the financial sector reforms.

While it is difficult to quantitatively calibrate any particular reform, the changes in the CRR and SLR rates could provide some quantifiable measure of how important financial reforms were. A relatively simple way of incorporating these reserve requirements is to assume that all household savings takes the form of deposits in a representative bank. The bank takes deposits from households, l_t, and gives out ρ_t as the deposit interest rate in return, while charging r_t as the lending rate to firms. The Government preempts σ_t fraction of the deposits. The deposits preempted by the Government, $\sigma_t l_t$, is transferred to households in a lump sum manner.[8] The firm borrows $(1-\sigma_t)l_t$ and converts it into capital $k_t = (1-\sigma_t)l_t$ and pays $(r_t - \delta)(1-\sigma_t)l_t$ at the end of production to the bank. The bank's profit is given by $(r_t - \delta)(1-\sigma_t)l_t - \rho_t l_t$, that under zero profit condition, implies that $\rho_t = (1-\sigma_t)(r_t - \delta)$.

The household's budget constraint is $c_t + \gamma_{t+1} n_{t+1} l_{t+1} - l_t = w_t e_t + (1-\sigma_t)(r_t - \delta)l_t + \pi_t$ and the economy's resource constraint is $c_t + \gamma_{t+1} n_{t+1} k_{t+1} - (1-\delta)k_t = y_t - (\pi_t + \sigma_t l_t - \gamma_{t+1} n_{t+1} \sigma_{t+1} l_{t+1})$. Previously, the net transfers on the household were the taxes needed to finance Government's expenditures g_t. Here $g_t = \pi_t + \sigma_t l_t - \gamma_{t+1} n_{t+1} \sigma_{t+1} l_{t+1}$. Thus depending on the sign of $\sigma_t l_t - \gamma_{t+1} n_{t+1} \sigma_{t+1} l_{t+1}$, the taxes needed to finance Government expenditure

---

[8] A more realistic but more complicated setting would be a transfer from the Government equivalent to the preempted deposits.

Deconstructing China's and India's Growth

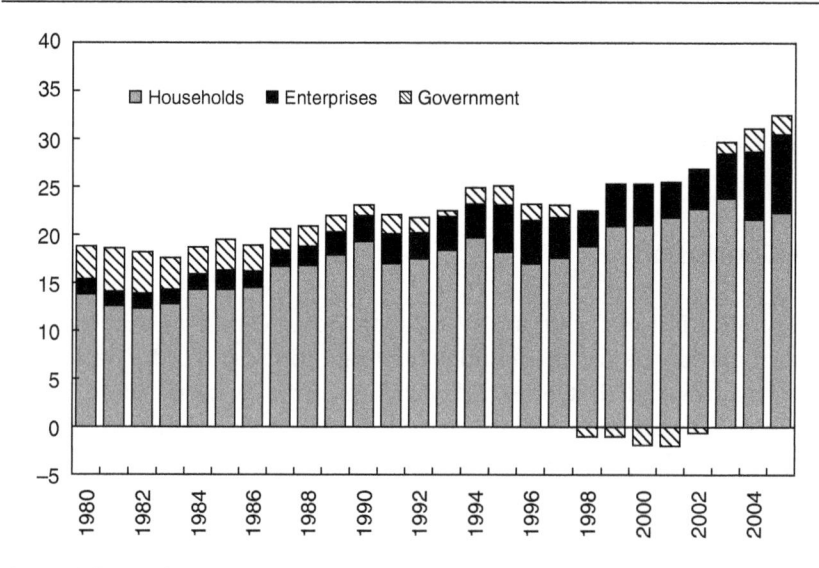

Figure 8.21. India: Domestic savings (% of GDP)

could be smaller or larger than before. In particular, if σ_{t+1} is not lowered too much compared to σ_t, then $\sigma_t l_t - \gamma_{t+1} n_{t+1} \sigma_{t+1} l_{t+1} > 0$ and the needed tax for a given level of Government spending will be less. This can be rewritten as $c_t + \gamma_{t+1} n_{t+1} k_{t+1} - (1 - \delta) k_t = (1 - g_t) y_t + (\sigma_t l_t - \gamma_{t+1} n_{t+1} \sigma_{t+1} l_{t+1})$. It is not difficult to construct a more realistic but complicated setting where $(\sigma_t l_t - \gamma_{t+1} n_{t+1} \sigma_{t+1} l_{t+1})$ is equivalent to the Government's net purchase of bonds. As a result, π_t can be thought of as the part of Government expenditure financed through taxes, with the remaining financed by net purchases of bonds that are partially or fully financed through the preempted deposits.

Turning to the consumption function, it turns out that

$$c_{t+1} = \frac{c_t}{\gamma_{t+1}} \beta \left[1 + (1 - \sigma_{t+1}) \left(\alpha \left(\frac{e_{t+1}}{k_{t+1}} \right)^{1-\alpha} - \delta \right) \right] \qquad (16)$$

which can be easily verified to be equivalent to (12) once more.

Two separate simulations were carried out. In the first, the sequence of $\{\sigma_t\}$ was proxied by the actual SLR for the period 1980–2005 and then assumed to be fixed at the average 2000–2005 level. In the second simulation $\{\sigma_t\}$ was proxied by both SLR and CRR. As shown in Figure 8.22, the results are encouraging. Using only SLR, the model mimics the data significantly better than under the standard Solow model set up. While the model does much better in the later years, in the earlier

275

years simulated consumption is still too low and investment too high. The results after adding CRR are much better. The gap between simulated and actual consumption and investment narrows markedly in the earlier years, while the fit in the latter years is preserved.

8.9 Conclusion

The implication of the analysis in the previous sections is that financial distortions may be crucial in understanding China's and India's economic performances and that financial sector reform may turn out to be key in China's quest to rebalance growth and India's pursuit to raise its growth rate. This is not to suggest that other factors put forward in the other studies are not relevant. Rather the analysis suggests that the explanatory power of financial distortions may be quantitatively large and

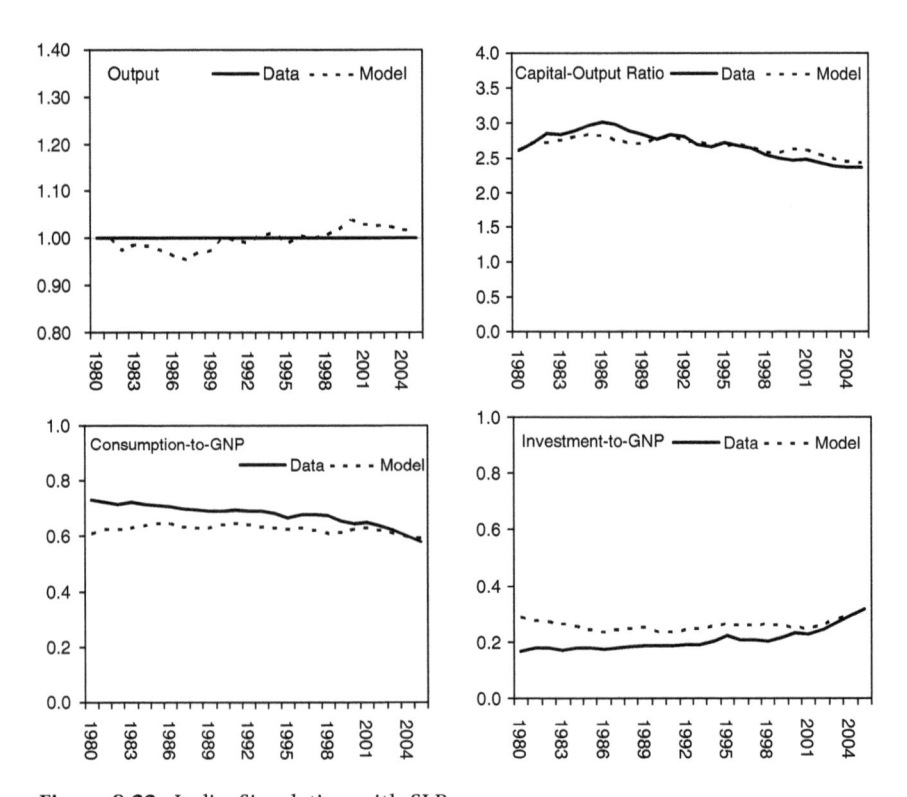

Figure 8.22. India: Simulation with SLR

Deconstructing China's and India's Growth

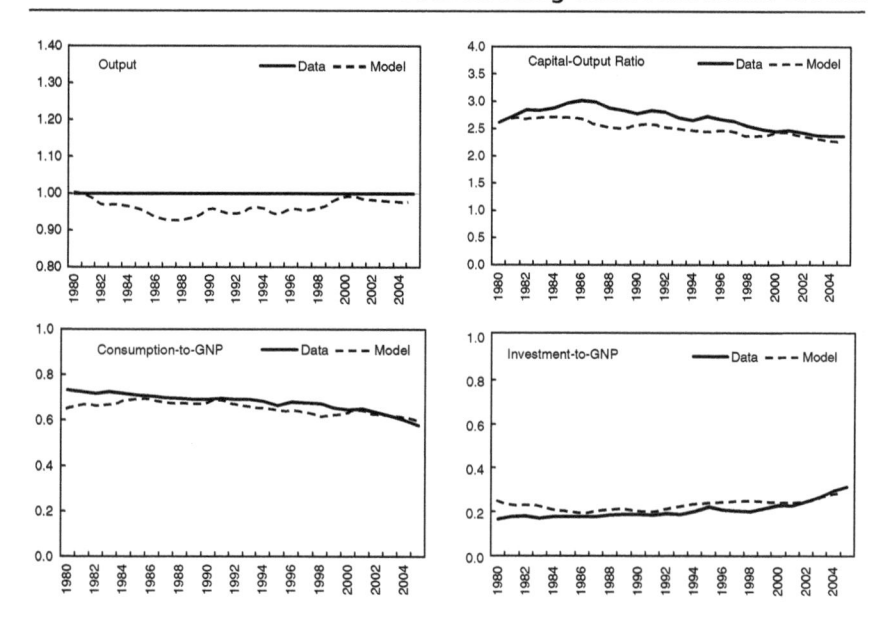

Figure 8.23. India: Simulation with SLR and CRR

that focusing on reforming this sector may be quite important. Indeed, simulations based on the prototype economy discussed in the previous sections indicate that in the case of China if financial reforms were to remove these distortions—for example, by raising the cost of capital to the effective capital income tax rate—the consumption-to-GNP could rise from its current level of below 40 percent to around 55 percent in steady state, which would imply that the investment-to-GNP ratio would fall to around 30 percent from its current level of over 45 percent. In the simulation, the average growth rate of output would fall by around 2 percentage points below the average of the 1990s and 2000s to around 8 percent. Similarly in the case of India, reforms that lower the cost of capital to its average effective rate of capital income tax would increase the investment-to-GDP ratio by another 5 percentage points over the medium term with 1–2 percentage points higher growth rate.[9]

Finally, a methodological issue: China's sustained double-digit growth rate over the last twenty-five years and India's rapid growth rate in the 2000s have, in a sense, surprised researchers, as they have been unprecedented. This has prompted many researchers to try to uncover the

---

[9] In simulating the impact of such reforms, it was assumed that financial sector restructuring cuts the wedge on capital income from its 2005 level to that of the average effective rate of capital income tax of the 1990s and 2000s. All other parameters were left unchanged.

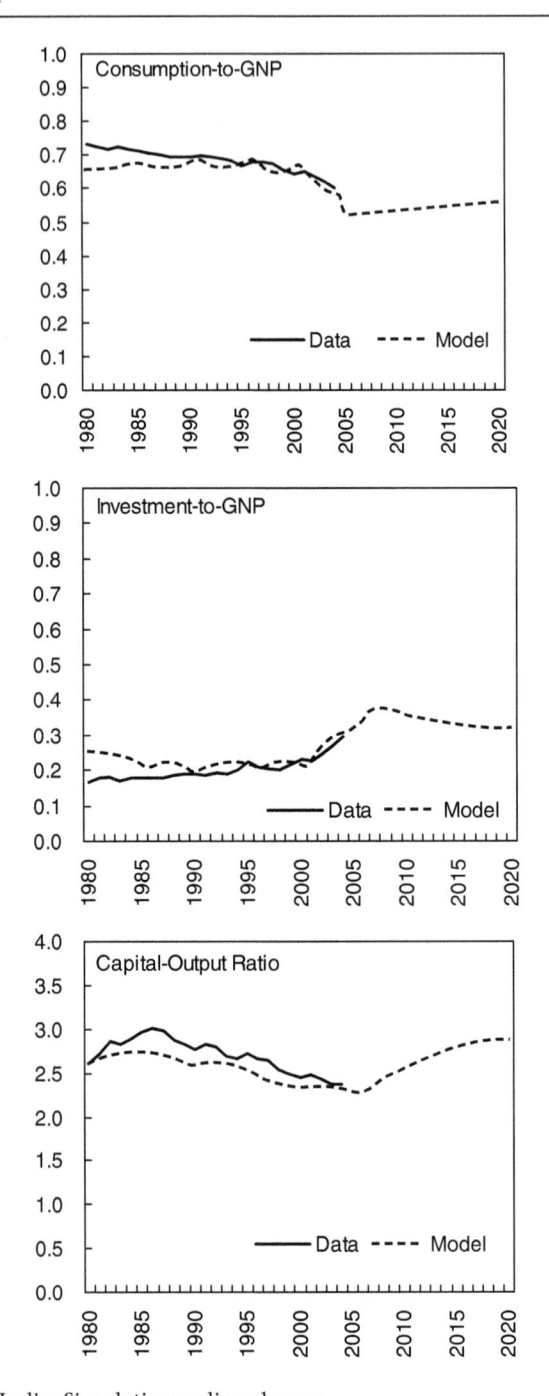

Figure 8.24. India: Simulating policy change

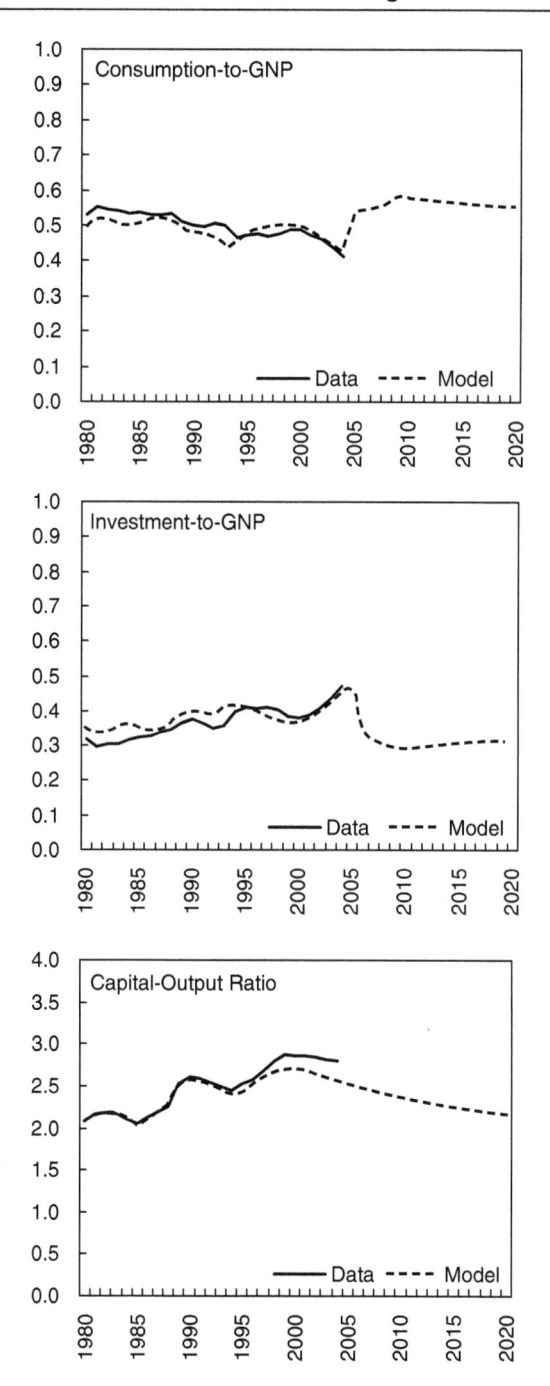

Figure 8.25. China: Simulating policy change

'China' or 'India' model of development. What this chapter suggests is that one need not look far beyond the neoclassical growth theory to uncover such a model. Many questions remain unanswered, such as what underlies the very high and sustained productivity growth? Is it really just technological progress or are some important elements being missed? Do the results change if the external sector for both China and India are endogenized? These are important questions for future research. Nonetheless, neoclassical growth theory provides empirically reasonable answers to some key questions: China's and India's high growth rate may just be the result of adding or removing distortions in financial incentives.

9
Pollution across Chinese Provinces

Catherine Yap Co, Fanying Kong, and Shuanglin Lin[*]

9.1 Introduction

The market-oriented economic reforms that started in 1978 have greatly transformed the Chinese economy. State-owned enterprises (SOEs) were allowed to operate and compete on free market principles, rather than under the direction and guidance of state planning; special economic zones were established along the coast for the purpose of attracting foreign direct investments, boosting exports, and importing high-technology products; and, private enterprises were legalized and promoted. With these reforms, the average annual growth rate of China's real GDP was close to 10 percent from 1979 to 2007, compared to a pre-reform growth rate of around 5 percent from 1960 to 1978. No country has ever lifted more people out of poverty faster than China since the adoption of these reforms. However, economic growth in China has been accompanied by severe environmental deterioration.

According to *The Economist* (2004), the World Bank estimates that direct damages from pollution (e.g. medical bills) are 8–12 percent of China's annual GDP. The World Bank has identified sixteen of the twenty most polluted cities in the world to be located in China. And close to two-thirds of the 300 cities tested by China's environmental protection agency failed

---

[*] The authors would like to thank Miaomiao Yu for invaluable research assistance; and Wang Xiaoping for help in collecting some of the pollution data. They would also like to thank discussants and participants at the following conferences and seminars: Eastern Economics Association conference (February 23, 2007; New York City), Development Economics and Policy Seminar Series at the University of Manchester (October 23, 2007; Manchester, UK), ICRIER's 'India and China's Role in International Trade and Finance' conference (December 6, 2007; New Delhi, India), and the American Economic Association's 2008 Poster Session (January 4, 2008; New Orleans).

to meet the air quality standards set by the World Health Organization. With negligent environmental protection, some areas have such high levels of toxins in the air and groundwater that cancer levels are fifteen to thirty times higher than the national figure (Lynch 2005).[1] Unsustainable environmental practices also pose increasing threats to China's water, forests, biodiversity, and food and energy supplies. Since China is a huge country, its pollution problems undoubtedly have serious negative effects on the global environment.[2]

Currently, forces that oppose more stringent rules and regulations in the name of free markets and economic growth are battling forces that favor greater environmental protection. It appears that the latter group is losing the battle. The general public and the central Government tend to favor more stringent environmental rules while local governments do not.[3] The current central and local Government tax revenue sharing scheme is one reason why local Governments in China have little incentive to call for more stringent environmental policies. Since 1994, local Governments have experienced budget deficits every year, and they have come to rely heavily on central Government transfers.[4] These transfers are largely dependent on value-added tax rebates. Since value-added tax rebates are related to local output increases, local Governments in China have strong incentives to increase production (thereby increasing revenue transfers),[5] but have little incentive to protect the environment.

In this chapter, we revisit the environmental Kuznets curve (EKC) hypothesis. According to the EKC hypothesis, an inverted-U characterizes the income-emission relationship.[6] However, a number of studies (Millimet et al. 2003) have shown that a cubic relationship may exist

---

[1] Economy (2004) also provides a description of the health effects of pollution in China.

[2] See *The Economist* (2007) for a popular account of how China's pollution problems affect the rest of the world.

[3] According to Cheng et al. (2007), a recent survey indicates that 86% of the people are not satisfied with China's environmental protection; 70% of the people blame local Governments for the environmental problems; and 78% of the people indicate willingness to sacrifice the speed of growth for a better environment.

[4] Even rich provinces largely depend on transfers from the central Government to cover their budget deficits. For example in 2004, 42% of Shanghai's budgetary revenues are rebates from the central Government; the rate for Jiangsu province is 48%.

[5] Another reason is that Chinese local Government officials are appointed by their superiors based mainly on local economic performance.

[6] See Grossman and Krueger (1995) for an early contribution. One of the explanations for the inverted-U EKC is that when regions reach a sufficiently high income level, people living in these regions will demand cleaner environments (and these regions also have the necessary institutions to enforce extant environmental rules); thus, emissions decline as income increases beyond this point. See De Bruyn and Heintz (1999) for a review.

between income and emissions. In particular, they may again be positively correlated at still higher income levels.

Our strategy is to first estimate income-emissions regressions using fixed effects panel regression using data for thirty Chinese provinces from 1987 to 1995.[7] We end the data coverage of the estimations in 1995 since a number of amendments to pollution laws were introduced after this year. This allows us to determine the trajectory of selected pollutants relative to income after 1995 if no changes to pollution policy occur (or, if no changes to the structure of the economy occur). In other words, we make off-sample predictions of pollution discharges using the estimated income-emissions regressions. We then compare these off-sample predictions to actual pollution discharges in 1996 to 2004 to partly quantify any effect pollution policy changes may have had on emissions.

A comparison of the off-sample predictions to actual pollution discharges in 1996 to 2004 indicates that actual industrial chemical oxygen demand (COD) pollution per capita discharge rates in 1996–2004 have leveled off and do not increase with income as the estimated income-emission regression predicts. Thus, environmental policies enacted by the Chinese Government to control industrial COD pollution may have been partly successful. However, actual industrial waste water per capita discharge rates in 1996–2004 increase with income; this is opposite to the prediction of the estimated income-emission regression. Also, actual industrial dust per capita discharge rates in 1996–2004 are larger than the predicted per capita discharge rates for most of the provinces. This is inconsistent with the notion that given the adoption of stricter environmental regulations, actual emissions should be lower than the predictions because the latter assumes no changes in environmental regulations.

Auxiliary regressions of the estimated province-specific fixed effects against several province characteristics show that conditional on income, northern provinces have lower levels of industrial waste water pollution (thus, may have been more willing to regulate this type of pollution); non-coastal provinces and provinces with smaller secondary industry shares have lower levels of three types of pollutants; provinces with a smaller state-owned enterprises share have lower levels of industrial COD pollution; finally, there is some evidence that a province's industrial dust

---

[7] To be precise, Beijing, Tianjin, and Shanghai are municipalities while Inner Mongolia, Guangxi, Tibet, Ningxia, and Xinjiang are Minority Autonomous Regions. We refer to all of these areas as provinces for convenience. Chongqing became a municipality in 1997 (it is part of Sichuan province in our data).

pollution level (thus, its commitment to control pollution) is related to its budget balance.

To put the current study in perspective, the environmental consequences of economic growth and policy responses to environmental problems since the establishment of the People's Republic of China are briefly described in the next section. In Section 9.3 a detailed description of the data and empirical methodology used is provided. The results are analyzed in Section 9.4. Concluding remarks are presented in the last section.

9.2 Pollution and environmental policy in China

Since the founding of the People's Republic of China, environmental degradation has accompanied economic growth. During the Great Leap Forward (1958–1960), people's communes were established in rural China. Trees were cut and used as fuel to make steel, causing a reduction in forest coverage. During the Cultural Revolution (1966–1976), farmers in the communes were mobilized to build terra fields in mountains to increase arable farmland, damaging the green coverage of mountains.[8] During the period of economic reforms that started in 1978, communes were dissolved and farmers and herdsmen were given freedom to engage in industrial production. SOEs became profit-oriented and private enterprises emerged. Using mostly outdated technologies, the emergence of these enterprises increased pollution in China substantially.

It was only in 1995 that the central Government fully realized the urgency of environmental problems in China. A number of environmental laws were amended to signal their strong commitment to protect the environment. For example, the Law on the Prevention and Control of Water Pollution was amended in 1996; the Law on the Prevention and Control of Atmospheric Pollution was amended in 1995 and 2000.[9] According to the Law on Prevention and Control of Water Pollution, all activities of any person or unit polluting surface and underground water

[8] Also see Edmonds (1999).

[9] National People's Congress of the People's Republic of China, Amendment to the Law on the Prevention and Control of Water Pollution, May 15, 1995; and, National People's Congress of the People's Republic of China, The Law on Prevention of Air Pollution, April 29, 2000. English translations of these laws are available from the State Environmental Protection Administration's (SEPA) website at http://english.mep.gov.cn/. According to Wang and Wheeler (2005), China's water pollution standards are stricter than those pertaining to air pollution. Muldavin (2000) provides an overview of China's environmental policy after 1949. Also see Ma and Ortolano (2000) for a detailed description of environmental regulations in China.

Pollution across Chinese Provinces

shall be punished with a fine. The Law on the Prevention and Control of Atmospheric Pollution sets standards for air pollution from burning coal, automobiles, and dust; it also specifies measures to punish violators.

Environmental policymaking devolved from the central Government to local Governments in the 1980s. This has introduced some amount of heterogeneity in environmental policy and enforcement across China's provinces.[10] For example, in 1998 Jiangsu passed the Regulations on Protection of Agricultural Ecology and Environment making dumping polluted water in agricultural areas illegal.[11] In 1998, Guangdong province passed the Regulations on Zhujiang Triangle Water Protection. This regulation set strict measures to punish water polluters.[12]

The passage of the Cleaner Production Promotion Law in 2002 is another signal of China's commitment to a path of sustainable development.[13] This has been preceded by a number of other environmental legislations with cleaner production provisions, such as the Law on the Prevention and Control of Water Pollution amended in 1996 (Article 22) and by the Law on the Prevention and Control of Atmospheric Pollution amended in 2000 (Article 19). Both legislations contain provisions encouraging firms to adopt cleaner production technologies to reduce pollution discharge.

Since a number of environmental laws were amended after 1995, we study the time path of various pollutants in two periods: 1987–1995 and 1996–2004. Table 9.1 presents summary statistics for per capita emissions across thirty Chinese provinces for various pollutants.[14] Means tests of the per capita emissions data show that the mean per capita discharge for three of the pollutants considered (industrial waste water, industrial

---

[10] See Ma and Ortolano (2000); Muldavin (2000); Economy (2004); and MacBean (2007) for details.

[11] See the 9th Standing Committee of Jiangsu People's Congress, 7th session, the Regulations on Protection of Agricultural Ecology and Environment, December 29, 1998 (Revised June 7, 2004).

[12] See the 9th Standing Committee of Guangdong People's Congress, 6th session, the Regulations on Zhujiang Triangle Water Protection, November 27, 1998.

[13] Cleaner production (CP) is referred to as pollution prevention (P2) in the United States. In 1990, the United States passed the Pollution Prevention Act. Prior to this legislation, pollution control efforts were focused at the 'end-of-the-pipe'. P2 refocuses pollution control efforts to the early stages of production whereby firms are encouraged to use production techniques that prevent pollution at the source.

[14] Industrial COD is the most important water pollutant in China (Wang and Wheeler 2003), and is commonly used as a measure of water quality. Sulfur dioxide is of concern because it contributes to acid rain. It is released primarily from burning fuels that contain sulfur (e.g. coal). Smoke and industrial dust pollution are also important concerns in China as a number of the provisions (e.g. Article 30) in the Prevention and Control of Atmospheric Pollution Law address these pollutants.

Table 9.1. Summary statistics, thirty Chinese provinces from 1987 to 2004

	Mean	Standard deviation	Coefficient of variation	Obs.	
A. 1987 to 1995					
Real income per capita (RGRPPC)[1/]	696.634[a/]	470.984	67.609	270	
Total industrial waste water (IWATER)[2/]	22.549[a/]	17.504	77.624	269	
Industrial COD (COD)[3/]	0.007[a/]	0.004	65.006	237	
Waste gas (GAS)[4/]	10359.320	7372.472	71.168	268	
Sulfur dioxide (SO$_2$)[3/]	0.016	0.010	63.752	267	
Total smoke (SMOKE)[3/]	0.014[a/]	0.010	69.780	266	
Industrial dust (IDUST)[3/]	0.007	0.005	73.178	267	
B. 1996 to 2004					
Real income per capita (RGRPPC)[1/]	1421.518	1105.391	77.761	270	
Total industrial waste water (IWATER)[2/]	16.307	10.905	66.876	270	
Industrial COD (COD)[3/]	0.005	0.004	70.309	270	
Waste gas (GAS)[4/]	n/a	n/a	n/a	n/a	
Sulfur dioxide (SO$_2$)[3/]	0.017	0.011	65.965	120	
Total smoke (SMOKE)[3/]	0.009	0.007	71.197	120	
Industrial dust (IDUST)[3/]	0.007	0.004	62.155	269	

Notes: [1/] 1950 yuan; [2/] Metric ton per capita; [3/] Ton per capita; [4/] Cubic meter per capita. [a/] Means test indicates that means in 1987–1995 and 1996–2004 are significantly different at the 99% confidence level.

COD, and smoke) declined between these two periods. Can this partly be attributed to changes in environmental laws enacted after 1995? Also, conditional on provinces' income levels, what other factors correlate with pollution discharges? These, and other, questions are tackled in the succeeding sections.

9.3 Data and empirical methodology

Data

Pollution discharge data for 1987 to 1995 are obtained from the Economics of Industrial Pollution Control research team of Development Research Group (DECRG) at the World Bank. Data are downloadable at www.worldbank.org/nipr/data/china/status.htm. The data compiled by the World Bank are from two sources: *China Environmental Quality Report* and *China Environment Yearbook*. Pollution discharge data for 1996 to 2004 are obtained from various editions of the *China Environment Yearbook*. From Table 9.1, it is evident that pollution data for 1996–2004 are sparse. Waste gas data are no longer available and data for sulfur dioxide and smoke are incomplete.

Gross regional product (in current yuan) and the general consumer price index (1950 = 100) data are obtained from the China National Bureau of Statistics, *China Compendium of Statistics 1949–2004*. In 2004, China conducted its first national economic census, a major piece of the comprehensive reform of the country's economic accounting system. For the most part, the new economic accounting system fixes the significant undercounting of activities in the tertiary sector (services) in China. The undercounting is a legacy of China's use of the Material Product System, commonly used by centrally planned economies. When economic reforms started in 1978, the number of private and individually run services increased, and these have been missed by an economic accounting system geared towards industrial production. In fact, for 2004, 93 percent of the upward revision in China's GDP can be attributed to the undercounting of the value added of tertiary industries under the old economic accounting system (Deshui 2005). The methodological change necessitated the issuance of revised gross domestic product figures for earlier years and revised data are available back to 1993. The revised figures are based on the 2004 GDP data using a trend deviation method.[15] Because the revised values only go as far back as 1993, we are not able to use them in our analysis.[16] More importantly, for our purposes, the unrevised gross product values are more appropriate. This is because tertiary industries are less polluting and using the revised GDP figures would 'overestimate' income (for most provinces) in our EKC estimations.[17]

Each province's ranking (from cleanest to dirtiest) in 1987–1995 for all pollution media appear in Table 9.2. For the most part, Tibet is the cleanest province while Liaoning is the dirtiest province. The southwest region is the cleanest region while the northeast

---

[15] According to China National Bureau of Statistics (2007, 56), 'historical trend values were first calculated with data from the census; next, the ratio between the actual value of the historical data and the trend value of historical data was calculated; and finally the ratio was applied to the historical trend values obtained from the census data to obtain the revised series of historical data'.

[16] It is not appropriate to use the estimated income-emissions regressions (based on unrevised 1987–1995 income data) to make off-sample predictions of pollution discharges (based on revised 1996–2004 income data).

[17] Using revised output data from the 2007 Statistical Yearbooks of each of the provinces, for 1995–2004, the mean revised GDP-to-unrevised GDP ratio for 12 provinces (6 northern and 5 coastal provinces) are less than 1. The mean ratio for Hubei is 0.85, followed by Anhui at 0.94, and Heilongjiang at 0.96. Beijing experienced the largest upward revision with a 1.25 mean ratio, followed by Shanxi at 1.11, and Guangdong at 1.10. Combining these ratios with information on Table 9.2, no clear pattern emerges as to a province's pollution ranking and the amount of upward or downward revision it experiences. For example, Liaoning is the dirtiest province, it experienced an average of 0.29% downward revision; Shanghai, another dirty region, experienced an average upward revision of 4.43%.

Table 9.2. Provincial unconditional rankings (cleanest = 1 to dirtiest = 30) in various pollutants, 1987–1995

Province	IWATER	COD	GAS	SO$_2$	SMOKE	IDUST
NORTH						
Beijing[1/2/]	28	24	29	28	25	17
Tianjin[1/2/]	24	29	25	26	23	9
Hebei[1/2/]	11	7	20	17	16	23
Shanxi[2/]	13	10	26	27	27	24
Inner Mongolia[2/]	9	22	24	25	30	26
NORTHEAST						
Liaoning[1/2/]	29	27	28	24	26	30
Jilin[2/]	17	28	23	13	28	16
Heilongjiang[2/]	23	23	22	11	29	18
EAST						
Shanghai[1/]	30	30	30	29	20	11
Jiangsu[1/]	27	19	16	19	15	10
Zhejiang[1/]	21	20	15	14	6	19
Anhui	14	16	7	5	12	4
Fujian[1/]	19	18	8	3	4	5
Jiangxi	16	6	6	10	11	21
Shandong[1/2/]	3	21	17	23	19	8
CENTRAL AND SOUTH						
Henan[2/]	5	8	9	4	9	3
Hubei	26	11	12	12	8	13
Hunan	25	12	5	9	5	12
Guangdong[1/]	18	15	13	7	3	22
Guangxi[1/]	20	26	3	15	10	28
Hainan[1/]	8	25	2	2	2	1
SOUTHWEST						
Sichuan	22	14	14	22	17	15
Guizhou	2	3	11	21	13	14
Yunnan	6	9	4	8	7	2
Tibet	1	1	1	1	1	6
NORTHWEST						
Shaanxi[2/]	7	4	10	20	21	7
Gansu[2/]	12	5	21	18	14	25
Qinghai[2/]	10	2	18	6	22	27
Ningxia[2/]	15	13	27	30	24	29
Xinjiang[2/]	4	17	19	16	18	20

Notes: [1/] Coastal province. [2/] Northern province. Classifications adopted from De Groot et al. (2004).

region is the dirtiest one.[18] Coastal provinces are dirtier—in four of the six pollution media, the mean rank of coastal provinces range from seventeen (waste gas) to twenty-two (industrial COD) while the mean rank of non-coastal provinces range from eleven (industrial

---

[18] Shanghai is the dirtiest province (municipality) and the central and south region is the cleanest region if median ranks are used instead of mean ranks.

Table 9.3. Spearman rank correlation coefficients, thirty Chinese provinces from 1987 to 1995

	IWATER	COD	GAS	SO$_2$	SMOKE	IDUST
IWATER	1.000					
COD	0.564[a/]	1.000				
GAS	0.383[b/]	0.404[b/]	1.000			
SO$_2$	0.298	0.318[c/]	0.774[a/]	1.000		
SMOKE	0.180	0.321[c/]	0.825[a/]	0.705[a/]	1.000	
IDUST	0.212	0.022	0.518[a/]	0.428[b/]	0.467[a/]	1.000

Notes: [a/b/c/] Significant at the 99%, 95%, and 90% confidence levels, respectively.

COD) to fourteen (SO$_2$). Non-coastal provinces ranked higher (dirtier) on average for smoke and industrial dust. Northern provinces ranked higher (dirtier) in all pollution media except industrial waste water. The mean ranks for northern provinces range from fourteen (industrial waste water) to twenty-two (smoke). For southern provinces, the mean ranks range from nine (smoke) to seventeen (industrial waste water).

Table 9.3 contains the Spearman rank correlation coefficients of the various pollutants for 1987–1995. The rank correlations range from 0.02 (industrial COD and industrial dust) to 0.83 (waste gas and smoke). Not surprisingly, the rank correlations are high among the various types of gas pollutants but low between water and gas pollutants. Also, although provinces with high water quality also tend to have high air quality, this relationship is not that strong (the rank correlation between industrial waste water and waste gas is 0.38).[19]

Empirical methodology

The following one-way fixed effects panel model is estimated:

$$poll_{it} = \alpha_i + \beta\, income_{it} + \gamma\, income_{it}^2 + \delta\, income_{it}^3 + \epsilon_{it}, \quad i = 1, \ldots, 30;\ t = 1, \ldots, 9 \qquad (1)$$

[19] Gas pollution in China is mostly from the use of coal and wood as fuels and from automobiles, while water pollution is mainly from pulp and paper, metallurgical, and chemical factories (Naughton 2007). In the late 1980s and the early 1990s, the environmental issue had not been emphasized. Thus, provinces with more water polluting industries might have higher levels of water pollution, while provinces with more air polluting industries might have more air pollution. In addition, the water distribution in China is largely uneven. There is a shortage of surface and underground water in the northern part of China. For example, in Beijing, we will only see air pollution, not much water pollution, since the Yongding River in Beijing has dried up. However, if we just look at the southern part, we may find a closer correlation between air and water pollution, i.e. less developed areas have less water and air pollution, while developed areas such as Shanghai have both high water and air pollution.

where i indexes provinces and t indexes time; $poll_{it}$ is one of the six pollutants measured in per capita terms in 1987 to 1995; $income$ is real per capita gross regional product for province i at time t; β, γ, and δ are coefficient parameters; α_i are province-specific fixed effects;[20] and, ϵ_{ij} is a well-behaved error term. We also estimate a quadratic specification for comparison.

We do realize that besides income, a number of other factors, such as environmental regulations, output composition, and the relative importance of state-owned enterprises, may affect pollution emissions across provinces.[21] However, these factors are somewhat related to income; thus, following standard practice (List and McHone 2000; Millimet et al. 2003) we exclude these other factors from equation (1) to focus on the total effect of income on emissions.[22] This is one of the limitations of the environmental Kuznets curve: The model per se does not explain why an income-emission relationship exists. De Bruyn and Heintz (1999) review some explanations for the EKC found in the literature. One explanation is that when people's income increases beyond a certain level, they start to demand a cleaner environment. Thus, emissions decline as income increases beyond this level. Likewise, a number of institutional changes occur as a country's income increases. For example, stricter environmental policies are enacted and enforced thereby leading to lower emissions. Next, economies generally transition to a service-oriented economy as incomes increase. And since services are less polluting than manufacturing, emissions decline. Thus, institutional and structural changes that occur as income increases can also explain the EKC.

Because equation (1) provides only reduced-form estimates, another limitation of the EKC is what its policy implications are. For example,

---

[20] The province-specific fixed effects capture unmeasured locational attributes or attributes that are non-time varying (e.g. north/south or coast/non-coast location) during the period of analysis.

[21] See Dasgupta et al. (2002) for a review.

[22] We are aware of the limitations of using equation (1) to estimate income-emissions regressions, see Stern (2004). In particular, equation (1) assumes that the slopes are homogeneous across the Chinese provinces. Using cross-country (Dijkgraaf and Vollegergh 2005) and cross-state panel data (List and Gallet 1999), studies have shown parameter heterogeneity across the cross-sectional units for selected pollutants. We do not implement slope heterogeneity in this chapter. Equation (1) is less likely to provide biased and inconsistent estimates since our cross-section units belong to a single country and not a cross-section of countries observed over time. The assumption of a common slope among cross-section units is more believable within than between countries. Also, given China's political set-up (that is, local Government officials being basically appointed by the central Government), pollution policies across Chinese provinces are expected to be less heterogeneous than pollution policies across US states.

if an inverted-U income-emissions relationship is found, it is not clear how this information could be used by policymakers. As Dasgupta et al. (2002, 147) observe, '[i]n developing countries, some policymakers have interpreted such results as conveying the message about priorities: Grow first, then clean up'.

To address the above limitations, auxiliary regressions are estimated whereby the estimated province-specific fixed effects from equation (1) are regressed against a number of provincial characteristics such as industrial structure (see equation (2) in the next section). Thus, conditional on income, do emissions increase with the share of secondary industries in total output? Equation (2) below answers this (and related) question(s).

9.4 Analysis of results

Table 9.4 contains the empirical results.[23] F-tests indicate that the inclusion of province-specific fixed effects is appropriate as the null hypothesis that the province-specific fixed effects are the same is rejected at the 1 percent significance level (the F statistic range from 4.56 to 137.71 for the cubic specification). Hausman tests of the null hypothesis that province characteristics are uncorrelated with income are also rejected in four of the models at the 1 percent significance level (for the cubic model, the Hausman test statistic ranges from 3.12 to 93.02). This is indicative of the appropriateness of using the fixed effects model (vs. the random effects model). The one-way fixed effects model controls for unmeasured province characteristics whereas the one-way random effects model treats these unmeasured characteristics as a component of the error term (see Greene 2000 for details). We focus on the results for four pollutants below: Total industrial waste water, industrial COD, waste gas, and industrial dust. This is because at least one of the income terms is statistically significant in all models dealing with these four pollutants. We also focus on the results from the cubic regressions (column (2) in Table 9.4) as the cubic term is statistically significant in the regressions for these four

---

[23] The province-specific fixed effects are available upon request. An unbalanced panel is estimated for all 6 models as pollution data are not available for selected provinces in selected years. Since missing data are at most only 12% (for industrial COD) of the 270 possible observations (30 provinces by 9 years), we do not think the results obtained are biased and inefficient. As a robustness check, we also omit observations whose standardized residuals are greater than 4. The results are qualitatively similar to those in Table 9.4.

Table 9.4. Fixed effects panel regression estimates[1]

	IWATER (1)	IWATER (2)	COD (1)	COD (2)	GAS (1)	GAS (2)
Income	−1.14E-0[a]	−3.23E-0[a]	−8.56E-07	8.86E-06	8.49[a]	15.90[a]
	(2.34E-03)	(5.15E-03)	(2.03E-06)	(5.39E-06)	(1.17)	(3.97)
Income²	−1.20E-07	1.69E-05[a]	−1.38E-09[a]	−9.29E-09[b]	−6.25E-04	−6.65E-03[b]
	(9.40E-07)	(3.90E-06)	(5.09E-10)	(3.67E-09)	(4.35E-04)	(3.32E-03)
Income³	—	−3.40E-09[a]	—	1.58E-12[b]	—	1.20E-06[c]
		(7.65E-10)		(6.81E-13)		(6.71E-07)
Constant	30.57[a]	36.75[a]	0.01[a]	0.01[a]	4871.76[a]	2684.47[b]
	(1.10)	(1.74)	(0.00)	(0.00)	(561.86)	(1188.92)
F-statistic[2]	138.93[a]	137.71[a]	8.12[a]	8.32[a]	84.30[a]	86.34[b]
Hausman test statistic[3]	92.74[a]	93.02[a]	40.34[a]	45.99[a]	8.40[b]	10.55[b]
R-sq.–within	0.349	0.393	0.113	0.128	0.389	0.408
R-sq.–between	0.710	0.618	0.457	0.370	0.585	0.558
Obs.	269	269	237	237	268	268

	SO$_2$ (1)	SO$_2$ (2)	SMOKE (1)	SMOKE (2)	IDUST (1)	IDUST (2)
Income	8.88E-06[a]	1.52E-05[b]	7.52E-07	3.92E-06	−1.35E-05[a]	−3.59E-05[a]
	(1.83E-06)	(6.35E-06)	(1.96E-06)	(7.41E-06)	(2.75E-06)	(9.19E-06)
Income²	−1.39E-09[a]	−6.53E-09	−6.22E-10	−3.20E-09	2.74E-09[a]	2.09E-08[a]
	(4.79E-10)	(5.10E-09)	(4.45E-10)	(6.02E-09)	(6.68E-10)	(6.37E-09)
Income³	—	1.03E-12	—	5.15E-13	—	−3.64E-12[a]
		(9.92E-13)		(1.16E-12)		(1.19E-12)
Constant	1.09E-02[a]	9.02E-03[a]	1.43E-02[a]	1.33E-02[a]	1.48E-02[a]	2.14E-02[a]
	(1.02E-03)	(1.94E-03)	(1.16E-03)	(2.22E-03)	(1.63E-03)	(3.40E-03)
F-statistic[2]	65.75[a]	64.09[a]	64.61[a]	63.81[a]	4.22[a]	4.56[a]
Hausman test statistic[3]	2.53	4.15	2.81	3.12	9.92[a]	12.31[a]
R-sq.–within	0.081	0.085	0.006	0.007	0.074	0.103
R-sq.–between	0.192	0.159	0.010	0.003	0.004	0.000
Obs.	267	267	266	266	267	267

Notes: The numbers in parentheses are robust standard errors. [a]/[b]/[c] Significant at the 99%, 95%, and 90% confidence levels, respectively.
[1] The province-specific fixed effects estimates are available upon request. [2] This tests the null hypothesis that the province-specific fixed effects are the same.
[3] The Hausman test is used to test the fixed effects model against the random effects model. A significant Hausman test statistic favors the fixed effects model.

pollutants. The (within group) R-square values of these models range from 0.10 to 0.41.[24]

Estimated income-emissions regressions

Substituting the estimated coefficients into equation (1), the estimated per capita emission values can be determined. Figure 9.1a contains the actual and estimated values of the industrial waste water per capita discharges from 1987 to 1995.[25] Although the cubic term is statistically significant, the coefficient estimate of the linear term for income dominates both the coefficient estimates of the square and cubic income terms. That is, the estimated industrial waste water per capita discharge declines with a rise in real income.

The actual and estimated values of the industrial COD per capita discharge appear in Figure 9.1b. A turning point in the estimated income-emissions relationship is evident here. A per capita discharge peak is observed at per capita income 556 yuan (in 1950 prices). According to the estimated income-emissions regression, industrial COD per capita emission is expected to decline as per capita income increases up to 3,291 yuan (the maximum real per capita income observed during the period). This is consistent with Wang and Wheeler's (2003) finding that COD pollution intensity across China's provinces declined between 1987–1989 and 1992–1995. The authors attribute this to increases in the pollution levy rates as incomes increase. As they suggest, '[t]he locally enforced price of pollution rises steadily with development because enforcement capacity and community valuation of damage both increase' (p. 466).

The coefficient estimate of the linear term for income once again dominates those of the square and cubic terms in the waste gas per capita discharge regression. From Figure 9.1c, we observe that emission per capita is expected to increase with real income. This result is consistent with those found by De Groot et al. (2004) who use a slightly longer data

---

[24] A two-way fixed effects panel is also estimated. In three of the models (industrial waste water, waste gas, and industrial dust), results indicate the appropriateness of including the time-specific fixed effects. These time effects capture unmeasured macroeconomic factors (e.g. change in environmental laws emanating from the central Government) that all provinces experience. However, when the time effects are included, the income variables (linear, square, and cubic terms) lose their significance. This suggests that the effects of changes in macroeconomic factors dominate those of changes in income as far as these types of emissions are concerned. With this result in mind, we focus on the one-way fixed effects panel results since income is an important variable in the EKC regressions.

[25] To focus on the relationship between income and emissions, unless indicated otherwise, all estimated values referred to in the chapter exclude the estimated province-specific fixed effects.

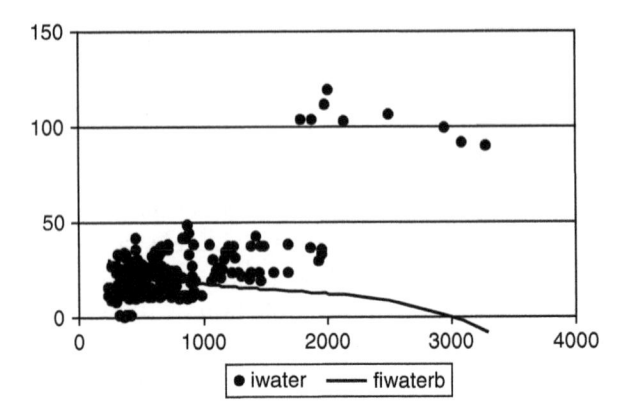

Figure 9.1a. Total industrial waste water per capita discharge (actual and estimated, 1987–1995)

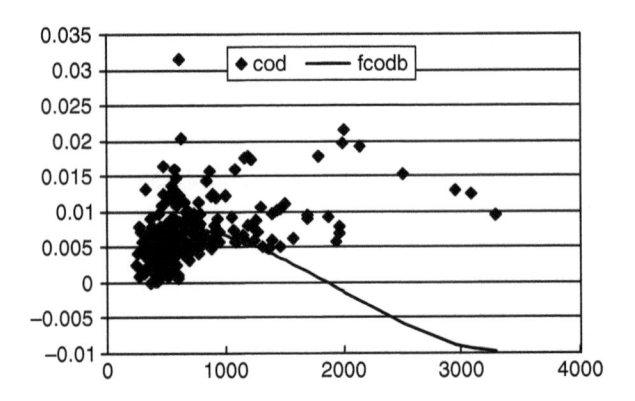

Figure 9.1b. Industrial COD per capita discharge (actual and estimated, 1987–1995)

series (1982–1997) for Chinese provinces. They also find that waste gas increases monotonically with per capita income.

Two turning points are evident in the estimated industrial dust per capita discharge regression, see Figure 9.1d. For the per capita income (at the 1950 constant price) range observed between 1987 and 1995, we see per capita emission at first decreases as per capita income increases up to 1,295 yuan; emission then increases with income up to an income level of 2,505 yuan; and, emission is expected to decrease as income increases up to the observe maximum per capita income of 3,291 yuan.

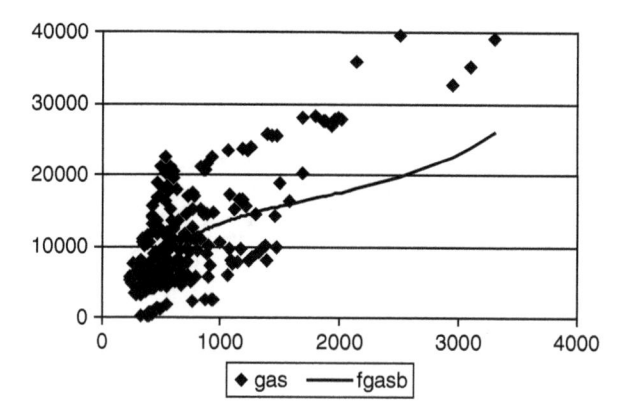

Figure 9.1c. Waste gas per capita discharge (actual and estimated, 1987–1995)

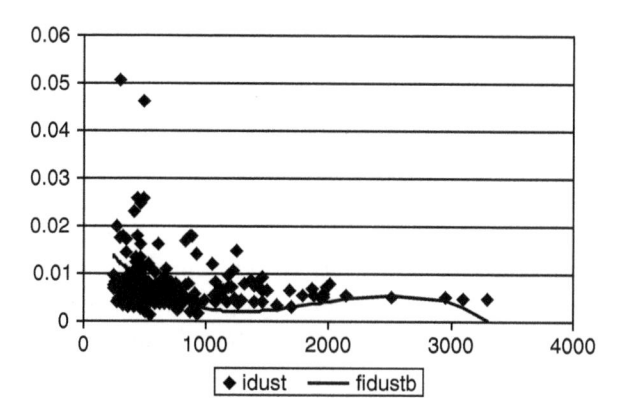

Figure 9.1d. Industrial dust per capita discharge (actual and estimated, 1987–1995)

Using the estimated income-emissions relationships, off-sample (1996 to 2004) predictions of per capita emission values are calculated. In other words, if the estimated income-emissions relationship remained the same after 1995, what are the expected per capita emission levels for each of these four pollutants? How do these compare with the actual per capita emission levels in 1996 to 2004? Since data for waste gas are no longer available after 1995, we can make such comparisons only for three pollutants.[26]

---

[26] By limiting our sample to 1987–1995, it is possible that we are not capturing the entire range of the income-emissions relationship. For example, if a cubic relationship exists between income and emissions, it is possible that we capture only the first increasing (decreasing) portion of the relationship and completely miss the subsequent declining (increasing)

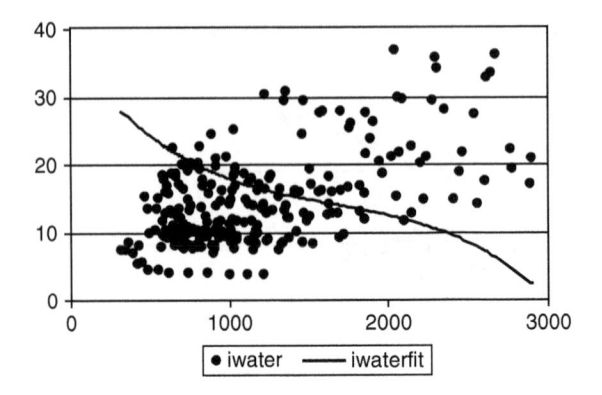

Figure 9.2a. Total industrial waste water per capita discharge (actual and predicted, 1996–2004)

Note: Excludes 22 observations with negative predicted values.

The estimated cubic income-emissions regression for industrial waste water predicts a decline in per capita emission as income increases up to the observed maximum real per capita income level of 8,343 yuan. In fact, the model predicts negative per capita emissions when income reaches around 3,000 yuan. Practically, this result suggests that if no changes occur (in the income-emission relationship), industrial waste water emissions per capita are expected to be negligible at around 3,000 yuan.[27] Figure 9.2a contains the actual and off-sample predictions (using the average province-specific fixed effects) excluding twenty-two observations with negative predicted values.

The estimated cubic income-emissions regression (using the average province-specific fixed effects) for industrial dust also predicts a decline in per capita industrial dust discharge as income increases beyond 3,291 yuan; and, per capita industrial dust discharge is also expected to be insignificant at around 3,280 yuan. Observations with negative predicted values are excluded in Figure 9.2b.

---

portion by limiting the data period to 1987 to 1995. To address this issue, we also estimate income-emissions regressions for these three pollutants using data for the entire 1987–2004 period. The results are qualitatively similar to those using the shorter sample—industrial waste water pollution increases then declines with an increase in income; industrial COD pollution declines and increases with an increase in income; and, the industrial dust estimated income-emission relationship flattens; however, it still predicts a decline in emissions as income increases.

[27] This translates to 19,809 yuan in 2004 prices; this is roughly US$2,390 at an exchange rate of 8.2768 yuan per US dollar.

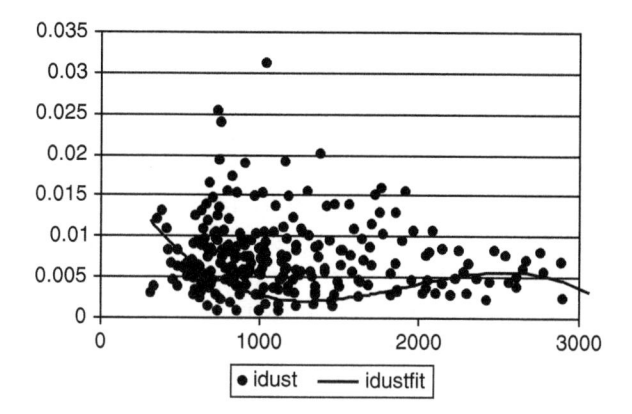

Figure 9.2b. Total industrial dust per capita discharge (actual and predicted, 1996–2004)

Note: Excludes 15 observations with negative predictive values.

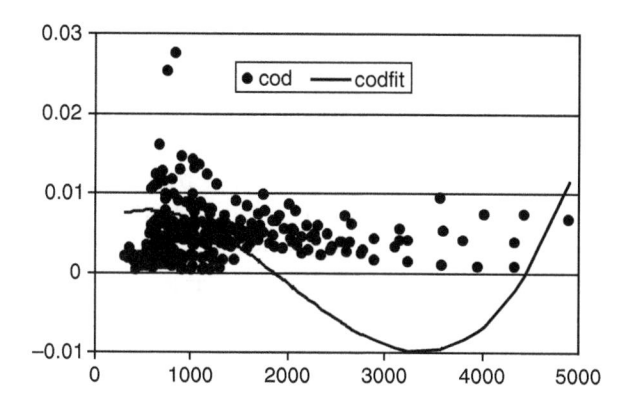

Figure 9.2c. Industrial COD per capita discharge (actual and predicted, 1996–2004)

Note: Excludes 5 observations with RGRPPC >5000 yuan.

Although the estimated income-emissions regression for industrial COD indicates that per capita industrial COD discharge declines as income increases up to 3,291 yuan (see Figure 9.1b), we see from Figure 9.2c that the estimates for industrial COD (using the average province-specific fixed effects) show a rise in per capita discharge as

297

income increases beyond 3,291 yuan (the observed maximum per capita income in the 1987–1995 period).[28]

Note that the estimates in Figures 9.2a to 9.2c also assume that the province-specific fixed effects remain the same between 1996 and 2004. Recall that the province-specific fixed effects for the most part capture the effect of unmeasured locational attributes; the effect of other factors that either did not change or changed very little during the period of analysis (e.g. north/south location; local authorities' attitude towards pollution) are also subsumed in the province-specific fixed effects. Thus, the predicted values in Figures 9.2a to 9.2c are calculated also assuming that the province-specific fixed effects remain the same between 1996 and 2004. That is, the off-sample predictions are based on a counterfactual—the relationship between income and emissions and the factors that are subsumed in the province-specific fixed effects remain the same (or change very little) after 1995.

It is evident from Figure 9.2a that actual industrial waste water per capita discharge increases with income—this is the opposite of the prediction of the estimated income-emission regression. This suggests that despite policies enacted by the Chinese Government after 1995,[29] perhaps these have not been stringent enough to bring the per capita discharge levels down to the level provided by the estimates.

Besides the adoption of stricter environmental rules, structural changes (e.g. sectoral changes in output) experienced by the Chinese economy between 1996 and 2004 could have contributed to the observed emission pattern.[30] The income-emissions relationships observed here is less likely due to structural changes. This is because large structural changes in the overall Chinese economy (i.e. shift to secondary industries) occurred in the early 1990s not after 1995. In particular, the share of secondary industries to total output in 1990 was 41.6 percent; this increased to 48.5

---

[28] We exclude observations with real income per capita greater than 5,000 yuan in Figure 9.2c to highlight the curvature in the estimated income-emissions regression. Actual data for these 5 observations are significantly lower than the predicted values.

[29] For example, Article 16 of the amended Law on the Prevention and Control of Water Pollution authorized 'national and provincial agencies to employ mass-based pollution control systems for water bodies that would not meet ambient standards even if all discharges met concentration-based effluent standards' (Ma and Ortolano 2000, 28). Prior to the amendment in 1996, China did not limit the mass (concentration and volume) flow rate of pollutants. Rather, concern was mostly over pollutant concentration.

[30] According to Dasgupta et al. (2002, 152), 'observed changes in pollution as per capita income rises could come from several different sources: shifts in the scale and sectoral composition of output, changes in technology within sectors, or the impact of regulation on pollution abatement'.

percent in 1995; by 2004, the share increased to 52.9 percent (China National Bureau of Statistics 2005).[31]

Output growth (scale effect) could have also contributed to the observed income-emissions relationships. Once again, it is not likely that the observed patterns after 1995 are due to significant growth in output. This is because between 1980 and 2004, China experienced its highest annual GDP growth prior to 1996. For example, annual GDP growth reached a high of 15 percent in 1984 and 14 percent in 1992. Annual growth rates after 1995 ranged from 7 percent to 10 percent (World Bank 2005).

Actual industrial dust per capita discharge rates are larger than the predicted per capita discharge rates for most of the provinces between 1996 and 2004, see Figure 9.2b. This is inconsistent with the notion that given the adoption of stricter environmental regulations, actual emissions should be lower than the predictions because the latter assumes no changes in environmental regulations. However, it should be noted that actual per capita emissions are closer to the predicted per capita emission values at income levels beyond 2,000 yuan. And, a negative income-emission relationship is observed in the actual data.

Policies enacted to lower industrial COD pollution discharge appear to have been partly successful.[32] That is, although actual per capita industrial COD pollution discharge rates are higher than the predicted discharge rates (see Figure 9.2c), the differences are for the most part not large and actual emission rates have not increased with income as the estimated income-emission regression model predicts. According to Wang and Wheeler (2005), industrial COD pollution is considered the most important water pollutant in China and has been monitored very closely by the Chinese environmental regulators. In fact, mass-based limits on industrial COD was included in the Ninth Five-Year Plan for Environmental Protection and Long Term Targets for the Year 2010 passed in 1996 (Ma and Ortolano 2000).

The above conclusions though need to be qualified. This is because the off-sample predictions were calculated assuming that the effect of factors that are subsumed in the province-specific fixed effects on emissions remain the same (or changed very little) after 1995. If these are not the case, then the above conclusions may not be correct. To partly address

---

[31] Using the revised GDP values in fact would strengthen our argument. The share of secondary industries to total output in 1990 was 41.3% increasing to 47.2% in 1995; the share dropped to 46.2% by 2004 (China National Bureau of Statistics 2007).

[32] A World Bank study (2006) arrives at a similar conclusion and partly attributes the reduction to improved industrial processes.

this concern, we also estimate a cubic income-emissions regression for the three pollutants using 1996–2004 data. We find that the structures of the fixed effects in the first (1987–1995) and second (1996–2004) periods are similar for industrial waste water and industrial COD—the Spearman (Pearson) correlations of the first and second period province-specific fixed effects are 0.91 (0.96) for industrial waste water, 0.72 (0.69) for industrial COD, and 0.26 (0.27) for industrial dust. This increases confidence in the results presented above.

Auxiliary regressions

Although China's State Environmental Protection Administration (SEPA) sets effluent standards, local Governments have the right to set stricter standards.[33] Thus, local conditions will have an influence on how stringent pollution prevention and control policies are. It was suggested earlier that the province-specific fixed effects could be related to provincial authorities' attitudes towards pollution control independent of income levels. Since the estimated fixed effects are parametric shifts, larger values indicate higher pollution discharge rates which could have resulted from less willingness to control pollution.

We test a number of additional hypotheses using the estimated province-specific fixed effects. In particular, we ask if the estimated province-specific fixed effects (which we take to be related to a province's commitment to control pollution) are related to a number of characteristics, such as a province's north/south and coast/non-coast location, unemployment rate, urbanization rate, and industrial structure. These fixed effects may also be related to the relative importance of state-owned enterprises and foreign direct investment (FDI) in a province's economy; and, whether the provincial Government is running a budget surplus/deficit. The following auxiliary regression model is estimated:

$$a_i = \phi + \theta' \mathbf{Z}_i + v_i, \qquad (2)$$

where a_i are the estimated province-specific fixed effects from equation (1), regressors included in $\mathbf{Z}_i$ are province attributes hypothesized to be related to emission levels and commitment to pollution control; and, v_i is a well-behaved error term.

The raw data clearly show that northern and coastal provinces are dirtier, thus we include a province's location in the auxiliary regression.

---

[33] See Ma and Ortolano (2000); Muldavin (2000); and Economy (2004) for details.

Since the problems caused by unemployment are immediate and visible while the problems caused by pollution may not be immediate and are less visible, provinces with higher unemployment rates are expected to be dirtier and may be less willing to enforce environmental protection laws. Urbanization may reduce pollution since urban areas have better sanitary facilities and people in urban areas usually use gas instead of coal. However, urbanization normally is accompanied by industrialization. More industries imply higher industrial pollution. Therefore, the correlation between the urbanization rate (proxied by population density) and emissions is ambiguous.

Provinces with a larger share of their output originating from secondary industries which include manufacturing are expected to be more polluted than provinces with a smaller output share from secondary industries. The managers of China's SOEs are appointed by the central Government. Thus, they may be more willing to follow pollution control rules. These enterprises also tend to have access to better pollution control technologies than other types of enterprises. Therefore, provinces with a larger share of their output coming from the SOEs are expected to have lower emissions. Since most foreign enterprises in China are from developed countries and these firms tend to have superior and cleaner technologies, provinces receiving relatively more FDI are expected to be cleaner.

Lester and Lombard (1990) argue that administrative units with greater fiscal resources may be more inclined to regulate pollution. This is because they are less dependent on polluters for tax revenues. In China, fiscal revenue shortage is the major obstacle for local Government enforcement of environmental protection laws. Thus, provinces experiencing relatively large budget deficits are expected to be more polluted and may be less willing to control pollution.

To mitigate potential endogeneity between the estimated province-specific fixed effects and the above mentioned regressors, we use the average values of these regressors in 1982–1986. In other words, since the effects of these factors may also be subsumed in the estimated province-specific fixed effects, these variables are measured in periods prior to 1987. Also, since the province-specific fixed effects capture unmeasured province characteristics that either did not change or changed very little, these variables should also not vary too much in each province. Some of these variables did not vary too much in each province. For example, the coefficients of variation for population density range from 1.3 percent (Jilin) to 4.5 percent (Beijing). The share of secondary industries to total regional output and the share of state-owned enterprises to total industrial output are also quite stable in most of the provinces. The provinces, however, experienced large changes in the rate of unemployment, the size of the budget surplus/deficit, and FDI relative to total regional output. For example, the coefficients of variation for the rate of unemployment range from 4.5 percent (Guangdong) to 69.4 percent (Beijing).

The estimates for the full model appear in column (1) of Table 9.5. There is no indication of a misspecification, multicollinearity, or heteroskedasticity problem. The fit of the models is quite good and ranges from 59 percent to 62 percent. Controlling for income, northern provinces, provinces with lower population densities, and provinces with smaller secondary industries shares have lower per capita industrial waste water pollution; industrial COD emissions per capita are lower in less urbanized areas; and, coastal provinces, provinces with larger secondary industries shares, and provinces experiencing smaller budget surpluses (or larger budget deficits) have larger industrial dust emissions per capita.

Since the rate of unemployment, the size of the budget balance, and FDI relative to total output experienced large changes in most provinces, we exclude them from equation (2). The results appear in column (2) of Table 9.5. For the most part, the results for the remaining variables are qualitatively similar to those in column (1) for industrial waste water and industrial dust. Coast, secondary industries share, and SOEs share are now statistically significant in the industrial COD regression. Non-coastal provinces and provinces with smaller secondary industries shares and smaller SOEs shares have lower industrial COD pollution per capita discharge rates. The latter is consistent with Wang and Wheeler's (2003) finding that state-owned plants are more pollution intensive. As a robustness check, we also test for the presence of influential observations using DFITS, Cook's distance, and Welsch Distance. We exclude observations (Shanghai and Guangdong for the first two pollutants; and only Shanghai in industrial dust) when at least two of these tests identify them as influential observations. The estimates appear in column (3). Population density loses significance in the industrial waste water and industrial COD regressions but become significant in the industrial dust regression. The results for the remaining variables are qualitatively similar.

Overall, the results indicate that provinces in the north have lower levels of industrial waste water pollution, after controlling for income. Northern provinces do not have much in the way of water resources, i.e. water is much more precious for them compared to the southern provinces, and therefore they may be more interested in controlling water pollution. Non-coastal provinces and provinces with smaller secondary

Table 9.5. Correlates of the estimated province-specific fixed effects in 1987–1995

	Industrial waste water [1]			Industrial COD [1]			Industrial dust [1]		
	(1)	(2)	(3)	(1)	(2)	(3)	(1)	(2)	(3)
North	−13.13[a]	−9.41[b]	−9.66[b]	−0.09	−0.10	−0.08	−0.18	0.24	0.21
	(4.14)	(3.43)	(3.55)	(0.20)	(0.14)	(0.14)	(0.17)	(0.17)	(0.14)
Coast	4.696	7.432[b]	8.398[b]	0.363	0.50[a]	0.450[a]	0.65[a]	0.388[b]	0.532[a]
	(4.33)	(3.11)	(3.43)	(0.21)	(0.12)	(0.13)	(0.18)	(0.15)	(0.13)
Unemployment	0.477	—	—	0.019	—	—	0.079	—	—
	(1.69)			(0.08)			(0.07)		
Population density	0.005[a]	0.005[a]	−0.003	0.000[b]	0.000[a]	0.001	0.000	0.000	−0.001[a]
	(0.00)	(0.00)	(0.01)	(0.00)	(0.00)	(0.00)	(0.00)	(0.00)	(0.00)
Secondary share	1.180[a]	0.835[a]	0.885[a]	0.013	0.016[b]	0.013[c]	0.035[a]	0.011	0.018[b]
	(0.28)	(0.16)	(0.17)	(0.01)	(0.01)	(0.01)	(0.01)	(0.01)	(0.01)
State enterprises share	0.130	0.125	0.070	0.010	0.012[b]	0.015[b]	0.001	0.002	−0.007
	(0.18)	(0.15)	(0.17)	(0.01)	(0.01)	(0.01)	(0.01)	(0.01)	(0.01)
FDI share	2.006	—	—	0.045	—	—	0.062	—	—
	(2.91)			(0.14)			(0.12)		
Budget balance share	−0.053	—	—	0.007	—	—	−0.031[b]	—	—
	(0.35)			(0.02)			(0.01)		
Constant	−58.84[a]	−46.22[a]	−42.59[a]	−1.50[c]	−1.78[a]	−1.97[a]	−2.03[a]	−0.83	−0.29
	(15.71)	(13.39)	(14.64)	(0.75)	(0.53)	(0.57)	(0.64)	(0.65)	(0.56)
N	23	30	28	23	30	28	23	30	29
F-statistic [2]	34.34[a]	54.60[a]	10.64[a]	7.58[a]	20.35[a]	7.13[a]	4.93[a]	4.59[a]	9.02[a]
Adj R	0.92	0.90	0.64	0.71	0.77	0.53	0.59	0.38	0.59
Ramsey Reset [3]	2.28	0.70	2.72[c]	0.65	1.78	1.29	0.59	0.73	1.76
Breusch-Pagan [4]	0.43	0.01	0.85	0.85	0.66	0.95	1.80	1.80	0.74
Mean VIF	3.50	1.94	1.97	3.50	1.94	1.97	3.50	1.94	1.98

Notes: The numbers in parentheses are standard errors. [a]/[b]/[c] Significant at the 99%, 95%, and 90% confidence levels, respectively. [1] Coefficients and standard errors are multiplied by 100. [2] Model significance test. [3] Specification test. [4] Heteroskedasticity test.

industries shares have lower levels of all three types of pollutants. Contrary to expectations, provinces with higher state-owned enterprises shares have higher levels of industrial COD pollution. Finally, there is also some evidence that a province's industrial dust pollution level is related to its budget balance. Industrial dust is a local public 'bad'; thus, local Governments may have more incentives to regulate this pollutant. Therefore, administrative units with greater fiscal resources may be more inclined to regulate industrial dust pollution.

9.5 Conclusion

This chapter has estimated income-emissions regressions using 1987–1995 data for Chinese provinces. Six pollutants have been considered. We find no evidence consistent with an inverted-U relationship between income and emissions. In fact, the estimated EKCs show no relationship between income and emissions (e.g. smoke pollution), a monotonically decreasing relationship (e.g. industrial waste water pollution), and a cubic relationship between income and emissions (e.g. industrial COD). Off-sample predicted values of selected pollutants for the period of 1996–2004 were compared with actual emission levels during this period. We find that actual industrial COD pollution per capita discharge rates in 1996–2004 have leveled off and do not increase with income as the estimated income-emissions regression predicts, indicating that environmental policies enacted by the Chinese Government may have been partly successful. However, we also find that the actual industrial waste water and industrial dust per capita discharge rates in 1996–2004 were higher than the predictions. And, contrary to the predictions of the estimated income-emission regression model, actual industrial waste water emissions increase with income. Clearly, more stringent rules are needed to fight industrial waste water pollution.

Auxiliary regressions show that conditional on income, northern provinces have lower industrial waste water pollution; non-coastal and provinces with smaller secondary industry shares have lower industrial (waste water, COD, and dust) pollution; provinces with smaller SOEs shares have lower industrial COD pollution; and, commitment to control industrial dust pollution is correlated with local Governments' budget balance.

Policymakers in China now admit that costs (e.g. health costs, ecological destruction) associated with pollution can no longer be ignored, and serious actions need to be undertaken to enforce extant pollution laws. China simply cannot continue to grow at 10 percent per year and ignore the associated harm to the environment. This line of thinking is clearly evident in a White Paper on environmental protection issued by the China State Council Information Office in 2006. The White Paper recognizes the trade-off between economic growth and a clean environment; and admits that a damaged environment may hinder China's future development, see China State Council Information Office (2006). The White Paper also summarizes what China has done to protect its environment in the last decade—from the passage of new environmental laws to closing firms that have caused serious environmental damage. China has also increased investments on environmental protection. According to *The Economist* (2004), in 2001–2005 environmental spending is about 1.3 percent of GDP; it was only 0.8 percent of GDP in the early 1990s. In 2006, environmental protection expenditure formally became a Government budgetary expenditure item (China State Council Information Office 2006).[34]

Despite these positive developments, a number of outstanding issues remain. First, enforcement of extant environmental laws is quite weak. There have been numerous reports of some administrators accepting bribes from violators and failing to enforce established laws on environmental protection.[35] Second, the role of local Governments in environmental protection is crucial. Thus, appropriate incentives need to be constructed to bring them in line with the public's demand for a cleaner environment (Cheng et al. 2007). Since fiscal resources are extremely limited, local Governments in China simply do not have much incentive for environmental protection. Thus, one way to put pressure on local Governments to regulate pollution is to create a mechanism whereby central Government transfers are tied not only to local output growth but to improvements in environmental outcomes as well. If appropriately constructed, this may prove popular with local Government officials.

---

[34] The Standing Committee of China's National People's Congress passed Energy Conservation Law of the People's Republic of China on October 28, 2007. This law requires households and enterprises to meet energy-conservation targets and requires Governments above the county level to annually report their energy saving achievements to the People's Congress of the corresponding level and requires provincial Governments to report energy saving achievements to the State Council. The law also allows the central Government to use policy tools to encourage energy savings. It is expected that local Government officials will be evaluated based on their energy savings achievements, in addition to their growth achievements. This law certainly is another step in tackling China's environmental problems (China Daily 2007a).

[35] See e.g. China Daily (2007b).

There has been an attempt to control pollution by using green GDP. Green GDP accounts for pollution costs in GDP calculations. A recent official estimate puts the cost of pollution at 3 percent of GDP in 2004 (*The Economist* 2007). Green GDP, however, is a controversial measure—both in how it is calculated and in its potential use in evaluating the performance of local Government officials. It is so controversial and unpopular that a report due in March 2007 has not been issued (Kahn and Yardley 2007). Perhaps rather than using green GDP to measure local Government officials' performance, a system rewarding those able to achieve targeted emission reductions would be more acceptable. Finally, the appearance of sixteen Chinese cities in the World Bank's list of the twenty most polluted cities in the world suggests that China has a long way to go in cleaning up its environment. This is a concern for the rest of the world as pollution in China affects other countries as well. In 2001, for example, dust from China reached the United States (*The Economist* 2004). Thus, China's participation in the international coordination of environmental protection is necessary.

Appendix 9A

Data used in equation (2) are collected from *China Compendium of Statistics 1949–2004*. **Unemployment rate** is the ratio of the number of the registered unemployed persons to the labor force in urban areas. **Population density** is the number of people per square kilometer. **Secondary share** (in percent) is the share of secondary industry output to the total regional product. Secondary industry includes mining and quarrying, manufacturing, production and supply of electricity, water and gas, and construction. **State enterprises share** (in percent) is the size of the gross industrial output of state-owned enterprises to gross industrial output of all enterprises in the province. **FDI share** (in percent) is the size of actually used foreign direct investment to the region's total output. **Budget balance share** (in percent) is the size of the budget balance relative to the region's total output. Budget balance is the difference between the local Government general revenue and expenditure.

10

What Constrains Indian Manufacturing?

Poonam Gupta, Rana Hasan, and Utsav Kumar[*]

10.1 Introduction

Many emerging countries in recent decades have relied on a development strategy focused on promoting the manufacturing sector and the export of manufactured goods. These include many East Asian countries and most recently, the People's Republic of China. India, too, hoped for a dynamic manufacturing sector when it introduced substantial product market reforms in its manufacturing sector starting in the mid-1980s. But the sector never took off as it did in other countries. India no doubt has grown impressively in the last fifteen years; but the main contribution to growth has come from the services sector rather than from the manufacturing sector. Moreover, insofar as subsectors within manufacturing have performed well, these have been the relatively capital- or skill-intensive industries, not the labor-intensive ones as would be expected for a labor-abundant country like India. What could be the reasons behind the rather lackluster performance of the manufacturing sector in India?

As Figure 10.1a shows, the manufacturing sector's share in GDP has been stagnant since the early 1990s despite several wide-ranging reforms in this sector. Similarly Figure 10.1b shows that the contribution to GDP growth has primarily been from the services sector and this contribution has been increasing over time.

Several hypotheses have been put forward to explain the lack of dynamism in India's manufacturing sector. Infrastructure related bottlenecks are widely believed to be a part of the explanation. In particular,

---

[*] The views presented here are those of the authors and not necessarily of the institutions they are affiliated with.

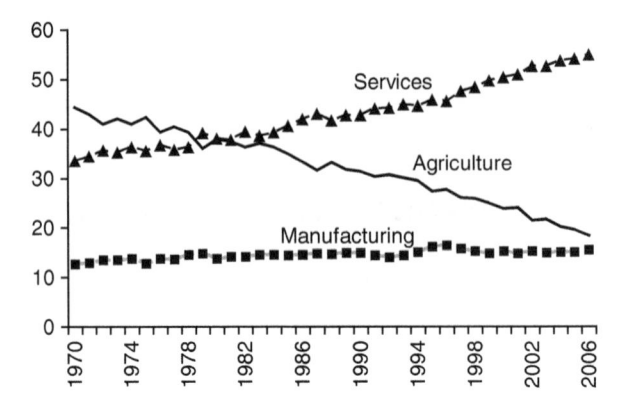

Figure 10.1a. Sectoral shares in GDP, India
Source: Authors' calculations using the data from Central Statistical Organization (India).

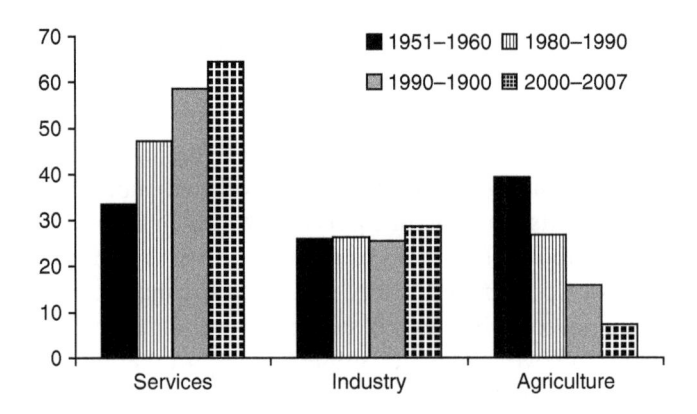

Figure 10.1b. Sectoral contribution to Indian GDP growth, 1951–2007
Source: Authors' calculations using the data from Central Statistical Organization (India).

poor quality of power supply, road networks, and ports and airports are believed to create significant disadvantages for Indian manufacturers by pushing up their costs of production, and making them uncompetitive in export markets.[1]

Besides infrastructure, some key policies remain unchanged. In particular, even though there have been extensive product market reforms,

---

[1] As indicated in Gordon and Gupta (2004), the nature of production of services is probably such that it is less affected by infrastructure bottlenecks.

it has been widely observed that the labor market reforms to complement these have not been undertaken (Kochhar et al. 2006; Panagariya 2006a; 2008). Moreover, credit constraints due to weaknesses in the financial sector may be holding back small- and medium-sized firms from expanding (Banerjee and Duflo 2004; Nagaraj 2005; McKinsey 2006).[2]

Finally, business regulations might have influenced key decisions of firms and potential investors. As the World Bank's Doing Business surveys of business regulations across the world have found, the procedures and costs for starting and, especially, closing a manufacturing business in India are among the most cumbersome in the world.[3]

It would be useful to empirically test the hypotheses related to the idea that various elements of the policy and institutional environment facing the manufacturing sector, either left untouched by the liberalizations of the 1990s or dealt with only partially, have emerged as significant bottlenecks to growth and employment generation.

One obvious way in which one can test for these hypotheses is to exploit the interstate heterogeneity in the policy and institutional environment, including labor market regulations; financial sector development; and infrastructure for different states of India and then test whether the industrial performance has been better in the states with better policy and institutional framework. This is precisely what has been done in the existing literature to show the importance of labor market flexibilities in explaining the gains from product market liberalizations. Besley and Burgess (2004), for example, exploit state-level amendments to the Industrial Disputes Act (IDA)—arguably the most important set of labor regulations governing Indian industry—over 1958–1992, and code legislative changes across major states as pro-worker, neutral, or pro-employer. These legislative amendments are then used in the regression analyses of various outcomes in the manufacturing sector,

---

[2] Banerjee and Duflo (2004) use firm-level data from the late 1990s and early 2000s and show that medium-sized firms—even those well above the 'small-scale' threshold—were subject to credit constraints and appeared to be operating well below their optimal scale.

[3] Another possibility is that hysteresis in the pattern of development in Indian manufacturing implies that the relative profitability of capital- and skill-intensive activities remains higher than that of labor-intensive activities despite the reforms of the early 1990s (Kochhar et al. 2006). Other factors often believed to be affecting the performance of Indian manufacturing are public ownership of enterprises, small-scale industries reservations, and stringent regulations on land use in India as discussed in Panagariya (2008). In recent years the availability of skilled labor has also emerged as a constraint on the growth of manufacturing and services.

including output, employment, investment, and the number of factories. Besley and Burgess find that pro-worker labor regulations have had a negative impact on output, employment, and investment in organized manufacturing.[4]

A related paper by Aghion et al. (2006) relates various dimensions of industrial performance to the extent to which an industry was covered by industrial licensing requirements, and state-level measures of the stance of labor regulations. They find that the effects of industrial delicensing were unequal across Indian states. In particular, delicensed industries located in states with pro-employer labor regulations grew faster in terms of both output and employment levels than those with pro-worker regulations. Similarly, Mitra and Ural (2007) show that industries experiencing larger tariff reductions grew faster in pro-employer states relative to pro-worker states.[5]

In this chapter we relate the pattern of growth in India's manufacturing sector to cross-industry heterogeneity in the reliance on infrastructure and financial sector and in the use of labor relative to capital. In particular, we calculate the dependence of industries on infrastructure, on the financial sector, and the labor intensity of industries. Using Annual Survey of Industries (ASI) data at the three-digit level and difference in differences estimation technique, we compare the performance of industries more dependent on infrastructure, on the financial sector, and labor-intensive industries post-delicensing with the performance of the control group.

Our results indicate that the aggregate performance of the manufacturing sector masks important inter-industry differences. Quite interestingly, we find that the industries with greater need for infrastructure; greater dependence on the financial sector; and greater labor intensity have performed relatively worse in the post-delicensing period. Quantitatively, the results indicate that in the post-delicensing period the above median infrastructure intensive industries grew 10 percent less than the industries below the median of infrastructure dependence. Similarly industries above median in the distribution of financial dependence grew 18 percent

---

[4] While, in principle, the approach of Besley and Burgess (2004) has considerable merit, it is not without controversy. Bhattacharjea (2006), in particular, has argued that deciding whether an individual amendment to the IDA is pro-employer or pro-worker in an objective manner is quite difficult. Even if individual amendments can be so coded, the actual workings of the regulations can hinge on judicial interpretations of the amendments. Moreover, if non-compliance with the regulations is widespread, then even an accurate coding of amendments which takes into account the appropriate judicial interpretation loses its meaning.

[5] There are some differences between Mitra and Ural and Aghion et al. in terms of the states deemed to have pro-employer or pro-worker labor regulations. See Mitra and Ural (2007) for details.

less than the industries below the median of financial dependence; and for labor intensity, industries with above median labor intensity grew 19 percent less than the below median industries post-delicensing.

There are two ways in which one can interpret our results. First, one can use these results to identify which industries have not benefited much from reforms. Second, to the extent that the heterogeneity across industries on parameters such as infrastructure dependence is exogenous and determined by factors such as production technology, one can probably draw causal inferences as well. Thus, for example, we can claim that if industries dependent on infrastructure have not benefited as much from reforms it is because of the unavailability of adequate infrastructure; and similarly for financial sector-dependent industries. For labor-intensive industries, an interpretation in terms of the limited supplies of labor would not be appropriate in the Indian context. A more natural interpretation would be to relate the relatively weak performance of labor-intensive industries to the quality of labor, skill mismatch and regulations on employment which make the effective price of hiring labor too high.

In order to ensure that the results are not driven by outliers; the standard errors are corrected for heteroskedasticity and autocorrelation; and that the estimates are not biased due to omitted variables, we conduct extensive robustness tests, and find our results to be robust to these sensitivity analyses.

There are two conclusions that one can draw from these results. First, product market reforms alone might not be sufficient to spur growth; for gains from these reforms to be maximized they may have to be complemented by reforms in other areas. Second, the potential benefits from product market reforms might not be realized unless these are matched by enabling conditions, such as high-quality infrastructure, availability of the right kind of labor, and financial markets that are deep enough. There is no room for complacency and efforts on a war footing should be made to remove these constraints if the manufacturing sector is to play the role that it did in the case of East Asian countries.

One point that needs to be noted about our analysis is that it only uses the data for organized (or registered) manufacturing sector and not for the unorganized sector. This is primarily because of the unavailability of detailed data for the latter. A question that comes up then is whether the lack of quality data on unregistered manufacturing should preclude any analysis of the registered manufacturing sector. Though there is no denying the fact that unorganized manufacturing sector is important when it comes to employment, but its output, wages, and productivity are very low. In terms of policy objectives, improving the performance of registered manufacturing is a key aspect to making India a powerhouse in manufacturing.

The rest of the chapter is organized as follows. In the next section we summarize the Indian policy framework and lay out the stylized facts related to the performance of the Indian registered manufacturing sector. In Section 10.3 we summarize evidence from two different firm-level survey data, Section 10.4 specifies the main econometric exercise, and presents and discusses our results. The last section concludes.

10.2 Stylized facts and preliminary evidence

Indian policy framework

Since the early 1950s up until the early 1980s the evolution of India's manufacturing sector was guided by industrial and trade policies that protected domestic industry and gave the state a central role in investment decisions. While a strict regime of import and export controls defined trade policy, industrial policy worked through an elaborate system of industrial licensing. Under the Industries Development and Regulatory Act of 1951 every investor over a very small size needed to obtain a license before establishing an industrial plant, adding a new product line to an existing plant, substantially expanding output, or changing a plant's location.

While the state-led import substitution policy framework had helped create a diversified manufacturing sector, industrial stagnation since the mid-1960s—increasingly blamed on the policy framework—led to some tentative steps aimed at liberalizing these regimes in the late 1970s and early 1980s (Ahluwalia 1987; 1991). Relaxations of the industrial licensing system were introduced and import licensing requirements were eased. However, by most accounts these reforms were marginal. Tariff rates as high as 400 percent were not uncommon, non-tariff barriers remained widespread, and the industrial licensing regime continued to impose binding constraints to entry and growth for most firms. The so-called small-scale sector reservations (introduced in 1969), which limited the entry and operations of firms above a certain size threshold in a number of labor-intensive industries, continued in full force. (This was largely the case until 2000, and reforms since then have left only a few items on the list.)

What Constrains Indian Manufacturing?

More serious liberalization efforts began in 1985 with delicensing—the exemption from the requirement of obtaining an industrial license—of twenty-five broad categories of industries (which maps into thirteen industries in our three-digit level data). The next major reform of the licensing regime came in 1991 when industrial licensing was abolished except in the case of a small number of industries (see Figure 10.2a and Table 10A.2 for the time path of delicensing). This was also the year in which a decisive break was made with the trade policies of the past. The liberalization of 1991 included the removal of most licensing and other non-tariff barriers on the imports of intermediate and capital goods, the simplification of the trade regime, devaluations of the Indian rupee, and the introduction of an explicit dual exchange market in 1992 (see Figure 10.2b).

Despite these impressive reform measures there are certain areas in which there has been little progress. One area in which there has been no major policy change is in the labor regulations that apply to India's industry sector. According to Panagariya (2008), it is rigidities introduced by these (unchanged) regulations that are holding back the manufacturing sector in general and its labor-intensive subsectors in particular. Since the issue of India's labor regulations is one of the most contentious ones in the context of debates on economic reforms, some details are in order.

While India's labor regulations have been criticized on many accounts including, for example, the sheer size and scope of regulations, their complexity, and inconsistencies across individual pieces of regulation, a few specific pieces of legislation are the controversial ones. First, as per Chapter VB of the IDA it is necessary for firms employing more than 100 workers to obtain the permission of state Governments in order to retrench or lay off workers.[6] While the IDA does not prohibit retrenchments, critics of the act argue that it is difficult to carry them out. Datta-Chaudhuri (1996) has argued, for example, that states have often been unwilling to grant permission to retrench.

Second, additional rigidities in using effectively a firm's existing workers are believed to stem from Section 9A of the IDA and the Industrial

---

[6] Until 1976, the provisions of the IDA on retrenchments or layoffs were fairly uncontroversial. The IDA allowed firms to lay off or retrench workers as per economic circumstances as long as certain requirements such as the provision of sufficient notice, severance payments, and the order of retrenchment among workers (last in first out) were met. An amendment in 1976 (the introduction of Chapter VB), however, made it compulsory for employers with more than 300 workers to seek the prior approval of the appropriate Government before workers could be dismissed. A further amendment in 1982 widened the scope of this regulation by making it applicable to employers with 100 workers or more.

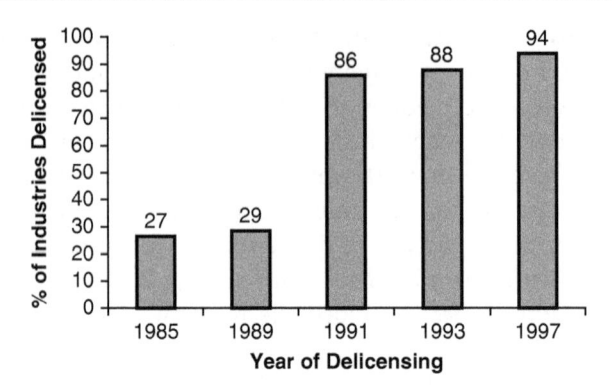

Figure 10.2a. Cumulative share of industries delicensed
Source: Constructed by the authors using data in Aghion et al. (2006).

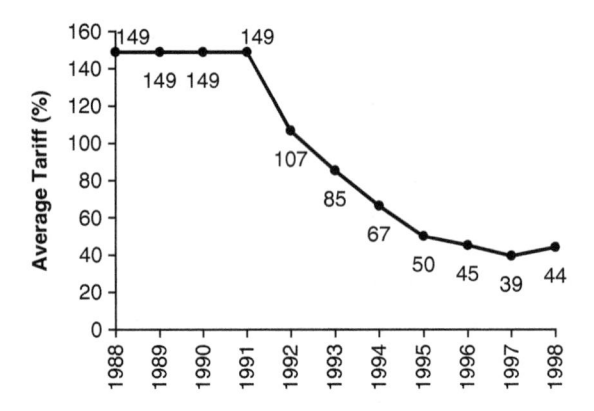

Figure 10.2b. Average nominal rate of protection, 1988 to 1998
Source: Constructed using the data in Hasan et al. (2007).

Employment (Standing Orders) Act —which pertain to procedures that must be followed by employers before changing the terms and conditions of work. While the two pieces of legislation seek to make labor contracts complete, fair, and legally binding they can constrain firms from making quick adjustments to changing conditions. In particular, worker consent is required in order to modify job descriptions or move workers from one plant to another in response to changing market conditions. In and of itself, this does not seem to be an unreasonable objective. The problem, according to some analysts, is that the workings of India's Trade Union Act (TUA) make it difficult to obtain worker consent. While the TUA allows any seven workers in an enterprise to form and register a trade union, it has no provisions for union recognition (e.g. via a secret ballot). The result, according to Anant (2000), has been multiple and rival unions, making it difficult to arrive at a consensus among workers.

Similarly, hiring contract workers can enable firms to get around many of the regulatory restrictions on adjusting employment levels, productions tasks, etc.; however, it is argued that Section 10 of the Contract Labor Act, which empowers the Government to prohibit the employment of contract labor in any industry, operation, or process, limits this course of action.

It is important to note that not all analysts agree that India's labor laws have made for a rigid labor market. In particular, a counter-argument to the views above is that the rigidity inducing regulations have been either ignored (Nagaraj 2002) or circumvented through the increased usage of temporary or contract labor (Dutta 2003; Ramaswamy 2003).[7] Ultimately, whether India's labor laws have created significant rigidities in labor markets or not is an empirical issue, as is the broader question of whether and to what extent various policies have been the main constraints on the growth of Indian manufacturing.

The state of India's infrastructure is widely believed to be a constraint on growth. According to the Deputy Chairman of the Planning Commission, Mr Montek Singh Ahluwalia, India needs to increase its investment in infrastructure from 5 percent of GDP to 8 percent of GDP by the end of the Eleventh Five-Year Plan, yielding an investment of US$400 billion in its infrastructure to sustain the current growth rates. A recent OECD survey of Indian economy compares Indian infrastructure with that of other countries and finds India to be badly lagging in most of the areas.[8]

An interesting comparison in this regard is with the infrastructure in China. Total investment anticipated in infrastructure in the Tenth Five-Year Plan (2002–2006) in India was 5 percent as compared to China's 12.6 percent in 2005 (Figure 10.3). Not only is China's investment as a share of GDP almost 2.5 times greater than that of India, China's GDP base is larger as well. In almost all sectors, investment as a share of GDP in China is far greater than that in India (Figure 10.3).

Another area in which there has been rather slow progress on reforms is the financial sector (or the banking sector, more narrowly). Reform efforts

---

[7] For a detailed review of Indian labor regulations and the debate surrounding the issue of rigidity, see Anant et al. (2006).

[8] Our exercise involving infrastructure is, therefore, in the *spirit* of the pioneering work of Robert Fogel and Albert Fishlow who independently evaluated the impact of railroad infrastructure on economic activity in the United States during the nineteenth century.

Infrastructure investment chart

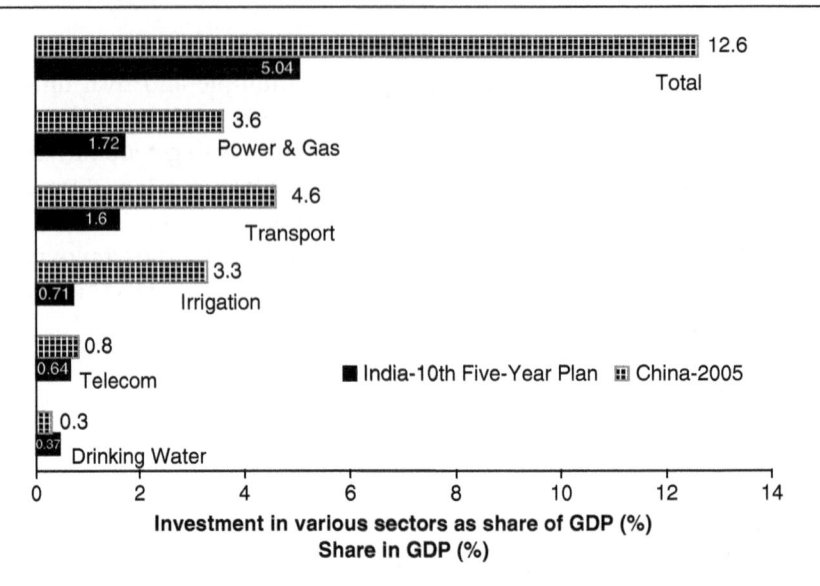

Sector	India-10th Five-Year Plan	China-2005
Total	5.04	12.6
Power & Gas	1.72	3.6
Transport	1.6	4.6
Irrigation	0.71	3.3
Telecom	0.64	0.8
Drinking Water	0.37	0.3

Investment in various sectors as share of GDP (%)
Share in GDP (%)

Figure 10.3. Infrastructure investment (% of GDP), China and India

Source: Authors' calculation using the data in Planning Commission (2007) (Sector-wise Investment Anticipated in the Tenth Five-Year Plan), and in Lall et al. (2007).

in this area have been directed at deregulating interest rates; some dilution of public ownership of banks; and limited opening up of the sector to private domestic and foreign banks. However as pointed out often, and most recently in OECD (2007a), some major challenges still remain. These include a very high share of public ownership in banks and low level of bank intermediation partly because of regulations on the allocation of credit which require banks to allocate a substantial percentage of their total advances into Government securities and other priority sectors.[9]

Performance of Indian manufacturing

We look at a fairly long time series of data on Indian registered manufacturing from 1973–2003.[10] Below we summarize some of the empirical

---

[9] In addition since the performance of the bank managers is not linked as tightly with the profitability of the banks, and is probably influenced more by the incidence of nonperforming loans, they have little incentive to provide credit to the private sector. Hence they play extremely cautiously and rather than lending to the private sector prefer to invest in safe Government securities (Banerjee and Duflo 2004).

[10] The reference period for ASI is the accounting year of the industrial unit ending on any day during the fiscal year. Therefore, in ASI 2003–2004, the data collected from the respective industrial units relates to their accounting year ending on any day between April 1, 2003 and March 31, 2004. When we say 2003 in the chapter it refers to the fiscal year 2003–2004.

What Constrains Indian Manufacturing?

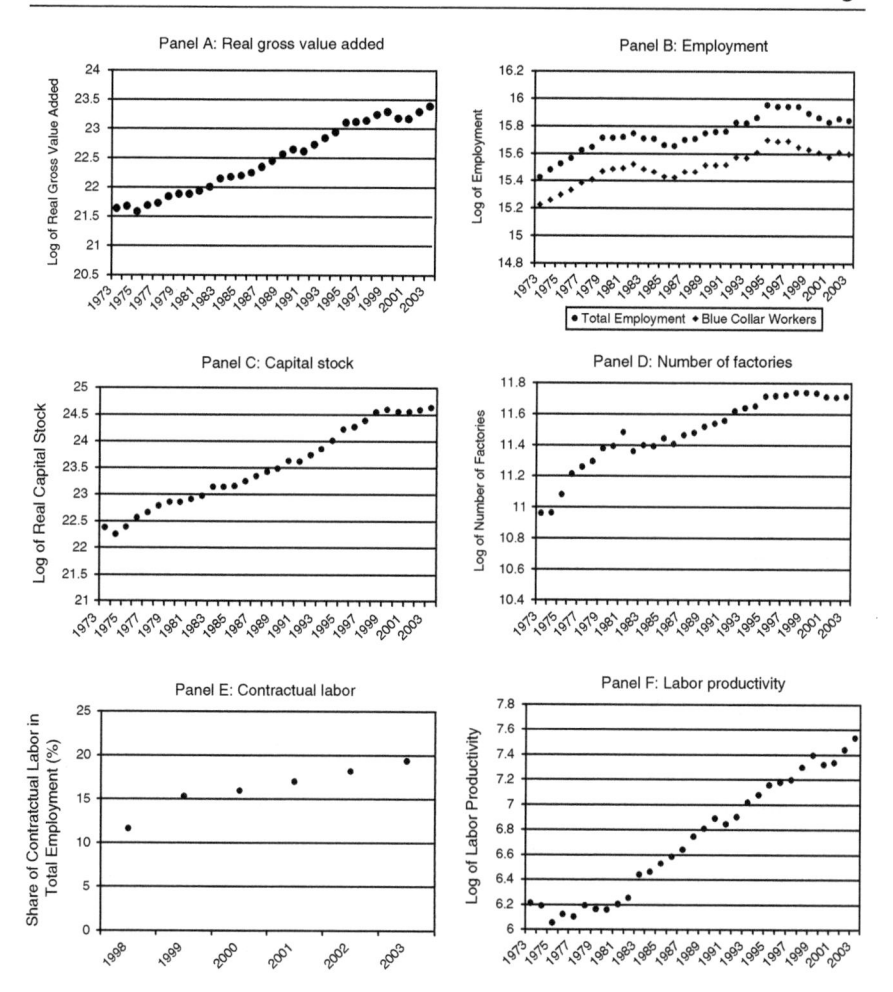

Figure 10.4. Performance of Indian manufacturing

Source: Authors' calculations using the data in Annual Survey of Industries.

regularities that we observe in the data on the various indicators of industrial performance and on employment related variables.[11] Various panels of Figure 10.4 show that the growth of value added, employment, capital formation, and factories has been stable throughout the last three

---

[11] The only comprehensive database available on Indian manufacturing is the ASI data which includes data on registered manufacturing, i.e. factories with more than 20 workers if not using power and factories employing more than 10 workers if using power. One caveat of using this data is that we are only looking at one component of total manufacturing. Registered manufacturing comprises 70% of the total output being produced in the manufacturing sector but only 20% of the total manufacturing employment.

317

Table 10.1. Pre- and post-reform performance of Indian manufacturing

	(1) Value added	(2) Capital stock	(3) Number of factories	(4) Total employment
Trend	5.997***	7.318***	2.703***	1.292***
	[21.82]	[27.16]	[7.75]	[5.26]
Trend*Post 1992	0.447**	0.838***	−0.375*	−0.013
	[2.18]	[4.55]	[2.04]	[0.08]
Observations	31	31	31	31
R-squared	0.98	0.99	0.87	0.77

Note: 3 digit ASI data from 1973–2003 has been used in the analysis. All variables are measured in log. Robust t statistics are given in brackets. * indicates significance at 10%; ** significance at 5%; *** significance at 1%.

decades and has not necessarily accelerated in the post-reform period. If anything, there is probably a stagnation starting sometime in the mid to late 1990s.

Panel B of the Figure shows separately the employment of blue collar workers and total employment. The trends seem to be broadly similar for both the variables. The data on contractual labor, is available only since 1998, but the trends show an increase in the share of contractual labor in total employment. The pace of growth of capital stock seems to be faster than that of employment. These different trends in employment and investment are probably reflected in the growth of labor productivity over time. Finally, the number of factories does not seem to have kept pace with the growth of value added.

The trends in these figures are also picked up in Table 10.1. In Table 10.1 we estimate the trend growth rates for the aggregate values of various performance indicators pertaining to the manufacturing sector. The regression equations include the dependent variables in logs, and regressed it on a linear trend and a dummy which takes the value 1 for the post-1992 period, and zero otherwise. Thus its coefficient measures the percentage change in the dependent variable post-1992 after accounting for its trend growth rate.

Thus the data show that the aggregate value added has increased at about 6 percent a year in the sample period, and there has been a modest annual growth acceleration of about half a percentage point between 1993 and 2003. This modest pickup in value added is not accompanied by an additional growth in employment or in the number of factories. Employment has grown at the rate of 1.3 percent a year, with no change in the rate of growth post-delicensing. New factories have come up at the rate of 2.7 percent a year; with the rate decelerating post-1992. Investment rate however has been commensurate with the growth of value added. Investment accelerated by about 8½ percent post-1992. Poor performance of employment is a very important question in itself and we cannot do full justice to this issue here; we propose to take it up in subsequent research.

Is this growth pickup impressive and does it imply that the reforms have paid off? When we compare this performance with the pace of growth in the manufacturing sector of many East Asian countries including China, we realize that not only in terms of employment, but also in terms of value added, the performance of Indian manufacturing has not been close to that of East Asian countries. For example, manufacturing value added in South Korea grew at an average annual real growth rate of approximately 17 percent between 1960 and 1980; China's manufacturing sector witnessed an average growth rate of 12 percent per year between 1990 and 2005.

10.3 Evidence from enterprise surveys

What lies behind this relatively lackluster performance? Before turning to the main econometric analysis of this chapter, it is useful to examine the views of managers based on two recent surveys of manufacturing firms: The Investment Climate Survey conducted by the World Bank and a survey of about 250 firms from some of the most labor-intensive sectors, conducted by ICRIER (*Field Survey on 'How to Enhance Employment Generation and Exports of Labour Intensive Firms'*).[12]

The World Bank's investment climate survey (ICS) data consists of the responses of managers to a wide range of questions including questions pertaining to managers' perceptions about how various regulatory and other factors influence their firms. A key question asks about the extent to which various factors are considered 'a problem for the operation and growth' of the surveyed firms business. For each factor listed, respondents can reply in terms of a five-point scale: 0 = no obstacle; 1 = minor obstacle; 2 = moderate obstacle; 3 = major obstacle; 4 = very severe obstacle.[13] It enables one to compare firms' responses about various factors, ranging

---

[12] This survey was conducted by a team led by Dr Deb Kusum Das. We thank him for sharing the data with us.

[13] We are aware that the phrasing of this question may not be ideal since it lumps together operations and growth. It is quite possible, for example, that some aspect of industrial regulations might not be a problem for the operations of a firm, unless the firm tried to expand its operations.

**Fraction reporting issue as "major" or "very severe" obstacle
All firms, 2005**

[Bar chart showing obstacles ranked from highest to lowest:
- Tax issues
- Infrastructure
- Governance
- Finance
- Regulations
- Skills
- Labor regulations
- Macro policy & uncertainty
- Land
- Anti-competitive practices

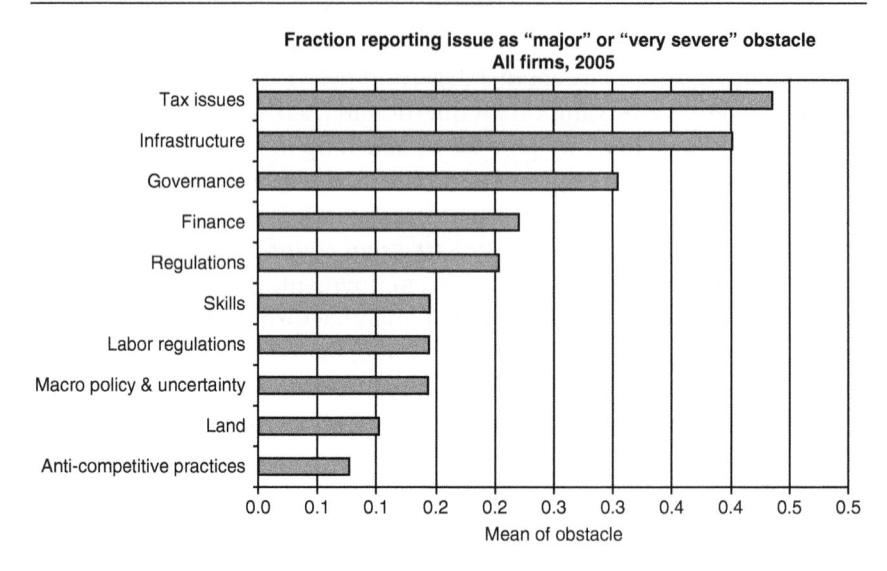

X-axis: Mean of obstacle, from 0.0 to 0.5]

Figure 10.5. Obstacles for operations and growth

from regulatory and governance issues to infrastructure-related concerns, in terms of how they influence firms' operations or growth prospects.

Figure 10.5 depicts the fraction of firms describing a given factor as a major or very severe obstacle in the 2005 ICS survey (similar patterns are observed in the 2002 ICS survey). Tax-related issues, incorporating difficulties with either the tax administration system or complaints about tax rates, are considered to be a major or severe constraint by more than 40 percent of respondents. Of course, it is not easy to interpret this finding given what is probably a natural penchant among firms to want to pay as little as possible in taxes. Ignoring tax-related issues then, the situation with infrastructure can be seen to be a critical obstacle for operations and growth from the perspective of the firms.[14] Almost 40 percent of respondents cite it as a major or severe obstacle. In addition to infrastructure, one-fifth or more respondents cite governance issues (which include concerns with corruption) and the cost and access to finance as the major obstacles. Surprisingly, an almost equal percent of respondents cite skills and labor regulations as major obstacles (around 15%).

A useful follow-up question entailed asking firms what constituted the *single* most important obstacle for firms' operation and growth (see

---

[14] Infrastructure includes electricity, telecommunications, and transportation. Disaggregating this variable shows that the concern with infrastructure is overwhelmingly driven by concerns with electricity. Telecommunications are hardly considered a problem.

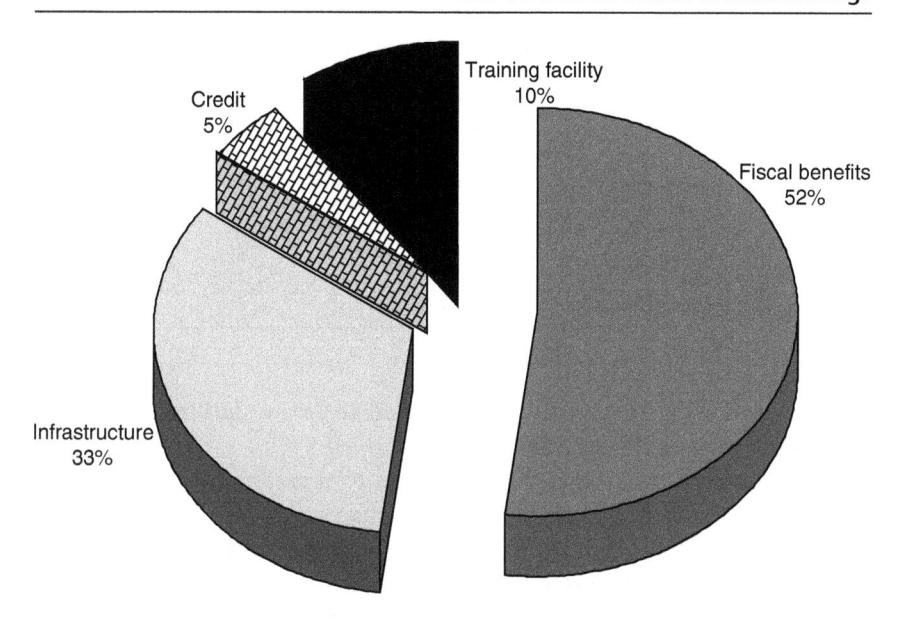

Figure 10.6. Areas for improvement
Source: Authors' calculation using data from the ICRIER survey.

Table 10.2). By far the biggest problem relates to infrastructure and within this, electricity was cited as the key issue. Indeed, 31 percent of firms listed electricity as the source of their single most important obstacle to operations and growth.

Another source of the views of manufacturing firm managers comes from the ICRIER survey of 250 enterprises engaged in manufacturing activities in five different sectors (apparel, bicycles, gems and jewelry, leather, and sports goods). It is useful to examine the results of this survey because it covers firms from some of the most labor-intensive manufacturing activities (see Figure 10.6). Thus to the extent that labor regulations create serious constraints and growth prospects of firms, the sample firms should be among those most affected.[15]

Broadly speaking, the respondents find electricity and infrastructure in general, financing, and skilled labor availability to be the most serious constraints on growth. Just like in the ICS survey they also point to

---

[15] Not all the firms covered responded to all the questions in the survey. For the purposes of the present study, we focus on the responses relating to the questions on the hurdles to the growth of the firms.

Table 10.2. Single most important obstacle for operation and growth of the firm

Factor	Number of responses	% of responses
Infrastructure	821	36
Tax issues	510	22
Governance	231	10
Finance	130	6
Skills	91	4
Labor regulations	82	4

specific regulations especially those related to taxes (and fiscal benefits, in general) among things that can be improved.[16,17]

In response to the questions on hurdles to increasing employment, a majority of the respondents reported shortage of labor (of mostly skilled and semi-skilled labor) as the key hurdle to hiring more labor.[18] Further, most of the firms (approximately 90%) responded in the negative to being affected by any labor disputes or to having labor unions in their organization and/or any impact of the unions on their activities.

Taken together, there are some striking similarities in the results of these two very different surveys. First, infrastructure-related issues are very high on the list of constraints faced by firms. Indeed, ignoring tax-related issues, concerns with electricity seem to be paramount. Second, finance-related issues also seem be a problem, especially for the smaller firms. Third, surprisingly labor regulations do not show up as a

---

[16] A look at the specific responses makes it clear that the concern with fiscal issues is very narrowly defined and is more in the nature of a personal issue to the firms, to the extent that taxes directly affect their bottom lines. In response to the question what would you like to see changed to help you, a majority of them answered that they would like the taxes to be lowered or subsidies from the Government.

[17] The survey also tried to find whether the technological changes are such that they are inhibiting employment growth. About two-thirds of the respondents acknowledged technological changes (either a lot or modest) taking place globally in their industry. Of those answering in the affirmative to worldwide changes in technology in their respective industries, 70% of the respondents adopted new technology during the 5 years prior to the year of the survey; but the majority of them still find a gap between the technologies they used and those used globally. In general, however, there is no clear evidence on the impact of adoption of new technologies on labor. One potential explanation for the lack of a clear pattern could be that while adoption of new technology, on the one hand, might be labor saving (substitution effect), growth resulting from adopting new technology might on the other hand be expansionary and lead to hiring of more labor (growth effect).

[18] Interestingly approximately 10% of the firms rue the lack of training facilities. This is consistent with shortage of labor or, more precisely, the shortage of the 'right' kind of labor for the 'right' kind of skills.

significant concern for firms. Indeed, both surveys suggest that concerns with skills-related issues are more important than those having to do with labor regulations.

While the concerns with electricity are not surprising for anyone with some familiarity with the Indian industrial scene, the low ranking of labor regulations as obstacles for operations and growth is surprising. One interpretation of these results could be that labor regulations may not matter much to firms in practice. This could happen, for example, if non-compliance with labor regulations is not costly. Alternatively, firms may be able to 'get around' restrictions on layoffs by hiring contract workers. A second interpretation of these results, however, is that labor regulations may not matter that much to *incumbent* firms. But it may matter to a non-incumbent investor contemplating entry into the manufacturing sector.

More generally, an investor's choice on which specific sectors (for example, services vs. manufacturing) and subsectors (for example, a more labor-intensive manufacturing industry vs. a less labor-intensive one) to enter, as well as the production technologies, scale, and desired levels of employment to adopt, can be expected to be influenced by the regulatory framework. In this way, there may be an *'ex ante'* effect of the law that would be very difficult, to capture through the surveys of incumbent manufactures. In other words, deterred by specific elements of labor regulations such as Chapter VB of the IDA, potential investors, especially those contemplating large investments, choose to avoid investing in manufacturing altogether, or if they do invest in manufacturing, they avoid subsectors, product lines, or scales of production for which the regulations have most bite.

In what follows, we turn to an approach which has the potential for getting around the 'selection' problem inherent in surveys of incumbent firms. In particular, we use industry-level data from India's organized manufacturing sector to examine the relative performance of industries with various characteristics.

10.4 Econometric analysis

We are interested in testing the variants of the following hypotheses: Did industries that are more labor intensive, or industries that rely more on infrastructure, or industries that rely more on the financial sector for their financing needs grow less than the control group of industries in the post-delicensing period? The econometric methodology is derived from Rajan and Zingales (1998), who analyze the effect of financial development on growth by comparing the growth of industries which depend more on the financial sector in countries with greater financial depth with the growth of these industries in countries with shallower financial markets. Thus if the financial sector indeed matters for growth then one would see higher growth in industries that rely on the financial sector in countries which have a deeper financial sector, and vice versa. This technique gets to the causality issue much more cleverly than the alternative econometric ways to measure this relationship. The methodology has subsequently been used in several different contexts.[19]

We use this technique to look at the constraints that Indian industry might have experienced post-delicensing. Hence we analyze the performance of the industries that rely more heavily on infrastructure; industries that depend on the financial sector; and the labor-intensive industries post-delicensing. An evidence of lackluster growth in these industries is attributed then to the unavailability of inputs or factors that the respective industries rely more heavily on. Thus if the infrastructure-dependent industries have not performed well post-delicensing then it is likely to be due to the fact that the infrastructure availability has not been adequate for these industries to gain the maximum benefit from the reforms.

Construction of variables

Reform Variables. As discussed in Section 10.2, industrial and trade policy has seen wide-ranging reforms over the period under study. While limited reforms were started from the mid-1980s onwards, major policy changes were undertaken following the crisis in 1991. Some of the reforms introduced were more generic, aimed at macroeconomic management; others were more specific to the industries. The reforms spanned several areas including delicensing of industries, trade reforms, and exchange rate reforms. In subsequent years these were complemented by the liberalization of foreign investment—both FDI and portfolio; dereservation of industrial sectors under small scale; financial sector liberalization; and privatization of public sector units.

---

[19] See Dell'Ariccia et al. (2005); Rajan and Subramanian (2005).

In our econometric exercise we look at the effect of delicensing on Indian manufacturing industries (see Appendix Table 10A.2). the reasons being that it is one of the most comprehensive programs which covered almost all the industries, and the information on it is readily available. The fact that these reforms were undertaken at different points in time allows us to include time-fixed effects to account for unobservable but common macroeconomic shocks in the regressions. We do not have complete data for trade reforms, but we do control for it in the robustness exercises.[20] In robustness tests we also estimate a specification in which we include the interaction of industry characteristics with a post-1992 dummy in the benchmark specification to account for the reforms which were more generic in nature, besides the delicensing. Results remain broadly unchanged and are presented selectively here.

Industrial Characteristics. We define three industrial characteristics of various industries: Labor intensity; dependence of industries on external finance; and infrastructure dependence. Rajan and Zingales (1998) assume that there are probably technological reasons why some industries depend more on external finance than others. We extend this reasoning to labor intensity and to infrastructure intensity. To the extent that these two characteristics define input usage, the technological requirement assumption is perhaps as valid as for defining the external financing dependence. We briefly describe the various industrial characteristics below, same as provided in Appendix 10A and Appendix Table 10A.3.

Labor Intensity. We define labor intensity as the ratio of total employment to capital stock. Since there are no comprehensive databases of employment at firm level we use the ASI industry-level data to calculate this ratio.

Dependence on External Finance. We calculate the external financial dependence of firms in two different ways and using two different databases: The first one uses the firm-level data from the Prowess database published by the CMIE, and employs the same definition as used by Rajan and Zingales (1998). The second measure is calculated using the ASI data as the ratio of outstanding loans to invested capital. The index of external finance dependence does not correlate well across two databases and across different definitions. Neither of these correlates too well with the index calculated by Rajan and Zingales (1998) which was calculated

---

[20] See Topalova (2005); Mitra and Ural (2007); Kumar and Mishra (2008), for the analyses of the effects of trade liberalization.

for industrial data at the 2-digit level for US industries. To the extent that our firm-level data (from Prowess) is only for listed firms whose access to financial markets is likely to be different from that of small and medium enterprises, and it might affect the cross-industry ranking, we use the financial dependence indicator calculated using the ASI data.

Infrastructure Dependence of Industries. We calculate it as the ratio of expenses on distribution (i.e. storage and transportation) and power and fuel to gross value added using the firm-level data. To the extent that we have data on expenses on fuel consumption in both CMIE and ASI, we calculate an indicator just as the ratio of fuel expenditure to gross value added. These are highly correlated across the two databases; and with the indicator which includes distribution expenses as well. Appendix 10A.3 indicates which industries qualify as below or above median for each of these characteristic.

In order to get around the concern that these characteristics would reflect the equilibrium conditions between the demand and supply of the respective inputs, we use the data from an earlier year (in general we use averages over the early 1990s, but where data are available we confirmed that the industry characteristics are correlated highly with the ones calculated using the data for earlier period) rather than contemporaneous data. Furthermore to smooth out the noise in the data we use five-year averages of the relevant variables to calculate the industry indicators. We also confirmed, where possible, that the relative industry rankings across various characteristics do not change over time. This robustness check gives credence to the belief that there are perhaps external technological reasons for why an industry uses more external finance; or uses more labor than capital; or depends more on infrastructure; and to the fact that using data from the early 1990s is legitimate.

The questions that come to mind about these industry features are whether they are capturing some other features of the industries, and how the three features are correlated with each other. The various industry characteristics are not correlated significantly with each other (not shown here).[21] The exceptions are that the labor-intensive industries are negatively correlated with imports and financial dependence and infrastructure dependence is negatively correlated with import and FDI intensity. Labor-intensive industries are also somewhat more export intensive.

---

[21] Please see the working paper version Gupta et al. (2008).

Table 10.3. Growth of gross value added post-delicensing across industries

	Infrastructure dependent		Dependent on external finance		Labor intensive	
	Above median	Below median	Above median	Below median	Above median	Below median
Delicensing	−0.15***	0.33***	0.08	0.18***	−0.01	0.24***
	[3.12]	[4.46]	[1.31]	[2.64]	[0.22]	[3.19]
Observations	682	679	682	679	682	679
Number of industries	22	22	22	22	22	22
Time FE	Yes	Yes	Yes	Yes	Yes	Yes
Industry FE	Yes	Yes	Yes	Yes	Yes	Yes
R-squared	0.77	0.66	0.71	0.70	0.69	0.72

Note: We have used 3-digit ASI data from 1973 to 2003 in the analysis. The industry characteristics have been defined as explained in Section III and Appendix 2. The dependent variable used is value added in log. Robust t statistics are given in brackets. * indicates significance at 10%; ** significance at 5%; *** significance at 1%.

Empirical results from the ASI data

We begin by exploring the possibility that the overall performance of the manufacturing sector masks significant inter-industry heterogeneity. Are there certain industries which have not benefited as much from the reforms?

In Table 10.3 we find that the performance varies across different sectors. In particular, we identify industries which depend more on infrastructure, industries which depend more on the financial sector for their financing needs, and the labor-intensive industries, see Appendix 10A.3. We divide the industries into those belonging to above or median values for each industry characteristic and estimate separate regressions for industries below and above median values. We use log of value added as the dependent variable and control for industry and year fixed effects and a dummy for delicensing which varies across industries and years in the regressions.

Results in Table 10.3 show that the industries which are more infrastructure intensive, on average, experience 15 percent lower growth in value added post-delicensing (i.e. in the delicensed period relative to the earlier period), as compared to 33 percent higher output growth in value added of industries which are less reliant on infrastructure. Similarly the industries more dependent on the financial sector or the labor-intensive industries have fared much worse than the industries that do not rely as much on the financial sector and are less labor-intensive industries. Thus, there seems to be significant heterogeneity in the performance of Indian manufacturing across industry groups.

Econometric framework

We use the following econometric specification to analyze the impact of delicensing on various performance indicators:

$$Y_{it} = \Sigma \alpha_i d_i + \Sigma \beta_t d_t + \gamma \text{ (delicensing dummy}_{it})$$
$$+ \delta(\text{characteristic of industry } i^* \text{ delicensing dummy}_{it}) + \epsilon_{it} \quad (1)$$

Where Y_{it} is the outcome variable measured in log. As before we consider gross value added at constant prices, employment, capital stock, and number of factories as the outcome variables.

In equation (1), d_is are industry specific dummies and α_is are their respective coefficients; d_ts are year specific dummies and β_ts are their respective coefficients. The fixed effects account for the industry specific omitted variables; and the year fixed effects control for year specific shocks that are common to all industries. Since we are using industry fixed effects and year fixed effects in the regression equation the only additional variables we can include are the ones that vary with both industry and year. The next term in equation (1) is the delicensing dummy which varies over time and industry. The dummy takes a value one from the year when the delicensing requirement for a particular industry was removed and remains one for the rest of the sample period.[22]

We are interested in testing the variants of the following hypotheses: Did industries that are more labor intensive (or industries that rely more on infrastructure or the financial sector for their financing needs) grow less than the control group of industries in the post-delicensing period? Testing for these hypotheses requires us to set up the regression equation for difference in differences estimates. Continuing with the specific hypothesis involving labor-intensive industries, consider the following possible cases for any given outcome variable:

	Outcome variable in pre-reform period	Outcome variable in post-reform period
For more labor intensive (treatment group)	$\Theta_{L,Pre}$	$\Theta_{L,Post}$
For less labor intensive (control group)	$\Theta_{C,Pre}$	$\Theta_{C,Post}$

[22] The delicensing dummy is based on the information provided in Aghion et al. (2006), which we updated ourselves until 2003. As of 2003 all but three industries had been delicensed, see Appendix Table 10A.2.

Essentially, we would like to test the hypothesis that $(\Theta_{L,Post} - \Theta_{L,Pre}) - (\Theta_{C,Post} - \Theta_{C,Pre})$ is significantly different from zero. The coefficient δ in equation (1) allows us to do this. We use the interaction with each of the industry characteristics discussed above with delicensing separately and together in the regression equations.

How do we interpret a negative and significant coefficient for the interaction term of a particular industry characteristic, let's say infrastructure-dependent industries? The coefficient indicates that the industries which use infrastructure more intensively have grown less post-delicensing as compared to the industries which use infrastructure less intensively. Can it be interpreted as a causal relationship between the lack of infrastructure and performance? As mentioned in the introduction, to the extent that an industry characteristic is exogenous of performance, e.g. it is some sort of a technical requirement; or if we can control for potential omitted variables, then we can probably claim causality in this result.

For exogeneity in our industry characteristics we use the data from the earliest possible period for which we have data (in our case early 1990s). We control for omitted variables varying only over industries and over years by including the respective fixed effects. To rule out other potential omitted variables we conduct extensive robustness tests as described later.

In Table 10.4 we present our results for the benchmark case as given by equation (1). Coefficients on both the industry and year fixed effects have been suppressed from the table. In the results in column 1 the coefficient for delicensing shows a 12 percent increase in value added per industry post-delicensing. Given that the average delicensing period is about fifteen years, it amounts to a less than 1 percent increase in value added per year in the post-delicensing period. However as we have seen in Table 10.3 certain industries did not fare as well during the post-delicensing period. Thus when we control for the different effects on these industries separately, the post-delicensing impact on growth of the control group improves substantially.

In columns 2–4 we include these characteristics with the interaction of delicensing one at a time. As expected the performance of the control group goes up considerably. From columns 2–4, we see that the industries more dependent on infrastructure, labor, and external finance respectively have witnessed slower growth as opposed to their respective control group. In column 5 we include them together and we find that industries ranking higher on each of our three industry characteristics have faired poorly in the post-delicensing period. Finally, the last column

Table 10.4. Value added post-delicensing

	(1)	(2)	(3)	(4)	(5)	(6)
Delicensing	0.12**	0.18***	0.26***	0.53***	0.93***	0.36***
	[2.50]	[3.10]	[3.31]	[4.65]	[7.35]	[5.61]
Infrastructure dependence* delicensing		−0.17**			−0.18***	
		[2.42]			[2.59]	
Labor intensity*delicensing			−0.30**		−0.51***	
			[2.02]		[3.55]	
External finance dependence*delicensing				−0.93***	−1.22***	
				[4.01]	[5.49]	
Infrastructure dummy* delicensing						−0.10*
						[1.88]
Labor intensity dummy* delicensing						−0.19***
						[4.07]
External finance dummy* delicensing						−0.18***
						[3.40]
Industry FE	Yes	Yes	Yes	Yes	Yes	Yes
Year FE	Yes	Yes	Yes	Yes	Yes	Yes
Observations	1,361	1,361	1,361	1,361	1,361	1,361
Number of industries	44	44	44	44	44	44
R-squared	0.70	0.70	0.70	0.70	0.71	0.71

Note: Dependent variable is log value added. Robust t statistics in brackets, * significant at 10%; ** significant at 5%; *** significant at 1%.

is the same as column 5 except that in this column instead of including the index of industry characteristics, we divide them into above and below median groups and include the interaction of the dummy variables, which takes the value one when an industry is above the median of the respective characteristic, with delicensing. Once again we find that the results hold and industries above the median in each of the three characteristics have not done as well as the control group in the post-delicensing period.[23]

Quantitatively the results, from column 6 of Table 10.4, indicate that in the post-delicensing period the above median infrastructure-intensive industries grew 10 percent less than the industries below the median of infrastructure dependence. Similarly industries above median in the distribution of financial dependence grew 18 percent less than the industries below the median of financial dependence; and for labor intensity,

---

[23] In unreported results, we test if availability of skill is emerging as a constraint. Based on US data we classify industries into as above median or below median skill-intensive industries. We find that the coefficient on the interaction term (skill intensity*delicensing) is positive and statistically significant. In other words, for the period under study we find that skill was not a constraint. Alternatively, the results could be interpreted to mean that more skill-intensive industries performed better post-delicensing as opposed to the less skill industries.

What Constrains Indian Manufacturing?

Table 10.5. Number of factories

	(1)	(2)	(3)	(4)	(5)
Delicensing	0.04	0.03	0.11**	0.15**	0.31***
	[1.09]	[0.86]	[2.20]	[2.41]	[3.42]
Infrastructure dependence*delicensing		0.02			0.01
		[0.39]			[0.23]
Labor intensity*delicensing			−0.16**		−0.22***
			[2.15]		[2.86]
External finance dependence*delicensing				−0.27**	−0.39***
				[2.24]	[3.05]
Industry FE	Yes	Yes	Yes	Yes	Yes
Year FE	Yes	Yes	Yes	Yes	Yes
Observations	1,361	1,361	1,361	1,361	1,361
Number of industries	44	44	44	44	44
R-squared	0.58	0.58	0.58	0.58	0.58

Note: Dependent variable is log number of factories. Robust t statistics in brackets, * significant at 10%; ** significant at 5%; *** significant at 1%.

industries with above median labor intensity grew 19 percent less than the below median industries post-delicensing.

In Table 10.5 results are presented for the dependent variable, number of factories (in log). The overall performance of Indian manufacturing seems to be even less impressive when we look at the number of factories. Overall there is no acceleration in the rate of expansion of factories post-delicensing. These results are on account of the fact that the performance has been particularly worse for the labor-intensive industries and industries dependent on the financial sector. Once we control for these as in the previous set of regressions, the performance of the control group (industries less dependent on infrastructure or financial sector or labor) is seen to be much better. The point remains that industries more dependent on external finance and labor-intensive industries have fared much worse post-delicensing in terms of new factories opening.

Next, we look at employment and capital stock. The issues related to employment are manifold and much more complex, and all of these probably cannot be addressed in this chapter. Some of the issues that merit attention include: Why has growth not been employment intensive; is technology displacing labor; how has the employment of unskilled vs. skilled workers evolved over time; how is the skill premium changing over time, etc. For brevity we look only at total employment here, which includes manual workers as well as supervisors and regular as well as contract employees.

We look at two econometric specifications here. The first is given in equation (1).[24] Results using this specification show that employment has increased by a mere 7 percent over the entire delicensing period. With the average delicensing period about fifteen years, this translates into a less than half a percent increase in employment per year post-product market reforms. As expected, once we introduce heterogeneity based on industry characteristics, the performance of the control group improves rather substantially. The maximum increase is for the industries less dependent on external finance. Notably, infrastructure- and external finance-dependent industries as well as labor-intensive industries are the weakest performers insofar as employment generation in the post-delicensing period is concerned.

Second, we estimate the following regression equation:

$$E_{it} = \Sigma \alpha_i d_i + \Sigma \beta_t d_t + \theta Y_{it} + \pi Y_{it} x \text{ delicensing dummy}_{it}$$
$$\lambda (Y_{it} x * \text{characteristic of industry } i * \text{delicensing dummy}_{it}) + \epsilon_{it} \quad (2)$$

In equation 2, E_{it} refers to log of employment (or log of invested capital in real terms), d_is are industry-specific dummies and d_ts are year-specific dummies as before. We also include log of gross value added in the equation; the coefficient θ can be interpreted as the employment elasticity of output. It measures the percentage change in employment for a 1 percent increase in output. The next term is the interaction of delicensing dummy with Y_{it}. Its coefficient π gives the employment elasticity of output post-delicensing. Finally, we include the interaction of Y_{it}, delicensing and industry characteristics. The coefficient λ measures the employment elasticity of output for the industry characteristic used in the interaction with post-delicensing. Thus if we are including labor intensity in the interaction term in equation (2) then it measures the change in the elasticity of employment post-delicensing in labor-intensive industries. If it is positive it implies that the employment elasticity in labor-intensive industries has increased post-delicensing and so on.

Results on employment from specification 2 are in Table 10.6. The results indicate that the employment elasticity of output is about 50 percent on average, though there are differences across industries. The elasticity is higher for labor-intensive industries than for infrastructure-dependent industries or for financially dependent industries. Results also indicate that there has been no change in the elasticity of employment

---

[24] For the sake of brevity, results are not shown here and the reader is kindly referred to the working paper version Gupta et al. (2008).

Table 10.6. Employment post-delicensing—results from equation 2

	(1)	(2)	(3)	(4)	(5)
Log gross value added (GVA)	0.52*** [20.76]	0.57*** [19.49]	0.47*** [17.30]	0.62*** [9.14]	0.55*** [7.03]
Delicensing*GVA	−0.000 [0.27]	−40.001 [0.35]	0.001 [0.48]	0.001 [0.28]	0.004 [0.86]
Infrastructure*GVA		−0.20*** [3.98]			−0.16*** [3.19]
Infrastructure* delicensing*GVA		0.003 [0.90]			0.001 [0.28]
Labor intensity*GVA			0.09*** [3.36]		0.08*** [2.70]
Labor intensity* delicensing*GVA			−0.000 [0.13]		−0.002 [0.66]
Financial dependence*GVA				−0.26* [1.92]	−0.107 [0.74]
Financial dependence* delicensing*GVA				−0.001 [0.10]	−0.004 [0.43]
Industry FE	Yes	Yes	Yes	Yes	Yes
Year FE	Yes	Yes	Yes	Yes	Yes
Observations	1,361	1,361	1,361	1,361	1,361
Number of industries	44	44	44	44	44
R-squared	0.69	0.70	0.70	0.70	0.70

Note: Dependent variable is log Employment. Robust t statistics in brackets, * significant at 10%; ** significant at 5%; *** significant at 1%. GVA refers to log value added in the above table.

post-delicensing, this is true on average for all industries, including for the industry characteristics that we control for explicitly in our regressions.

These results have two implications: First, if growth were to accelerate in Indian manufacturing it would probably generate employment at the same rate as before; and second, in order to generate more employment in Indian manufacturing it is imperative that the labor-intensive sectors grow faster. As we mentioned earlier, aggregate employment masks several nuances related to different kinds of employment, but we do not have space to discuss them all here.

For analyzing the patterns in investment we use both the specifications used for employment (see Table 10.7).[25] Thus we look at the capital elasticity (i.e. how investment changes) of value added and compare it with the behavior of investment post-delicensing. We also compare the investment behavior across industries and see whether there are any patterns in the investment changes across industries post-delicensing. Here we find that the capital elasticity is higher than that for employment elasticity.

[25] Please see the working paper version, Gupta et al. (2008) for results from estimation of equation (1).

Table 10.7. Investment post-delicensing—results from equation 2

	(1)	(2)	(3)	(4)	(5)
Gross value added (log)	0.85***	0.81***	0.88***	0.71***	0.73***
	[36.17]	[25.27]	[26.53]	[10.28]	[8.19]
Delicensing*GVA	0.01***	0.01***	0.004	0.02***	0.01
	[4.29]	[2.69]	[1.51]	[3.47]	[1.58]
Infrastructure*GVA		0.16**			0.12*
		[2.23]			[1.69]
Infrastructure* delicensing*GVA		0.001			0.004
		[0.21]			[0.73]
Labor intensity*GVA			−0.06*		−0.038
			[1.76]		[1.05]
Labor intensity* delicensing*GVA			0.01*		0.007
			[1.74]		[1.57]
Financial dependence* GVA				0.36**	0.28
				[2.34]	[1.64]
Financial dependence* delicensing*GVA				−0.02**	−0.02*
				[2.22]	[1.76]
Industry FE	Yes	Yes	Yes	Yes	Yes
Year FE	Yes	Yes	Yes	Yes	Yes
Observations	1,361	1,361	1,361	1,361	1,361
Number of industries	44	44	44	44	44
R-squared	0.90	0.90	0.90	0.90	0.90

Note: Dependent variable is log real invested capital. Robust t statistics in brackets, * significant at 10%; ** significant at 5%; *** significant at 1%.

Across industries, infrastructure and financially dependent industries see higher investment than the labor-intensive industries as value added increases. Investment has also increased somewhat post-delicensing; quite interestingly this is on account of a higher investment in the labor-intensive industries. Thus over time and especially post-delicensing, the labor-intensive industries seem to be substituting away from labor and adopting relatively more capital intensive technology! In addition, we find that industries which are more dependent on external finance see a decline in investment in the post-delicensing period.

Robustness of results

We do extensive tests for the robustness of our results. These include checking the robustness to different time periods, to omitted variables, and to potential outliers. We account for the lags between policy and implementation; we also account for the possibility that the outcomes might be correlated by the industries or by the year of delicensing. While we do obtain small variations in coefficients and in the standard errors across these different specifications, overall the results are quite robust to various sensitivity tests. One result which does seem a bit sensitive to some of the corrections for autocorrelation is the result on infrastructure dependence. In some of the corrections for autocorrelations the coefficients of the interaction between infrastructure and delicensing become less significant, but even here its effect holds at about the 20 percent level of significance. Details on each robustness test follow.

In the methodology used here the omitted variables that vary only by industries or only by year have been accounted for through the respective fixed effects, thus the estimates remain susceptible to the omission of variables that vary over industry-year dimensions of the data. In particular, there might have been the following two types of omissions: First, the interaction of delicensing with industry characteristics other than the ones included; and second, the interaction of policy variables other than delicensing and their interactions with the industry characteristics included.

We explicitly control for only one of the major policy changes pertaining to Indian industries. What about the other policy changes? In order to address these concerns we carry out two robustness tests. First, to control for the reforms which were more generic rather than specific to industries, we include in our regressions interaction of industrial characteristics with a post-1992 dummy. Second, we construct a trade policy measure which is industry specific and interact it with industrial characteristics. Results that infrastructure-dependent, external finance-dependent, and labor-intensive industries have not benefited as much from reforms are fairly robust across these various specifications.

While we are unable to conduct these tests for some of the other reforms, the results are unlikely to change. The reason is that the reforms are highly correlated over time and across sectors. Thus even if we get a somewhat different coefficient when we include interaction of industry characteristics with different reforms instead of delicensing, the basic message we want to bring home, that without sufficient infrastructure development, financial depth, and progress on factors inhibiting labor-intensive industries, Indian industry is unlikely to realize its potential, would hold. For this argument it is really immaterial what kind of reforms we are talking about. Second, if we include the interactions of industry characteristics with different reform measures, e.g. delicensing and trade reforms, in the same specification, then the coefficient for a particular policy measure would become weaker and probably even lose their statistical significance. Such a specification will be of little use since again

Table 10.8. Robustness tests (dependent variable is log value added)

	(1) 1980s and beyond	(2) Newey 2	(3) w/o tobacco, petroleum	(4) Trade reform	(5) Trade and delicensing	(6) Delicensing lagged two years	(7) Cluster SEs
Delicensing	0.71*** [4.69]	0.9*** [5.12]	1.1*** [8.41]		0.62*** [3.18]	0.95*** [7.80]	0.93** [2.86]
Trade openness				1.04*** [6.33]	0.72*** [3.46]		
Infrastructure* delicensing	−0.22** [2.57]	−0.18* [1.83]	−0.18*** [2.62]		0.03 [0.29]	−0.23*** [3.43]	−0.18 [1.37]
Labor intensity* delicensing	−0.45*** [2.97]	−0.51** [2.32]	−0.60*** [4.08]		−0.30* [1.94]	−0.50*** [3.38]	−0.51*** [4.26]
External finance* delicensing	−0.94*** [3.52]	−1.2*** [3.80]	−1.37*** [6.21]		−1.09*** [2.88]	−1.11*** [4.97]	−1.22 [1.57]
Infrastructure*trade openness				−0.41*** [5.26]	−0.45*** [5.01]		
Labor intensity*trade openness				−0.05 [0.97]	0.03 [0.55]		
Financial dep*trade openness				−0.52** [2.01]	0.13 [0.36]		
Industry FE	Yes	Yes	Yes	Yes	Yes	Yes	Yes
Time FE	Yes	Yes	Yes	Yes	Yes	Yes	Yes
Observations	1,056	1,361	1,299	1,056	1,056	1,361	1,361
Number of industries	44	44	42	44	44	44	44
R-squared	0.67	0.71	0.71	0.68	0.69	0.71	0.71

Note: Dependent variable is log value added. Robust t statistics in brackets, * significant at 10%; ** significant at 5%; *** significant at 1%.

the interest is in a composite reform measure rather than specific reform measures. Thus, even if the coefficients might be biased in the benchmark specification, to the extent that we do not really care about attributing it to delicensing per se, we are fine. For omitted industry characteristics we include other industrial characteristics in the regressions such as export intensity or FDI intensity interacted with delicensing and find the results to be robust.

We report results for some of the robustness tests in Table 10.8. The reported results are for the dependent variable log value added. In order to address the concerns related to autocorrelation we reduce the sample length to the period from 1980 onwards, column 1, Table 10.8. We can restrict the period further but then we would start losing our control period. In the results reported in column 2 of the table we calculate the standard errors corrected for Newey West adjustment.

We also drop two industries, tobacco and petroleum (these industries typically show extreme measures on various accounts such as labor productivity and size) in column 3 and the results are unchanged. In columns 4 and 5 of Table 10.8 we include the trade reform variable. Here as expected we find that the trade reforms have had a growth enhancing effect on Indian industries, and again the effect has varied across industries along the same dimension as we have seen in the earlier tables.

To control for the fact that there may be a lag between reform and actual implementation or the effect of the reform is felt with a delay, in column 6 we lag the delicensing dummy by two years. In other words, if an industry was delicensed in 1991, we assume that the effect was felt two years later, i.e. 1993 onwards. Our benchmark results hold qualitatively.

10.5 Conclusion

In this chapter, we have analyzed the performance of registered Indian manufacturing sector in using data from the ASI. In line with some recent studies, we find that industrial performance has improved with industrial delicensing. However, our analysis also indicates that there is considerable heterogeneity in the response of industries to policy reforms. In particular, the industries more dependent on infrastructure, industries with greater dependence on sources of finance external to the firms, as well as those with high labor intensity have not performed well.

From a policy perspective, the important question then is what features of India's policy and institutional landscape explain this pattern?

The ongoing policy debates in India suggest several leading candidates. In the case of infrastructure-dependent industries, the inadequacy of existing infrastructure is probably the main culprit. Similarly, the failure to improve the Indian financial sector's ability to identify and finance creditworthy firms and investors may well lie behind the relatively weak performance of industries especially dependent on external finance.

A complementary analysis of two firm-level surveys of managers in the manufacturing sector lends further support to these arguments, especially in the case of infrastructure and finance. Taken together, the results of the World Bank's investment climate survey and ICRIER survey of labor-intensive manufactures support the notion that weak provision of infrastructure and finance has constrained the growth of the manufacturing sector.

As regards the weak performance of labor-intensive industries, India's labor regulation may well be responsible as argued by a number of observers of the Indian economy. In particular, certain elements of the IDA may have raised significantly the effective cost of hiring workers, thereby hitting the relative profitability of labor-intensive industries disproportionately. Since this is more likely to be the case for larger firms (due to the nature of the regulations), labor regulations may have led to relatively weaker performance of labor-intensive industries in two ways: First, by discouraging entry by large firms; and second, by reducing incentives among small firms to expand.

However, other factors cannot be ruled out—such as the policy of reserving a whole range of labor-intensive products for production by small-scale firms as recently as 2001. One way to make headway on this issue—i.e. establishing whether certain elements of the policy or institutional framework are causal drivers of the pattern of industrial performance we find—is to extend our analysis to the state level. To the extent that India's states present sufficient variability in the provision of infrastructure and finance and in the stance of labor regulations (as they actually apply to firms and not just on paper), extending this chapter's analysis at the state level should be very useful. We take up this issue in our forthcoming work.

In the meantime, our econometric analysis has served to highlight from where relatively weaker performance in India's manufacturing sector is coming. Unlike previous work that has highlighted mainly the role of labor regulations in influencing industrial performance, our econometric results interpreted in conjunction with perceptions of managers suggest that steps to improve infrastructure and the financial system should go a long way in improving manufacturing performance. Additionally, our results also point to the urgency of identifying the constraints on labor-intensive manufacturing in India and relaxing these.

Appendix 10A. Data sources and construction of variables

We have primarily used ASI data at the 3-digit level. After the concordance from NIC87 and NIC70 into NIC 98 classification, we have data on forty-nine industries. Data are available from 1973 to 2003. Data in general seem good and comparable pre- and post-1998, when there was a change in the sampling framework. The following industries were excluded from the analysis. The first three—dressing and dyeing of fur, saw milling, and publishing—were excluded because of lack of data on infrastructure dependence from CMIE. The others that were dropped included processing of nuclear fuels and reproduction of recorded media. As noted by Aghion et al. (2006), processing of nuclear fuels is likely to be affected by non-economic factors and hence we drop them from our sample. Finally, reproduction of recorded media was introduced as a new category in 1998. There are no data for this industry for the period 1973–1998 and they are therefore excluded from the sample. We exclude less than 1% of the registered manufacturing sector, whether we look in terms of employment or gross value added.

Appendix Table 10A.1. Summary statistics of the ASI data

Variable	Observations	Mean	Standard deviation	Minimum	Maximum
Log (number of factories)	1,361	6.86	1.42	1.39	21.74
Log (total employment)	1,361	11.11	1.31	6.996	14.31
Log (blue collared workers)	1,361	10.81	1.36	6.38	14.18
Log (white collared workers)	1,361	9.68	1.23	5.84	12.92
Log (real gross value added)	1,361	17.88	1.42	13.94	21.74
Log (real invested capital)	1,361	18.76	1.51	14.36	22.65
Log (productivity)	1,361	6.77	0.75	4.62	9.95
Size-log (labor per factory)	1,361	4.25	0.70	2.85	6.94
Size-log (gross value added per factory)	1,361	11.02	1.09	8.30	14.71
Infrastructure dependence	44	0.30	0.25	0.04	1.17
Financial dependence	44	0.52	0.48	0.04	3.27
Labor intensity	44	0.42	0.14	0.09	0.83

Appendix Table 10A.2. Delicensing

Year of delicensing	Industry code	description
1985	151, 191, 210, 252, 261, 281, 300, 311, 319, 321, 322, 331, 341 Total number of industries delicensed: 13	meat, fish, fruit, vegetables, etc.; leather; paper; plastic products; glass; metal products; office/computing machinery; electric motors; other electric equipment; electronic components; television; radio transmitters; medical appliances and motor vehicle.
1989	251 Total number of industries delicensed: 14	rubber products
1991	152, 153, 154, 155, 171, 172, 173, 181, 182, 192, 202, 221, 222, 233, 241, 269, 271, 272, 289, 313, 314, 332, 333, 351, 352, 359, 361, 369 Total number of industries delicensed: 42	dairy products; grain mill products; other food products; beverages; spinning, weaving; other textiles; knitted fabrics; weaving apparel; articles of fur; footwear; wood products; publishing; printing; processing of nuclear fuels; basic chemicals; non-metallic; iron and steel; basic precious/non-ferrous metals; fabricated metal products; insulated wire and cable; accumulators, cells/batteries; optical and photographic equipment; watches; ships and boats; railway locomotives; transport equipment nec; furniture; and manufacturing nec.
1993	293 Total number of industries delicensed: 43	domestic appliances
1997	201, 223, 232 Total number of industries delicensed: 45	saw milling; recorded media; and refined petroleum products.

Note: Based on the data provided in Aghion et al. (2006), mapped into our 3-digit classification, and updated up to the year 2003.

Analysis from here onwards, when it refers to total manufacturing output, employment, etc., refers to the registered manufacturing excluding the above five industries. The real values have been calculated by using respective WPI deflators (unless otherwise noted, e.g. for the capital formation or capital stock variables).

Construction of variables

Value added (ASI): Increment to the value of goods and services that is contributed by the factory and is obtained by deducting the value of total input.

Workers (blue collared) (ASI): Blue collared workers are defined to include all persons employed directly or through any agency whether for wages or not, and engaged in any manufacturing process or in cleaning any part of the machinery or premises used for manufacturing process or in any other kind of work incidental to or connected with the manufacturing process or subject of the manufacturing process.

Appendix Table 10A.3. Industry characteristics

NIC98 3-digit	Industry description	Infrastructure dependence	Financial sector dependence	Labor intensive
151	Meat, fish, fruit, vegetables etc.	1	0	0
152	Dairy products	1	1	1
153	Grain mill products	1	0	1
154	Other food products	1	0	1
155	Beverages	1	1	0
160	Tobacco products	0	0	1
171	Spinning, weaving and finishing of textiles	1	1	1
172	Other textiles	1	0	1
173	Knitted and crocheted fabrics	1	0	1
181	Wearing apparel	0	0	1
191	Leather products except footwear	1	0	1
192	Footwear	1	1	1
202	Wood products	1	1	1
210	Paper and paper products	1	1	0
222	Printing	0	0	1
231	Coke oven products	0	0	0
232	Refined petroleum products	1	0	0
241	Basic chemicals	1	1	0
251	Rubber products	1	1	0
252	Plastic products	1	1	0
261	Glass and glass products	1	1	1
269	Non-metallic mineral products	1	1	0
271	Basic iron and steel	1	1	0
272	Basic precious & non-ferrous metals	1	0	0
281	Metal products	0	0	1
289	Fabricated metal products	1	1	1
293	Domestic appliances, electric lamps & equipment	0	0	1
300	Office, accounting and computing machinery	0	0	0
311	Electric motors, generators & transformers	0	1	0
313	Insulated wire and cable	0	1	0
314	Accumulators, cells & batteries	0	0	0
319	Other electric equipment	0	0	1
321	Electronic components	0	1	0
322	Television, radio transmitters etc	0	1	0
331	Medical appliances and instruments	0	0	1
332	Optical instruments & photographic equipment	0	1	0
333	Watches & clocks	0	1	0
341	Motor vehicles, trailers, parts and accessories	0	1	0
351	Ships and boats	0	1	0
352	Railway locomotives	1	0	1
353	Aircraft & spacecraft	0	0	0
359	Transport equipment nec	0	0	1
361	Furniture	0	1	1
369	Manufacturing not elsewhere classified	0	0	1

Total employment (ASI): Total employment is defined to include all blue collared workers as defined above and persons receiving wages and holding clerical or supervisory or managerial positions or engaged in administrative office, store keeping section and welfare section, sales department as also those engaged in purchase of raw materials, etc. or production of fixed assets for the factory and watch and ward staff.

Capital stock (ASI): Sum of fixed capital and physical working capital. Fixed capital represents the depreciated value of fixed assets owned by the factory and covers all types of assets, new or used or own constructed, deployed for production, transportation, living or recreational facilities, hospitals, schools, etc. for factory personnel. Physical working capital includes all physical inventories owned, held, or controlled by the factory as on the closing day of the accounting year, such as the materials, fuels and lubricants, stores etc.

Capital formation (ASI): It represents the excess of fixed capital at the end of accounting year over that at the beginning of the year.

Number of factories (ASI): Factory for the purposes of ASI is defined as the one which is registered under sections 2m (i) and 2m (ii) of the Factories Act, 1948. Broadly, according to these sections. Premises whereon ten or more workers with the aid of power or twenty or more workers without the aid of power is referred to as a factory.

Labor productivity (ASI): Ratio of Value Added to Total Employment.

Labor intensity (ASI): Labor intensity: (employment/real invested capital)*1,000. Where deflator used is the WPI for the NIC classification 319 (other electrical equipment, to proxy for the capital goods).[26]

Infrastructure dependence (CMIE): Ratio of distribution and power & fuel expenses to gross value added. It is the average of the ratio over the period 1994–1998.

Dependence on external finance (ASI): Ratio of outstanding loans to invested capital, averaged over 1991 to 1995.

Export intensity (CMIE): Ratio of total foreign exchange earnings to GVA.

Trade reforms (Hasan et al. 2007): Nominal Rate of Protection.

---

[26] Results do not depend on the deflator used or whether we use only fixed capital, rather than invested capital which included working capital as well to define labor intensity. It is not surprising since the correlation of the WPI series is of the order of 0.94 with the WPI for electrical goods; and the correlation of fixed capital with invested capital is of the same order of magnitude.

References

Aghion, P., R. Burgess, S. Redding, and F. Zilibotti. 2006. 'The Unequal Effects of Liberalization: Evidence from Dismantling the License Raj in India', CEP Discussion Paper no. 728.

Ahluwalia, Isher. 1987. *Industrial Growth in India: Stagnation since the Mid-Sixties*, Oxford University Press, Delhi.

—— 1991. *Productivity and Growth in Indian Manufacturing*, Oxford University Press, Delhi.

Ahluwalia, Montek. 2002. 'Economic Reforms in India since 1991: Has Gradualism Worked?' *Journal of Economic Perspectives*, 16 (3), 67–88.

Ahmad, Sultan. 1983. 'International Comparison of Chinese Prices', Working Paper, Economic Analysis and Projections Department, World Bank.

Allen, Franklin, and Douglas Gale. 2000a. *Comparing Financial Systems*, MIT Press, Cambridge, Mass.

—— —— 2000b. 'Corporate Governance and Competition', in X. Vives (ed.), *Corporate Governance: Theoretical and Empirical Perspectives*, Cambridge University Press, London, 23–94.

—— Jun Qian, and Meijun Qian. 2005. 'Law, Finance, and Economic Growth in China', *Journal of Financial Economics*, 77, 57–116.

—— Rajesh Chakrabarti, Sankar De, Jun Qian, and Meijun Qian. 2006. 'Financing Firms in India', World Bank Policy Research Working Paper no. 3975. Available at SSRN: http://ssrn.com/abstract=923282.

—— —— —— —— —— 2007. 'Financing Firms in India', Working Paper, The Wharton School, University of Pennsylvania.

Amiti, Mary, and Caroline Freund. 2007. 'An Anatomy of China's Trade', IMF Working Paper.

Anant, T. C. A. 2000, 'Reforming the Labour Market', in S. Gangopadhyay and W. Wadhwa (eds.), *Economic Reforms for the Poor*, Konark, Delhi.

—— R. Hasan, P. Mohapatra, R. Nagraj, and S. K. Sasikumar. 2006. 'Labor Markets in India: Issues and Perspectives', in J. Felipe and R. Hasan (eds.), *Labor Markets in Asia: Issues and Perspectives*, Palgrave Macmillan for the Asian Development Bank, London.

Anderson, James E., and Eric van Wincoop. 2004. 'Trade Costs', NBER Working Paper no. 10480.

References

Anderson, Jonathan. 2003. 'The Complete RMB Handbook', UBS Investment Research, Asian Economic Perspectives.

—— 2004. 'Can China Manage a Full Float?', paper presented to IMF Seminar on 'The Foreign Exchange System', Dalian, China, May 26–27.

—— 2006. 'How Real Is China's Bank Cleanup?', UBS Investment Research, Hong Kong, www.ubs.com/economics.

Annual Survey of Industries. 2007. 'A Data Base on the Industrial Sector in India (1973–74 to 2003–04)', vol. ii, Economic and Political Weekly Research Foundation (EPWRF).

Ark, Bart van. 1993. 'International Comparisons of Output and Productivity', Monograph Series no. 1, Groningen Growth and Development Centre (http://www.eco.rug.nl/GGDC/ThesisArk.html).

—— Judith Banister, and Catherine Guillemineau. 2006. 'Competitive Advantage of "Low-Wage" Countries Often Exaggerated', Executive Action Series no. 212 (October).

Asian Development Bank. 2007. *Purchasing Power Parity: Preliminary Report 2005*, International Comparison Program in Asia and the Pacific, Manilla (July).

Aten, Bettina. 2006. 'Interarea Price Levels: An Experimental Methodology', *Monthly Labor Review*, (September).

Athukorala, P, and Kunal Sen. 2002. *Saving, Investment, and Growth in India*, Oxford University Press, Oxford.

Atkins, A., and E. Dyl. 1997. 'Transaction Costs and Holding Periods for Common Stocks', *Journal of Finance*, 52 (1997), 309–25.

Ayyagari. M., A. Demirgüç-Kunt, and V. Maksimovic. 2005. 'Formal versus Informal Finance: Evidence from China', World Bank Policy Research Working Paper.

Aziz, Jahangir. 2006. 'Rebalancing China's Economy: What Does Growth Theory Tell Us?' IMF Working Paper WP/06/291, IMF, Washington.

—— 2007. 'Rebalancing China's Economy: What Does Growth Theory Tell Us?', ICRIER, December 6–7.

—— and Li Cui. 2007. 'Explaining China's Low Consumption: The Neglected Role of Household Income', IMF Working Paper WP/07/181, IMF, Washington.

—— and C. Duenwald. 2003. 'Growth-Financial Intermediation Nexus in China', in W. Tseng and M. Rodlaluer (eds.), *China: Competing in the Global Economy*, IMF, Washington, 30–51.

Baily, Martin Neil, and Robert Z. Lawrence. 2006. 'Competitiveness and the Assessment of Trade Performance', in Michael Mussa (ed.), *C. Fred Bergsten and the World Economy*, Peterson Institute for International Economics, Washington, 215–42.

Banerjee, A., and E. Duflo. 2004. 'Do Firms Want to Borrow More? Testing Credit Constraints Using a Directed Lending Program', mimeo, MIT; also BREAD WP 2003–5, 2003.

—— S. Cole, and E. Duflo. 2004. 'Banking Reform in India', BREAD Policy Paper no. 006.

References

Banister, Judith. 2005. 'Manufacturing Earnings and Compensation in China', *Monthly Labor Review*, August, 22–40.

Barnett, Steve, and Ray Brooks. 2006. 'What's Driving Investment in China?', IMF Working Paper WP/06/265, IMF, Washington.

Beck, T., R. Levine, and N. Loayza. 2000. 'Finance and the Sources of Growth', *Journal of Financial Economics*, 58, 261–300.

——Asli Demirgüç-Kunt, and Ross Levine. 2005. 'SMEs, Growth and Poverty: Cross-Country Evidence', *Journal of Economic Growth*, 10, 199–229.

Bencivenga, V. R., and Bruce Smith. 1991, 'Financial Intermediation and Endogenous Growth,' *Review of Economic Studies*, 58, 195–209.

Bergeoing, R., P. J. Kehoe, T. J. Kehoe, and Raimundo Soto. 2002. 'A Decade Lost and Found: Mexico and Chile in the 1980s', *Review of Economic Dynamics*, 5 (1), 166–205.

Berkowitz, Daniel, Katharina Pistor, and Jean-Francois Richard. 2003. 'Economic Development, Legality, and the Transplant Effect', *European Economic Review*, 47, 165–95.

Bernanke, B., and Mark Gertler. 1989. 'Agency Costs, Net Worth, and Business Fluctuations', *American Economic Review*, 79 (1), 14–31.

Bertrand, M., E. Duflo, and S. Mullainathan. 2004. 'How Much Should We Trust Differences-in-Differences Estimates?', *Quarterly Journal of Economics*, 119 (1), 249–75.

Bery, S., and K. Singh. 2005. 'Domestic Financial Liberalization and International Financial Integration', in J. Aziz et al. (ed.), *China and India: Learning from Each Other*, IMF, Washington.

Besley, T., and R. Burgess. 2004. 'Can Labor Regulation Hinder Economic Performance? Evidence from India', *Quarterly Journal of Economics*, 119 (1), 91–134.

Bhattacharjea, A. 2006. 'Labor Market Regulation and Industrial Performance in India: A Critical Review of the Empirical Evidence', *Indian Journal of Labor Economics*, 49 (2), 211–32.

Blanchard, Olivier, and Francesco Giavazzi. 2005. 'Rebalancing Growth in China: A Three-Handed Approach', MIT Department of Economics Working Paper WP05/32.

——and A. Shleifer. 2001. 'Federalism with and without Political Centralization: China vs. Russia', IMF staff working papers, Special Issue.

Bosworth, B., and Susan Collins. 2008. 'Accounting for Growth: Comparing China and India', *Journal of Economic Perspectives*, 22 (1; Winter), 44–66.

————and A. Virmani. 2007. 'Sources of Growth in the Indian Economy', NBER Working Paper no. 12901.

Botero, Juan, Simeon Djankov, Rafael La Porta, Florencio Lopez-de-Silanes, and Andrei Shleifer. 2004. 'The Regulation of Labor', *Quarterly Journal of Economics*, 119, 1339–82.

References

Bowles, Paul, and Baotai Wang. 2006. 'Flowers and Criticism: The Political Economy of the Renminbi Debate', *Review of International Political Economy*, 13 (2), 233–57.

Brandt, Loren, and Carsten Holz. 2004. 'Spatial Price Differences in China: Estimates and Implications', *Economic Development and Cultural Change*, 55 (1), 43–86.

Branstetter, Lee, and C. Fritz Foley. 2007. 'Facts and Fallacies about U.S. FDI in China', presented at NBER conference on China's Growing Role in World Trade, available at http://www.nber.org/books/china07/index.html.

Bris, A., W. Goetzmann, and Zhu, N. 2003. 'Efficiency and the Bear: Short Sales and Markets around the World', unpublished working paper, Yale University.

Bruton, G., and D. Ahlstrom. 2002. 'An Industrial View of China's Venture Capital Industry: Explaining the Differences between China and the West', *Journal of Business Venturing*, 17, 1–27.

Burkart, Mike, Fausto Panunzi, and Andrei Shleifer. 2003. 'Family Firms', *Journal of Finance*, 58, 2167–201.

Bussière, M., and A. Mehl. 2008. 'China and India's Role in Global Trade and Finance: Twin Titans for the New Millennium?', Occasional Paper Series no. 80 (January), European Central Bank.

Carlstrom, C. T., and T. S. Fuerst. 1997. 'Agency Costs, Net Worth, and Business Fluctuations: A Computable General Equilibrium Analysis', *American Economic Review*, 87 (5), 893–910.

Cassel, Gustav. 1918. *Theory of Social Economy*. C. F. Winter, Leipzig.

Chakrabarti, Rajesh. 2006. *The Financial Sector in India: Emerging Issues*, Oxford University Press, New Delhi.

Chakraborty, Suparna. 2005. 'Real Estate Prices, Borrowing Constraints and Business Cycles: A Study of the Japanese Economy', Working Paper, Department of Economics, University of Minnesota.

Chamon, Marcos, and Eswar Prasad. 2007. 'The Determinants of Household Savings in China', forthcoming IMF Working Paper.

Chang, Gene Hsin. 2007. 'Is the Chinese Currency Undervalued? Empirical Evidence and Policy Implications', *International Journal of Public Administration*, 30 (2), 137–48.

——and Qin Shao. 2004. 'How Much is the Chinese Currency Undervalued? A Quantitative Estimation', *China Economic Review*, 15 (3), 366–71.

Chari, V. V., P. J. Kehoe, and Ellen R. McGrattan. 2002a. 'Accounting for the Great Depression', *American Economic Review*, 92 (2), 22–7.

—————2002b. 'Technical Appendix: Accounting for the Great Depression', Working Paper no. 619, Federal Reserve Bank of Minneapolis Research Department.

—————2007. 'Business Cycle Accounting', *Econometrica*, May, 75(3), 781–836.

References

Chen, Shaohua, and Martin Ravallion. 2008. 'China is Poorer than We Thought but no Less Successful in the Fight against Poverty', Policy Research Working Paper 4621, World Bank, May.

Chen, Vivian, Bart van Ark, Harry Wu, and Qin Xiao. 2007. 'The Convergence of Provincial Unit Labor Cost in China, 1995 and 2004', The Conference Board, paper presented at IARIW-NBS International Conference on Experiences and Challenges in Measuring National Income and Wealth in Transition Economies (September), Beijing.

Cheng, Y., S. Chen, and Y. Guang. 2007. 'Expected Decisions from the Two Meetings', *Liaowang Dongfang Weekly Journal*, March 12.

Cheung, Yin-Wong, Menzie Chinn, and Eiji Fujii. 2007. 'The Overvaluation of Renminbi Undervaluation', *Journal of International Money and Finance*, forthcoming.

China Daily. 2007a. 'Local Governments 'Ignoring' Green Model,' (July 23). Available at www.chinadaily.com.cn/china/2007-07/23/content_5441271.htm, (last accessed August 27, 2007).

——2007b. 'Green Performance Goals May Decide Careers', October 25. Available at en.chinagate.com.cn/environment/2007-10/25/content_9123473.htm (last accessed February 1, 2008).

China Editorial Board of China Environmental Yearbook. Various years. *Environmental Yearbook of China*, China Environmental Science Press, Beijing.

China National Bureau of Statistics. 2005. *China Compendium of Statistics* (1949–2004), China Statistics Press, Beijing.

——2007. *China Statistical Yearbook 2007*, China Statistics Press, Beijing.

China State Council Information Office. 2006. *Environmental Protection in China* (1996–2005). Available at www.china.org.cn/english/2006/Jun/170355.htm (last accessed January 18, 2007).

Chow, Gregory C. 1993. 'Capital Formation and Economic Growth in China', *Quarterly Journal of Economics*, 108 (3), 809–42.

——2002. *China's Economic Transformation*, Blackwell Publishing, London.

——and K. Li. 2002. 'China's Economic Growth 1952–2010', *Economic Development and Cultural Change*, 15 (1), 247–56.

Claessens, Stijn, Simeon Djankov, and Larry Lang. 2000. 'The Separation of Ownership and Control in East Asian Corporations', *Journal of Financial Economics*, 58, 81–112.

————Joseph Fan, and Larry Lang. 2002. 'Disentangling the Incentive and Entrenchment of Large Shareholdings', *Journal of Finance*, 57, 2741–71.

Clark, Colin. 1965. 'Economic Growth in Communist China', *China Quarterly*, 21 (March), 148–67.

——1976. 'Economic Development in Communist China', *Journal of Political Economy*, 84 (21), 239–64.

Cline, William. 2005. '*The United States as a Debtor Nation*', Institute for International Economics, Washington.

References

Coe, David T., Arvind Subramanian, and Natalia T. Tamirisa. 2007. 'The Missing Globalization Puzzle: Evidence of the Declining Importance of Distance', *IMF Staff Papers*, 54 (1), 34–58.

Dasgupta, S., B. Laplante, H. Wang, and D. Wheeler. 2002. 'Confronting the Environmental Kuznets Curve', *Journal of Economic Perspectives*, 16, 147–68.

Datta-Chaudhuri, Mrinal. 1996, 'Labor Markets as Social Institutions in India', IRIS-India Working Paper no. 10, University of Maryland at College Park.

Deardorff, Alan V. 1998. 'Determinants of Bilateral Trade: Does Gravity Work in a Neoclassical World?', in Jeffrey A. Frankel (ed.), *The Regionalization of the World Economy*, University of Chicago Press, Chicago, 7–32.

Debroy, Bibek. 2000. 'Some Issues in Law Reform in India', in Jean-Jacques Dethier (ed.), *Governance, Decentralization and Reform in China, India and Russia*, Kluwer Academic Publishers, Boston, 339–68.

De Bruyn, S. M., and R. J. Heintz. 1999. 'The Environmental Kuznets Curve Hypothesis', in J. van den Bergh (ed.), *Handbook of Environmental and Resource Economics*, Edward Elgar, Cheltenham, 656–77.

De Groot, H. L. F., C. A. Withagen, and M. Zhou. 2004. 'Dynamics of China's Regional Development and Pollution: An Investigation into the Environmental Kuznets Curve', *Environment and Development Economics*, 9, 507–37.

Dell'Ariccia, G., E. Detrigache, and R. Rajan. 2005. 'The Real Effect of Banking Crises', IMF Working Paper WP/05/63.

Demirgüç-Kunt, Asli, and Ross Levine. 2002. *Financial Structure and Economic Growth: Cross-Country Comparisons of Banks, Markets, and Development*, MIT Press, Cambridge, Mass.

——— 2008. 'Finance, Financial Sector Policy, and Long-Run Growth', World Bank Policy Research Working Paper, 4.469.

Deshui, L. 2005. 'Key Achievements of the First National Economic Census with New Changes of China's GDP Aggregates and its Structure', Press Conference by the Commissioner of the National Bureau of Statistics in Beijing, China (December 20).

Dijkgraaf, E., and H. Vollegergh. 2005. 'A Test for Parameter Homogeneity in CO_2 Panel EKC Estimations', *Environmental and Resource Economics*, 32, 229–39.

Dimaranan, B., E. Ianchovichina, and W. Martin. 2007. 'China, India and the Future of the World Economy: Fierce Competition or Shared Growth', Policy Research Working Paper no. 4304, World Bank, Washington.

Djankov, Simeon, Rafael La Porta, Florencio Lopez-de-Silanes, and Andrei Shleifer. 2002. 'The Regulation of Entry', *Quarterly Journal of Economics*, 117, 1–37.

——— 2003. 'Courts', *Quarterly Journal of Economics*, 118, 453–517.

——— 2007a. 'The Law and Economics of Self-Dealing', *Journal of Financial Economics*. Forthcoming.

References

——Caralee McLiesh, and Andrei Shleifer. 2007b. 'Private Credit in 129 Countries', *Journal of Financial Economics*, 84, 299–329.

Dobson, Wendy, and Anil Kashyap. 2006. 'The Contradiction in China's Gradualist Banking Reforms', *Brookings Papers on Economic Activity*, Fall, 103–48.

Dollar, David, and Aart Kraay. 2006. 'Neither a Borrower Nor a Lender: Does China's Zero Net Foreign Asset Position Make Economic Sense?', *Journal of Monetary Economics*, 53 (5), 943–71.

—— and Shang-Jin Wei. 2007. 'Das (Wasted) Kapital: Firm Ownership and Investment Efficiency in China', IMF Working Paper WP07/9.

Dunaway, Steven, and Eswar Prasad. 2004. 'Interest Rate Liberalization in China,' Op-ed article in *International Herald Tribune*, December 3.

Dunaway, Steven, Lamin Leigh, and Xiangming Li. 2006. 'How Robust are Estimates of Equilibrium Real Exchange Rates: The Case of China', IMF Working Paper WP06/220.

Dutta, Ramesh. 2003. 'Labor Market, Social Institutions, Economic Reforms and Social Cost', in Shuji Uchikawa (ed.), *Labour Market and Institution in India, 1990s and Beyond*, Manohar, New Delhi.

Eckstein, Alexander. 1977. *China's Economic Revolution*, Cambridge University Press, Cambridge.

Economist, The. 2004. 'China's Environment: A Great Wall of Waste', August 19.

—— 2007, 'Grim Tales', March 31.

Economy, E. 2004. *The River Runs Black: The Environmental Challenge to China's Future*, Cornell University Press, Ithaca, NY.

Edmonds, R. L. 1999. 'The Environment in the People's Republic of China 50 Years On', *China Quarterly*, 159, 640–9.

Eichengreen, Barry. 2004. 'Chinese Currency Controversies', CEPR Discussion Paper 4375, London.

—— 2005. 'Is a Change in the Renminbi Exchange Rate in China's Interest?', *Asian Economic Papers*, 4 (1).

—— and Ricardo Hausmann. 2007. 'Exchange Rates and Financial Fragility', NBER Working Paper 7418.

Engman, M., O. Onodera, and E. Pinali. 2007. 'Export Processing Zones: Past and Future Role in Trade and Development', OECD Trade Policy Working Paper no. 53.

Erumban, Abdul Azeez. 2007. 'Productivity and Unit Labor Cost in Indian Manufacturing: A Comparative Perspective', GGDC Research Memorandum GD-96, Groningen Growth and Development Centre, University of Groningen.

ESCAP. 1999. *Comparisons of Real Gross Domestic Product and Purchasing Power Parities, 1993*, United Nations Economic and Social Commission for Asia and the Pacific (ST/ESCAP/1918), Bangkok.

Feenstra, Robert C. 2002. 'Border Effects and the Gravity Equation: Consistent Methods for Estimation', *Scottish Journal of Political Economy*, 49, 491–506.

References

Feenstra, Robert C., Wen Hai, Wing-Thye Woo, and Schunli Yao. 1999. 'Discrepancies in International Data: An Application to China-Hong Kong Entrepot Trade', *American Economic Review*, Papers and Proceedings, 89, 338–43.

—— Alan Heston, Marcel P. Timmer, and Haiyan Deng. 2009. 'Estimating Real Production and Expenditures across Nations: A Proposal for Improving the Penn World Tables', *Review of Economics and Statistics*, February.

Fehr Hans, Sabine Jokisch, and Laurence J. Kotlikoff. 2005. 'Will China Eat our Lunch or Take Us Out to Dinner? Simulating the Transition Paths of the U.S., EU, Japan, and China', NBER Working Paper no. 11668.

Finger, J. Michael, and M. E. Kreinin. 1979. 'A Measure of "Export Similarity' and its Possible Uses', *Economic Journal*, 89, 905–12.

Fisman, Raymond, and Shang-Jin Wei. 2004. 'Tax Rates and Tax Evasion: Evidence from "Missing Trade" in China', *Journal of Political Economy*, 112 (2), 471–96.

Fontagne, Lionel, Guillaume Gaulier, and Soledad Zignago. 2007. 'Specialisation across Varieties within Products and North–South Competition', CEPII Working Paper no. 2007-06 (May).

Frankel, Jeffrey. 2006. 'On the Yuan: The Choice between Adjustment under a Fixed Exchange Rate and Adjustment under a Flexible Rate', *CESifo Economic Studies*, 52 (2), 246–75.

Frye, T., and A. Shleifer. 1997. 'The Invisible Hand and Grabbing Hand', *American Economic Review*, 87, 354–8.

Fujita, M., P. Krugman, and A. J. Venables. 1999. *The Spatial Economy: Cities, Regions, and International Trade*, MIT Press, Cambridge, Mass.

Fung, K. C., and Lawrence J. Lau. 1996. 'The China–United States Bilateral Trade Balance: How Big Is It Really?', Occasional Paper, Asia/Pacific Research Center (April), Institute for International Studies, Stanford University.

———— 2003. 'Adjusted Estimates of United States–China Bilateral Trade Balances: 1995–2002', *Journal of Asian Economics*, 14, 489–96.

———— and Yanyan Xiong. 2006. 'Adjusted Estimates of United States–China Bilateral Trade Balances: An Update', Stanford Center for International Development, Working Paper no. 278 (June).

Gagnon, Joseph. 2003. 'Long-Run Supply Effects and the Elasticities Approach to Trade', International Finance Discussion Papers no. 692, Board of Governors of the Federal Reserve, Washington.

Ghosh, Saibal. 2006. 'Did Financial Liberalization Ease Financing Constraint? Evidence from Indian Firm-Level Data', *Emerging Markets Review*, 7, 176–90.

Glaeser, Edward, Simon Johnson, and Andrei Shleifer. 2001. 'Coase Versus the Coasians', *Quarterly Journal of Economics*, 116 (3), 853–99.

Goldstein, Morris. 2005a. 'Renminbi Controversies', manuscript, Peterson Institute for International Economics, Washington.

References

—— 2005b. 'What Might the Next Emerging-Market Financial Crisis Look Like?', Working Paper 05–7, Institute for International Economics, Washington.

—— 2007. 'A (Lack of) Progress Report on China's Exchange Rate Policies', Peterson Institute, Working Paper 07–5.

—— and Nicholas Lardy. 2003. 'A Modest Proposal for China's Renminbi', *Financial Times*, August 26.

—— —— 2004. 'What Kind of Landing for the Chinese Economy?', Policy Brief no. PB04–7, Institute for International Economics, Washington.

—— —— 2005. 'Exchange Rate and Monetary Policy in China', *Cato Journal*, 25.

Gollin, Douglas. 2002. 'Getting Income Shares Right', *Journal of Political Economy*, 110, 458–74.

Gomes, J., A. Yaron, and L. Zhang. 2002. 'Asset Prices and Business Cycles with Costly External Finance', Working Paper, The Wharton School, University of Pennsylvania.

Goodfriend, Marvin, and Eswar Prasad. 2007. 'A Framework for Independent Monetary Policy in China', *CESifo Economic Studies*, 53 (1), 2–41.

Gordon, Jim, and Poonam Gupta. 2003. 'Understanding India's Services Revolution', paper prepared for the IMF-NCAER Conference 'A Tale of Two Giants: India's and China's Experience with Reform'.

—— —— 2004. 'Understanding India's Services Revolution', IMF Working Paper WP/04/171.

Graham, J., and C. Harvey. 2001. 'The Theory and Practice of Corporate Finance: Evidence from the Field', *Journal of Financial Economics*, 61, 1–35.

Greene, M., N. Dihel, P. Kowalski, and D. Lippoldt. 2006. 'China's Trade and Growth: Impact on Selected OECD Economies', OECD Trade Policy Working Paper no. 44, OECD, Paris.

Greene, W. H. 2000. *Econometric Analysis*, 4th edn., Prentice Hall, Upper Saddle River, NJ.

Greenwood, J., and Boyan Jovanovic. 1990. 'Financial Development, Growth, and Distribution of Income', *Journal of Political Economy*, 98, 1076–107.

Greif, A. 1989. 'Reputation and Coalitions in Medieval Trade: Evidence on the Maghribi Traders', *Journal of Economic History*, 49, 857–82.

—— 1993. 'Contract Enforceability and Economic Institutions in Early Trade: The Maghribi Traders' Coalition', *American Economic Review*, 83, 525–48.

Grossman, G. M., and A. B. Krueger. 1995. 'Economic Growth and the Environment', *Quarterly Journal of Economics*, 110, 353–77.

Gupta, Poonam, Rana Hasan, and Utsav Kumar. 2008. 'What constrains Indian manufacturing?' Working Paper no. 211, Indian Council for Research on International Economic Relations.

References

Hale, Galina, and Cheryl Long. 2006. 'What Determines Technological Spillovers of Foreign Direct Investment: Evidence from China', Working Paper 2006-13, Federal Reserve Bank of San Francisco.

Hallack, Juan Carlos. 2006. 'Product Quality and the Direction of Trade', *Journal of International Economics*, 68 (1), 238-65.

—— and Peter Schott. 2005. 'Estimating Cross-Country Differences in Product Quality', Working Paper, Yale University.

Hansen, Gary, and E. C. Prescott. 1998. 'Needed: A Theory of Total Factor Productivity', *International Economic Review*, 39, 525-52.

Hasan, R., D. Mitra, and K. V. Ramaswamy. 2007. 'Trade Reforms, Labor Regulations, and Labor-Demand Elasticities: Empirical Evidence from India', *Review of Economics and Statistics*, 89, 466-81.

Hausmann, Ricardo, Jason Hwang, and Dani Rodrik. 2005. 'What you Export Matters', NBER Working Paper 11905. Forthcoming in *Journal of Economic Growth*.

Hayashi, Fumio, and Edward C. Prescott. 2002. 'The 1990s in Japan: A Lost Decade', *Review of Economic Dynamics*, 5 (1), 206-35.

Helpman, Elhanan, Marc Melitz, and Yona Rubenstein. 2007. 'Estimating Trade Flows: Trading Partners and Trading Volumes', NBER Working Paper no. 12927 (February).

Herd, Richard, and Sean Dougherty. 2007. 'Growth Prospects in China and India Compared', *European Journal of Comparative Economics*, 4 (1), 65-89.

Hertel, T. W. 1997. *Global Trade Analysis*, Cambridge University Press, Cambridge.

Heston, A. 2007. 'What Can Be Learned about the Economies of China and India from the Results of Purchasing Power Comparisons?', Working Paper no. 229, Indian Council for Research on International Economic Relations, New Delhi.

—— and Terry Sicular. 2007. 'China and Development Economics', in Loren Brandt and Tom Rawski (eds.), *China's Great Transformation: Origins, Mechanism, and Consequences of the Post-Reform Economic Boom*, Cambridge University Press, Cambridge, ch. 2.

Heytens, Paul., and H. Zebregs. 2003. 'How Fast Can China Grow?', in W. Tseng and M. Rodlauer (eds.), *China: Competing in the Global Economy*, IMF, Washington, 8-29.

Hollister, William W. 1958. *China's Gross National Product and Social Accounts: 1950-57*, The Free Press, Glencoe, Ill.

Holz, Carsten. 2006. 'China's Reform Period Economic Growth: How Reliable are Angus Maddison's Estimates', *Review of Income and Wealth*, 52 (1), 85-119.

—— and Y. Lin, 2001. 'The 1997-1998 Break in Industrial Statistics Facts and Appraisal', *China Economic Review*, 12, 303-16.

Houser, Trevor, and Daniel Rosen. 2007. 'China Energy: A Guide for the Perplexed', Policy Brief, Peterson Institute for International Economics, PB09-8.

References

Huang, Yasheng. 2003. *Selling China: Foreign Direct Investment during the Reform Era*, Cambridge University Press, Cambridge.

——2008. 'The Next Asian Miracle', *Foreign Policy*, July/August, 32–41.

Hummels, David. 2001. 'Toward a Geography of Trade Costs', mimeo, Purdue University, obtained at http://www.mgmt.purdue.edu/faculty/hummelsd/research.htm.

——and Peter Klenow. 2005. 'The Variety and Quality of a Nation's Exports', *American Economic Review*, 95, 704–23.

IMF. 2006. *Staff Report for 2006 Article IV Consultation with China*, Washington.

Jeanne, Olivier. 2007. 'International Reserves in Emerging Market Countries: Too Much of a Good Thing?', *Brookings Papers on Economic Activity*, forthcoming.

Johnson, Simon, John McMillan, and Christopher Woodruff. 2002. 'Property Rights and Finance', *American Economic Review*, 92, 1335–56.

Kahn, J., and J. Yardley. 2007. 'As China Roars, Pollution Reaches Deadly Extremes', *New York Times*, August 26.

Kansal, Satish M. 1971. 'A Comparison of the Cost of Living in India and Japan', *The Developing Economies*, Institute of Developing Economies, Tokyo (June).

Karacadag, Cem. 2003. 'Financial System Soundness and Reforms', in Wanda Tseng and Markus Rodlauer (eds.), *China: Competing in the Global Economy*, IMF, Washington.

Keidel, Albert. 2007. 'Assessing China's Economic Rise: Strengths, Weaknesses and Implications', International Conference on Experiences and Challenges in Measuring National Income and Wealth in Transition Economies, Organized by the International Association for Income and Wealth and the National Bureau of Statistics of China, (September).

King, R., and R. Levine. 1993. 'Finance and Growth: Schumpeter Might Be Right', *Quarterly Journal of Economics*, 108, 717–37.

Klein, Lawrence R., and Suleyman Ozmucur. 2003. 'The Estimation of China's Economic Growth Rate', *Journal of Economic and Social Measurement*, 28 (4), 187–202.

Kobayashi, Keiichiro, and Masaru Inaba. 2005. 'Borrowing Constraints and Protracted Recessions', Discussion Paper no. 06011, Research Institute of Economy, Trade and Industry (RIETI), Japan.

Kochhar, K., U. Kumar, R. Rajan, A. Subramanian, and I. Tokatlidis. 2006. 'India's Pattern of Development: What Happened, What Follows?', *Journal of Monetary Economics*, 53, 981–1019.

Koeva, Petya. 2003. 'The Performance of Indian Banks during Financial Liberalization', IMF Working Paper no. WP03/150.

Koopman, Robert, Zhi Wang, and Shang Jin Wei. 2008. 'How Much of Chinese Exports is Really Made in China? Assessing Domestic Value-Added when Processing Trade is Pervasive', NBER Working Paper 14109.

Kortum, S., and J. Lerner. 2000. 'Assessing the Contribution of Venture Capital to Innovation', *RAND Journal of Economics*, 31, 674–92.

References

Kose, M. Ayhan, Eswar Prasad, Kenneth Rogoff, and Shang-Jin Wei. 2006. 'Financial Globalization: A Reappraisal', IMF Working Paper WP06/189.

Kowalski, P., and N. Dihel. 2009. 'India's Trade Integration, Realising the Potential', OECD Trade Policy Working Paper no. 88, OECD, Paris.

Kraay, Aart. 2000. 'Household Saving in China', *World Bank Economic Review*, 14 (3; September), Washington.

Kravis, I. B. 1981. 'An Approximation of the Relative Real Per Capita GDP of the People's Republic of China', *Journal of Comparative Economics*, 5, 60–78.

—— A. Heston, and R. Summers. 1982. *World Product and Income: International Comparisons of Real GDP*. Johns Hopkins University Press, Baltimore.

—— A. Heston, Z. Kenessey, and R. Summers. 1975. *A System of International Comparisons of Gross Product and Purchasing Power*, Johns Hopkins University Press, Baltimore.

Krugman, P. 1991. 'Increasing Returns and Economic Geography', *Journal of Political Economy*, 49, 137–50.

Kuijs, Louis. 2005. 'Investment and Savings in China', World Bank China Research Paper no. 1, World Bank, Washington.

Kumar, U., and P. Mishra. 2008. 'Trade Liberalization and Wage Inequality: Evidence from India', *Review of Development Economics*. Forthcoming.

Kydland, Finn, and Carlos Zarazaga. 2002. 'Argentina's Lost Decade', *Review of Economic Dynamics*, 5 (1), 152–65.

Lall, R., A. Rastogi, and R. Anand. 2007. 'Financing and Implementation of Infrastructure Projects', mimeo, IDFC.

La Porta, Rafael, Florencio Lopez-de-Silanes, Andrei Shleifer, and Robert Vishny. 1997a. 'Legal Determinants of External Finance', *Journal of Finance*, 52, 1131–50.

—— —— —— —— 1997b. 'Trust in Large Organizations', *American Economic Review* (proceedings issue), 87, 333–8.

—— —— —— —— 1998. 'Law and Finance', *Journal of Political Economy*, 106, 1113–55.

—— —— —— —— 1999a. 'The Quality of Government', *Journal of Law, Economics, and Organization*, 15, 222–79.

—— —— —— 1999b. 'Corporate Ownership around the World', *Journal of Finance*, 54, 471–517.

—— —— —— and Robert Vishny. 2000. 'Agency Problems and Dividend Policy around the World,' *Journal of Finance* 55, 1–34.

—— —— —— 2002a. 'Government Ownership of Banks', *Journal of Finance*, 57, 265–302.

—— —— —— and Robert Vishny. 2002b. 'Investor Protection and Corporate Valuation,' *Journal of Finance* 57, 1147–1170.

—— —— Cristian Pop-Eleches, and Andrei Shleifer. 2004. 'Judicial Checks and Balances', *Journal of Political Economy*, 112, 445–70.

—— —— and Andrei Shleifer. 2006. 'What Works in Securities Laws?', *Journal of Finance*, 61, 1–32.

References

Lardy, Nicholas. 1994. *China in the World Economy*, Institute for International Economics, Washington.

——1998. *China's Unfinished Economic Revolution*, Brookings Institution, Washington.

——2006. 'China: Toward a Consumption-Driven Growth Path', Policy Brief 06-6, Peterson Institute for International Economics, Washington.

Lau, L., Y. Qian, and G. Roland. 2000. 'Reform without Losers: An Interpretation of China's Dual-Track Approach to Transition', *Journal of Political Economy*, 108, 120–43.

Lee, Boon L., D. S. Prasada Rao, and William Shepherd. 2007. 'Comparisons of Real Output and Productivity of Chinese and Indian Manufacturing, 1980–2002', *Journal of Development Economics*, 84 (1; September), 378–416.

Lehman Brothers. 2007. *India: Everything to Play for*. Global Economics, Lehman Brothers.

Leigh, Lamin, and Richard Podpiera. 2006. 'The Rise of Foreign Investment in China's Banks: Taking Stock', IMF Working Paper WP06/292.

Lester, J. P., and E. N. Lombard. 1990. 'The Comparative Analysis of State Environmental Policy', *Natural Resources Journal*, 30, 301–19.

Leuz, Christian, Dhananjay Nanda, and Peter Wysocki. 2003. 'Earnings Management and Investor Protection: An International Comparison', *Journal of Financial Economics*, 69, 505–27.

Levine, Ross. 2002. 'Bank-Based or Market-Based Financial Systems: Which is Better?', *Journal of Financial Intermediation*, 11, 1–30.

List, J. A., and C. A. Gallet. 1999. 'The Environmental Kuznets Curve: Does One Size Fit All?', *Ecological Economics*, 31, 409–23.

List, J. A., and W. McHone. 2000. 'Ranking State Environmental Outputs: Evidence from Panel Data', *Growth and Change*, 31, 23–39.

Lowe, Jeffrey. 2008. 'An Ownership-Based Framework for the U.S. Current Account, 1997–2006', *Survey of Current Business*, January, 59–61.

Lynch, D. J. 2005. 'Pollution Poisons China's Progress', *USA Today*, July 4.

Ma, X., and L. Ortolano. 2000. *Environmental Regulation in China: Institutions, Enforcement, and Compliance*, Rowman & Littlefield, Lanham, Md.

MacBean, A. 2007. 'China's Environment: Problems and Policies', *World Economy*, 30, 292–307.

McKinnon, Ronald. 2007. 'Why China Should Keep its Exchange Rate Pegged to the Dollar: A Historical Perspective from Japan', *International Finance*. Forthcoming.

McKinsey. 2006. *Accelerating India's Growth through Financial System Reform*, McKinsey Global Institute, McKinsey & Company, San Francisco.

McMillan, J. 1995. 'China's Nonconformist Reform', in Edward P. Lazear (eds.), *Economic Transition in Eastern Europe and Russia: Realities of Reform*, Hoover Institution Press, Stanford, Calif., 419–33.

References

McMillan. 1997. 'Markets in Transition', in D. Kreps and K. Wallis (eds.), *Advances in Economics and Econometrics 2*, Cambridge University Press, Cambridge, 210–39.

——and Christopher Woodruff. 1999a. 'Interfirm Relationships and Informal Credit in Vietnam', *Quarterly Journal of Economics*, 114, 1285–320.

————1999b. 'Dispute Prevention without Courts in Vietnam', *Journal of Law, Economics, and Organization*, 15, 637–58.

Maddison, Angus. 1998. *Chinese Economic Performance in the Long Run*, OECD, Paris.

——2007. 'Shape of Things to Come', in *Contours of the World Economy, 1–2030 AD: Essays in Macroecomic History*, Oxford University Press, Oxford, ch. 7.

——and Bart van Ark. 2002. 'The International Comparison of Real Product and Productivity', in A. Maddison, D. S. Prasada Rao, and W. F. Shepherd (eds.), *The Asian Economies in the Twentieth Century*, Edward Elgar, Cheltenham, 5–26.

——and Harry Wu. 2007. 'China's Economic Performance: How Fast has GDP Grown? How Big is it Compared with the USA?', paper presented at the University of Queensland (December).

Malenbaum, Wilfred. 1982. 'Modern Economic Growth in India and China: The Comparison Revisited, 1950–1980', *Economic Development and Cultural Change*, 31 (1), 45–84.

Mann, Katherine. 1999. *Is the S. Trade Deficit Sustainable?*, Institute for International Economics, Washington.

Mauro, P. 1995. 'Stock Markets and Growth: A Brief Caveat on Precautionary Savings', *Economic Letters*, 47, 111–16.

Millimet, D. L., J. A. List, and T. Stengos. 2003. 'The Environmental Kuznets Curve: Real Progress or Misspecified Models?', *Review of Economics and Statistics*, 85, 1038–47.

Mitra, D., and B. P. Ural. 2007. 'Indian Manufacturing: A Slow Sector in a Rapidly Growing Economy', World Bank Working Paper WPS 4233.

Mitra, S. 2008. 'Special Economic Zones in India: White Elephants or Race Horses'. Available at SSRN, http://ssrn.com/abstract=969274.

Mizoguchi, Tohiyuki. 1968. 'A Comparison of Level of Consumption of Urban Households in Japan and on Mainland China', Technical Paper no. 3, Institute of Economic Research, Hitotsubashi University, Japan.

Modigliani, Franco, and Shi Cao. 2004. 'The Chinese Saving Puzzle and the Life-Cycle Hypothesis', *Journal of Economic Literature*, 42 (March), 145–70.

Mohan, Rakesh. 2005. 'Financial Sector Reforms in India: Policies and Performance Analysis', *Economic and Political Weekly*, 40, 1106–21.

Morck, Randall, Bernard Yeung, and Wayne Yu. 2000. 'The Information Content of Stock Markets: Why do Emerging Markets Have Synchronous Stock Price Movement', *Journal of Financial Economics*, 58, 215–60.

Muldavin, J. 2000. 'The Paradoxes of Environmental Policy and Resource Management in Reform-Era China', *Economic Geography*, 76, 244–71.

References

Myers, S. C., and N. S. Majluf. 1984. 'Corporate Financing and Investment Decisions when Firms have Information that Investors do not have', *Journal of Financial Economics*, 13, 187–221.

Nagaraj, R. 2002. 'Trade and Labour Market Linkages in India: Evidence and Issues', Economic Series Working Paper no. 50, East West Center, Hawaii.

——2005. 'Industrial Growth in China and India: A Preliminary Comparison', *Economic and Political Weekly*, 40 (21) 21–7.

Naughton, B. 2007. *The Chinese Economy*, MIT Press, Cambridge, Mass.

Nehru, Vikram, E. Swanson, and A. Dubey. 1993. 'A New Database on Human Capital Stock: Sources, Methodology, and Results', World Bank Policy Research Working Paper WPS 1124.

Nikomborirak, Deunden. 2007. 'A Comparative Study of the Role of the Service Sector in the Economic Development of China and India', in L. Alan Winters and Shahid Yusuf (eds.), *Dancing with Giants*, World Bank Publications, Washington.

Nordas, H. K., S. Miroudot, and P. Kowalski. 2006. 'Dynamic Gains from Trade', Trade Policy Working Paper no. 43, Organization for Economic Co-operation and Development, Paris.

OECD. 2003. *China: Progress and Reform Challenges*, OECD, Paris.

——2005. *Economic Survey of China*, OECD, Paris.

——2006a. *OECD Economic Surveys: China*, volume 13, Paris (October).

——2006b. *OECD's FDI Regulatory Restrictiveness Index: Revision and Extension to More Economies*, Working Papers on International Investment no. 2006/4, OECD, Paris.

——2006c. *China: Open Policies towards Mergers and Acquisitions*. OECD, Paris.

——2007a. *Economic Surveys: India*, volume 13, OECD, Paris.

——2007b. *International Direct Investment by Country*, OECD, Paris.

——2007c. *Modal Estimates of Services Barriers*, OECD Trade Policy Working Paper no. 51.

Orts, E. 2001. 'The Rule of Law in China', *Vanderbilt Journal of Transitional Law*, 34, 43–115.

Oura, O., and R. Kohli. 2008. 'Financial Development and Growth in India: A Growing Tiger in a Cage?', IMF Working Paper. Forthcoming.

Pagano, M. 1993. 'Financial Markets and Growth: An Overview', *European Economic Review*, 37, 613–22.

Panagariya, A. 2004. 'India in the 1980s and 1990s: A Triumph of Reforms', IMF Working Paper WP/04/43.

——2006a. 'Transforming India', paper presented at the conference 'India: An Emerging Giant', Columbia University (October).

——2006b. 'India and China: Trade and Foreign Investment', paper presented at the Stanford Pan Asia Conference, June 1–3. Available at http://scid.stanford.edu/events/PanAsia/Papers/papersonly.html.

References

Panagariya, A. 2008. *India an Emerging Giant*, Oxford University Press, Oxford.

Perkins, Dwight, and Thomas Rawski. 2007. 'Forecasting China's Economic Growth over the Next Two Decades', manuscript, Harvard University.

——2008. 'Forecasting China's Economic Growth over the Next Two Decades', in Loren Brandt and Tom Rawski (eds.), *China's Great Economic Transformation*, Cambridge University Press, Cambridge.

Planning Commission. 2007. 'Projections of Investment in Infrastructure during the Eleventh Plan', The Secretariat for the Committee on Infrastructure, Planning Commission, Government of India.

Podpiera, Richard. 2006. 'Progress in China's Banking Sector Reform: Has Bank Behavior Changed?', IMF Working Paper WP06/71.

Poirson, H. 2006. 'The Tax System in India: Could Reform Spur Growth', IMF Working Paper WP/06/93.

Prasad, Eswar, and Raghuram Rajan. 2006. 'Modernizing China's Growth Paradigm', *American Economic Review*, 96 (2), 331–6.

——and Shang-Jin Wei. 2007. 'China's Approach to Capital Inflows: Patterns and Possible Explanations', in Sebastian Edwards (ed.), *Capital Controls and Capital Flows in Emerging Economies: Policies, Practices and Consequences*, University of Chicago Press, Chicago. Forthcoming.

——Thomas Rumbaugh, and Qing Wang. 2005. 'Putting the Cart before the Horse? Capital Account Liberalization and Exchange Rate Flexibility in China', *China and the World Economy*, 13 (4), 3–20.

Pye, L. 1982. *Chinese Commercial Negotiating Style*, Rand Corporation, Santa Monica, Calif.

Rajan, R., and A. Subramanian. 2005. 'What Undermines Aid's Impact on Growth', IMF Working Paper WP/05/126.

——and L. Zingales. 1998. 'Financial Dependence and Growth', *American Economic Review*, 88 (3), 559–86.

Ramaswamy, K. V. 2003. 'Liberalization, Outsourcing and Industrial Labor Markets in India: Some Preliminary Results', in Shuji Uchikawa (ed.), *Labour Market and Institution in India, 1990s and Beyond*, Manohar, New Delhi.

Ravallion, Martin, and Shaoshua Chen. 2007. 'China's (Uneven) Progress against Poverty', *Journal of Development Economics*, 82 (1), 1–42.

Reserve Bank of India, Balance of Payments Statistics Division. 2005. 'Computer Services Exports from India: 2002–03', *Reserve Bank of India Bulletin*, September, 821–9.

Richardson, J. David. 1993. *Sizing up U.S. Export Disincentives*, Institute for International Economics, Washington, DC.

Rodrik, Dani. 2006. 'What's so Special about China's Exports?', NBER Working Paper 11947. Forthcoming in *China & World Economy*.

Rouen, Ren. 1997. *China's Economic Performance in International Perspective*, OECD, Paris.

Schindler, John W., and Dustin H. Beckett. 2005. 'Adjusting Chinese Bilateral Trade Data: How Big is China's Trade Surplus?', *International Journal of Applied Economics*, 2, 27–55.

Schipani, C., and J. Liu. 2002. 'Corporate Governance in China: Then and Now', *Columbia Business Law Review*, 1–69.

Schneider, F. 2002. 'Size and Measurement of the Informal Economy in 110 Countries around the World', World Bank.

——and D. Enste. 2000. 'Shadow Economies: Sizes, Causes, and Consequences', *Journal of Economic Literature*, 38 (1), 77–114.

Schott, Peter. 2004. 'Across-Product versus Within-Product Specialization in International Trade,' *Quarterly Journal of Economics*, 119 (2), 647–78.

——2006. 'The Relative Sophistication of Chinese Exports', NBER Working Paper 12173.

Schumpeter, J. A. 1911. *The Theory of Economic Development*, reprinted 1969, Oxford University Press, Oxford.

Shleifer, A., and D. Treisman. 2000. *Without a Map: Political Tactics and Economic Reform in Russia*, MIT Press, Cambridge, Mass.

Sicular, Terry, Ximing Yue, Bjorn Gustafsson, and Shi Li. 2007. 'The Urban–Rural Gap and Income Inequality in China', *Review of Income and Wealth*, 53(1), 93–126.

Singh, A. 1997. 'Financial Liberalisation, Stock Markets and Economic Development', *Economic Journal*, 107, 771–82.

Singh, C. 2004. 'Financial Sector Reforms in India', SCID Working Paper no. 241.

Srinivasan, T. N. 1994. 'Agriculture and Trade in India', ICS Press, San Francisco, Calif.

Stern, D. I. 2004. 'The Rise and Fall of the Environmental Kuznets Curve', *World Development*, 32, 1419–39.

Summers, R., A. Heston, and D. Nuxoll. 1994. 'The Differential Productivity Hypothesis and Purchasing Power Parities: Some New Evidence', *Review of International Economics*, October.

Swamy, Subramanian. 1973. 'Economic Growth in China and India, 1952–70: A Comparative Appraisal', *Economic Development and Cultural Change*, 21 (4; part II), 1–84.

Szirmai, A., and R. Ren. 2000. 'Comparative Performance in Chinese Manufacturing, 1980–92', *China Economic Review*, 11 (1), 16–53.

—————and M. Bai. 2005. 'Chinese Manufacturing Performance in Comparative Perspective, 1980–2002', Working Papers 920, Economic Growth Center, Yale University.

Timmer, M. P. 2000. *The Dyanmics of Asian Manufacturing: A Comparative Perspective in the late Twentieth Century*, Edward Elgar, Cheltenham.

Topalova, P. 2005. 'Trade Liberalization: Evidence on Poverty and Inequality: Evidence from Indian Districts', NBER Working Paper 11614.

References

UBS. 2007. 'Is China Export-Led?', UBS Investment Research, Asian Focus, Global Economic Research, UBS.

UNCTAD. 2002. *The Least Developed Countries Report*. New York and Geneva.

—— 2005. 'World Investment Report 2005: Transnational Corporations and the Internationalisation of R & D', Geneva.

United Nations Economic and Social Commission for Asia and the Pacific. 1999. ESCAP Comparisons of Real Gross Domestic Product and Purchasing Power Parities, 1993 (ST/ESCAP/1918), Bangkok.

United States General Accountability Office. 2004. 'International Trade: Current Government Data Provide Limited Insight into Offshoring of Services, Report to Congressional Committees (September). Available at http://www.gao.gov/new.items/d04932.pdf.

—— 2005. 'International Trade: U.S. and India Data on Offshoring Show Significant Differences', Report to Congressional Committees (October). Available at http://www.gao.gov/new.items/d06116.pdf.

van Ark, Bart, Abdul Azeez Erumban, Vivian Chen, and Utsav Kumar. 2007. 'The Cost Competiveness of Manufacturing Sector in China and India: An Industry and Regional Perspective', ICRIER, December 6–7.

Visaria, Sujata. 2005. 'Legal Reform and Loan Repayment: The Microeconomic Impact of Debt Recovery Tribunals in India', Working Paper, Columbia University.

Wan, G. 2007. 'Understanding Regional Poverty and Inequality Trends in China: Methodological Issues and Empirical Findings', *Review of Income and Wealth*, 53 (1), 28–34.

Wang, H., and D. Wheeler. 2003. 'Equilibrium Pollution and Economic Development in China', *Environment and Development Economics*, 8, 451–66.

—— —— 2005. 'Financial Incentives and Endogenous Enforcement in China's Pollution Levy System', *Journal of Environmental Economics and Management*, 49, 174–96.

Wang, Qing. 2007. 'Impact of Stock Bubble Burst: An Update', Morgan Stanley China Economics Research Note, October 19.

Wang, Zhi, and Shang-Jin Wei. 2008. 'What Accounts for the Rising Sophistication of China's Exports?', NBER Working Paper 13771 (February).

—— M. Gehlhar, and S. Yao. 2007. 'Reconciling Bilateral Trade Statistics in the Presence of Re-exports via Third Countries: The Case of China, Hong Kong and their Major Trading Partners', unpublished manuscript, United States International Trade Commission, Washington. Available at https://www.gtap.agecon.purdue.edu/resources/res_display.asp?RecordID=2415.

World Bank. 2004. 'India: Investment Climate Assessment 2004, Improving Manufacturing Competitiveness', World Bank, Washington.

—— 2005. *2005 World Development Indicators CD-Rom*, World Bank, Washington, DC.

——2006. 'China Water Quality Management: Policy and Institutional Considerations', Environment and Social Development Discussion Paper (September).

——2007. *Dancing with Giants: China, India, and the Global Economy*, World Bank, Washington.

——2008. *Global Purchasing Power Parities and Real Expenditures: 2005 International Comparison Program*, Washington, DC.

WTO. 2001a. 'WTO Successfully Concludes Negotiations on China's Entry', WTO Press Release, Geneva, 17 (September).

——2001b. Section 18 of the 'Protocol on the Accession of the People's Republic of China', WTO [WT/L/432], 23 (November).

Wu, Harry X. 2001. 'China's Comparative Labor Productivity Performance in Manufacturing, 1952–1997: Catching Up or Falling Behind?', *China Economic Review*, 12, 162–89.

——2007. 'The Chinese GDP Growth Rate Puzzle: How Fast has the Chinese Economy Grown?' *Asian Economic Paper*, 6 (1), 1–23.

——Boon L. Lee, and D. S. Prasada Rao. 2007. 'Comparative Performance of Indian and Chinese Manufacturing Industries, 1980–2004', paper presented at IARIW-NBS International Conference on Experiences and Challenges in Measuring National Income and Wealth in Transition Economies, Beijing (September).

Xiang, B. 1998. 'Institutional Factors Influencing China's Accounting Reforms and Standards', *Accounting Horizons*, 12, 105–19.

Xu, Bin. 2007. 'Measuring China's Export Sophistication', China Europe International Business School.

——and Jiangyong Lu. 2007. 'The Impact of Foreign Firms on the Sophistication of Chinese Exports', Working Paper, China Europe International Business School and Tsinghua University.

Yu, Yongding. 2007. 'Ten Years after the Asian Financial Crisis: The Fragility and Strength of China's Financial System', manuscript, Chinese Academy of Social Sciences, Beijing.

Index

Affiliate transactions 40
Aghion, Phillip 310, 310 n. 5, 314, 328 n. 22, 339, 340
Ahlstrom, D. 139
Ahluwalia, Isher 312
Ahmad, Sultan 5 n. 3
Allen, Franklin 125–81, 245, 274
Anant, T. C. A. 315, 315 n. 7
Anderson, E. James 261 n. 4, 263
Anderson, Jon 212 n. 119, 215
Annual Survey of Industries 93, 97, 120, 310, 317
Asian Development Bank 10
Aten, Bettina 12 n. 11, 15
Athukorala, P. 244
Atkins 137 n. 6
Average labor compensation 89, 115
Average labor productivity 89
Ayyagari, M. 245
Aziz, Jahangir 25, 243–80

Bai, M. 93, 93 n. 5, 93 n. 7, 93 n. 8, 96
Baily, Martin Neil 57 n. 20, 61
Balanced growth path 252, 255
Balassa–Samuelson effect 29, 92
Banerjee, Abhijit 309, 309 n. 2, 316 n. 9
Banister, Judith 93 n. 8
Barnett, Steve 252 n. 2
Baumol's disease 27–30
Beck, Thorsten 244
Beckett, Dustin H. 38 n. 6
Bencivenga, V. R. 243
Bergeoing, R. 245, 259
Berkowitz, Daniel 132, 146
Bernanke, Ben 266
Bery, S. 273
Besley, T. 309, 310, 310 n. 4
beta convergence 89, 107, 109, 110, 117
Bhattacharjea, A. 310 n. 4
Bilateral trade flows 38, 47, 209 n. 16
Blanchard, Olivier 151, 192 n. 111

Bosworth, Barry 32–61
Botero, Juan 143
Brandt, Loren 13, 13 n. 12, 15
Bris, A. 137
Brooks, Ray 252 n. 2
Bruton, G. 139
Bureau of Economic Analysis 41, 54, 61 n. 22
Burgess, R. 309, 310, 310 n. 4
Burkart, Mike 158, 179
Business cycle accounting 245
Business regulations 309
Bussière, M. 184, 206

Capital income tax 245, 258, 262, 263, 263 n. 5, 271, 272, 277, 277 n. 9
Capital Issues Act 2
Capital–labor ratio 229
Capital per worker 18, 27, 254
Carlstrom, C. T. 266
catching-up 65, 107
Chakrabarti, Rajesh 125–81
Chakraborty, Suparna 266
Chamon, Marcos 232
Chari, V. V. 245, 257
Chaudhuri, Mrinal D. 313
Chen, Kai 5 n. 3
Chen, Shaohua 12, 13
Chen, Vivian 87–118
Cheng, S. 231 n. 127, 251
China State Council Information Office 305
Chow, G. 178
Chow, Gregory C. 253 n. 3
Claessens, Stijn 126, 128, 158, 179
Clark, Colin 4, 12 n. 10
Cline, William 59 n. 21
Cobb–Douglas technology 250
Coe, David T. 47 n. 12
Coefficient of variation 101, 102, 111
Collins, Susan M. 22, 23, 27, 32–61, 246

Index

Competitiveness measure 89–92
Conditional convergence 107, 108
Corporate governance 126, 127, 146, 154–7, 167, 177–81, 239, 247
Corruption Perception Index 131, 145, 150
Cossel, Gustav 28, 29
Credit constraints 247, 309, 309 n. 2
Cui, Li 244, 252 n. 2, 267

Das, Deb Kusum 319 n. 12
Dasgupta, S. 290 n. 21, 291, 298 n. 30
De, Sankar 125–83, 282 n. 6
Deardoff, Alan V. 47 n. 12
Debroy, Bibek 147
De Bruyn, S. M. 282 n. 6, 290
Deflators 6, 6 n. 6, 90, 120–1, 340
De Groot, H. L. F. 293
Delicensing 310, 311, 313, 314, 318, 324, 325, 327–35, 337, 340
Dell'Ariccia, G. 324 n. 19
Demirgüç-Kunt, Asli 125, 149, 244
Deng, Haiyan 21
Depreciation rate 251, 253, 254
Deshui, L. 287
Detrigache, E. 324 n. 19
Dihel, N. 184, 199, 199 n. 8, 200, 201, 218, 220, 221
Dijkgraaf, E. 290 n. 22
Dimaranan, B. 188
Direction of Trade Statistics 48
Disclosure Requirement index 132
Djankov, Simeon 128, 128 n. 2, 128 n. 3, 131, 132, 134, 145, 178
Dobson, Wendy 261 n. 4
Dollar, David 235
Dougherty, Sean 23, 27
Dubey, A. 253
Duenwald, C. 244
Duflo, E. 309, 309 n. 2, 316 n. 9
Dutta, Ramesh 315
Dyl, Edward 137 n. 6

Eckstein, Alexander 4, 5 n. 3
Economic and Technological Development Areas 74
Edmonds, R. L. 284 n. 8
Efficiency wedge 252, 255
Eichengreen, Barry 239 n. 6
Employment elasticity of output 332
English common-law origin 127, 181
Engman, M. 220
Enste, D. 146 n. 9

Environmental Kuznets curve 282, 287, 290, 293 n. 25, 304
Erumban, Abdul Aziz 87–124
EU-15 33, 33 n. 1, 37–40, 42, 43, 46–52, 54, 56, 57, 59, 60
Exchange rate 4, 8–10, 11, 14, 20–2, 21 n. 22, 28–30, 48 n. 14, 58, 59, 59 n. 21, 61, 90–2, 93 n. 7, 118, 130, 130 n. 4, 144, 185, 187, 227, 228, 232–5, 237–41, 296 n. 27, 324
Exchange rate elasticity 58
Exchange rate flexibility 235, 237, 239–41
Export Dissimilarity Index 66, 67, 69
Export Processing Zones 70, 73–5, 78, 80, 206, 219
Export sophistication 63, 64, 69–80

Fan, Joseph 126, 128, 179
Feenstra, Robert C. 21, 38 n. 6, 47 n. 12
Financial development 135, 238, 243–5, 324
Financial frictions 25, 260–72
Financial intermediation 243, 244, 248, 265, 273
Financial policies 243–80
Financial repression 25–7, 227, 247, 272
Finger, Michael J. 67
Fishlow, Albert 315 n. 8
Fisman, Raymond 73 n. 2
Focus Markets scheme 215
Focus Products scheme 215
Fogel, Robert 315 n. 8
Foley, Fritz C. 46
Fontagne, Lionel 62, 66 n. 1, 69–70
Foreign direct investment 33, 44, 149 n. 12, 151, 169, 175, 209, 281, 300, 306
Foreign invested enterprises 44
Frye, T. 180
Fuerst, T. S. 266
Fujita, M. 118
Fung, K. C. 38, 38 n. 6

Gale, Douglas 139, 178, 179
Gallet, C. A. 290 n. 22
GATS schedule 209
Gehlhar, M. 38 n. 6
Gertler, Mark 266
Giavazzi, Francesco 237 n. 2
Glaeser, Edward 138
Goetzmann, W. 137
Goldstein, Morris 232
Gollin, Douglas 253
Goodfriend, Marvin 239
Gordon, J. 308 n. 1
Gosh, Saibal 245, 274

Index

Gravity equations 33, 47, 49, 50, 52, 54, 55, 57, 60
Greene, M. 184, 191, 194, 195, 206, 208, 209
Greene, W. H. 291
Greenwood, J. 243
Grossman, G. M. 282 n. 6
Guang, Y. 282 n. 3, 305
Guillaume, Gaulier 62, 66, 69
Guillemineau, Catherine 93 n. 8
Gupta, Poonam 307–42
Gustafsson, Bjorn 13 n. 12

Hai, Wen 38 n. 6
Hale, Galina 71
Hans, Fehr 246
Hasan, Rana 307–42
Hausman tests 291, 292
Hayashi, Fumio 245, 255, 257, 259
Heintz, R. J. 282 n. 6, 290
Helpman, Elhanan 47 n. 12, 50
Herd, Richard 23, 27
Heston, A. 3–31, 184, 184 n. 1, 188, 188 n. 3
Heytens, Paul 253 n. 3
Hi-Technology Industry Development Areas 74
Hollister, William W. 5 n. 3
Holz, Carsten 5 n. 4, 13
Huang, Yasheng 265

Ianchovichina, E. 188
Inaba, Masaru 267
Income-emissions regression 283, 287, 290, 293–300, 304
Industrial Disputes Act 309, 310, 313, 323, 338
Industrial dust per capita 283, 294, 295, 297, 299, 304
Industrial waste water 283, 285, 289, 291, 293, 294, 296, 298, 300, 302, 304
Industries Development and Regulatory Act of 1951 312
Inflation targeting 240
Influential observations 302
Informational asymmetry 244, 246
Infrastructure 61, 135, 219, 221, 224, 229, 241, 248, 307–11, 315, 315 n. 8, 316, 320–32, 334, 335, 337, 338
Infrastructure dependence 310, 311, 325, 326, 330, 335, 339, 342
Internal Financing 25, 151, 154, 164–5, 173, 244
International comparison of productivity 24, 88, 92–6

International Labor Organization 249
International Monetary Fund 8, 9, 35–7, 40, 45, 46, 48, 57, 62, 87, 130–2, 190, 194, 196, 202, 212, 233, 234
International reserves 235
Intertemporal equilibrium condition 257
Investment Climate Survey 163, 319–21, 338
Investment wedge 257–60, 262, 264, 267, 272–4
Investor protection 126–9, 131, 137, 139, 145, 150, 161, 172, 179, 181, 182

Jahangir, Aziz 25, 243–80
Job creation 244
Johnson 168
Jokisch, Sabin 246
Jovanovic, Boyan 243

Kahn, J. 306
Karacadag, Cem 261 n. 4
Kashyap, Anil 261 n. 4
Kehoe, P. J. 245, 259
Kennessey, Z. 3–31, 184, 184 n. 1, 188, 188 n. 3
King, R. 244
Klein 6
Kobayashi, Keiichiro 267
Kochhar, Kalpana 309, 309 n. 3
Koeva, Petya 150
Kohli, R. 245, 274
Koopman, Robert 64
Kortum, S. 139
Kose, Ayhan M. 239 n. 5
Kotlikoff, Laurence J. 246
Kowalski, P. 184–224
Kraay, Aart 25 n. 24
Kravis, I. B. 5 n. 3
Kreinin, E. M. 67
Krueger, A. B. 282 n. 6
Krugman, P. 118
Kumar, Utsav 87–124, 307–42
Kydland, Finn 245

Labor market regulations 309
Labor regulations 99, 143, 146, 222, 309, 310, 310 n. 5, 313, 315 n. 7, 320–3, 338
Lang, Larry 126, 128, 158, 179
Laplante, B. 290 n. 21, 291, 298 n. 30
La Porta, Rafael 127–32, 134, 135, 137–9, 145–8, 150, 151, 154, 158, 160, 160 n. 13, 160 n. 14, 161, 180
Lardy, Nicholas 140, 229, 232, 261 n. 4

Index

Lau, Lawrence J. 38 n. 6
Lawrence, Robert Z. 57, 61
Lee, Boon L. 93
legal institutions 125, 128, 129, 131, 146, 181
Legality Index 132, 146, 150
Lehman, Brothers 185, 188, 222
Lerner, J. 139
Lester, J. P. 301
Leuz, Christian 132, 146
Levine, Ross. 135, 147 n. 10, 149, 244
Li, K. 253 n. 3
Li, Shi 13 n. 12
Lin 119
Lippoldt, D. 184, 191, 209
List, J. A. 282, 290, 290 n. 22
Liu, J. 155
Lombard, E. N. 301
Long, Cheryl 71
Lopez-de-Silanes, Florencio 128 n. 2, 130, 132, 135, 139, 143, 145, 158, 160, 160 n. 13, 178
Lowe, Jeffrey 56
Loyaza, N. 244
Lynch, D. J. 282

Ma, X. 233 n. 9, 285 n. 10, 298 n. 29, 299, 300 n. 33
MacBean, A. 285 n. 10
McGrattan, Ellen R. 245, 257
McHone, W. 290
McKinnon–Shaw hypothesis 243
McKinsey 309
McLeish 128, 128 n. 2, 131–4, 145, 178
McMillan, John 169, 176, 178
Maddison, Angus 5n. 3, 5 n. 4, 7, 8, 27, 30, 92, 184 n. 1
Majluf, N. S. 244
Maksimovic, V. 245
Malenbaum, W. 3, 4
Mann, Katherine 59 n. 21
Manufacturing sector 92, 93, 116, 120, 144, 188, 191, 196, 210, 223, 307, 309, 310, 311, 312, 318, 319, 323, 327, 337, 338, 339
Market frictions 246
Martin, W. 188
Mauro, P. 243 n. 1
Mehl, A. 206
Melitz, Marc 47 n. 12, 50
Merchandise trade 38, 189, 191, 199, 201, 219
Millimet, D. L. 282, 290
Mishra, P. 325 n. 20

Mitra, D. 310, 310 n. 5, 325 n. 20
Mitra, S. 220
Mizoguchi, Tohiyuki 12 n. 10
Mohan, Rakesh 273
Mohapatra, P. 315
Monetary policy 228, 235, 238, 239, 241, 242
Morck, Randall 137
Muldavin, J. 284 n. 9, 285 n. 10, 300 n. 33
Multifiber Arrangement 36
Multinational companies 41, 44
Multinational corporations 33, 44–54
Myers, S. C. 244

Nagaraj, R. 309, 315
Nanda, Dhananjay 132, 146
National Bureau of Statistics 13, 118, 287, 299
Naughton, B. 289 n. 19
Nehru, Vikram 253
Neoclassical growth model 249–54
New Economic Geography models 116
New Foreign Trade Policy 219, 221
Nikomborirak, Deunden 39 n. 8
Nonperforming loans 25, 140, 228, 247, 260–75
Nuxoll, D. 29 n. 26

Onodera, O. 220
Ortolano, L. 284 n. 9, 285 n. 10, 298 n. 29, 300 n. 33
Orts, E. 134
Oura, O. 245, 274
Ozmucur 6

Pagano, M. 243
Panagariya, A. 38 n. 7, 273, 309, 309 n. 3, 313
Panunzi, Fausto 158, 179
Penn World Table 4, 92
People's Bank of China 235
Per capita emission 285, 293–6, 299
Perkins, Dwight 25, 26
Perpetual inventory method 253
Physical capital 23, 24, 229
Pinali, E. 220
Pistor, Katherina 132, 146
Podpiera, Richard 264
Poirson, H. 272
Pop-Eleches, Cristian 134
Prasad, Eswar 227–47
Prasada Rao, D. S. 93
Prescott, Edward C. 245, 255, 257, 259
Processing exports 70, 73–81, 206, 219

Index

Product-level data 62, 92
Product market liberalizations 309
Product market reforms 307, 308, 311, 332
Purchasing power parities 4, 88, 92, 116, 144, 188
Pye, L. 178

Qian, Jun 125–83
Qian, Meijun 125–83
Qian, Y. 180

Rajan, Raghuram 125, 237 n. 2, 244, 324, 324 n. 19, 325
Ramaswamy, K. V. 315
Ravallion, Martin 12, 13
Rawski, Tom 25, 26
Real exchange rate 58
Redding, S. 310, 310 n. 5, 314, 328 n. 22, 339, 340
Registered manufacturing 93, 97, 98, 98 n. 9, 120, 311, 312, 317, 339, 340
Remittances 37, 196
Ren, R. 93 n. 5, 95, 122
Representative household 249
Richard, Jean-Francois 132, 146
Richardson, David J. 61
Robinson–Patman Act 28
Rodrik, Dani 62
Rogoff, Kenneth 239 n. 5
Roland, G. 180
Rubenstein, Yona 47 n. 12, 50
Rumbaugh, Thomas 237 n. 2
Rouen, Ren 5 n. 3

Samuelson, Paul 29
Sasikumar, S. A. 315 n. 7
Schindler, John W. 38 n. 6
Schipani, C. 155
Schneider, F. 146 n. 9
Schott, Peter 62, 63, 66 n. 1, 67
Schumpeter, J. A. 243
SEBI Act of 1992 273
Sen, A. K. 3
Sen, Kunal 244
Services exports 39, 189, 200, 201, 202
Shanghai Stock Exchange 126, 137
ShenZhen Stock Exchange 126, 155
Shepherd, William 93
Shleifer, Andrei 128, 128 n. 2, 128 n. 3, 131–4, 143, 145, 158, 178–80
Shooting algorithm 255
Sicular, Terry 13 n. 12
sigma convergence 111–16
Simulation 255–61, 268, 269, 275–7

Singh, A. 243 n. 1
Singh, C. 273
Singh, K. 273
Skill-intensive 63, 309 n. 3
Skill-intensive industries 115, 118, 307, 330 n. 23
Smith, Bruce 243
Socialist market economy 206
Solow growth model 245, 246, 247, 255–57, 259, 264, 272
Solow residuals 252
Soto, Raimundo 245, 259
Special economic zones 74, 214, 219–21
'Special mention' loans 262
Srinivasan, T. N. 3
State-Owned Enterprises 25, 119, 126, 265, 281, 283, 290, 301, 304
Stengos, T. 282, 290
Sterilization 235
Stern, D. I. 290 n. 22
Subramanian, Arvind 47 n. 12, 309, 309 n. 3, 324 n. 19
Summers, R. 9, 18 n. 16, 29 n. 26
Swamy, S. 3, 4
Swanson, E. 253
Szirmai, A. 93, 93 n. 5, 93 n. 7, 93 n. 8, 95, 96, 122

Tamirisa, Natalia T. 47 n. 12
Tariff reductions 212, 213, 310
Tertiary sector 6 n. 6, 23, 27–28, 30, 31, 287
Timmer, Marcel P. 21, 93 n. 5
Tinbergen, Jan 47
Tokatlidis, I. 309, 309 n. 3
Topalova, P. 325 n. 20
Total factor productivity 23, 24, 250
Trade deficit 32, 37, 38, 39, 42, 55–59, 60, 61 n. 22
Trade policy 188, 189, 206–23, 312, 325
Trade resistance 47, 48
Transparency International 131, 145
Treisman, D. 180
Turnover velocity 137, 137 n. 6, 138

UN COMTRADE 64, 66, 68, 69, 204
UN International Comparison Programme 3, 188
Unit labor cost 29, 88–118, 120, 121
Ural, B. P. 310, 310 n. 5, 325 n. 20
Urbanization 301

Van Ark, Bart 29, 87–124
Venables, A. J. 118
Virmani, A. 246

367

Index

Visaria, Sujata 146
Vishny, Robert 128, 132, 135, 139, 145, 154, 160, 160 n. 13, 14, 161
Vollegergh, H. 290 n. 22

Wang, H. 285 n. 14, 290 n. 21, 291, 293, 298 n. 30, 302
Wang, Qing 38 n. 6, 239 n. 6
Wang, Zhi 62–84
Wei, Shang-Jin 62–84, 235, 237, 238 n. 4, 239 n. 5
Wheeler, D. 284 n. 9, 285 n. 14, 290 n. 21, 291, 293, 298 n. 30, 299, 302
Wincoop, Eric van 47 n. 12
Withagen, C. A. 288, 293
Woo, Wing-Thye 38 n. 6
Woodruff, Christopher 168, 169, 176
World Bank 3, 4, 8–11, 20 n. 20, 30, 34, 34 n. 2, 48, 130, 132, 135, 145, 146, 146 n. 9, 147 n. 10, 156, 157, 163, 164, 184–6, 195, 214, 222, 265, 265 n. 6, 267, 281, 286, 299, 299 n. 32, 306, 309, 319, 338
World Economic Outlook 9, 131, 132

WTO accession 206–8
Wu, Harry 7, 27, 184 n. 1, 87, 93 n. 5, 115, 118, 119
Wysocki, Peter 132, 146

Xiang, B. 135
Xiao, Qin 87, 115, 118, 119
Xiong, Yanyan 38 n. 6
Xu, Bin 62, 66 n. 1

Yao, Schunli 38 n. 6
Yardley, J. 306
Yeung, Bernard 137
Yu, Wayne 137
Yu, Yongding 239 n. 6
Yue, Ximing 13 n. 12

Zarazaga, Carlos 245
Zebregs, H. 253 n. 3
Zhou, M. 288, 293
Zhu, N. 137
Zignago, Soledad 62, 66 n. 1, 69
Zilibotti, F. 310, 314, 328 n. 22, 339, 340
Zingales, L. 244, 324, 325

Ingram Content Group UK Ltd.
Milton Keynes UK
UKHW020906240323
419093UK00004B/200